THE WORKS

OF

JAMES

ARMINIUS

VOLUME THREE

a lamp post book

THE WORKS OF JAMES ARMINIUS, VOLUME THREE
By James Arminius

ISBN# 1-60039-114-1

Layout and Design Copyright © 2008 by Lamp Post Inc.
Additional Content Copyright © 2008 by Lamp Post Inc.
Electronic Version Copyright © 2008 by Christian Classics Ethereal Library.

Requests for information should be addressed to:
LAMP PoST Inc.
www.lamppostpubs.com

THE WORKS OF JAMES ARMINIUS VOL. 3.

A FRIENDLY DISCUSSION
BETWEEN
JAMES ARMINIUS
& FRANCIS JUNIUS,
CONCERNING PREDESTINATION,
CONDUCTED BY
MEANS OF LETTERS

Jacobus Arminius
Dutch Reformed theologian
(1560-1609)

Jacobus Arminius (aka Jacob Arminius, James Arminius, and his Dutch name Jacob Harmenszoon), was a Dutch theologian, best known as the founder of the anti-Calvinistic school in Reformed Protestant theology, thereby lending his name to a movement which resisted some of the tenets of Calvinism—known popularly as Arminianism. The early Dutch followers of Arminius' teaching were also called the Remonstrants, after they issued a document containing five points of disagreement with classic Calvinism, entitled "Remonstranti" (1610).

Arminius became a professor of theology at Leiden in 1603, and remained there for the rest of his life. The theology of Arminianism was not fully developed during Arminius' time, but was systematized after his death and formalized in the Five articles of the Remonstrants in 1610. The works of Arminius (in Latin) were published at Leiden in 1629, and at Frankfort in 1631 and 1635. After his death the Synod of Dordrecht (1618-1619) judged his theology and its adherents anathemas and published the five points of Calvinism (later knows as TULIP) as a point-by-point response to the five points of the Arminian Remonstrants.

CONTENTS

- Arminius And Junius' First Correspondence
- First Proposition Of Arminius
- Second Proposition Of Arminius
- Third Proposition Of Arminius
- Forth Proposition Of Arminius
- Fifth Proposition Of Arminius
- Sixth Proposition Of Arminius
- Seventh Proposition Of Arminius
- Eighth Proposition Of Arminius
- Ninth Proposition Of Arminius
- Tenth Proposition Of Arminius
- Eleventh Proposition Of Arminius
- Twelth Proposition Of Arminius
- Thirteenth Proposition Of Arminius
- Fourteenth Proposition Of Arminius
- Fifteenth Proposition Of Arminius
- Sixteenth Proposition Of Arminius
- Seventeenth Proposition Of Arminius
- Eighteenth Proposition Of Arminius
- Ninteenth Proposition Of Arminius
- Twentyth Proposition Of Arminius
- Twentyfirst Proposition Of Arminius
- Twentysecond Proposition Of Arminius
- Twentythird Proposition Of Arminius
- Twentyfourth Proposition Of Arminius
- Twentyfifth Proposition Of Arminius
- Twentysixth Proposition Of Arminius
- Twentyseventh Proposition Of Arminius

INTRODUCTION

The origin of this discussion is thus stated by the elder Brandt: "On the subject of Predestination, he [Junius] endeavoured to defend the opinion of Calvin, by rendering it a little more palatable. For he did not maintain that the divine predestination had respect to mankind either ANTECEDENT TO THE DECREE OF THEIR CREATION, or SUBSEQUENT TO THEIR CREATION, ON A FOREKNOWLEDGE OF THEIR FALL, but that it had respect only to MAN ALREADY CREATED, so far as BEING ENDOWED BY GOD WITH NATURAL GIFTS, HE WAS CALLED TO A SUPERNATURAL GOOD. On that account James Arminius, then one of the ministers of the church at Amsterdam, entered into an epistolary conference with him, and tried to prove that the opinion of Junius, as well as that of Calvin, inferred the NECESSITY OF SIN, and that he must therefore, have recourse to a third opinion, which supposed man, not only AS CREATED but AS FALLEN, to have been the object of predestination. Junius answered his first letter with that good temper, which was peculiar to him, but seemed to fabricate out of the various opinions concerning predestination one of his own, which, Arminius thought contradicted all those which it was his endeavour to defend. Arminius was induced to compose a rejoinder to the answer of Junius, which he transmitted to the Professor, who retained it full six years, to the time of his death, without attempting to reply."

The letter of Arminius was divided by Junius into twenty-seven propositions in answering it, and each of them is here presented, with the answer of Junius, and the reply of Arminius, corresponding to it.

LETTER

**TO THE MOST DISTINGUISHED MAN,
FRANCIS JUNIUS, D.D.,
A BROTHER IN CHRIST, WORTHY OF
MY MOST PROFOUND REGARD,
JAMES ARMINIUS WISHES YOU HEALTH.**

MOST DISTINGUISHED AND VENERATED SIR:

They who do not give their assent to the sentiments of others, seem to themselves, and wish to seem to others, to be, in this, under the influence of sound judgment; but sometimes, ignorance of the sentiments of others is the cause of this, which, nevertheless, they by no means acknowledge. I have not hitherto been able to agree, in the full persuasion of my mind, with the views of some learned men, both of our own and of former ages, concerning the decrees of predestination and of reprobation.

Consciousness of my own lack of talents does not permit me to ascribe the cause of this disagreement to sound judgment: that I should ascribe it to ignorance is hardly allowed by my own opinion, which seems to me to be based on an adequate knowledge of their sentiments. On this account I have been till this time in doubt; fearing to assent to an opinion of another, without a full persuasion in my own mind; and not daring to affirm that which I consider more true, but not in accordance with the sentiments of most learned men. I have, therefore, thought it necessary for the tranquillity of my mind, to confer with learned men concerning that decree, that I might try whether their erudite labours might be able to remove my doubt and ignorance, and produce in my mind knowledge and certainty. I have already done this with some of my brethren; and with others, whose opinions have authority, but thus far, (to confess the truth,) with a result useless, or even injurious to me. I thought that I must have recourse to you, who, partly from your published works, and partly from the statements of others, I know to be a person such that I may, without fear, be permitted to hope from you some certain result.

REPLY OF FRANCIS JUNIUS TO THE MOST LEARNED MAN, AND MY VERY DEAR BROTHER, JAMES ARMINIUS GREETING:

TERTULLIAN, On whose works, as you know, I have now been long engaged, has been the cause of my long silence, respected brother. In the mean time, I placed your letter on a shelf plainly in my view, that I might be reminded of my obligation to you, and might attend, at the earliest possible opportunity, to your request. You desire from me an explication of a question of a truly grave character, in which the truth is fully known to God: that which is sufficient He had expressed in His written word, which we both consult with the divine help. You may set forth openly what you think and do not think. You desire that I should present my views, that from this mutual interchange and communication of sentiments, we may illustrate the truth of divine grace. I will do what I can according to the measure, which the Lord has admeasured to me; and whatever I may perceive of this most august mystery, I will indicate it, whether I regard it as truth or as a merely speculative opinion, that you with me may hold that which belongs to the Deity. Whatever pertains to my opinion, if you have a more correct sentiment, you may, in a kind and brotherly manner, unfold it, and by a salutary admonition recall me into the way of truth. I will here say nothing by way of introduction, because I prefer to pass at once to the subject itself, which may rather be "good to the use of edifying," as the apostle teaches. I judge that all desire the truth in righteousness: but all do not therefore see the truth in righteousness. "We know in part, and we prophesy in part," (1 Cor. xiii. 9,) and "when he, the Spirit of truth, is come, he will guide you into all truth." (John xvi. 13.) We perceive a part of the truth: and present a part; the rest will be given in his own time, by the Spirit of truth to those who seek. May he therefore grant to both of us that we may receive and may present the truth.

That we may both realize greater advantage from this brotherly discussion, and that nothing may carelessly fall from me, I will follow the path marked out in your letters, writing word for word, and distinguishing the topics of your discussion into propositions; and will subjoin to them, in the same order, my own opinion concerning each point, that in reference to all things you may be able to see clearly, and according to the Divine will, determine from the mode of my answer, what I think and what I do not think. The following is your first proposition, in which you may recognize yourself as speaking.

FIRST PROPOSITION OF ARMINIUS

I see, then, most renowned sir, that there are three views in reference to that subject, [predestination] which have their defenders among the doctors of our church. The first is that of Calvin to Beza; the second that of Thomas Aquinas and his followers; the third that of Augustine and those who agree with him. They all agree in this, that they alike hold that God, by an eternal and immutable decree, determined to bestow upon certain men, the rest being passed by, supernatural and eternal life, and those means which are the necessary and efficacious preparation for the attainment of that life.

THE REPLY OF FRANCIS JUNIUS TO THE
FIRST PROPOSITION OF ARMINIUS

If one should wish to accumulate a variety of opinions, he would in appearance have a large number of them; but let these be the views of men to whom will readily be assigned the first place in relation to this doctrine. But in reference to the points of agreement among them all, of which you speak, there are, unless I am deceived, two things most worthy of explanation and notice. First, that what you say is indeed true, that "God, by an eternal and immutable decree, determined to give eternal, supernatural life to certain men;" but that eternal life is not here primarily, or per se the work of that divine predestination, but rather in a secondary manner, and dependent, by consequence, on adoption th~v uiJoqesiav The apostle demonstrates this in Ephes. i. 5.

"Having predestinated us unto the adoption of children by Jesus Christ to himself, according to the good pleasure of his will." And in verse 11, "which He hath purposed in Himself; that in the dispensation of the fullness of time, He might gather together in one all things in Christ," &c.

Also, Romans viii. 17, "if children, then heirs; heirs of God, and joint-heirs with Christ," &c. We must not, however, forget that if an effect is substituted for the distinguishing part of the essence the definition of the thing is defective. Predestination, if we regard its peculiar and distinguishing quality, is, according to the testimony of the Scripture, to filiation, (so to speak,) or the adoption of children, the effect and sequence of which is eternal life. It is thus true that we are predestinated to life, but, accurately speaking, we are predestinated to adoption by the special grace of our heavenly Father. He who proposes one, supposes the other; but it is necessary that the former should be always set forth distinctly in the general discussion. Hence it seems that the arrangement of this whole argument will be less encumbered, if we consider that saving decree of the divine predestination in this order; that God has predestinated us to the adoption of children of God in Christ "to himself," and that he has pre-arranged by his own eternal decree the way and the end of that adoption; the way of that grace, leading us in the discharge of duty, by our vocation and justification, but its end, that of life, which we shall obtain when our glorification is perfected, (Rom. 8,) which are the effects of that grace, and the most certain consequences of our adoption. The statement that God has predestinated certain persons to life, is a general one; but it is not sufficiently clear or convenient for the purpose of instruction, unless gratuitous adoption in Christ is supposed, prior to justification and life and glory.

There is still another statement, made by you, which seems to me to need consideration, that "God has bestowed on certain men those means which are the necessary and efficacious preparation for the attainment of that life." For though that assertion is true, yet it must be received with cautious discrimination and religious scrupulousness. Our filiation is (so to speak) the work of the divine predestination, because God is our father, and by His grace unites us to himself as sons. But whatever God has ordained for the consummation of this adoption in us, it is, in respect to that adoption, not a means but a necessary adjunct or consectary. That eternal life, bestowed on us, is a consectary of our adoption "to himself." But in respect to the adjuncts and consequence, they may be called mutually, the means one of another; as calling is said to be the means of justification, and justification of glorification, (Rom. 8.) Yet though they are means, most of them are necessary and efficacious in certain respects, not per se and absolutely. For if they were, per se and absolutely necessary and efficacious, they would be equally necessary and efficacious in all the pious and elect. Yet most of them are not of this character; since even infants and they who come in their last hours, being called by the Lord, will obtain eternal life without those means. These things have been said, the opportunity being presented.

We agree generally in reference to the other matters.

THE REPLY OF JAMES ARMINIUS TO
THE ANSWER OF FRANCIS JUNIUS

To that most distinguished person, Doctor Francis Junius, and my brother in Christ, to be regarded with due veneration.

REVEREND SIR:

I have read and reviewed your reply, and used all the diligence of which I was capable, considering it according to the measure of my strength, that I might be able to judge with greater certainty concerning the truth of the matter which is under discussion between us. But while I consider everything in the light of my judgment, it seems to me that most of my propositions and arguments are not answered in your reply. I venture, therefore, to take my pen and to make some comments in order to show wherein I perceive a deficiency in your answer, and to defend my own arguments. I am fully persuaded that you will receive it with as much kindness as you received the liberty used in my former letter, and if any thing shall seem to need correction and to be worthy of refutation, you will indicate it to me with the same charity; that, by your faithful assistance, may be able to understand the truth which I seek with simplicity of heart, and explain it to others to the glory of God and their salvation, as occasion shall demand. May that Spirit of truth be present with me, and so direct my mind and hand, that it may in no respect err from the truth. If however any thing should fall from me not in harmony with its meaning, I shall wish that it had been unsaid, unwritten.

THE REPLY OF ARMINIUS TO THE ANSWER
TO HIS FIRST PROPOSITION

In my former letter I laid down three views held by our doctors in reference to the decree of Predestination and Reprobation, diverse, not contrary. Others might perhaps have been adduced, but not equally diverse among themselves or from others. For each of these are distinguished by marks which are manifest and have reference to the essence and nature of the subject itself, which is under discussion.

First, they give the object of the decree (man) a different mode or form, since the first presents him to the Deity as an object to be created, the second as created, the third as fallen.

Secondly, they adapt to that decree attributes of the Deity, either different or considered in a different relation. For the first presents mercy and justice as preparing an object for themselves; the third introduces the same attributes as finding their object prepared; the second places grace, which holds the relation of genus to mercy, over predestination; and liberty of grace over non-election or the preparation of preterition, and justice over punishment.

Thirdly, they differ in certain acts. The first view attributes the act of creation to that decree, and makes the fall of man subordinate to the same decree; the second and the third premises creation; the third also supposes the fall of man to be antecedent in the order of nature to the decree, regarding the decree of election which flows from mercy and that of reprobation which is administered by justice, as having no possible place except in reference to man considered as a sinner, and on that account meriting misery.

It is hence apparent that I have not improperly separated those views which are themselves separated and discriminated by some marked distinction. But you will perhaps persuade me that our doctors differ only in their mode of presenting the same truth, more easily than you will persuade them or their adherents. For Beza in many places sharply contends that God, when predestinating and reprobating man, considers him, not as created, not as fallen, but as to be created, and he claims that this is indicated by the term "lump," used in Rom. ix. 21, and he charges great absurdities on those who hold different views. For example, he says that they "who present man as created to God decreeing, consider the Deity as imprudent, creating man before he had his own mind arranged any thing in reference to his final condition. He accuses those who present man as fallen, of denying, divine providence, without the decree or arrangement of which sin entered into the world, according to their view. But I can readily endure, indeed I can praise any one who may desire to harmonize the views of the doctors, rather than to separate them more widely, only let this be done by a suitable explanation of views, apparently diverse, not by change in statement, or by any addition, differing from the views themselves. He, who acts otherwise, does not obtain the desired fruit of reconciliation, and he gains the emolument of an erroneously stated sentiment, the displeasure of its authors.

As to those two respects in which you think that my explanation of the agreement of those views needs animadversion, in the former I agree, in the latter I do not much disagree with you. For Predestination is, immediately, to adoption, and, through it, to life; but when I propose the sentiments of others, I do not think that they should be corrected by me. Yet I cheerfully receive the correction; though I consider that it has little or nothing to do with this controversy. Indeed I think that it tends to confirm my view. For adoption in Christ not only requires the supposition of sin as a condition requisite in the object, but of a certain other thing also, of which I did not in my former letter think it best to treat. That thing is faith in Jesus Christ, without which adoption is in fact bestowed on no man, and, apart from the consideration of which, adoption is prepared for no one by the divine predestination. (John i. 12.) For they who believe are adopted, not they who are adopted receive the gift of faith: adoption is prepared for those who shall believe, not faith is prepared for those who are to be adopted, just as justification is prepared for believers, not faith is prepared for the justified. The Scripture demonstrates that this is the order in innumerable passages. But I do not fully understand in what sense you style vocation and justification the way of adoption. That may be called the way of adoption which will lead to adoption, and that also by which adoption tends to its own end. You seem to me to understand the term way in the latter sense, from the fact that you make justification subsequent to adoption, and you speak of the way of grace leading us in the discharge of duty, by our vocation and justification. Here are two things not unworthy of notice. The first is that you connect vocation with adoption as antecedent to it, which I think can scarcely be said of vocation as a whole. For the vocation of sinners and unbelievers is to faith in Christ; the vocation of believers is to conformity to Christ and to communion with him. The Scripture makes the former antecedent to adoption. The latter is to adoption itself, which is included in conformity and communion with Christ. The second is that you made adoption prior to justification; both of which I regard as bestowed on believers at the same time, while in the order of nature, justification is prior to adoption. For the justified person is adopted, not the adopted person is justified. This is proved by the order both of the attainment of those blessings made by Christ, and that of the imputation of the same blessings made by God in Christ. For Christ obtained the remission of sins, before he obtained adoption, before in the order of nature: and righteousness is imputed before sonship. For "when we were enemies, we were reconciled to God by the death of his Son," (Rev. v. 10,) but being reconciled, we are adopted as sons.

Let us consider also what are opposed to these, namely, imputation of sins and non-adoption. From these it is clearly seen that such is the order. Sin is the cause of exclusion from filiation by the mode of demerit. Imputation of sin is the cause of the same exclusion by the mode of justice, punishing sin according to its demerit. In reference to your remarks concerning means, I observe that this term is applied by the authors to whose sentiments I refer, to those things which God makes subordinate to the decree of Predestination, but antecedent to the execution of that decree, not those by which or in respect to which Predestination itself is made, whether to adoption or to life. But I think it may be most useful to consider whether these, either as adjuncts, or consectaries, or means, or by whatever other name they may be called, are only effective to consummate the adoption already ordained for certain individuals, or whether they were considered by the Deity in the very act of predestination to sonship, as necessary adjuncts of those to be predestinated.

SECOND PROPOSITION OF ARMINIUS

They differ in this, that the first presents men as not yet created, but to be created, to God, electing and predestinating, also passing by and reprobating, (though, in the latter case, it does not so clearly make the distinction):

the second presents them created, but considered in a natural state, to God electing and predestinating, "to be raised from that natural state above it; it presents them to Him in the act of preterition, as considered in the same natural state, and to Him in that of reprobation, as involved in sin by their own fault: the third presents them to Him both electing and predestinating, and passing by and reprobating as fallen in Adam, and as lying in the mass of corruption and perdition.

THE ANSWER OF JUNIUS TO THE
SECOND PROPOSITION

That, in this statement of views (which are apparently, not really, contradictory) you have, in some manner, fallen into error, we shall, in its own place, demonstrate. I could wish that in this case an ambiguity, in the verb reprobate, and the verbal reprobation, had been avoided. This word is used in three ways; one general, two particular. The general use is when non-election, or preterition and damnation, is comprehended in the word, in which way Calvin and Beza frequently understood it, yet so as to make some distinction. A particular mode or signification is when it is opposed to election, and designates non-election or preterition (a Latin phrase derived from forensic use) in which sense the fathers used it according to the common use of the Latins. There is also a particular use of the word, when reprobation is taken for damnation, as I perceive that it is used by you in this whole letter. The first mode is synecdochical, the second common, the third metonymical; I add that the third might properly be called catachrestic if we attend to the just distinction of these members. I wholly approve the second meaning and shall adhere to it in this whole discussion.

THE REPLY OF ARMINIUS TO THE ANSWER
TO THE SECOND PROPOSITION

I have made a difference, not a contrariety between those views, and have already explained that difference according to my judgment. I do not, however, wish to be tedious in the proof of this point. For, in this matter, it is my aim that of a number of positions, any one being established, others, perhaps before unsettled, may be demonstrated.

The word reprobation may be sometimes used ambiguously, but it was not so used by me: and, if it had been, blame for that thing ought not to be laid on me, who have used that word in the sense and according to the use of those, whose views I presented, but especially according to the sense in which it has been used by yourself, with whom I have begun this discussion. For I had examined various passages in your writings, and in them I found that the word was used by you in the last sense, which you here call catachrestic. I will adduce some of those passages, from which you will see that I have used the word in accordance with your perpetual usage. In your Notes on Jude, (fol 27-6,) "The proper cause of reprobation is man himself; of his own sin, dying in sins." So in your Sacred Axioms concerning Nature and Grace, prefaced to the Refutation of the Pamphlet of Puccius, Axioms xliv, xlv, xlvi, xlvii, xlviii, and especially xlix and l, the words of which I here quote. Axiom xlix, "Nor is preterition indeed the cause of reprobation or damnation, but only its antecedent. But the peculiar and internal efficient cause of this is the sin of the creature, while the accidental and external cause is the justice of God." Axiom i, "Therefore Reprobation (that we may clearly distinguish the matter) is understood either in a wider sense, or in one which is more narrow and peculiar to itself. In a wider sense, if you consider the whole subject of the divine counsel from preterition, as the antecedent and commencement, to damnation, as the end and consequent, with the intervention of the peculiar cause of damnation, namely, sin; in a more narrow and appropriate sense, if you consider only the effects of sin." We might add, also, what is said in the 51st axiom. Of the theses concerning Predestination, discussed by Coddaeus under you, the 14th has this remark:

"Preterition is the opposite of preparation of grace and reprobation or preparation of punishment is the opposite of preparation of glory. But preparation of punishment is the act in which God determines to punish his creatures, &c." In theses 17 and 18, "reprobate on account of sins, from the necessity of justice." Here you seem to have wished to use those words properly: which you also signify more plainly in the Theses concerning election discussed by the younger Trelcatius under your direction. Thesis xii, "But if reprobation is made the opposite of election, (as it really is,) it is a figurative expression, that is either by synecdoche, or by catachresis. By synecdoche, if it refers to the whole series of acts opposed to Predestination; by catachresis, if it refers to non-election. For non-election is the first limit of the divine purpose, dependent on his will alone. Reprobation is the ultimate limit, next to the execution, dependent on the supposition of antecedent causes." Hence it is apparent that I have used that word in the sense which you have styled "appropriate." I will state, in a few words, what I think in reference to the same word, and its use. I am wholly of the opinion that the word reprobation, according to the use of the Latin language, properly signifies non-election, if election does not consist without reprobation. But I think that it is never used in the Scripture for an act which is merely negative, and never for an act which has reference to those who are not sinners. If at any time Augustine and others of the fathers use it for preterition, non-election, or any negative act, they consider it as having reference to a reelection in sin, and in the mass of corruption, or for a purpose to withhold mercy, the latter term being used for a deliverance from sin and actual misery. Calvin and Beza use it in almost every case, for the mere preparation of punishment, or for both acts.

THIRD PROPOSITION OF ARMINIUS

The first theory is this, that God determined from eternity to illustrate his own glory by mercy and justice: and as these could be exercised in fact only in reference to sinners, that he decreed to make man holy and innocent, that is, after his own images yet, good in such a sense as to be liable to a change in this condition, and able to fall and to commit sin: that he ordained also that man should fall and become depraved, that He might thus prepare the way for the fulfillment of his own eternal counsels, that he might be able mercifully to save some and justly to condemn others, according to his own eternal purpose, to the declaration of his mercy in the former, and of his justice in the latter.

ANSWER OF JUNIUS TO THE THIRD PROPOSITION

This view seems to have been stated not with sufficient fullness; for Calvin in his Institutes, (lib. 3,) eloquently refers to the words of Paul in Ephes. i, "He predestinated us unto the adoption of children by Jesus Christ to himself, &c.," and explains them, preserving the order which we noticed under Proposition I. God therefore from eternity determined to illustrate most wisely his own glory by the adoption of these and the preterition or non-adoption of those with the introduction also of mercy and justice. This being settled, that statement may be very well conceded, that "God determined to illustrate his own glory by mercy and justice, if it is rightly understood. But this will be hereafter explained in a summary manner. But it cannot be conceded, nor can I think that Calvin or Beza would have said simply that "mercy and justice cannot in fact be exercised except in reference to sinners. For in the first place (that we may sooner or later explain these things), sinners are such in act, in habit, or in capability. We are sinners in act when the depravity of our nature has carried out its own operations; we were sinners in habit in the womb and from the womb, before we wrought the works of the flesh. Adam was such in capability in some sense before the fall, when he had the power to lay aside his holy habits of life, and make himself the bond-slave of sin. So also they are miserable, in act, in habit, or in capability, who now endure miseries or have put on the habit of them, are capable of falling into them. The latter, however, are sinners and miserable, not absolutely but relatively; not fully but in a certain sense (kata ti) and only in a comparative mode of speaking as Job iv. 18, "Behold He put no trust in his servants; and his angels he charged with folly." Augustine refers to this (Lib. contra. Priscill et Origen, cap 10) concluding his remarks with this most elegant sentence: "for by participation in whom they are righteous, by comparison with Him they are unrighteous."

But in the second place it is not true that "mercy cannot be exercised except in reference to sinners," for all creatures, even the angels from heaven, when compared, according to their own nature, with the Deity, are wretched, since in comparison with Him they are not righteous, and because, by their own nature, they can sink into misery, (which is certainly the capability of misery; as, on the contrary, not to be capable of misery, is the highest happiness), they are miserable by capability. Therefore, He who has freed them from possible misery by His own election, has bestowed mercy on them; in reference to which they are called "elect angels" by Paul. (1 Tim. v. 21.) We may here merely refer to the fact that the word mercy (the Latin term misericordia being used in a more contracted sense) does not necessarily suppose misery, as will be seen by a reference to the original languages, the Hebrew and Greek, in which the men of God wrote. The Hebrews expressed that idea by two words dsj and symjr neither of which had reference properly and necessarily to misery e]leov of the Greeks does not necessarily suppose misery, if we regard the common usage of the Scriptures; for parents exercise it towards their children, though happy and free from misery. In the third place, it is by no means more true that "he can exercise justice only in reference to sinners." For he who renders to each his due, exercises justice: but God would clearly not be just if he did not render their due to the righteous as well as to the unrighteous. For even towards Adam, if he had remained righteous, God would have exercised justice both by the bestowment of his own reward upon him, analogous to his righteousness, and by that supernatural gift, analogous to his own power and grace, which He adumbrated to man by the symbol of the tree of life. It was possible that God should exercise justice in reference even to those who were not sinners. But concerning judgment to death, the case is different. From what has already been said, we readily conclude in reference to the rest. In reference to the word ordain, we shall speak under the sixth proposition.

REPLY OF ARMINIUS TO THE ANSWER
TO HIS THIRD PROPOSITION

I might show that the sentiments of Calvin and Beza were well and fully set forth by me in those words, by many passages selected from their writings. For though sometimes, when they make mention of adoption, and non-adoption, which is its contrary by logical division and opposition, yet they do not set forth their views, as it was explained by you in answer to my first proposition, and as you have just explained it in these words: "God, therefore, from eternity, determined to illustrate most wisely his own glory by the adoption of these, and the preterition or non-adoption of those, with the introduction of mercy and justice." For in two respects there is a departure in those words from their sentiment.

In the first place, because they do not consider that the illustration of the glory of God is effected immediately by the adoption of these and the non-adoption or preterition of those, but by a declaration of mercy and justice, which are unfolded in the acts of adoption or election, and of non-adoption or reprobation. It seems proper, according to the rule of demonstration, that this order should be preserved; the glory of God consists in the declaration of the attributes of God; the attributes of God are illustrated by acts suitable to those attributes.

Secondly, mercy and justice are not said by them to be introduced into the decree of predestination and reprobation. For those words signify that God, according to other attributes of his nature, decreed the adoption of these and the non-adoption of those, to the illustration of his own glory, in which deed he used also mercy and justice for the execution of that decree, and indeed with the condition of a change in the object. But this was not their view, but it was as I have already set it forth, namely, "God determined from eternity to illustrate his own glory by mercy and justice: since the glory of God can be neither acknowledged nor celebrated, unless it be declared by his mercy and his justice. But they consider mercy the appropriate cause of adoption, but justice the cause of non-adoption or reprobation, and they regard his purpose of illustrating both as the whole cause of predestination, that is, of election and reprobation; for they divide predestination into these parts or species. Therefore in my statement less was ascribed to mercy and justice in that decree than those authors think ought to be ascribed to those attributes, and than they do ascribe to them in the explanation of their entire view. Nor is it with justice denied that it is a part of their sentiment that mercy and justice can only be exercised in fact in reference to actual sinners. For they assert this most clearly, not indeed restricting the word justice to punitive justice, which, indeed, is my view, as is evident from my sixth proposition, and I think that this can be understood from them. I will adduce a few passages from many.

Beza (adversus calumnias Nebulonis, ad art. 2) "God, having in view the creation of man, to declare the glory both of his mercy and of his justice, as the result showed, made Adam in his own image, that is, holy and innocent; since as he is good, nothing depraved can be created by him. But they must be depraved on whom he determines to have mercy, and they also whom he justly determines to condemn." From this passage I quoted the words in which I stated this view. The same Beza again says (lib. 1, quest. et reap. fol. 126, in 8,) "Since God had decreed from eternity, as can be learned from events, to manifest in the highest degree his own glory in the human race, which manifestation might consist partly in the exercise of mercy, partly in the demonstration of hatred against sin, he made a man inwardly and outwardly pure, and endowed with right understanding and will, but susceptible of change. He, as supremely good, could not and would not indeed create any evil thing, and yet unless evil had entered into the world, there would have been no place for mercy or judgment." He expresses himself, in the plainest manner possible, in his conference with Mombelgartes; "Let us," says Beza "lay down these principles. God, an infinitely wise architect, and whose wisdom is unlimited, when He determined to create the world, and especially the human race had a certain proposed end, &c. For the eternal and immutable purpose of God was antecedent to all causes, because He decreed in Himself from eternity to create all men for His own glory. But the glory of God is neither acknowledged nor celebrated, unless his mercy and justice is declared. Therefore, He made an eternal and immutable decree by which He destined some particular individuals, of mere grace, to eternal life, and some, by an act of judgment, to eternal damnation, that He might declare His mercy in the former, but His justice in the latter. Since God had proposed this end to Himself in the creation of men, it was necessary that He should also devise the way and the means by which He could attain that end, that His mercy and His justice might be equally manifested. For since mercy presupposes misery, it can neither have place nor be declared where misery does not exist, it was then necessary that man should be created, that in him there might be a place for the mercy of God. This could not be found without preceding misery. So also, since justice presupposes crime, without which justice cannot be exercised, (for where there is no crime, there justice has no place,) it was necessary that man should be so created that, without the destruction of his nature, he might be a fit subject, that in him God might declare His own justice. For He could not declare His own justice in man unless He should have destined him to eternal damnation. Therefore, God proposed, &c." These things were published by James Andreas, but acknowledged by

Beza, for in his answer to that discussion he does not say that views, not his own, are attributed to him. You see, therefore, that I have adapted the proper object to those attributes according to their opinion, which sentiment they without doubt think that they have derived from the Scripture; in which this is fixed that God cannot justly punish one who is not a sinner; in which also the same author will deny that the word mercy is so used that, when attributed to God, it may signify salvation from possible misery; since, in their view, it every where designates salvation from the misery which the sinner has merited, and which either has been or can be justly inflicted by the Deity. But I shall not wish to contend strenuously that it is not possible that mercy should be exercised towards those not actually miserable, and I can easily assent to those things which you have said concerning that subject, if they may have the meaning which I will give in my own words, namely, that all creatures, even angels and men, when compared with God, are miserable, misery being here taken for non felicity, not for that which is opposed to felicity in a privative sense, but for that which is opposed to it in a contradictory sense; as nothing more is proved by the reason from analogy. In comparison with God they are not just, therefore, in comparison with him they are not happy. For there are three antecedents, each of which has its consequent; just, unjust, not just; happy, unhappy or miserable, not happy. From justice results happiness, from injustice misery, from non-justice non-felicity.

But creatures as such can be compared with God, both in relation of the limit whence they proceed, and in relation to the limit to which they advanced by the Deity. In relation to the latter, angels and men exist, are just, are happy; in relation to the former, they do not exist, are not just, are not happy, since they come from nothing and can therefore be returned to nothing. But in this relation they cannot be called unjust or unhappy, since the limit, from which they were brought forward, is opposed, by contradiction, not by privation, to the limit to which they are borne by the divine goodness, or more briefly, since they are brought from possibility to actuality, which possibility and actuality are contradictory not privative, one of the other. Now, since they consist of possibility and actuality, it is not possible that they, if deserted by divine support, should return to nothing, but it is necessary that they, if thus deserted, should return to nothing. It is moreover possible that, continuing to exist by the divine power, yet being left to themselves and having power to decide their own course, they should, in their second action, not live according to the dictates of justice, by which they were governed in their first action, but do something contrary to it, and by this act become unrighteous and sinners, and, having become such, should put on the habit of unrighteousness, the habit of righteousness having been removed, either as an effect or on the ground of demerit, so that they would become miserable first by desert, next by act, and finally by habit. But if God should hinder them from deserving that misery that is from sinning and becoming actually miserable, I do not see why that act may not be ascribed to mercy since it originates in the desire to prevent misery, which desire pertains to mercy. I concede, indeed, that this is so, and that it is not therefore absolutely true that mercy can only be exercised towards actual sinners. But I wish that it should be observed that mercy is not used, in that sense, by Calvin and Beza, and indeed if mercy, thus understood, should be substituted for the same affection, as it is used by Calvin and Beza, the whole relation and description of the decree would be changed. I remark also that mercy, understood as you present it, does not come under consideration when the subject treated of is the predestination of men: for it is not exercised by God towards man, as one who has not been saved from possible misery by the divine predestination. Finally, it should also be considered that the relation between mercy understood in the latter, and mercy understood in the former sense is such that both cannot concur to the salvation of a man. For if there be occasion for the mercy, which saves from possible misery, there can be no place for that which delivers from actual misery, as the opportunity for the exercise of its peculiar functions is taken away, or, rather, precluded by the former; if on the contrary the mercy, which frees from actual misery, is necessary, the other does not act, and so the former excludes the latter in the relation of both cause and effect, and the latter consequently excludes the former, not succeeding after the fulfillment of its office, but existing by the necessity of its own action, as the man has failed of the former.

We remark in reference to justice that it is indeed very true that it can have place, and can be exercised towards those who are not sinners. For it is the rewarder not only of sinful, but of righteous conduct. But why may it not be deduced from these things, so considered by you, that the necessary existence of sin cannot be inferred even from the necessary declaration of the mercy and justice of God, since both, considered in a certain light, can be exercised towards those who are not sinners. In this way the order of predestination established by Calvin and Beza is wholly overthrown. But as mercy, saving from possible misery, and justice, rewarding virtue do not need the pre-existence of actual misery and sin, yet it is certain that mercy, freeing from actual misery and justice, punishing sin, can only be exercised towards the actually miserable and sinful. But Calvin and Beza every where use the terms, mercy and justice, in this sense, when they discuss the decree of predestination and probation. Since, also, mercy and justice, understood in the former sense, have no place in the predestination and reprobation of men, but only as they are received in the former signification, mercy, saving from possible misery and justice, rewarding

precedes the affirmative. From this it follows that if that negative act is posterior, in the order of nature, to the affirmative act of predestination, as is the case, then the functions of mercy must be prior; for from mercy originates the affirmative act of predestination, which is antecedent to the negative act of reprobation. SECONDLY, that the punishment, due to sin, is by this decree destined for no one, unless so as it is not removed by mercy; and in this respect, though justice may in its own right claim the punishment of the sinner, yet it exacts that punishment, according to the decree of predomination which is made by justice, in view not of the fact that it is due to the sinner, but of the fact that it has not been remitted to him of mercy; else all men universally would be predamned, since they all have deserved punishment. Hence, this ought also to be considered whether the justice, which is the administratrix of the decree of reprobation or predamnation is revealed according to the Law or the Gospel, of legal rigor or softened by some mercy and forbearance. If mercy, the administratrix of predestination is revealed according to the Gospel, as is true, it seems from what has already been said, that justice the opposite of mercy, which is prior to it, in the order of nature, should be also revealed according to the Gospel. If any one thinks that these views are vain and useless, let him consider that what is said in the Scripture concerning legal righteousness is not useless—

"The man which doeth those things shall live by them," (Rom. x. 5,) and "cursed is every one that continueth not in all things which are written in the book of the law to do them." (Gal. iii. 10.)

Let him also consider what is said concerning Evangelical righteousness, "He that believeth in the Son hath everlasting life, (John iii. 36,) and "He that believeth not is condemned. (John iii. 18.) I wish that these things may be considered thoroughly by the thoughtful, and I ask a suspension of their decision until they have accurately weighed the matter.

FOURTH PROPOSITION OF ARMINIUS

The second theory is this—God, from eternity, considering men in their original native condition determined to raise some to supernatural felicity and ordained for the same persons supernatural means which are necessary, sufficient and efficacious to secure that felicity to them, to the praise of his glorious grace; and to pass by others, and to have them in their natural state, and not to bestow on them those supernatural and efficacious means, to declare the liberty of his own goodness; and that he reprobated the same individuals, so passed by, whom he foresaw as not continuing in their original condition, but falling from it of their own fault, that is, he prepared punishment for them to the declaration of his own justice.

THE ANSWER OF JUNIUS TO THE
FOURTH PROPOSITION

This theory is stated, in these words, not more nearly in accordance with the sentiment of its authors than the preceding. For in the first place, I do not remember that I have read these words in Thomas Aquinas, or others: in the second place, if any have used this phraseology, they have not used it in that sense, as shall be proved under the sixth proposition. But in the phrase supernatural felicity, understand th<n uiJoqesian, the adoption of the sons of God with all its adjuncts and consectaries. After the words "declare the liberty of his own goodness," add, if you please, "and the perfection of his manifold wisdom." The word reprobation is to be taken catachrestically, as we have before observed. I should prefer that words should be variously distinguished in referring to matters which are distinct.

THE REPLY OF ARMINIUS TO THE ANSWER
TO THE FOURTH PROPOSITION

If I have stated this second theory as nearly in accordance with the sentiments of its authors as in the preceding case, it is well; but I fear on this point since I do not, with equal confidence claim a knowledge of the second. Yet I think that I have derived the explanation of this from the Theses discussed under your direction in which I recognize your style and mode of discussion. Thus in Thesis 10 of those which were discussed, Coddaeus being the respondent, is this statement. "Human beings" (that is, one part of the material of predestination, as is stated in Thesis 7, of the same disputation concerning predestination) "are creatures in a condition of nature (which can effect nothing natural, nothing divine) to be exalted above nature, and to be transmitted to a participation of divine things by the supernatural energy of the Deity." The same assertion is found in the Thesis 4 of your tenth theological disputation, in which the subject of the predestination of human beings alone is discussed, as is the case with the first Thesis, that no one may think that things, said in common concerning the predestination of angels and of men, ought to be expressed in general terms. which might afterwards be attributed specially to each of these classes, according to their different condition to the elect angels, an exaltation from that nature, in which they were created by the Deity, but to elect human beings on elevation from their corrupt nature into which they fell, of their own fault. If, however, this matter is thus understood, there is now no discrepancy between us in this respect.

But I think that it is evident from those words of your Theses that human beings, considered in their original condition are the material of predestination, or its adequate object. Human beings I say in their original condition, both in the fact that nothing supernatural or divine has been bestowed upon them, and that they have not yet fallen into sin.

Considered in their original condition, I say again, in view of the fact that even if they have either supernatural and divine gifts or sin, they are not considered with reference to these by Him who determined to perform any certain act concerning them, which is equivalent to an assertion that neither supernatural or divine gifts, nor sin, held, in the mind of Him who considered them the position of a formal cause in the object, From these words I deduce this conclusion: Human beings, considered in their natural state which can admit nothing supernatural or divine, are the object or material of predestination;- But human beings, considered in their natural condition, are here as beings considered in that natural state, which can do nothing supernatural or divine, or rather they are the same in definition;- Therefore, human beings in their natural state are the object and material of predestination, that is, according to the views embraced in your Theses. The Major Proposition is contained in the Thesis. For if the will or decree of God in reference to the exaltation of men from such a state of nature to a state above nature is predestination, then men, considered in that natural state, are the true material of predestination; since the acts of God, both the internal, which is the decree concerning the exaltation of certain human beings, and the external, which is the exaltation itself, (as it ought to be, if we wish to consider the mere object) leave to us man in his mere natural state which can do nothing supernatural or divine.

If it is said that, in these words, the condition of sin is not excluded, since even sinners may be raised from their corrupt nature, I reply, in the first place, that this cannot be the meaning of those words, both because it is not necessary that it should be said of such a nature that can do nothing supernatural or divine, for this is understood from the qualifying term, when it is spoken of as "corrupt," and because, in the definition of preterition, Thesis 15, that act, by which the pure nature of some creatures is not confirmed, is attributed to preterition, which preterition is the leaving of some created beings in their natural condition. I reply, in the second place, that there is here an equivocation in the definition, and that the decree is equivocal and only true on the condition of its division, of which I will say more hereafter. The Minor is true, for this is evident from the reciprocal and equivalent relation of the antecedent and consequent to each other. But what pertains to predestination is enunciated in these words, "to be exalted above nature, and to be transferred to a participation of divine things by the supernatural energy of the Deity, which divine things pertain to grace and glory," as in your Thesis 9. It is not doubtful that my words, in which I have described the second theory, are in harmony with these statements, but if any one thinks that there is a discrepancy because, in your Theses, grace and glory are united, and that it can be understood from my words that I designed to indicate that glory first, and grace afterwards, are prepared for men in predestination, I would inform him that I did not wish to indicate such an idea, but that I wished to set forth, in those words, what the predestinate obtain from predestination.

I come now to the second part, which refers to preterition, and in reference to this, your Theses make this statement "Preterition is the act of the divine will, by which God, from eternity, determined to leave some of his creatures in their natural state, and not to communicate to them that supernatural grace by which their nature might be preserved uncorrupt, or, having become corrupt, might be restored to the declaration of the freedom of his own goodness." Also in your theological axioms Concerning Nature and Grace, axiom 44. "To this purpose of election in Christ is opposed the eternal purpose of non-election or preterition, according to which some are passed by as to be left in their own natural state." These are my words: "but he determined to pass by some and to leave them in their natural state, and not to impart to them those supernatural and especially those efficacious means, to declare the freedom of his own goodness." He, who compares our statements, will see that one and the same sentiment is expressed in different words. For "supernatural grace" and "supernatural means" signify the same thing, "the grace by which nature, when uncorrupt, might be strengthened, and when corrupt, might be restored," is what I have described in the phrase "efficacious means." For "efficacious means" either confirm nature when uncorrupt or restore it when corrupt; as sufficient means are those which have the power to confirm or restore. Moreover the end, which I have proposed, is expressed in your second Thesis, "to the praise of his glorious grace," and again, in the second Thesis of the tenth disputation, "to the praise of his most glorious grace," and in Thesis 15 of the disputation concerning predestination, in which Coddaeus is the respondent, you have stated the end of preterition to be "the declaration of the freedom of the divine goodness, with no additional remark; yet I do not object to what you wish to add in this place, "the perfection of his manifold wisdom." However, the freedom of goodness and the perfection of wisdom cannot be at the same moment engaged in the acts of predestination and preterition. For the office of wisdom takes precedence, in pointing out all possible methods of illustrating the glory of God, and that which may especially conduce to the glory of God. But the freedom of his goodness is subsequent in its operation, in making choice of the mode of illustration, and in carrying it out into the action, in the exercise (so to speak) of power. In reference to the third part, I make the same remark, namely, concerning reprobation, or the preparation of punishment, that I have also explained it correctly according to your view, for thus is reprobation or the preparation for punishment defined in Thesis seventeen. "It is the act of the divine pleasure, by which God from eternity determined for the declaration of his own justice to punish his creatures, who should not continue in their original state, but should depart from God, the author of their origin, by their own deed and depravity. But I have used the same words with only this addition, "the same individuals, so passed by," by which addition I have only done that which was made requisite by the arrangement and distinction in character which I have adopted; for those, for whom punishment is prepared, are not different from those who are passed by, though punishment was prepared for them, not because they are included in the latter class, the passed by, but because they were foreseen as those who would be sinners.

I cannot, therefore, yet persuade myself that this sentiment has been incorrectly set forth by me. If I shall see it hereafter, I will freely acknowledge it, though this may not be of so much importance.

This indeed I desire, that whether the first view, or the second, or any other view whatever be presented, it may be clearly and strongly proved from the Scriptures, and be defended, with accuracy, from all objections. In reference to the word "reprobate," I have spoken before in reply to your second answer, and I am prepared to use it hereafter according to your later explanation, as you have given it in your last answer. I should perhaps have so used it, in my former letter, if I had found it so used by yourself in your own writings, for I know that equivocal meaning has always been the mother of error, and that it ought to be carefully avoided in all serious discussions.

FIFTH PROPOSITION OF ARMINIUS

The third theory is that God determined of his grace to free some of the human race, fallen, and lying in the "lump" (Rom. ix. 21) of perdition and corruption, to the declaration of his Mercy; but to leave in the same "lump," or at least to damn, on account of final impenitence, others, to the illustration both of the freedom of his gratuitous grace towards the vessels of glory and mercy, and of his justice towards the vessels of dishonour and wrath. I do not state these views, that I may instruct you in reference to them, but that you may see whether I have correctly understood them, and may direct and guide me, if I am, in any respect, in error.

THE REPLY OF JUNIUS TO THE FIFTH PROPOSITION

This theory agrees with the first and second in all respects, if you make this one exception, that, in the latter case, the election and reprobation of men is said to have been made after the condition of the fall and of our sin, in the former case without reference to the fall, and to our sin. But neither of them seems properly and absolutely to pertain altogether to the relation of election and reprobation since all admit that the cause of election and reprobation is placed in the consent only of the Being, who alone predestinates. For, whether it is affirmed that election and reprobation are made from among human beings in their original state, or from those, who are fallen and sinful, there was not any cause in them, who, in either state, were equal in all respects, according to nature, but only in the will and liberty of God electing, who separated these from those, and adopted them unto himself "of his own will" boulhqeiv as James says (ch. 1, vers. 18,) or according to the counsel of his will. But yet this circumstance is worthy of notice, and we will, hereafter in its own place, give our opinion concerning it, according to the Scriptures, as there will be an appropriate place for speaking of this subject.

THE REPLY OF ARMINIUS TO THE ANSWER
TO THE FIFTH PROPOSITION

The circumstance of sin and of the fall is of very great importance in this whole subject, not indeed as a cause but as a quality, requisite in the object, without a consideration of which I do not think that election or reprobation was or could have been made by the Deity, which matter we will hereafter more fully discuss. There are also many men learned, and not unversed in the sacred Scriptures, who say that God could not be defended from the charge of sin, if he had not in that decree, considered, man as a sinful being. But I cannot, for a two-fold reason, assent to your denial that the formal cause of the object properly pertains to the subject of that decree, because all fully agree in admitting that the cause of the decree is placed in Him, who predestinates. First, because the formal cause of the object, and not the cause of the act only, is necessarily required for the definition of that act. Secondly, because it is possible that the cause of the act may be of such a nature, that, in its own act, it cannot exert influence on the object which is presented to it, unless it be furnished with that formal relation, which I think is the fact in this case, and will prove it. Nor is there any reason why it should be said that the freedom of God, in the act of predestination, is limited though the circumstance of sin may be stated to be of necessity presupposed to that decree.

But since frequent mention has been made, in this whole discussion of divine freedom, it will not be out of place to refer to it at somewhat greater length, and to affix to it its limits from the Scripture, according to the declaration of God himself. The subject of freedom is the will, its object is an act. In respect to the former, it is an affection of the will, according to which it freely tends towards its one object; in respect to the latter, it is the power and authority over its own act. This freedom is, in the first place and chiefly, in God, and it is in rational creatures by a communication made by God. But freedom is limited, or, which is the same thing, it is effected that any act should not be in the power of the agent in three ways, by natural and internal necessity, by external force and coaction, and by the interposition of law. God can be compelled by no one to an act, he can be hindered by no one in an act, hence, this freedom is not limited by that kind of restriction. Law also cannot be imposed on God, as He is the highest, the Supreme Lawgiver. But He can limit Himself, by His own act. There are, then, but two causes which effect that any act should not be in the power of God; the former is the nature of God, and whatever is repugnant to it is absolutely impossible; the latter is any previous act of God, to which another act is opposed. Examples of the former are such as these; God cannot lie, because He is, by nature, true. He cannot sin or commit injustice, because he is justice itself. Examples of the latter are these; God cannot effect that what has previously occurred may not have occurred, for, by an antecedent act, he has effected that it should be; if now can effect that it may not have been, He will destroy his own power and will. God could not but grant to David that his seed should sit on his throne, for this was promised to David, and confirmed by an oath. He cannot forget the labour of love, performed by the saints, so as not to bestow upon it a reward, for He has promised that reward. If, then, any one wishes to inquire whether any act belongs to the free will and the power of God, he must see whether the nature of God may restrict that act, and if it is not so restricted, whether the freedom of God is limited by any antecedent act, if he shall find that the act is not restricted in either mode, then he may conclude that the act pertains to the divine power; but it is not to be immediately inferred that it has been or will be performed by God, since any act which depends on His free will, can be suspended by Him, so as not to be performed. It is also to be observed here that many things are possible for God, in respect to this absolute power, which are not possible in respect to justice. It is possible in respect to His power that He should punish one who has not sinned, for who could resist Him, but it is not possible, in respect to justice, for it would be at variance with the Divine justice. God can do whatever He wills with His own, but He cannot will to do with His own that which he cannot do of right. For His will is restricted by the limits of justice. Nor is the creature, in such a sense, in the power of God, the Creator, that he can do, of right, in reference to it, whatever he might do of His absolute power, for the power of God over the creature depends, not on the infinity of the Divine essence, but on that communication by which he has communicated to us our limited essence. This permits that God should deprive us of that being which he has given us without merit on our part, but does not permit that He should inflict misery upon us without our demerit. For to be miserable is worse than not to be, as happiness is better than mere existence. And, therefore, there is not the same liberty to inflict misery on the creature without demerit, as to take away being without previous sin. God takes away that which He gave, and He can do as He wills, with His own, but He cannot inflict misery, because the creature does not so far belong to God. The potter cannot, from the unformed lump, make a man to dishonour and condemnation, unless the man has previously made himself worthy of punishment and dishonour by his own transgression.

SIXTH PROPOSITION OF ARMINIUS

I am not pleased with the first theory because God could not, in his purpose of illustrating his glory by mercy and punitive justice, have reference to man as not yet made, nor indeed to man as made, and considered in his natural condition. In which sentiment I think that I have yourself as my precedent, for, in discussing predestination, you no where make mention of mercy, but every where of grace, which transcends mercy, as exercised towards creatures, continuing in their original, natural state, while it coincides with mercy in being occupied with the sinner, but when you treat of the passed by and the reprobate, you mention justice, and only in the case of such. Besides, according to that opinion, God is, by necessary consequence, made the author of the fall of Adam and of sin, from which imputation he is not freed by the distinctions of the act and the evil in the act, of necessity and coaction, of the decree and its execution, of efficacious and permissive decree, as the latter is explained by the authors of this view, in harmony with it, nor a different relation of the divine decree and of human nature, nor by the addition of the proposed end, namely that the whole might redound to the divine glory, &c.

ANSWER OF JUNIUS TO THE SIXTH PROPOSITION

There are three things to be laid down in order, before I come to the argumentation itself. First, in reference to the meaning of the first view; secondly, in reference to its agreement with the second and third; thirdly, in reference to a few fundamental principles necessary to the clearness of this question. In the first place, then, if that view be fully examined, we shall perceive with certainty that its authors did not regard man absolutely and only before his creation, &c., but in a general view and with a universal reference to that and to all times. For though they make the act of election and predestination, (as one which exists in the Deity,) as from eternity, in reference to the creation of man, yet they teach that its object, namely mankind, was predestinated without discrimination, and in common, and that God, in the act of predestination, considered the whole human race as various parts inwrought by the eternal decree into its execution. Thus Beza, very clearly on Ephes. i. 4, says, "Christ is presented to us as mediator. Therefore, the fall must, in the order of causes, necessarily precede in the purpose of God, but previous to the fall there must be a creation in righteousness and holiness." So afterwards, on ch. iv, 24, "As God has made for Himself a way both for saving, by his mercy, those whom He had elected in Christ, and for justly punishing those who, having been conceived in sin, should remain in their depravity," &c.

This view he also learnedly presents in a note on verses 4 and 5. Thus those authors embrace the first, and, at the same time, the second and third theories.

But this first theory has an agreement with the second and also with the third, indeed it is altogether the stone, though in appearance it seems otherwise, if you attend to the various objects of these theories. For while the authors of the first regard man universally, in the argument of predestination, election and reprobation, the authors of the second have made a restriction to the case of man before transgression only, and this with the design to show that, in predestination, the cause of election and of reprobation was only in the being predestinating, which is very true. When they assert, therefore, that the election of man was made before his fall, they do not exclude the idea of the eternity of that decree, but consider this to be sufficient if they may establish the fact that eternal predestination, that is, election and reprobation, was made by God, without reference to sin, which the apostle has demonstrated in the example, by no means obscure, of Jacob and Esau. (Rom. 9) The first, therefore, differs from the second less in substance than in the manner of speaking. But those, who adhere to the third theory, have looked, properly speaking, not so much to the cause of election and reprobation, as to the order of causes, of which damnation is the consequence; which damnation, many in former times, confounding with reprobation, that is, non-election or predestination, exclaimed that the doctrine of predestination was impious, and accused the servants of God, as is most clearly evident from the writings of Augustine and Fulgentius. The little book of Augustine, which he wrote in answer to the twelve articles falsely charged against him, most opportunely explains the matter. Neither those who favour the second theory, therefore, nor those who favour the third, have attacked the first, but have rather presented in a different mode, parts of the same argument, distinct in certain respects. It seems then that, as to the sum of the whole matter, they do not differ so much as some suppose, but have attributed to parts of its execution, (to all of which the decree has reference,) certain circumstances, not indeed ineptly in respect to the decree.

Let us now come to certain fundamental principles necessary to this doctrine, by the application of which its truth may be confirmed, and those things which seem to operate against it, may be removed. These seem to me capable of being included under four heads, the essence of God, His knowledge, His actions, and their causes, to each of which we will here briefly refer. We quote first from Mal. iii. 6, "I am the Lord, I change not;" also from James i. 17, "with whom is no variableness, neither shadow of turning," and many similar passages. The truth of this fundamental principle is very certain; from it is deduced the inevitable necessity of this conclusion, that in the Deity nothing is added, nothing is taken away, nothing is changed in fact or relation; for such have philosophers themselves decided to be the nature of eternity; but God is eternal. Also that God is destitute of all movement in His essence, because He is immortal; in His power because He is pure and simple action; and in intellect, because "all things are naked and opened unto His eyes," and He sees all and each of them eternally, by a single glance; in His will and purpose, for He "is not a man that he should lie, neither the son of a man that He should repent," (Num. xxiii. 19,) but He is always the same; and lastly in operation, for the things which vary are created, while the Lord remains without Variation, and has in Himself the form of immutable conception of all those things which exist and are done mutably in time. The second fundamental principle is that the knowledge of the eternal, immutable and infinite mind is eternal, immutable and infinite and knows things to be known as such, and those to be done as such, (gwstw~v) eternally, immutably and infinitely. God has a knowledge practically (praktikw~v) of all evil as a matter of mere knowledge and finally of all things of all classes, (which consist of things the highest, the intermediate, and the lowest of things good and evil,) energetically (ejnerghtikw~v) according to his own divine mode. There is a three-fold relation in all science, if comparison is made with the thing known according to the measure of the being who knows or takes cognizance of it; inferior, equal, and superior, or supereminent, which may be made clear by an illustration from sight. I see the sun, but the light of my vision is inferior to its light; I take cognizance of natural objects, but as owls do of the light of the sun, as Aristotle says. Here is the inferior mode of knowledge, which never exists in God. In him alone exists equal knowledge, and that knowledge which is supereminent after the divine mode, for He has equal knowledge of Himself; He is that which He knows Himself to be, and he knows adequately what He is. All other things He knows in the supereminent mode, and has them present to himself from eternity; if not, there would be two very grievous absurdities, not to mention others; one, that something might be added to the Deity, but that nothing can be added to eternity; the other, that knowledge could not belong to God univocally as the source of all knowledge. But nature herself teaches that in every class of objects there is some one thing which they call univocal, from which are other things in an equivocal sense; as, for example, things which are hot, are made so by fire. Here the fire is hot univocally, other things equivocally. God has knowledge univocally, other beings equivocally; unless perhaps some may be so foolish as to place a possessor of knowledge above the Deity, which would be blasphemy. The third point is that the actions of God in Himself are eternal, whether they pertain to His knowledge or His essence, to His intellect, will or power, and whatever else there may be of this nature; but from Himself they flow, as it were, out of himself according to His own mode, or according to that of the creature according to his eternal decree, yet in an order which is his own, but adapted to time. According to the mode of the Deity, action is three-fold; that of creation, that of providence, so far as it is immediate, and that of saving grace.

For many things proceed from the Deity without the work of the creature, but they are things which He condescends to accomplish mediately in nature and in grace. He does, as a universal principle according to the mode of the creature and, as Augustine says, (lib. 7, de. civit. Dei. cap. 30) "He so administers all things which He has created, as to permit them also to exercise and to perform their own motions." But "their own motions" pertain, some of them to nature and to natural instinct and are directed invariably to one certain and destined end, and others to the will in the rational nature, which are directed to various objects either good or evil, to those which are good, by the influence of the Deity, to those which are evil by His influence only so far as they are natural, and by his permission so far as they are voluntary. From which it can be established in the best and most sacred manner that all effects and defects in nature and in the will of all kinds, depend on the providence of God; yet in such a manner that, as Plato says, the creature is in fault as the proximate cause, and "God is wholly without blame."

The fourth point is that the first and supreme cause is so far universal, that nothing else can be supposed or devised to be its cause, since if it should depend on any other cause, it could be neither the first nor the supreme cause, but there must be another, either prior or superior, or equal to it, so that neither would be absolutely first or supreme. In the next place, all causes exist, either as principles or derived from a principle; "as principles" nature and the will exist; "from a principle" are mediate causes, from nature, natural causes, and from the will voluntary causes. The mode of the latter has been made two-fold by the Deity, necessary and contingent. The necessary mode is that which cannot be otherwise, and this is always good, in that it is necessary; but the contingent is that which is as it happens to be, whether good or bad. But here a three-fold caution is to be carefully observed; first, that we hold these modes of the causes to be from the things themselves and in themselves, according to the relation of the principles from which they proceed, for we speak now not of the immediate actions of God, which are above these principles, as we have before noticed, the natural causes, naturally, and the voluntary causes, voluntarily; secondly, that we make both these modes to be from God, but not in God; for mode in God is only divine, that is, it surpasses the necessary and contingent in all their modes; since there can occur to the Deity neither necessity from any source, nor any contingency, but all things in the Deity are essential, and in a divine mode; thirdly, that we should consider those modes as flowing from God to created things, in such a manner that none of them should be recipro-cated, and, as it were, flow back to God. For God is the universal principle; and if any of these should flow back to Him, He would from that fact cease to be the principle. The reason, indeed, of this is manifest from a comparison of natural examples, since this whole thing proceeds not from natural power simply, in so far as it is natural, but from the rational power of God. For it is a condition of natural power, that it always produces one and the same thing in its own kind, and that if it should produce any thing, out of itself, it must produce something like itself from the necessity of nature, or something unlike from contingency. A pear tree produces a pear tree, a bull begets one of its own species, and a human being begets a human being; that is, in accordance with the distinct form which exists in the nature of each thing.

But the operation of rational power, which is capable of all forms, is of all kinds; to which three things must concur in the agent, knowledge, power, and will. But the mode of those things, which rational power effects, is not consti-tuted according to the mode of knowledge or power, but to the mode of the will which actually forms the works, which virtually are formed in the knowledge and power, as in a root; and this from the freedom of the will and not from the necessity of nature. If we would illustrate this by an example in divine things, let it be this: the person of the Father begat the person of the Son by nature, not by the will; God begat his creatures by the will, not by nature. Therefore, the Son is one with the Father, but created things are diverse from the Deity, and are of all classes, degrees, and conditions, made by His rational power voluntarily to demonstrate His manifold wisdom. It is indeed nothing new that those things which are of nature should be reciprocated and refluent, since many of them are adequate, while many indeed are essential. But it is a new idea that those things which are of the will should be either reciprocated or made adequate. But if this is true in nature, as it surely is, how much more must it be believed in reference to God, if He be compared with created things. It was necessary that these should be laid down by me, my brother, rather copiously, that the sequence might be more easily determined by certain limits.

You say that the first opinion does not please you, because you think that God cannot, in his purpose to illustrate his glory by mercy and punitive justice, have had reference to the human race, considered as not yet made. You add, in amplifying the idea, that God did not have reference even to the human race, considered as created, and in his natural condition. That we may each understand the other, I remark that I understand by your phrase, "have reference to the human race," to have man as the object or instead of the object of action. But let us consider, if you please, or rather, because it does please you and you request it, how far your view is correct. Indeed, from the first fundamental principle, which I have before laid down, (from which I trust that you do not dissent,) I consider man as not yet created, as created, as fallen, and, in fine, man in general, in whatever light he may be viewed, to be the object of the power, knowledge, will, mercy and justice of God; for if this is granted, it will then be a complete sequence that there is something, aside from common providence and the special predestination of the sons of God, not an object of the action of the Deity. Then there can be some addition to God, if something can be added to His power, knowledge, will, &c., since the power, knowledge, will, &c., of God, is either God, or a divine, that is, an infinite act. Whatever eternity looks upon, if it does not look upon it eternally, it ceases to be eternity; it loses the nature of eternity. If infinity does not look on infinite things, in an infinite manner, if it is limited by parts, it ceases to be infinity. To God and His eternity, it is not is, was or shall be, but permanent and enduring being, all at once, and without bounds. The creature exists indeed in time, but is present to God, in a peculiar, that is, a divine mode, which is above all consideration of time, and from eternity to eternity; and this is true not only of the creature itself, but of all its feelings, whatever may be their origin. You will perhaps say that this principle is acknowledged in the abstract, but that here, as it is considered in the concrete, it has a different relation, in that it has reference to mercy and punishment, which can really be supposed only in view of antecedent misery and sin. But these also, my brother, are present with God as really as those; I do not say in the mode of nature, which is fleeting, but in that of the Deity, which is eternal, and in all respects surpasses nature. They, who think differently, are in danger of denying the most absolute and eternal essence of the Deity itself. We said also, under proposition three, that in created things misery and sin may be considered in relation to the act, the habit, or the capability also in an absolute and in a relative sense. But in God, (whom also Aristotle acknowledges to be "energy in its most simple form," mercy and judgment exist by an eternal act, and not by a temporal one; and contemplates the misery and sin of man in all their modes, previous to all time, and does not merely take cognizance of them as they occur in time.

Lastly, that we may disclose the fountain of the matter, this whole idea originates in the fact that the third fundamental principle which, we before laid down, has not been sufficiently regarded by those who so think. For since all action is either internal or external, or both united together. The internal is in God, as the maker: the external is in the creature in its own time and place, and in the thing made just as the house is formed in the mind of the builder, before it is built materially (as it is said). But when both acts are united and from them is produced a work, numerically a unit, which they style a result, then the internal act is the formal cause; the external act is the material cause. Nothing in God is temporary; action in God is alone eternal, for it is internal, it is therefore not temporary; so, on the contrary, all things out of God are temporary, therefore the external act is temporary, for it is out of God. "What, then, do you prove?" you will ask. "That God in his mercy and punitive justice acts with reference to man as not yet created, or indeed as created, but considered in his natural condition?" I indeed admit that whatever it may be, which can be predicated of man, it can sacredly and in truth be predicated of him. Yet I see that two statements may be made of a milder character, and in harmony with the words of Christ and the apostles, which are clearly intimated, if not fully expressed by them; the former, that, in this question, we must consider, not only the mode and the consequent event (which some call, catechrestically, the end), namely, mercy and punitive justice, also life and eternal death, but the fountain and the genus from which these result, and to which they hold the relation of species, namely, grace and non-grace, adoption or filiation, and non-adoption, which is reprobation, as we have said above (Prop. 2), the latter, that, in the argument of election, we must propose not any particular relation of the human race, but the common or universal relation so that we may consider him as not yet created, as created, as fallen &c., yet present in all respects in the conception of God, so that in this election, grace towards mankind in the abstract, and mercy towards man as fallen and sinful, which is of grace, concur, but in reprobation, the absence of the grace of adoption and the absence of mercy concur. If these statements are correct, I do not see in what respect a pious mind can be offended. For Christ says that they are blessed of God, the Father who "inherit the kingdom prepared for them from the foundation of the world." (Matt. xxv. 34.)

And Paul says that God "hath blessed us with all spiritual blessings in heavenly places in Christ, according as he hath chosen us in him, before the foundation of the world, that we should be holy and without blame before him in love, having predestinated us unto the adoption of children by Jesus Christ to himself, according to the good pleasure, to the praise, &c." (Ephes. i. 3-6.) "What then? is there no special reference?" I answer that properly in the argument of election and reprobation (for the matter of damnation is a different one) there is no particular reference to men as a cause, but our separation from the reprobate is wholly of the mere will of God: in that God has separated and made a distinction among men, whether not yet created, created or fallen, and indeed among all things, present alike to Him, yet equal in all respects by nature and condition, by electing and predestinating some to the adoption of the sons of God, and by leaving others to themselves and to their own nature, not calling them to the adoption of the sons of God, which is gratuitous and can be ascribed only to grace. This grace, also, unique in itself only, may be two-fold in the elect, for either it is grace simply, if you look even from eternity on man without reference to the fall, which grace is communicated to the elect, both angels and men, or it is grace joined to mercy, or gracious mercy, when you come down to the special matter of the fall and of sin. God dealt with the angels according to His grace, with us according to His grace and mercy, if you do not also have reference to possible misery (of which we spoke, Prop. 3, and misery.) For in this sense mercy is, and can, with propriety, be called a divine work of grace. But what is there here which can be reprehended in God? What is there, which can be denied by us? God has bestowed human nature on all; it is a good gift; on certain individuals he has bestowed mercy and the grace of adoption; this is a better gift. He was not under obligation to bestow either; He bestowed both, the former on all, the latter on some men. But it may perhaps be said that reprobation is one thing, and punitive justice and damnation, which is under discussion, is another. Let that be conceded; then there is agreement between us in reference to reprobation, let us then consider punitive justice and damnation. It is certain that, as the vessels of mercy which God has prepared for His glory that He might demonstrate the riches of His glory, are from eternity fully present to Him in a divine and incomprehensible manner, without any motion or change in Himself, so also "the vessels of wrath fitted to destruction" that he might "show His wrath and make His power known," (Rom. ix. 22,) are eternally presented to his eyes, according to the mode of Deity. As vessels, therefore, they are of God, for He is the maker of all things: as vessels of wrath, they are of themselves and of their own sin, into which they rush of their own will, for we all are by this nature the children of wrath, (Ephes. ii. 3,) but not in our original constitution. Moses affirms in Gen. i. 31, that "God saw every thing that He had made, and, behold, it was very good."

God, who is good, does not hate that which is good. All things, at their creation, were good, therefore at their creation, God did not hate any one of all created things: He hates that which is alien from Himself, but not that which is His own: He is angry with our fall and sin, not with His own creation. By creation they are vessels; by the fall, they are vessels of wrath, and fitted to destruction, as the most just consequence of the fall and of depravity: for "neither shall evil dwell with God." (Psalm v. 4.) As in the knowledge of God is the good of the elect, with whom he deals in mercy, so in the knowledge of God, as Isaiah says, chapter xlviii, 4 and 8, is the evil of others: the latter He hated and damned from the period of His knowledge of it. But He knew and foreknew from eternity; therefore, He hates and damns, and even pre-damns from eternity.

As this is the relation of the former proposition, the relation of the other also, added by way of amplification, "nor indeed to man as made and considered in his original condition," is also the same. For the consequence is plainly deduced in the same mode, in reference to the latter as in reference to the former; and you are not ignorant that universal affirmations follow by fair deduction from that which is general to that which is particular. God has reference from eternity in election and reprobation to mankind in general; therefore He had reference to man as not created, created and fallen, and if there is any other term, by which we can express our ideas. In the case of election, and of reprobation, I say, He regarded man abstractly, with whatever relation you may invest him. In the case of damnation, He regarded the sinner, whom He had not given to Christ in the election of grace, and whom He from eternity saw as a sinner. Those holy men, therefore rightly stated that the election and reprobation of man was made from eternity: some considered them as having reference to man, not yet created, others to man as not yet fallen, and yet others to man as fallen: since in whatever condition you regard him, a man is elected or reprobated without consideration of his good or evil deeds. Nor indeed can it be proved that they are at variance in this matter, unless a denial of other conditions is shown in plain terms. For such is the common statement by universal consent. In which, if any one affirms that the supposition of one involves the disavowal of the other he opposes the truth of natural logic and common usage. But if such is the relation of election and reprobation in a general sense, it is a complete sequence that they who say that men, as not created, were elected, speak very truly, since God elected them by the internal act, before He did by the external act; and that they who affirm that the election was of man, as created, have reference to the principle of the external act; and so with the rest. But all these things are not in reference to His act per se, but in reference to the condition of the act, which does not affect its substance. You say that in this opinion you have me as a precedent since, in the discussion of predestination, I "no where make mention of mercy, but every where of grace, which transcends mercy." Indeed, my brother, I have never thought that I should seem to exclude the other parts when I might use the term grace, nor do I see how that inference can be made from the phrase itself. Grace is the genus; it does not exclude mercy, the species. Grace includes, so to speak, the path for all times; therefore it includes that of mercy. Nor do they, who mention mercy, in presenting the species, exclude the genus, nor, in presenting a part, do they exclude all which remains. And we, in presenting the genus, do not deny the species, nor in presenting the whole, do we disavow a part. Both are found in the Scriptures, which speak of grace in respect to the whole and its single parts, and in a certain respect, of mercy: but they take away neither by the affirmation of the other. I would demonstrate this by quotations, did I not think that you with me, according to your skill and intelligence would acknowledge this. Predestination is of grace: the same grace, which has effected the predestination of the saints, also includes mercy: this I sufficiently declared a little while since. I mentioned grace simply, in the case of simple predestination, that is, predestination expressed in simple and universal terms. I speak of mercy, also, in relation to a man who is miserable, spoken of absolutely, or relatively. You add that when I treat of the passed by and the reprobate, I mention justice, and only in the case of such. Let us, if you please, remove the homonymy; then we shall expedite the matter in a few words. We exposed the homonymy in the second proposition; we speak of the reprobate either generally or particularly. If you understand it generally, the mention of justice is correctly made, as we shall soon show. If particularly, either reprobates and those passed by refer to the same, which is the appropriate signification, or the term reprobate is applied to the damned, which is catachrestic. I do not think that you understand it in the former sense, if you understand it in the latter (as you do), what you say is certainly very true, that I spoke of justice only when treating of the damned. However, I do not approve that you write copulatively of the passed by and the reprobate, that is, the damned. For although they are the same in subject, and all the passed by are damned, and all the damned are passed by, yet their relation as passed by or reprobate is one thing, and their relation as damned is another.

Preterition or reprobation is not without justice, but it is not of justice, as its cause: damnation is with justice and of justice. Election and reprobation or preterition are the work of free will according to the wisdom of God; but damnation is the work of necessary will according to the justice of God; for God "cannot deny Himself" (2 Tim. ii. 13.) As a just judge, it is necessary that He should punish unrighteousness, and execute judgment. This, I say, is the work of the manifold wisdom of God, which in those creatures, in whom he has implanted the principle of their own ways, namely, a free will, He might exhibit its two-fold use, good and bad, and the consequent result of its use in both directions. Hence he has, in His own wisdom, ordained, both in angels and in men, the way of both modes of its use, without any fault or sin on His own part. But it is a work of justice to damn the unrighteous. Therefore also it is said truly that the passed by are damned by the Deity, but because they were to be damned, not because they were passed by or reprobated.

Now I come to your argumentation, in which you affirm that, "according to that theory, God is, by necessary consequence, made the author of the fall of Adam, and of sin &c." I do not, indeed, perceive the argument from which this conclusion is necessarily deduced, if you correctly understand that theory. Though I do not doubt that you had reference to your own words, used in stating the first theory, "that he ordained also that man should fall and become depraved, that he might thus prepare the way for the fulfillment of his own eternal counsels, that he might be able mercifully to save some, &c." This, then, if I am not mistaken, is your reasoning. He, who has ordained that man should fall and become depraved, is the author of the fall and of sin; God ordained that man should fall and become depraved; therefore, God is the author of sin. But the Major of this syllogism is denied, because it is ambiguous; for the word ordain is commonly, though in a catachrestical sense, used to mean simply and absolutely to decree, the will determining and approving an act; which catachresis is very frequent in forensic use. But to us, who are bound to observe religiously, in this argument, the propriety of terms, to ordain is nothing else than to arrange the order in acts, and in each thing according to its mode. It is one thing to decree acts absolutely, and another to decree the order of acts, in each thing, according to its mode. The former is immediate, the latter, from the beginning to the end, regards the means, which in all things, pertain to the order of events. In the former signification, the Minor is denied; for it is entirely at variance with the truth, since God is never the author of evil (that is, of evil involving guilt). In the latter signification the Major is denied, for it is not according to the truth, nor is it necessary in any respect that the same person who disposes the order of actions and, in each thing, according to its mode: should be the author of those actions. The actor is one thing, the action is another,-and the arranger of the action is yet another. He who performs an evil deed is the author of evil. He, who disposes the order in the doer and in the evil deed, is not the author of evil, but the disposer of an evil act to a good end. But that this may be understood, let us use the fourth fundamental principle, which we have previously stated, according to this, we shall circumscribe this whole case within this limit; every fault must always be ascribed to the proximate, not to the remote or to the highest cause. In a chain, the link, which breaks, is in fault; in a machine, the wheel, which deviates from its proper course, is in fault, not any superior or inferior one. But as all causes are either principles, or from principles, (in this case, however, principles are like wheels, by which the causes, originating from the principles, are moved), God is the universal principle of all good, nature is the principle of natural things, and the rational will, turning freely to good or evil, is the principle of moral actions. These three principles, in their own appropriate movement, perform their own actions, and produce mediate causes, act in their own relations, and dispose them; God in a divine mode, nature in a natural mode, and the will in an elective mode. God, in a divine mode, originates nature; nature, in its own mode, produces man; the will, in its own appropriate mode, produces its own moral and voluntary actions. If, now, the will produces a moral action, whether good or evil, it produces it, of its own energy, and this cannot be attributed to nature itself as a cause, though nature may implant the will in man, since the will, (though from nature) is the peculiar and special principle of moral actions, instituted by the Deity in nature. But if the blame of this cannot be attributed to nature as a cause, by what right, I pray, can it be attributed to God, who, by the mode and medium of nature, has placed the will in man? I answer then, with Augustine, in his book against articles falsely imputed to him, artic. 10.

"The predestination of God neither excited, nor persuaded, nor impelled, the fall of those who fell, or the iniquity of the wicked, or the evil passions of sinners, but it clearly predestinated His own judgment, by which He should recompense each one according to his deeds, whether good or bad, which judgment would not be inflicted, if men should sin by the will of God." He proceeds to the same purpose in art. 11, remarking, "If it should be charged against the devil, that he was the author of certain sins, and the inciter to them, I think he would be able to exonerate himself from that odium in some way, and that he would convict the perpetrators of such sins from their own will, since, although he might have been delighted in the madness of those sinners, yet he could prove that he did not force them to crime. With what folly, what madness, then, is that referred to the counsel of God, which cannot at all be ascribed to the devil, since he, in the sins of wicked men, aids by enticements, but is not to be considered the director of their wills. Therefore God predestinated none of these things that they should take place, nor did He prepare that soul, which was about to live basely and in sin, that it should live in such a manner; but He was not ignorant that such would be its character, and He foreknew that He should judge justly concerning a soul of such character."

But if this could be imputed neither to nature, nor to the devil, how much less to God, the most holy and wise Creator? God, (as St. Augustine says again, book 6) "does not predestinate all which he foreknows. For He only foreknows evil. He does not predestinate it, but He both foreknows and predestinates good." But it is a good, derived from God, that, in His own ordination, He disposes the order in things good and evil; if not, the providence of God would be, for the most part, indifferent (may that be far from our thoughts). God does not will evil, but He wills, and preserves a certain order even in evil. Evil comes from the will of man; from God is the general and special arrangement of His own providence, disposing and most wisely keeping in order even those things which are, in the highest degree, evil.

Here a two-fold question will perhaps be urged upon me:

first, how can these be said, in reference to the will, to be its own motions, when we acknowledge that the will itself, that is, the fountain of voluntary motions, is from nature, and nature is from God? Secondly, why did God place in human beings this will, constituted in the image of liberty? I will reply to both in a few words. To the first; the will is certainly from nature, and nature is from God, but the will is not, on that account, the less to be called the principle of those motions, than nature is called the principle of natural motions. Each is the principle of its own action, though both are from the supreme principle, God. It is one thing to describe the essence of a thing, another to refer to its source. What is essential to nature and the will? That the former should be the principle of natural motions, the latter, of spontaneous motions. What is their source? God is the only and universal source of all things. Nor is it absurd that a principle should be derived from another principle: for although a principle, which originates in another, should not be called a principle in the relation of origin or source, yet, in the relation of the act it does not on that account, cease to be an essential principle. God is, per se, a principle. Nature and our wills are principles derived from a principle. Yet each of them has its own appropriate motions. Nor is there any reason, indeed, why any should think that these are philosophical niceties: they are natural distinctions, and that, which is of nature, is from God. But if we are unwilling to hear nature, let us listen to the truth of God, to Christ speaking of the devil (John viii. 44), "when he speaketh a lie, he speaketh of his own: for he is a liar and the father of it." Here he is called "the father of a lie," and is said "to speak of his own."

According to Christ's words, then, we have the origin and the act of sin in the devil. For the act has a resemblance to himself, for he speaks of his own. What, I pray, can be more conclusive than these words? Hence Augustine, in the answer already quoted, very properly deduces this conclusion. "As God did not, in the angels who fell, induce that will, which they did not continue in the truth; so he did not produce in men that inclination by which they imitate the devil. For he speaketh a lie of his own; and he will not be free from that charge, unless the truth shall free him." He indeed gave free will, namely, that essential power to Adam: but its motion is, in reference to Adam, his own, and, in reference to all of us, our own. In what sense is it our own, when it is given to us by God? Whatever is bestowed on us by God, is either by the law of common right, or of personal and private property. He gave the will to angels and men by the law of personal possession. It is therefore, one's own and its motion belong to the individual. "This," says Augustine, (lib. de Genes. ad litt. in perf. cap. 5,) "He both makes and disposes species and natures themselves, but the privations of species and the defects of natures he does not make, He only ordains." Therefore God is always righteous, but we are unrighteous.

To the second question, namely, why did God create in us this will, and with such a character? I reply; -- it was the work of the highest goodness and wisdom in the universe. Why should we, with our ungrateful minds, who have already made an ill use of those minds, obstruct the fountain of goodness and wisdom? It was the work of goodness to impress his own image on both natures, in the superior, on that of angels, and in the inferior, on that of men: since, while other things in nature are moved by instinct, or feeling, as with a dim trace of the Deity, these alone, in the freedom of their own will, have the principle of their own ways in their own power by the mere goodness of God. It was the work of wisdom to make these very species, endued with His own image, together with so many other objects, and above the others, as the most perfect mirror of His own glory, so far as is possible in created things. But why did he make them of such a character, with mutable freedom? He made His own image, not himself.

The only essential image of God, the Father, is the Lord Jesus Christ, one God, eternal and immutable, with the Father and the Holy Spirit. Whoever thou mayest be, who makest objections to this, thou hearest the serpent whispering to thee, as he whispered once to Eve, to the ruin of our race. Let it suffice thee that thou wast made in the image of God, not possessing the divine perfection. Immutability is peculiar to the divine perfection. This pertains by nature to God. The creature had in himself His image, communicated by God, and placed in his will: but he, whether angel or man, who fell, rejected it of his own will. Not to say more, this whole question was presented by Marcion, and Tertullian, with the utmost fluency and vigour, discussed it in its whole extent, in a considerable part of his second book against Marcion, the perusal of which will, I trust, be satisfactory to you.

You remark, finally, that they are not freed from the necessity of that conclusion "by the distinctions of the act, and the evil in the act, of necessity and creation, of the decree and its execution, &c." Indeed, my brother, I think that, from those things, which have just been said, you will sufficiently perceive in what respects your reasoning is fallacious. For God does not make, but ordains the sinner, as I say, with Augustine, that is, He ordains the iniquity of the sinner not by commanding or decreeing particularly and absolutely that he should commit sin, but by most wisely vindicating His own order, and the right of His infinite providence, even in evil which is peculiar to the creature.

For it was necessary that the wisdom of God should triumph in this manner, when He exhibited His own order in the peculiar and voluntary disorder of His own creature. This disorder and alienation from good the creature prepared for himself by the appropriate motion of free-will, not by the impulse of the Deity. But that freedom of the will, says Tertullian against Marcion (lib. 2, cap. 9) "does not fix the blame on Him by whom it was bestowed, but on him by whom it was not directed, as it ought to have been." Since this is so, it is not at all necessary that I should speak of those particular distinctions, which, in their proper place, may perhaps be valid; they do not seem to me to pertain properly to this argument, unless other arguments are introduced, which I cannot find in your writings. Besides all those distinctions pertain generally to the subject of providence, not particularly to this topic. I am not pleased that the discussion should extend beyond its appropriate range. But here some may perhaps say; "Therefore, the judgments of God depend on contingencies, and are based on contingencies, if they have respect to man as a sinner, and to his sin." That consequence is denied: for, on the contrary, those very things which are contingencies to us, depend on the ordination of God, according to their origin and action. To their origin, for God has established the contingency equally with the necessity: To their action, for He acts in the case of that which is good, fails to act in that which is evil, in that it is evil, not in that it is ordained by His special providence. They are not, therefore, contingencies to the Deity, whatever they may be to us; just as those things, which are contingent to an inferior cause, can by no means be justly ascribed to a superior cause. But I have already stated this matter with sufficient clearness, in the discussion of the fourth fundamental principle. Let us, therefore, pass to other matters.

THE REPLY OF ARMINIUS TO THE ANSWER
TO THE SIXTH PROPOSITION

The meaning of the first theory is that which I have set forth in the third proposition. But it is of little importance to me, whether the object, generally and without distinction, or with a certain distinction, and invested with certain circumstances, is presented to God, when predestinating and reprobating, for that is not, now, the point before me. If, however, it may be proper to discuss this also in a few words, I should say that it cannot seem to one who weighs this matter with accuracy, that the object is considered in general and without any distinction by God, in the act of decreeing, according to the sentiment of the authors of the first theory. For the object was considered by God, in the act of decreeing, in the relation which it had at the time. when it had, as yet, been affected by no external act of God, executing that decree; for this, in a pure and abstract sense, is an object, free from every other consideration, which can pertain to an object, through the action of a cause operating in reference to it. But since, according to the authors of the first theory, the act of creation pertains to the execution of the decree, of which we now treat, it is, therefore, most certainly evident, that man, in that he was to be made, was the object of predestination and reprobation. If any one considers the various and manifold sets of that decree, it is not doubtful that some of these must be accommodated and applied to this and others to that condition of man, and in this sense, I would admit the common and general consideration of the object. But all those acts, according to the authors of that first theory, depend on one primary act, namely, that in which God determined to declare, in one part of that unformed "lump," from which the human race was to be made, the glory of his mercy, and, in another part, the glory of his justice, and it is this very thing which I stated to be displeasing to me in that first theory; nor can I yet persuade myself that there exists, in the whole Scripture, any decree, by which God has determined to illustrate his own glory, in the salvation of these and in the condemnation of those, apart from foresight of the fall.

The passage which you quote from Beza, on Ephes. i. 4, plainly proves that I have done no injustice to those authors in explaining their doctrine. He says, in that passage, that God, by the creation and corruption of man, opened a way for himself to the execution of that which he had before decreed."

In reference to the harmony of those theories, I grant that all agree in this, that this decree of God was made from eternity, before any actual existence of the object, whatever might be its character, and however it might be considered. For "known unto God are all his works from the beginning of the world." (Acts xv. 18.)

It is necessary also that all the internal acts of God should universally be eternal, unless we wish to make God mutable; yet in such a sense that some are antecedent to others in order and nature. I admit also that they agree in this, that there exists, in the predestinate or the reprobate, no cause why the former should be predestinated, the latter reprobated; and that the cause exists only in the mere will of God. But I affirm that some ascend to a greater height than others, and extend the act of decree farther. For the advocates of the third theory deny that God, in any act of predestination and reprobation, has reference to man, considered as not yet fallen, and those of the second theory say that God, in the act of that decree, did not have reference to man as not yet created. The advocates of the

first, however, openly assert and contend that God, in the first act of the decree, had reference to man, not as created, but as to be created. I, therefore, distinguished those theories according to their objects, as each one presented man to God, at the first moment of the act of predestination and reprobation, as free from any divine act predestinating and reprobating, either internal, by which he might decree something concerning man, or external, by which He might effect something in man; this may be called pure object, having as yet received no relation from the act of God, decreeing from eternity, and no form from the external act. But when it has received any relation or form from any act of God, it is no longer pure object, but an object having some action of God concerning it, or in it, by which it is prepared for receiving some further action, as was also a short time since affirmed. We will hereafter examine your idea that they substantiate their theory by the example of Jacob and Esau in Romans 9.

I may be permitted to make some observations or inquiries concerning what you lay down as fundamental principles of this doctrine, and of your reply to my arguments. In reference to the first, concerning the essence of the Deity,

God is in such a sense immutable in essence, power, intellect, will, counsel and work, that, nevertheless, if the creature is changed, he becomes to that creature in will, the application of power, and in work, another than that which he was to the same creature continuing in his primitive state; bestowing upon a cause that which is due to it, but without any change in Himself. Again if God is immutable, He has, for that very reason, not circumscribed or determined to one direction, by any decree, the motion of free-will, the enjoyment and use of which He has once freely bestowed on man, so that it should incline, of necessity, to one direction, and should not be able, in fact, to incline to another direction, while that decree remains. Thirdly, God has the form and an eternal and immutable conception of all those things which are done mutably by men, but following, in the order of nature, many other conceptions, which God has concerning those things which He wills both to do Himself, and to permit to men.

In reference to the second, concerning the knowledge of God;

I am most fully persuaded that the knowledge of God is eternal, immutable and infinite, and that it extends to all things, both necessary and contingent, to all things which He does of Himself, either mediately or immediately, and which He permits to be done by others. But I do not understand the mode in which He knows future contingencies, and especially those which belong to the free-will of creature, and which He has decreed to permit, but not to do of Himself, not, indeed, in that measure, in which I think that it is understood by others more learned than myself. I know that there are those who say that all things are, from eternity, presented to God, and that the mode, in which God certainly and infallibly knows future contingencies, is this, that those contingent events coexist with God in the Now of eternity, and therefore they are in Him indivisibly, and in the infinite Now of eternity, which embraces all time. If this is so, it is not difficult to understand how God may certainly and infallibly know future contingent events. For contingencies are not opposed to certainty of knowledge, except as they are future, but not as they are present. That reasoning, however, does not exhaust all the difficulties which may arise in the consideration of these matters. For God knows, also, those things which may happen, but never do happen, and consequently do not co-exist with God in the Now of eternity, which would be events unless they should be hindered, as is evident from 1 Samuel xxiii. 12, in reference to the citizens of Keilah, who would have delivered David into the hands of Saul, which event, nevertheless, did not happen. The knowledge, also, of future events, which depend on contingent causes, seems to be certain, if those causes may be complete and not hindered in their operation. But how shall the causes of those events, which depend on the freedom of the will, be complete, among which, even at that very moment in which it chose one, it was free not to choose it, or to choose another in preference to it? If indeed at any time your leisure may permit, I could wish that you would accurately discuss, in your own manner, these things and whatever else may pertain to that question. I know that this would be agreeable and acceptable to many, and that the labour would not be useless.

The knowledge of God is called eternal, but not equally so in reference to all objects of knowledge. For that knowledge of God is absolutely eternal, by which God knows Himself, and in Himself all possible things. That, by which He knows beings which will exist, is eternal indeed as to duration, but, in nature, subsequent to some act of the divine will concerning them, and, in some cases, even subsequent to some foreseen act of the human will. In general, the following seems to me to be the order of the divine knowledge, in reference to its various objects. God knows

1. Himself what He, of Himself is able to do.

2. All things possible what can be done by those beings which He can make.

3. All things which shall exist by the act of creation.

4. All things which shall exist by the act of creatures and especially of rational creatures. Whether moved by those actions of His creatures and

5. What He Himself especially of His rational shall do. creatures; Or at least receiving occasion from them.

From this, it is apparent that the eternity of the knowledge of God is not denied by those, who propose, as a foundation for that knowledge, something dependent on the human will, as foreseen.

But I do not understand in what way it can be true that, in every genus, there must be one thing univocal, and from this, other things in an equivocal sense. I have hitherto supposed that those things which are under the same genus are univocal or at least analogous; but, that things equivocal are not comprehended with those which are univocal, under the same genus, either in logic, or metaphysics, and still less in physics. Then I have not thought that the univocal could be the cause of the equivocal. For there is no similarity between them. But if there exists a similarity as between cause and effect, they are no longer equivocal. Thus those things, which are heated by the fire as I should say, are heated neither univocally, nor equivocally, but analogically. God exists univocally, we, analogically. This they admit, who state that certain attributes of the divine nature are communicable to us according to analogy, among which they also mention knowledge.

In reference to the third, concerning the actions of the Deity; the actions of God are, in Himself, indeed eternal, but they preserve a certain order; some are prior to others by nature, and indeed necessarily precede them, whether in the same order, in which they proceed from Him, I could not easily say; but I know that there are those who have thus stated, among whom some mention George Sohnius. Some also of the internal actions in God, are subsequent in nature to the foresight of some act dependent on the will of the creature. Thus the decree concerning the mission of His Son for the redemption of the human race is subsequent to the foresight of the fall of man. For although God might have arranged to prevent the fall, if he had not known that He could use an easy remedy to effect a restoration, (as some think,) yet the sure decree for the introduction of a remedy for the fall by the mission of His Son, was not effected by God except on the foresight of the disease, namely, the fall.

The mode in which God, as the universal principle, is said to flow into His creatures, and especially his rational creatures, and concurs with their nature and will, in reference to an action, has my approbation, whatever it may be, if it does not bring in a determination of the will of the creature to one or two things which are contrary, or contradictory. If any mode introduces such a determination, I do not see how it can be consistent with the declaration of Augustine, quoted by yourself, that God so governs all things which He has created as also "to permit them to exercise and put forth their own motions," or with the saying of Plato, in which God is declared to be free from all blame.

I could wish that it might be plainly and decisively explained how all effects and defects in nature, and the will, of all kinds universally, are of the providence of God, and yet God is free from fault, the whole fault, (if any exists,) residing in the proximate cause. If any one thinks that God is exempted from fault because He is the remote cause, but that the creature, as the proximate cause, is culpable, (if there is any sin,) he does not seem to me to present a correct reason why any cause may be in fault, or free from fault, but, concerning this also, I will hereafter speak at greater length. In reference to the fourth, concerning the causes of the actions of God; the universal cause has no cause above itself, and the first and supreme cause does not depend on any other cause, for the very terms include that idea; but it is possible that there may be afforded to the universal, first and supreme cause, by another cause, an occasion for the production of some certain effect, which, without that occasion, the first cause would neither propose to be produced in itself, nor in fact produce out of itself, and indeed could neither produce nor propose or decree to be produced. Such is the decree to damn certain persons, and their damnation according to that decree.

I readily assent to what you have said in reference to the modes of necessary and contingent causes, as also those things which you have remarked in reference to the distinction between natural and rational power. I am, however, certain that nothing can be deduced from them against my opinion, or against those things, which have been presented by me for the refutation of the first theory.

Having made these remarks, I come to the consideration of your answer to my arguments. In my former argument, I denied that man, considered as not yet created, is the object of mercy rescuing from sin and misery, and of punitive justice, and I persist in that sentiment; for I do not see that any thing has been presented, which overthrows it, or drives me from that position. For man is not, by that consideration, removed from under the common providence or the special predestination of God, but providence must, in this case, be considered as according to mercy and justice thus administered, and predestination, as decreed according to them. But the reasoning from the relative to the absolute is not valid; and the removal, in this case, is from under the providence of God, considered relatively, not absolutely; so also with predestination. You foresaw that I would make this reply, and consequently you have presented a three-fold answer; but, in no respect, injurious to my reasoning. For as to the first, I admit that sin and misery were, in the most complete sense, present with God from eternity, and, as they were present, so also there was, in reference to them, a place for mercy and justice. But the theory, which I oppose, does not make them, (as foreseen,) present to mercy and justice, but, according to the decree for illustrating mercy and justice, it presents a necessity for the existence of sin and misery, as, in their actual existence, there could be in fact, a place, for the decree, made according to mercy and justice. As to the second, I grant also that there could be, in one who was in fact neither a sinner, nor miserable, a place for mercy saving from sin and possible misery, but we are not here treating of mercy so considered: and it is certain that mercy and judgment exist in the Deity, by an eternal act, but it is in the first action of those attributes. In a second act, God cannot exercise those attributes, understood according to the mind of the authors of that theory, except in reference to a sinful and actually miserable being. Lastly, what you say concerning the internal, and external action of the Deity, and these conjoined, does not disturb, in any greater degree, my argument. For neither the internal action, which is the decree of God in reference to the illustration of his glory, by mercy and punitive justice, nor the external action, which is the actual declaration of that same glory through mercy and justice, nor both conjoined can have any place in reference to a man who is neither sinful, nor miserable. I know, indeed, that, to those who advocate this theory, there is so much difference between internal and external action, that is, as they say, between the decree and its execution, that God may decree salvation according to mercy and death according to justice to a person who is not a sinner, but may not really save, according to mercy, any one, unless, He is a sinner, or damn, according to justice, any except sinners. But I deny that distinction; indeed I say that God, can neither will nor decree, by internal act, that which He cannot do, by external act, and thus the object of internal and external action is the same, and invested with the same circumstances: whether it be present to God, in respect to his eternal intelligence and be the object of His decree, or be, in fact, in its actual existence, present to Him and the object of the execution of the decree. Hence, I cannot yet decide otherwise concerning that theory, than that it cannot be approved by those, who think and desire to speak according to the Scriptures.

The "two statements" which you think "may be made, of a milder character, and in harmony with the words of Christ and the apostles," do not serve to explain that first theory, but are additions, by which it is very much changed, and which its advocates would by no means acknowledge, as, in my opinion, was made sufficiently manifest in my statement of the same theory in reply to your third answer, and may be, at this time, again demonstrated in a single word. For those very things, which you make the mode and the consequent event of predestination and reprobation, are styled, by the authors of that first theory, the cause, and the principle of that same decree, and also the end, though not the final one, which, they affirm, is his glory, to be declared by mercy and justice. Again they acknowledge no grace in predestination which is not mercy, and correctly so, for the grace, which is towards man considered absolutely, is not of election: also they do not acknowledge any non-grace, or non-mercy, which is not comprehended in punitive justice. Here I do not argue against that theory thus explained, not because I approve it in all respects, but because I have, this time, undertaken to examine what I affirm to be the view of Calvin and Beza; other matters will be hereafter considered. I will notice separately what things are here brought forward, agreeing with that view, thus explained. The passages of Scripture quoted from Matthew 25, and Ephesians 1, in which it is taught that "God, from all eternity, of the good pleasure of his will, elected some to adoption, sanctification, and a participation of his kingdom," so far fail to prove the common view that on the contrary there may be inferred from them a reference to sin, as a condition requisite in the object of benediction and election. In the former passage, the blessed are called to a participation of the kingdom, which God has prepared for them from eternity; but in whom and by whom? Is it not in Christ and by Christ? Certainly; then it was prepared for sinners, not for men considered in general, and apart from any respect to sin. For "thou shall call his name Jesus; for he shall save his people from their sins." (Matt. i. 2.)

The passage from Ephesians 1, much more plainly affirms the same thing, as will be hereafter proved in a more extended manner, when I shall use that passage, avowedly to sustain the theory which makes sin a condition requisite in the object. I did not present a particular reference to men, as a cause, which I wished to have kept in mind, but according to a condition, requisite in the object, namely, misery and sin. This I still require. The distinction, which you make between grace and mercy, is according to fact and the signification of terms, but in this place is unnecessary. For no grace, bestowed upon man, originates in predestination, as there is no grace, previous to predestination, not joined with mercy. God deals with angels according to grace, not according to mercy saving from sin and misery. He deals with us according to mercy, not according to grace in contradistinction to mercy. I speak here of predestination. According to that mercy, also, is our adoption; it is not, then, of men, considered in their original state, but of sinners. This is also apparent from the phraseology of the apostle, who calls the elect and the reprobate "vessels," not of grace and non-grace but of "mercy" and "wrath." The relation of "vessels" they have equally and in common from their divine creation, sustainment, and government. That they are vessels worthy of wrath, deserving it, and the "children of wrath," (Ephes. ii. 3), in this also there is no distinction among them. But that some are "vessels of wrath," that is, destined to wrath, of their own merit, indeed, but also of the righteous judgment of God, which determines to bring wrath upon them; while others are "vessels" not "of wrath" but "of mercy" according to the grace of God, which determines to pardon their sin, and to spare them, though worthy of wrath, this is of the will of God, making a distinction between the two classes; which discrimination has its beginning after the act of sin, whether we consider the internal or the external act of God. From this it is apparent that they are not on this account vessels of wrath because they have become depraved, the just consequence of which is wrath, if the will of God did not intervene, which determines that this, which would be a just consequence in respect to all the depraved, should be a necessary consequence in respect to those, whom alone He refuses to pardon, as He can justly punish all and had decreed to pardon some. That which is "added by way of amplification" is confirmed by the same arguments. For there is no place for punitive justice except in reference to the sinner; there can be no act of that mercy, of which we treat, except towards the miserable. But man, considered in his natural condition is neither sinful nor miserable, therefore that justice and mercy have no place in reference to him. Hence, you, my brother, will see that the object of predestination, made according to those attributes and so understood, cannot be man, considered in general, since it requires, in its object, the circumstance of sin and misery, by which circumstance man is restricted to a determinate condition, and is separated from a general consideration. I know, indeed, that, if the general consideration is admitted, no one of those particular considerations is excluded, but you also know that if any particular relation is precisely laid down, that universal relation is excluded. I do not think that it is to be altogether conceded that, in the case of election and reprobation, there is no consideration of well-doing or of sin. There is no consideration of well-doing, it is true, for there is none to be considered; there is no consideration of sin as a cause why one, and not another, should be reprobated, but there is a consideration of sin as a meritorious cause of the possibility of the reprobation of any individual, and as a condition requisite in the object, as I have often remarked, and shall, hereafter, often remark, as occasion may require. In what respects, those theories differ was briefly noticed in reply to your first answer. When God is said to have elected persons, as not created, as created but not fallen, or as fallen, all know that it is understood, not that they are in fact such, but that they are considered as such, for all admit that God elected human beings from eternity, before they were created, that is, by the internal act; but no one says, that man was elected by the external act before he was created; therefore a reconciliation of those theories was unnecessary, since the object of both acts is one and the same, and considered in the same manner. Besides the questions, when the election was made, and in what sense it was considered, are different. I wished to confirm my words by the authority of your consent; whether ignorantly, will be proved from these statements. You make man, considered as a sinner, the subject of the preparation of punishment according to justice, which I, agreeably to your Theses, have called reprobation, and you, according to your opinion, presuppose sin in him; but, in the first theory, they make sin subordinate to that same decree. The preterition, which the same theory attributes to punitive justice, you attribute to the freedom of the divine goodness, and you exclude punitive justice from it, when you make man, not yet a sinner, the subject of preterition. Predestination, which the first theory ascribes to mercy, in contra-distinction to grace, your Theses, already cited (answers 2 and 4) assign to grace, spoken of absolutely, since they consider man in the state of nature in which he was created; but you make man, as a sinner, the subject of grace, as conjoined with mercy, and you presuppose sin. That first theory, on the other hand, makes sin subordinate to that predestination, both of which cannot, at the same time, be true, therefore, in this you seem to agree with me, as you ascribe election to mercy, only so far as man is considered miserable, and preparation of punishment to justice, only so far as man is considered sinful. You reply, that, when grace is presented, as the genus, mercy, as the species, is not excluded, and mercy being presented, as the species, grace, as the genus, is not excluded. I grant it, but affirm, first, that grace cannot be supposed here as the genus, for grace, spoken of generally, cannot be supposed to be the cause of any act, that is, any special act, such as predestination. Again, the relation of grace and mercy in this case, is different from that of genus and species: for they are spoken of, in an opposite manner, as two different species of grace, the term grace, having the same appellation with that of the genus, referring to that grace which regards man as created, the term mercy, receiving its appellation from its object, referring to that grace which regards man as sinful and miserable. If man is said to be predestinated according to the former, the latter can have no place; if according to the latter, then it is certain that the former can have no place, otherwise the latter would be unnecessary. Predestination cannot be said to have been made conjointly according to both. My conclusion was, therefore, correct, when I excluded one species by the supposition of the other. If man is to be exalted to supernatural glory from a natural state, this work belongs to grace, simply considered, and in contra-distinction to mercy; if from a corrupt state, it belongs to grace conjoined with mercy, that is, it is the appropriate work of mercy. Grace, simply considered and opposed to mercy, cannot effect the latter, mercy is not necessary for the former. But predestination is of such grace as is both able and necessary to effect that which is proposed in predestination.

What I wrote copulatively, in reference to the passed by and the reprobate, was written thus, because they are one subject. But that they are not the same in relation, is admitted: and I expressed this when I remarked that you referred to justice only in the case of the latter, namely, the reprobate, that is, the damned. In my second proposition, however, I signified that, according to the view of those to whom I ascribed the second theory, the relation of preterition was different from that of predamnation, which I there called reprobation. The homonymy of the term reprobation is explained in my second answer, and all fault is removed from me, who have used that word every where according to your own idea. But it is very apparent, from what follows, that you dissent from the authors of the first theory. For you assert that "predestination is of justice," but that preterition or reprobation is according to justice, but not "of justice;" while the authors of the first theory ascribe to justice the cause of reprobation, however understood, whether synecdochically, or properly, or catachrestically, that is, they affirm that both preterition and predamnation are of justice.

But how are election and preterition "the work of flee-will according to the wisdom of God and damnation, the work of necessary will according to the justice of God? I have hitherto thought, with our theologians, that this whole decree was instituted by God, in the exercise of most complete freedom of will, and I yet think that the same idea is true, according to the declaration, "I will have mercy on whom I will have mercy," and "He hath mercy on whom He will have mercy, and whom He will He hardeneth." (Rom. ix. 15, 18.)

In each of these acts God exercises equal freedom. For, if God necessarily wills in any case to punish sin, how is it that He does not punish it in all sinners? If he punishes it in some, but not in others, how is that the act of necessary will? Who, indeed, does not ascribe the distinction which is made among persons, equally meriting the punishment, to the freewill of God? Justice may demand punishment on account of sin, but it demands it equally in reference to all sinners without distinction; and, if there is any discrimination, it is of free-will, demanding punishment as to these, but remitting sin to those. But it was necessary that punishment should be at least inflicted on some. If I should deny that this was so after the satisfaction made by Christ, how will it be proved? I know that Aquinas, and other of the School-men, affirm that the relation of the divine goodness and providence demands that some should be elected to life, and that others should be permitted to fall into sin and then to suffer the punishment of eternal death, and that God was free to decree to whom life, and to whom death should appertain, according to his will, but their arguments seem to me susceptible of refutation from their own statements, elsewhere made concerning the price of our redemption paid by Christ. For they say the price was sufficient for the sins of all, but if the necessity of divine justice demands that some sinners should be damned, then the price was not sufficient for all. For if justice, in him who receives that price, necessarily demands that some should be destitute of redemption, then it must have been offered by the redeemer with the condition that there must always remain to the necessity of justice, some satisfaction, to be sought elsewhere and to be rendered by others. Let no one think that the last affirmation of the school-men (that concerning the sufficiency of the price), which, however, they borrowed from the fathers, is to be rejected, for it could be proved, if necessary, by plain and express testimonies from the Scripture.

Let us now come to my second argument, which was this. A theory, by which God is necessarily made the author of sin, is to be repudiated by all Christians, and indeed by all men; for no man thinks that the being, whom he considers divine, is evil; -- But according to the theory of Calvin and Beza God is necessarily made the author of sin; -- Therefore it is to be repudiated. The proof of the Minor, is evident from these words, in which they say that "God ordained that man should fall and become corrupt, that in this way he might open a way for His eternal counsels." For he, who ordains that man should fall and sin, is the author of sin This, my argument, is firm, nor is it weakened by your answer. The word ordain is indeed ambiguous, for it properly signifies to arrange the order of events or deeds, and in each thing according to its own mode, in which sense it is almost always used by the school-men. But it is also applied to a simple and absolute decree of the will determining an action. What then? Does it follow, because I have used a word, which is ambiguous and susceptible of various meanings that I am chargeable with ambiguity? I think not; unless it is proved that, in my argument, I have used that word in different senses. Otherwise sound reasoning would be exceedingly rare, since, on account of the multitude of things and the paucity of words, we are very frequently compelled to use words, which have a variety of meanings. Ambiguity may be charged when a word is used in different senses in the same argument. But I used that word, in the same sense in the Major and in the Minor, and so my argument is free from ambiguity. I affirm that this is evident from the argument itself. For the added phrase "that man should fall" signifies that the word ordain, in both propositions, is to be applied to the simple decree in reference to an action, or rather to a simple decree that something should be done. It cannot, on account of that phrase, be referred to a decree disposing the order of actions.

Let us now state the syllogism in a few words, that we may be able to compare your answer with the argument.

He who ordained that man should fall and become depraved, is the author of the fall and of sin; God ordained that man should fall and become depraved; Therefore, God is the author of sin.

You deny the Major, if the word ordain is understood to mean the disposal of the order of actions. You deny the Minor if the same word is used to mean a simple decree as to actions, or things to be done. This is true, and, in it, I agree with you. But what if the same word in the Minor signifies a simple decree, &c.? Then, indeed, even by your own admission, the Major will be true. Else your distinction in the word is uselessly made, if the Major is false, however the word may be understood. But that the word is used in the Major in this sense, is proved by the phraseology, "He who ordained that man should fall." Then you say that the Minor is false if the word is used in the same sense in which we have shown that it is used in the Major, and so the conclusion does not follow. I reply, that the question between us is not whether that Minor is true or false, the word ordain being used for the decreeing of things to be done, but whether they affirm it, to whom the first theory is attributed. If, then, they affirm this, and the Major is true, then it follows (and in this you agree with me,) that God is the author of sin. For you admit that he is the author of sin, who, by the simple decree and determination of the will, ordains that sin shall be committed. Calvin and Beza assert this in plain and most manifest declarations, needing no explanation, and by no means admitting that explanation of the word ordain, which, as you say and I acknowledge, is proper. I wish also that it might be shown in what way the necessity of the commission of sin, can depend on the ordination and decree of God otherwise than by the mode of cause, either efficient or deficient, which deficiency is reduced to efficiency, when the efficiency of that which is deficient is necessary to the avoidance of sin. Beza himself concedes that it is incomprehensible how God can be free from and man be obnoxious to guilt, if man fell by the ordination of God, and of necessity.

This, then, was to be done: their theory was to be freed from the consequence of that absurdity, which, in my argument, I ascribe to it. It was not, however, necessary to show how God ordained sin, and that He is not indeed the author of sin. I agree with you, both in the explanation of that ordination, and in the assertion that God is not the author of sin. Calvin himself, and Beza also, openly deny that God is the author of sin, although they define ordination as we have seen, but they do not show how these two things can be reconciled.

I wish, then, that it might be shown plainly, and with perspicuity, that God is not made the author of sin by that decree, or that the theory might be changed, since it is a stumbling block to many, indeed to some a cause of separating from us, and to very many a cause of not uniting with us. But I am altogether persuaded that you also perceive that consequence, but prefer to free the theory of those men from an absurd and blasphemous consequence, by a fit explanation, than to charge that consequence to it. This is certainly the part of candour and good will, but used to no good purpose, since the gloss, as they say, is contrary to the text, which is manifest to any one who examines and compares the text with the gloss. Those two questions, which you present to yourself, do not affect my argument, when the matter is thus explained.

Yet I am delighted with your beautiful and elegant discussion of those questions. But I would ask, in opposition to the theory of Calvin and Beza, "How can these movements of the will be called its own and free, when the act of the will is determined to one direction by the decree of God?" Then, "Why did God place the will in man, if He was unwilling that he should enjoy the liberty of its use?" For these questions are necessarily to be answered by those authors, if they do not wish to leave their theory without defense. It is therefore, apparent from these things that my argument does not fail, but remains firm and unmoved, since all things which you have adduced, are aside from that argument, which did not seek to conclude, as my own views, that God is the author of sin (far from me be even the thought of that abominable blasphemy), but to prove that this is a necessary consequence of the theory of Calvin and Beza: which (I confidently say) has not been confuted by you: nor can it be at all confuted, since you use the word ordain in a sense different from that in which they use it, and from that sense, according to which if God should be said to have ordained sin, nothing less could be inferred than that He is the author of sin.

I said, moreover, that the theory of Calvin and Beza, in which they state that God ordained that man should fall and become depraved, could not be explained so that God should not be made by it the author of sin, by the distinctions of the act, and the evil in the act, of necessity and coaction, of the decree and its execution, of efficacious and permissive decree, as the latter is explained by the authors of that theory agreeably to it, nor by the different relation of the divine decree and of human nature or of man, nor by the addition of the end, namely, that the whole ordination was designed for the illustration of the glory of God. You seem to me, reverend sir, not to have perceived for what purpose I presented these things, for I did not wish to present any new course of reasoning against that first theory, but to confirm my previous objection by a refutation of those answers, which are usually presented by the defenders of that theory, to the objection which I made, that, by it, God is made the author of sin. For they, in order to repel the charge from their theory, never make the reply which has been presented by you, for, should they do this, they would necessarily depart from their own theory, which is wholly changed, if the word ordain, which they use, signifies not to decree that sin should be committed, but to arrange the order of its commission, as you explain that word. But to show that it does not follow from their theory, that God is the author of sin, they adduce the distinctions to which I have referred, and have diligently gathered from their various writings; which ought to be done before that accusation should be made against their theory. For, if I could find any explanation of that theory, any distinction, by which it could be relieved of that charge, it would have pertained to my conscience, not to place upon it the load of such a consequence. Your distinction in the word ordain indeed removes the difficulty, but, in such a way, that, by one and the same effort, it removes the theory from which I proved that the difficulty followed. Prove that the authors of that theory assert that God ordained sin in no other sense than that, in which you have shown that the word is properly used, and I shall obtain that which I wish, and I will concede that those distinctions were unnecessary for the defense of that theory. For the word ordain used in your sense, presupposes the perpetration of sin; in their sense, it precedes and proposes its perpetration, for "God ordained that man should fall and become depraved," not that from a being, fallen and depraved, He should make whatever the order of the divine wisdom, goodness, and justice might demand.

There is here, then, no wandering beyond the appropriate range of the discussion. You say that all those distinctions pertain in common to the question of providence, and therefore the ordination of sin pertains in common to the question of providence. If, however, the authors of the first theory have ascribed the ordination of sin to the divine predestination, why should it cause surprise, that those distinctions should also be referred to the same predestination? There is, in this case, then, no blame to be attached to me, that I have mentioned these distinctions. On the contrary, I should have been in fault, if, omitting reference to those distinctions, I should have made an accusation against their theory, which they are accustomed to defend against this accusation by means of those distinctions. But since you do not, by your explanation, relieve their theory from that objection, and I have said that those distinctions do not avail for its relief and defense, it will not be useless that I should prove my assertion, not for your sake, but for the sake of those, who hold that opinion, since they think that it can be suitably defended by these distinctions.

They use the first distinction thus: "In sin there are two things, the act and its sinfulness." God, by his own ordination, is the author of the act, not of the sinfulness in the act. I will first consider the distinction, then the answer which they deduce from it. This distinction is very commonly made, and seems to have some truth, but to one examining, with diligence, its falsity, in most respects, will be apparent. For it is not, in general or universally, applicable to all sin. All sins, especially, which are committed against prohibitory laws, styled sins of commission, reject this distinction. For the acts themselves are forbidden by the law, and therefore, if perpetrated, they are sins. This is the formal relation of sin, that it is something done contrary to law. It is true that the act in that it is such, would not be sin, if the law had not been enacted, but then it is not an act, having evil or sinfulness. Let the law be absent, the act is naturally good: introduce the law, and the act itself is evil, as forbidden, not that there is any thing in the act which can be called unlawfulness or sin. I will make the matter clear by an example. The eating of the forbidden fruit, if it had been permitted to the human will as right, would, in no way, be sin, nor any part of sin, it would not contain any element of sin; but the same act, forbidden by law, could not be otherwise than sinful, if perpetrated; I refer to the act itself, and not to any thing in the act to which the term evil can be applied. For that act was simply made illicit by the enactment of the law. I shall have attained my object here in a single word, by simply asking that the sinfulness in that act may be shown separately from the act itself. That distinction, however, had a place in acts which are performed according to a perceptive law, but not according to a due mode, order, or motive. Thus he, who gives alms, that he may be praised does a good act badly, and there is, in that deed both the act and the evil of the act according to which it is called sin. But the sin which man perpetrated at the beginning, of the ordination of God, was a sin of commission; it therefore affords no place for that distinction. This fundamental principle having been established, the answer, deduced from that distinction, is at once refuted. Yet let us look at it. "God," they say, "is, by ordination, the author of the act, not of the evil in the act." I affirm, on the contrary, that God ordained that act, not as an act, but as it is an evil act. He ordained that the glory of His mercy and justice should be illustrated, of his pardoning mercy, and His punitive justice; but that glory is illustrated not by the act as such, but as it is sinful, and as an evil act. For the act needs remission, not as such, but as evil; it deserves punishment, not as such, but as evil. The declaration, then, of His glory by mercy and justice, is by the act as it is evil, not as it is an act; therefore that ordination which had its end, the illustration of that glory, was not of the act as such, but as evil, and of sin, as sin and transgression. That distinction, therefore, is useless in repelling the objection, which I have urged against that theory. I add, for the elucidation of the subject, that if God efficaciously determines the will to the material of sin, or to depraved objects, though it may be affirmed that He does not determine the will to an evil decision, in respect to the evil, He is still made the author of sin, since man himself does not will the evil in respect to the evil and the devil does not solicit to evil in respect to the evil, but in respect to that which is delectable, and yet he is said to induce persons to sin.

The second distinction is that of necessity and coaction. They use it in this way. If the decree of God, in which he ordained that man should fall, compelled him to sin, then would God, by that decree, become the author of sin, and man would be free from guilt: but that decree did not compel man. It only imposed a necessity upon him so that he could not but sin; which necessity does not take away his liberty. Therefore, man, since he sins freely, the decree being in force, is the cause of his own fall, and God is free from the responsibility. Let us now consider this distinction, and the use made of it.

Necessity and coaction differ as genus and species. For necessity comprehends coaction in itself. Necessity also is twofold, one from an internal, the other from an external cause; the one, natural, the other, violent. Necessity, from an external cause and violent, is also called coaction, whether it be used contrary to nature, or against the will, as when a stone is projected upwards, and a strong man makes use of the hand of a weaker person to strike a third person. The former has the name of the genus, necessity, but is referred to a specific idea, by a contraction of the mental conception. There is, then, between these two species, some agreement, as they belong to the same genus, and some discrepancy, since each has its own form. But it is now to be considered whether they so differ that coaction alone, and not that other species of necessity, is contrary to freedom; and whether he who compels to sin is the cause of sin, and not he who necessitates without compulsion. They indeed affirm this, who use this distinction. First, in reference to freedom; it is opposed directly to necessity, considered in general, whether natural or compulsive, for each of these species causes the inevitability of the act. For a cause acts freely when it has the power to suspend its action. Some say that freedom is fully consistent with natural necessity, and refer to the example of the Deity, who is, by nature and freely, good. But is God freely good? Such an affirmation is not very far from blasphemy. His own goodness exists in God, naturally and most intimately; it does not then exist in Him freely. I know that a kind of freedom of complacency is spoken of by the School-men, but contrary to the very nature and definition of freedom. We say, in reference to sin, that he is the cause of sin, who necessitates to the commission of sin, by any act whatever of necessitation, whether internal or external, whether by internal suasion, motion, or leading, which the will necessarily obeys, or by an application of external violence, which the will is not able, though it may desire, to resist; though, in that case, the act would not be voluntary. He, indeed sins more grievously, who uses the former act, than he, who uses the latter. For the former has this effect, that the will may consent to the sin, but the latter has no such effect, though that consent is not according to the mode of free-will, but according to that of nature, in which mode only, God can so move the will, that it may be moved necessarily, that is, that it cannot but be moved. And in this relation, the will, as it consents by nature to sin, is free from guilt; for sin, as such, is of free-will, and tend towards its object, according to the mode of its own freedom. The law is enacted not for nature but for the will, for the will as it acts not according to the mode of nature, but according to the mode of freedom. That distinction is, therefore, vain, and does not relieve the first theory from the objection made against it. If any one wishes, with greater pertinacity, still to defend the idea, that one and the same act can be performed freely and necessarily, in different respects, necessarily in respect to the first cause, which ordains it, but freely and contingently in respect to the second cause, let him consider that contingency and necessity differ not in certain respects, but in their entire essence, and that they divide the whole extent of being, and cannot, therefore, be coincident. That is necessary which cannot fail to be done; that is contingent which can fail to be done. These are contradictions which can in no way be attributed to the same act. The will tends freely to its own object, when it is not determined, to a single direction, by a superior power; but, when that determination is made by any decree of God, it can no longer be said to tend freely to its own object; for it is no longer a principle, having dominion and power over its own acts. Did it not pertain to the nature of the bones of Christ, (which they present as an example,) to be broken? Yet they could not be broken on account of the decree of God. I reply, that the divine determination being removed, they could be broken; but, that determination, being presented by the decree of God, they could not at all be broken, that is, it was necessary, not contingent, that they should remain unbroken. Did God, therefore, change the nature of the bones? That was not necessary. He only prevented the act of breaking the bones, which were liable by their nature to be broken, which act could have been performed, and would have been, if God had not anticipated it by His decree, and by an act according to that decree. For our Lord gave up the ghost when the soldiers were approaching the cross to break his bones, and were about to use the breaking of his legs to accelerate his death. That I may not be tedious, I will not refute all the objections; but I am persuaded, from what has been presented, that they are all susceptible of refutation. The third distinction is that of the decree and its execution. They use it thus; though God may have decreed from eternity to devote certain persons to death, and, that this may be possible, may have ordained that they should fall into sin, yet he does not execute that decree, by their actual condemnation, until after the persons themselves have become sinful by their own act, and, therefore, He is free from responsibility. I answer that the fact that the execution of the decree is subsequent to the act of sin, does not free from responsibility him, who, by his own decree, has ordained that sin should occur, that he might afterwards punish it; indeed he, who has ordained and decreed that sin should be committed, cannot justly punish sin after its commission; he cannot justly punish a deed, the doing of which he has ordained; he cannot be the ordainer of the punishment, who was the ordainer of the crime. Augustine rightly says, "God can ordain the punishment of crimes, not the crimes themselves," that is, He can ordain that they should take place. I have already demonstrated that man does not become depraved of his own fault, if God has ordained that he should fall and become depraved.

The fourth distinction is that of efficacious and permissive decree: which distinction, rightly explained, removes the whole difficulty, but it removes also the theory, by which God is affirmed to have ordained that sin should take place. The authors, however, of the first theory endeavour to sustain that theory by reference to permissive decree. They affirm that God does not effect, but decrees and ordains sin, and that this is done not by an efficacious, but by a permissive decree; and they so explain a permissive decree, that it coincides with one, which is efficacious. For they explain permission to be an act of the divine will, by which God does not bestow, on a rational creature, that grace, which is necessary for the avoidance of sin. This action, joined with the enactment of a law, embraces in itself the whole cause of sin. For he, who imposes a law which cannot be observed without grace, and denies grace to him, on whom the law is imposed, is the cause of sin by the removal of the necessary hindrance. But more on this point hereafter.

On the contrary, if permissive decree be rightly explained, it is certain that he, who has decreed to permit sin, is by no means the cause of sin; for the action of his will has reference to its own permission, not to sin. Nor are these two things, God, in the exercise of His will, permits sin, and, God wills sin, equivalent. For, the object of the will is, in the former case, permission, in the latter, sin. On the contrary rather, the conclusion, God permits, therefore, He does not will, a sinful act, is valid, for he who wills any thing does not permit the same thing. Permission is a sign of want of action in the will. That distinction, then, does not relieve the first theory. The fifth distinction is that of the divine decree and human nature, which they use thus: -- sin, if you consider the divine decree, is necessary; but if you have reference to human nature, which is equally free and flexible in every direction, it is freely and contingently committed; and, therefore, the whole responsibility is to be placed on human nature, as the proximate cause. We have discussed this, previously, in reference to the second distinction, and have sufficiently refuted it. They make another use of the same distinction, by a diverse respect of the ends, which God has proposed to Himself in His decree, and which are proposed to man in the commission of sin. "For," they say, "God intends, in His decree, to illustrate His own glory, but man intends to gratify his own desire; and though man does the very thing, which is divinely decreed, he does not do it because it is decreed, but because his will so inclines him. I reply, first; a good end does not approve, or make good, an action which is unlawful in itself; for "we are not to do evil that good may come;" but it is evil to ordain that sin shall be committed. Secondly, that man, to satisfy his own desire, should do that which God has forbidden, also results from the decree of God, and, therefore, man is relieved from responsibility. Thirdly, though the fulfillment of the divine decree is not the end which moves man to the commission of sin, yet that same thing is the cause which, by a gentle, silent, and imperceptible, yet efficacious, movement effects that man should sin, or, rather, commit that act which God had decreed should be committed, which, then, in respect to man, cannot be called sin. Finally, the last defense consists in a reference to the end, of which they make this use: "We are accustomed to state the decree of God, not in these terms, that 'God has determined to adjudge some men to eternal death and condemnation,' but we add, ' that His justice may be illustrated to the glory of his name.'"

I answer, that the addition does not deny the previous statement, (for this is confirmed by the rendering of the cause,) and the addition, even of the best end, does not justify an action which is not in itself formally good, as has before been stated. From these things, then, it is apparent, that these grounds of defense are insufficient, and avail nothing for the defense of that theory which states that God ordained that men should fall and become depraved, in order to open to Himself, in that manner, a way for the execution of the decree which He had, from eternity, determined and proposed to Himself, for the illustration of His own glory by mercy and justice. If any one may think that any other distinction or explanation can be presented, by which that theory may be defended and vindicated, I shall be, in the highest degree, pleased, if this is done. But let him be cautious not to change the theory or add to it any thing inconsistent with it. You mention, at the end of your sixth answer, an objection to your view; -- "Then the judgments of God depend on contingency, and are based on things contingent, if they have reference to man as a sinner, and to his sin." I must examine this with diligence, since it also lies against my view, in that I think that sin must be presupposed in the object of the divine decree. It is most manifest, from the Scriptures, that many of the judgments of God are based on sin, which, yet, cannot be said, to depend on sin. It is one thing to make sin the object and occasion of the divine judgments, and another to make it the cause of the same. The judgment, which God pronounces in reference to sin, He pronounces freely, nor does this depend on sin, for He can suspend it, or substitute another in its place; yet it is based on sin, because, apart from sin, He could not thus judge. But sin is contingent, or contingently committed.

Therefore, the judgments of God are based on things contingent. I deny the consequence. The judgments of God are based on sin, not as it is committed contingently, but as it is certainly and infallibly foreseen by God. Therefore, the sight of God intervenes between sin and judgment, and thus, judgment is based on the certain and infallible vision of God. Then that which exists, so far as it exists, is necessary. But the judgments of God are based on sin, already committed and in existence. In your answer, however, I could wish that it might be explained to me how those things, which are contingent, depend on the ordination of God, whether according to the source or the act, the word ordination having reference to a decree that certain things shall be done, not to the disposal of the order in which they shall be done, for so the word is to be understood in this place. For, though God has appointed the mode of contingency in nature, yet it does not follow from this that contingencies have their source in the ordination of God. For a cause, which is free and governs its own action, can suspend or carry forward a contingent act, according to its own will; so also in reference to the act. I do not, therefore, understand in what way contingencies, which are such in themselves, are not contingencies to God, from the fact that He has established the mode of contingency in nature. Sin is not, in any mode and in respect to anything, necessary. Therefore, sin is also contingent to God, that is, it is considered by God as done contingently, though in His certain and infallible sight, on account of the infinity of the divine knowledge. Nor is it the same idea, that a thing should be really contingent to the supreme cause, and that a thing, truly contingent in itself, should be considered as contingent by that supreme cause. For it is understood that nothing can be accidental or contingent to God, for He is immutable, He is entirely uncompounded, and, as Being and Essence, belongs to Himself alone. But the knowledge of God considers things as they are, though with vision far exceeding the nature of all things.

SEVENTH PROPOSITION OF ARMINIUS

I will not now adduce other reasons why that theory is not satisfactory to me, since I perceive that you treat it in a mode and respect different from mine. I come then to the theory of Thomas Aquinas, to which, I think, you also gave your assent, and presented proofs from the Scriptures, and I will openly state that, of which I complain. I would pray you not to be displeased with the liberty, which I take, if your good will towards me was not most manifest.

ANSWER OF JUNIUS TO THE SEVENTH PROPOSITION

I should prefer that those "other reasons," whatever they might be, had been presented, that I might dispose of the whole matter, (if possible,) at the same time, for I desire that my opinion should be known to you without any dissimulation, and that your expectation should be satisfied. Nevertheless, I hope, that, in your wisdom, you will perceive, from what I have already said, and shall yet say, either what my opinion is concerning those reasons, or what there may be, according to my view, in which your mind may rest, (which may the Lord grant). The theory of Thomas Aquinas I unite with the other, I do not follow it. But I will, briefly and in a few words, explain what I shall state in this argument, and in what mode, from the word of God, and what does not please me in that theory, noticing the words of your writing in the same order.

REPLY OF ARMINIUS TO THE ANSWER
TO THE SEVENTH PROPOSITION

If I thought, indeed, that you considered that first theory, as it is explained by its authors, to be in accordance with the Scriptures, I would, in every way, attempt to divest you of that idea, but I see that you so explain it, as greatly to change it; on which account I am persuaded that you judge that, unless it be explained according to your interpretation, it is, by no means, in accordance with the Scriptures. You will also allow me, my brother, to repeat, that, in your entire answer, you have not relieved that theory from any objection. For it remains valid, that "God is made the author of sin, if He is said to have ordained that man should fall and become depraved that He might open to Himself a way for the declaration of His own glory, in the way in which He had already determined by eternal decree." Yet, that no one may think that my promise was vain, I will attempt by other arguments also the refutation of that theory, which presents, as an object to God, in the act of predestination, man not yet created or to be created. I used two arguments, one a priore, the other, a posteriore or by absurdity of consequence. The argument a priore was as follows; -- Predestination is the will of God in reference to the illustration of His glory by mercy and justice; but that will has no opportunity for exercise in a being not yet created. The argument a posteriore was as follows; If God ordained that man should fall and become depraved, that He might open to Himself a way for the execution of that purpose of His will (predestination,) then it follows that He is the author of sin by that ordination. These arguments have been already dwelt upon at sufficient length.

I adduce my third argument. Predestination is a part of providence, administering and governing the human race; therefore, it was subsequent to the act of creation or to the purpose of creating man. If it is subsequent to the act of creation, or to the purpose of creating man, then man, considered as not yet created, is not the object of predestination. I will add a fourth. Predestination is a preparation of supernatural benefits, it is, therefore, preceded by the communication of natural gifts, and, therefore, by creation, in nature, or act, or in the decree of God. Also a fifth. The illustration of the wisdom of God in creation, is prior to that illustration of the wisdom of God, which is the business of predestination. (1 Cor. i. 21.) Therefore, creation is prior to predestination, in the purpose of God. If creation is prior, man is considered by God, in the act of predestination, as existing, not as to be created.

So also in reference to goodness and mercy, the former of which, in the act of creation, was illustrated in reference to Nothing, the latter, in the act of predestination, concerning that which was subsequent to Nothing. To the same purpose can all the arguments be used, by which it was proved that "sin is a condition requisite in the object of predestination."

EIGHTH PROPOSITION OF ARMINIUS

I shall, therefore, consider three things in that theory.

1. Did God elect from eternity, of human beings, considered in their natural condition, some to supernatural felicity and glory, and non elect or pass by others?

2. Did God prepare for those whom He elected, that is, for human beings to be raised from a natural to a supernatural state, and to be translated to a participation of divine things, according to the purpose of election, those means which are necessary, sufficient, and efficacious to the attainment of that supernatural felicity, but passed by others, that is, determine not to communicate those means to them, but to leave them in their natural state?

3. Did God, foreseeing that those persons, thus passed by, would fall into sin, reprobate them, that is, decree to subject them to eternal punishment?

ANSWER OF JUNIUS TO THE EIGHTH PROPOSITION

Let this be the rule which shall guide us in our future discussion. If any use the term, "in their natural condition," they do not exclude supernatural endowments, which God communicated to Adam, but use it in opposition to sin, (which afterwards supervened,) and to native depravity. They, who use these words otherwise, seem to me to be deceived by a diversity of relation. The word reprobation is here used, (as we have before observed,) in its third signification, which we have called catachrestic; but sufficient on that point. We will come to those three points in their order.

THE REPLY OF ARMINIUS TO THE ANSWER
TO THE EIGHTH PROPOSITION

Natural condition I have opposed both to supernatural endowments, and to sin and native depravity, for I have supposed the former term to be used, to the exclusion of the latter; -- not incorrectly, whether we consider the force of the terms themselves, or their use by the school-men. Natural condition has a relation to supernatural endowments, which they exclude as transcending it, and to sin and depravity which they, in like manner, exclude, as corrupting it. Though I have used the term reprobation in the sense in which it is used in your Theses and other writings, yet I shall desist from it hereafter, (if I can keep this in my mind,) and use, in its place, the words preterition and non-election, except when I wish to include both acts, by Synecdoche, in one word. For the term reprobation, as it is used by me, I will substitute preparation of punishment or predamnation.

NINTH PROPOSITION OF ARMINIUS

In the first question, I do not present as a matter of doubt, the fact that God has elected some to salvation, and not elected or passed by others for I think that this is certain from the plain words of Scripture; but I place the emphasis on the subject of election and non election; -- Did God, in electing and not electing, have reference to men, considered in their natural condition. I have not been able hitherto to receive this as truth.

THE ANSWER OF JUNIUS TO THE
NINTH PROPOSITION

We remarked, in the sixth proposition, that, though the mode of regarding man can and ought to be distinguished by certain respects or relations, yet the authors of the first theory have stated that mankind was considered in common by the Deity in the case of election and reprobation; but the authors of the second have not excluded that common relation of the human race, which they have referred to a special relation; but they have only desired that the contemplation of supervenient sin should not affect the case of election and reprobation, according to the declaration of the apostle, "neither having done any good or evil," (Rom. ix. 11,) and according to those words "natural condition," mean only the exclusion of any reference to supervenient sin from the case of election. If this observation is correct, the latter state of the question, properly considered, will not be at variance with the former. For he, who states that man, as not yet created, as not yet fallen, and as fallen, was considered by the Deity in the case of election and reprobation, he certainly affirms the latter, and both the former. The question, therefore, is, properly, not whether God, in electing and in passing by or reprobating, had reference to men in their natural condition, that is, apart from the contemplation of sin, as sin, but the question should be, whether God had reference, in this case, to man, apart from any contemplation of sin as a cause. We deny this, on time authority of the word of God. Nor did Augustine, to whom the third theory is ascribed, mean any thing else, as he has most abundantly set forth (lib. 1, quaes. ad Simplicianum), for what he asserts concerning Jacob and Esau is either to be understood, in the same manner, in the ease of Adam and Eve, or the rule of election and reprobation will be different in different cases, which is certainly absurd. Before, then, Adam and Eve were made, or had any thing good or evil, the Divine election, as we have plainly stated in the same argument, was already made according to the purpose of grace, which election preceded both persons, and all causes originating from, or situated in, persons. The truth of this is proved from authority, reason, and example. From authority, in Romans 9, Ephesians 1, and elsewhere. From reason; for, in the first place, election is made in Christ, not in the creatures, or in any condition in them; secondly, it is admitted by all, (which you afterwards acknowledge in part, though in a different sense,) that predestination and reprobation suppose nothing in the predestinate or the reprobate, but only in Him who predestinates, as the apostle affirms "not of works, but of Him that calleth." (Rom. ix. 11.) Augustine presents a most luminous exposition of that passage, showing, from the reasoning of the apostle, that neither works, nor faith, nor will, was foreseen in the case. The procreation of the child depends, in nature, on the parent only; much more does the adoption of His children originate in God alone (to whom it peculiarly pertains to be the cause and principle of all good), not in any consideration of them. Finally the example of angels demonstrates the same thing, of whom some are called elect, others are non-elect. Of the angels, the elect were such apart from any consideration of their works, and those, who are non-elect, passed-by; or reprobate, are non-elect, apart from the consideration of their works. For, as Augustine conclusively argues in reference to men, "if, because God foresaw that the works of Esau would be evil, He, therefore, predestinated him to serve the younger, and, because God foresaw that the works of Jacob would be good, He, therefore, predestinated him to have rule over the elder, that which is affirmed by the apostle, would be false, 'not of works,'" &c. The state of the case is the same in reference to angels. For God provided against the possible misery of these, by the blessing of election; He did not provide against the possible misery of those, in the work of reprobation and preterition. But how? by predestinating the elect angels, to the adoption of sons, who are so styled in Job 1, 2 & 38, and not predestinating the others. God begat them as sons, not by nature, but by will, which will is eternal, and preceded from eternity their existence, which belongs to time. What does the child contribute towards his procreation? He does not indeed exist. What does an angel contribute towards his sonship? If nothing, what does man contribute? In reply to both these, Augustine, in the place already cited, surely with equal justice, thunders forth that inquiry of St. Paul, "who maketh thee to differ from another? and what hast thou that thou didst not receive?" &c. (1 Cor. iv. 7.)

God, therefore, regards man in general; He does not find any cause in man; for the cause of that adoption or filiation is from His sole will and grace. But if any one should say that sin is the cause of reprobation or preterition, He will not establish that point. For, in the first place, the reasoning of Augustine, which we have just adduced, remains unshaken, based on a comparison of works foreknown; in the second place, since we are, by nature, equally sinners before God, one of these three things must be true; -- either all are rejected on account of sin, as a common reason, or it is remitted to all, or a cause must be found elsewhere than in sin, as we have found it. Lastly, "who makes us to differ," if it be not God, according to the purpose of His own election? Therefore, the affirmation stands, that God, in the case of election and reprobation made from eternity, considered man in general, so that He has in Himself, not in man, the cause of both acts. Yet let us accurately weigh the arguments, which are advanced here, though, properly, they are not opposed to this theory.

THE REPLY OF ARMINIUS TO THE ANSWER
TO THE NINTH PROPOSITION

I think it is sufficiently evident how the authors of the first theory considered man, from what was said in reply to your answer to Prop. 6. But that the authors of the second theory, by the addition of that special relation, did not exclude the universal relation, seems hardly probable to me. For he, who says that sin supervened to election and preterition originating in their own causes, excluding sin not only from the cause of election and preterition, but from the subject and the condition requisite in it, he denies that man, universally, considered as fallen, is presented to him who elects and passes by, and if he denies this, he denies also that man is considered in general, by God, in the act of decree. In other respects I assent to what you affirm. Sin is not the cause of election and preterition, yet this statement must be rightly understood, as I think that it is here understood, namely, that sin is not the cause that God should elect some, and pass by others: let it be only stated that sin is the cause that God may be able to pass by some individuals of the human race made in His own image. In the former statement there is agreement between us, in the latter we disagree, if at all. It is not, then, the question, "Did God have reference, in His own decree, to men apart from any consideration of sin, as a cause, that is, as a cause that He should elect these, and pass by those." For this is admitted even by Augustine, who, nevertheless, presupposes to that decree sin, as a requisite condition in its object. But the question is this; "Is sin a condition requisite in the object, which God has reference in the acts of election and preterition, or not?" This is apparent by the arguments presented by myself, which prove, not that sin is a cause of that decree, but a condition, requisite in the object. Augustine affirms this, and I agree with him. Let us look at some passages from his works. In Book 1, to Simplicianus, he excludes sin as a cause that God should elect or reprobate, but includes it as a cause that He might have the power to pass by or reprobate, or as a condition requisite in the object of election and reprobation. The latter, I prove by his own words, (there is no necessity of proof as to the former, for in reference to that, there is agreement between us). "God did not hate Esau, the man, but He did hate Esau, the sinner," and again, "Was not Jacob, therefore, a sinner, because God loved him? He loved in him not sin, of which he was guilty, but the grace which Himself had bestowed, &c., and again, "God hates iniquity, therefore He punishes it in some by damnation, and removes it from others by justification." Again, "The whole race from Adam is one mass of sinful and wicked being, among whom both Jews and Gentiles, apart from the grace of God, belong to one lump." If you say that Augustine was here discussing, not preterition, but predamnation, I reply that Augustine knew no preterition which was not predamnation, for he prefixes to preterition hatred as its cause, as he prefixes love to election. Then, I conclude, according to the theory of Augustine, that what is affirmed in the case of Esau and Jacob, is not to be understood in that of Adam and Eve, and it does not, hence, follow that there would be a diverse mode of election and reprobation, unless it be first proved that God, in election, had reference to Adam and Eve, considered in their primitive state, which, throughout this discussion, I wholly deny. But there is a manifest difference between Esau and Jacob, and Adam and Eve. For the former, though not yet born, could be considered as sinners, for both had been already conceived in sin; if they had not been created, they could not be considered as such, for they were such in no possible sense; not even when they had been created by God, and remained yet in their original integrity. It cannot be inferred from this, that "persons, and all causes originating from, or situated in persons" preceded the act of election. For sin, in which Jacob and Esau were then already conceived, did not precede. Yet I admit that sin was not the cause that God should love one and hate the other, should elect one and reprobate the other, but it was a condition requisite in the object of that decree. Those arguments, however, which you present, do not injure my case. For they do not exclude sin from the object of that decree as a requisite condition, nor as a cause without which that decree could not be made, but only as a cause, on account of which one is reprobated, another elected.

This is apparent from Romans 9. For Esau had been conceived in sin when those words were addressed by God to Rebecca. In the same chapter also, the elect and the reprobate are said to be "vessels of mercy" and "of wrath," which terms could not be applied to them apart from a consideration of sin. I will not now affirm, as I might do with truth, that Jacob and Esau are to be considered, not in themselves, but as types, the former being the type of the children of the promise, who seek the righteousness which is of faith in Christ, the latter, the type of the children of the flesh, who followed after the righteousness of the law, which subject requires a more extended explanation, but here not so necessary. The first chapter to the Ephesians clearly affirms the same thing, as it asserts that the election is made in Christ, because it is of the grace, by which we have redemption in the blood of Christ, &c.

Your arguments "from reason" do not militate against the position, which I have assumed, they rather strengthen it. For in the first place, "the election is made in Christ," therefore, it is of sinners, as will be hereafter proved at greater length. Secondly, "predestination and reprobation suppose nothing in their subject." Therefore, whatever character the subject may have, which receives grace, for such a character, and considered in the same relation, is the grace prepared. But the sinner receives, and he only, the grace prepared in predestination. Therefore, also for the sinner alone, is grace prepared in predestination, but of this, also, more largely hereafter. Thirdly, men are the sons of God, not by generation, but by regeneration; the latter, presupposes sin, therefore, adoption is made from sinners.

The example of angels in this case proves nothing. Their election and reprobation and those of men are unlike, as you in many places acknowledge, for their salvation is secured by the grace of preservation and confirmation, that of men by the grace of restoration. He begat angels, as sons to Himself, according to the former grace; He regenerated men as sons to Himself by the latter grace. Therefore, God regarded man not in general, but as sinful, in reference to which point is this question between us, though he might find in man no cause that He should adopt one and pass by another, in reference to which we have no controversy. The question then remains between us, did God, in His decree of predestination and reprobation, have reference to man considered in his natural purity, or to man considered as in his sins? I assert the latter, and deny the former, and I have presented many arguments in support of my opinion; but I will now consider, in their order, those things, which you have presented against it.

TENTH PROPOSITION OF ARMINIUS

First, in general. 1. Since no man was ever created by God in a merely natural state; whence also no man could ever be considered in the decree of God, since that, which exists in the mind, is the material of action and exists in the relation of capability of action, but takes its form from the will and decree by which God determined actually to exert His power, at any time, in reference to man. Hence, whatever distinction may be made, in the mind, between nature, and a supernatural gift, bestowed on man at the creation, that is not to be considered in this place. For the creation of the first man, and, in him, of all men, was in the image of God, which image of God in man is not nature, but supernatural grace, having reference not to natural felicity, but to supernatural life. It is evident, from the description of the image of God, that supernatural grace in man is that divine image. For, according to the Scripture, it is "knowledge after the image of Him that created him," (Col. iii. 10,) and "righteousness and true holiness" pertaining to the new man which is created after" (according to) "God." (Ephes. iv. 24.) In addition to this, all the fathers, seem, without exception, to be of the sentiment that man was created in a gracious state. So, also, our Catechism, ques. 62. Since there is found, in the Scriptures, no reference to the love of God according to election, no divine volition and no act of God concerning men, referring to them in different respects, until after the entrance of sin into the world, or after it was considered as having entered.

ANSWER OF JUNIUS TO THE TENTH PROPOSITION

Before I refer to arguments, an ambiguity must be removed, which is introduced here, and which will be frequently introduced whenever reference is made to a "merely natural state." Things are called natural from the term "nature." But nature is two-fold, therefore, natural things are also two-fold. I affirm that nature is two-fold, as it is considered, first in relation to this physical world, situated nearer and lower in elementary and material things, which is described by Philosophers in the science of Physics, secondly, in relation to that spiritual world, namely, that which is more remote and higher, consisting in spiritual and immaterial things, which is treated of in Metaphysics, rightly so called. From the former nature we have our bodies, and by it we are animals; from the latter, we have our spirits, and by it we are rational beings, which is also observed by Aristotle (lib. 2, de gener. animalium cap. 3) in his statement that the mind alone "enters from without" into the natural body, and is alone divine; for there is no communion between its action and that of the body. Hence, it is, that natural things must, in general, be considered in three modes; physically, in relation to the body according to its essence, capability, actions and passions; metaphysically, in relation to the intelligent mind, according to its essence and being; and conjointly in relation to that personal union, which exists in man, as a being composed of both natures. But particularly, a distinction must be made in these same natural things, in respect to nature as pure and as corrupt. Therefore, all those things, which pertain to the nature of man in these different modes, are said to belong to the mere natural state of man, sin being excluded.

Now, I come to the particular members of your Proposition. First, you affirm, "that no man was ever created in a merely natural state." If you mean that he was created without supernatural endowments, I do not see how this can be proved, (though many make this assertion). The Scripture does not any where make this statement. But you are not ignorant that it is said in the schools, that a negative argument from authority, as, "it is not written, therefore, it is not true" is not valid. Again, the order of creation, in a certain respect, proves the contrary, since the body was first made from the dust, and afterwards the soul was breathed into it. Which, then, is more probable, that the soul was, at the moment of its creation, endowed with supernatural gifts, or that they were superadded after its creation? I would rather affirm that, as the soul was added to the body, so the supernatural endowments were added to the soul. If God did this in relation to nature, why may He not have done it, in the case of grace, which is more peculiar. Lastly, I do not think that it follows, if man was not made in a merely natural state, but with supernatural endowments, that grace, therefore, pertains to creation, and also that supernatural gifts would therefore, pertain, in common, to the whole race. That this consequence is false, is proved by the definition of nature, and the relation of supernatural things. For what else is nature than the principle of motion and rest, ordained by God? If, then, supernatural things are ordained on this principle, they cease to be supernatural and become natural. Besides the relation of supernatural things is such that they are not natural, as they are not common; for those things which are common to all men belong to nature, but supernatural things are personal, and do not pass to heirs. I acknowledge that Adam and Eve received supernatural gifts, but for themselves not for their heirs; nor could they transmit them to their heirs, except by a general arrangement or special grace. If this be so, then man is without supernatural endowments, though, as you claim, the first man may not have been made without them; and he is justly considered by us as not possessing them, and much more would he have been so considered by the Deity. Indeed, my brother, God contemplated man, in a merely natural state, and determined in His own decree to bestow upon him supernatural endowments. He could then be so considered in the decree of God. He contemplated nature, on which He would bestow grace; the natural man, on whom He would bestow, by His own decree, supernatural gifts. Was it not, indeed, a special act of the will, to create man, and another special act of the will to endow Him with supernatural gifts? Which acts, even though they might have occurred at the same time (which does not seem to me necessary, for the reasons which have been just advanced) cannot be together in the order of nature, since one may be styled natural, and the other supernatural. I know that you afterwards speak of the image of God, but we shall soon see that this has no bearing, (as you think), on this case. Meanwhile, I wish that you would always keep in view the fact, that, though all these things should be true, yet they are not opposed to that doctrine which asserts that in this decree, God considered man in general.

I will leave without discussion those subsequent remarks on the material and the formal relation of the decree of God, since the force of the argument does not depend on them, and pass to the proof. "The creation of the first man," you affirm, "and, in him, of all men, was in the image of God," (I concede and believe it,) "which image of God in man is not nature but supernatural grace, having reference not to natural felicity but to supernatural life." What is this, your statement, my brother? Origen formerly affirmed the same thing, and on this account received the reprehension of the ancient church in its constant testimony and harmonious declarations, as is attested by Epiphanius, Jerome and other witnesses. I do not, however, believe that you agree in sentiment with Origen, in opposition to the united and wise declaration of that church, but some ambiguity, which you have not observed, has led you into this mistake. Let us then expose and free from its obscurity this subject, by the light of truth.

The first ambiguity is in the word nature, the second in the term supernatural. We have just spoken in reference to the former, affirming that this term may refer to the lower nature of elementary bodies, or to that higher nature of spiritual beings, or finally to our human nature, composed of both natures in one compound subject; and that this latter nature is itself two-fold, pure and depraved.

The latter ambiguity consists in the fact, that the term supernatural is applied, at one time, to those things which are above this inferior nature, and pertain to the superior, spiritual, or metaphysical nature; at another, to those things which are above even that higher and metaphysical nature, that is, to those which are properly and immediately divine; and at another, to those things which are above the condition of this our corrupt nature, as they are bestowed upon us only of supernatural grace, though they might have pertained to that pure nature. The body, for example, is of this lower nature, and in comparison with it, the soul is supernatural. Again, our souls are of the higher nature, which pertains to angels. In reference to both the soul and the body, all divine things are supernatural as they are superior to all corporeal and mental nature. How you say that "the image of God in man is not nature but supernatural grace;" that is, as I think, it is not of nature, but of grace, or not from nature, but from grace. Here consider, my brother, the former ambiguity. "The image of God is not of nature," if the lower or corporeal nature is referred to, is a true statement, but if the higher nature is referred to, it is not a true statement. For what is nature? It is the principle, ordained of God, of motion and rest in its own natural subject, according to its own mode. Place before your mind the kinds of motion, which occur in the lower nature, generation, corruption, increase, diminution, alteration, local transition, which they style fora &c. You will find this difference, that the subjects of this lower nature experience these motions according to their own essence and all other matters, that is, according to their material, form, and accidents, but the subjects of that higher nature are moved by no means according to their essence, but only according to their being; but that divine things surpass both natures, in an infinite and divine mode, because they are, in all respects, destitute of all motion. The body is mortal; whence, if not from this inferior nature? The soul is immortal; whence, if not from that superior nature? But both natures are ordained of God, and so perform their work, immediately, that God performs, by both mediately, all things which pertain to nature. But the image of God is from that superior nature, by which God performs mediately in the children of Adam, as He instituted our common nature in Adam, our first parent. It is indeed true, that it was supernatural grace by which God impressed His own image on Adam; just as he also performed the work of creation by the same grace. God bestowed its principle not on nature, of nature, but of Himself; but when nature has received its existence, that which existed by nature, was produced by nature in the species and individuals. Though, in its first origin, it is of grace, yet it is now, in its own essence, of nature, and is to be called natural. But the image of God is produced, in the species and in the individuals, by nature. Therefore, it must be called natural We shall hereafter consider its definition, for it is necessary first to elucidate the statement that "the image of God has reference, not to felicity, but to supernatural life." Let us remove the ambiguity, as we shall thus speak more correctly of these matters. Natural felicity pertains either to the nature from which we have the body, or to that from which we have the spirit, or to both natures united in a compound being. To this latter felicity the image of God has, naturally, its reference; to that of the body as its essential and intimately associated instrument; to that of the spirit, as its essential subject; to that of the man, as the entire personal subject. If you deny this, what is there, I pray you, in all nature, which does not seek its own good? But, to every thing, its own good is its felicity. If, in this lower nature, a stone, the herds, an animal, and, in that higher nature, spirits and intelligent forms do this, surely it cannot be justly denied to man, and to the image of God in man. You add that "it has reference to supernatural life." This, however, is a life dependent on grace, as all the adjuncts show. If you understand that it has reference to that life only, we deny such exclusive reference. If to this (natural) life, and to that life conjointly, we indeed affirm this, and assent to your assertion that the image of God in man has respect to both kinds of felicity, both natural and supernatural; by means of nature, in a natural mode, and of grace, in a supernatural mode.

I would now explain this, in a more extended manner, if it was not necessary that a statement should first be made of the subject under discussion. Perceiving this very clearly, you pass to a definition of that image, in proof of your sentiment. "It is evident," you say, "from the description of the image of God, that supernatural grace, in man, is that divine image." You will permit me to deny this, since you ask not my opinion. You add, "According to the Scripture, it is 'knowledge after the image of Him that created him,' (Col. iii. 10,) and righteousness and true holiness pertaining 'to the new man which is created after God.' (Ephes. v. 25)". I acknowledge that these are the words of the apostle, and I believe them, but I fear my brother, that you wander from his words and sentiment.

In the former passage, he does not assert that the image of God is "knowledge after the image etc," but that the "new man is renewed in knowledge after the image of him that created him." The subject of the proposition is man, one in substance, but once "old," now "new." In this subject there was old knowledge, there is new knowledge. According to the subject, the knowledge is one, but it differs in mode; for the old man and the new man understand with the same intellect, in the previous case as the old, afterwards as the new man. What, therefore, is the mode of that knowledge! "After the image of God." This is the mode of our knowledge and intelligence. The former (that which is old) according to the image of the first Adam who "begat a son in his own likeness;" (Gen. v. 3;) the latter according to the image of the second Adam, Christ and God, our Creator. The image of God is not said to be knowledge, but knowledge is said to be renewed in us after the image of God. What, then, is knowledge? An act of the image of God. What is the image of God? The fountain and principle of action, fashioning in a formal manner, the action, or the habit of that image. The mode, in which this may be understood, is a matter of no interest to me. Consider, I pray you, and I appeal to yourself as a judge, whether this can be justly called a suitable description; -- "The image of God is knowledge according to the image of God." This description, indeed, denies that the image of God is either one thing or another; either knowledge or the image of God, if, indeed, knowledge is according to the image of God. You will, however, understand these things better, from your own skill, than they can be stated by me in writing. I now consider the other passage. "The image of God is ' righteousness and true holiness' pertaining 'to the new man, which is created after God.'" Here you affirm something more than in the previous case, yet without sufficient truth. That knowledge, of which you had previously spoken, is a part of truth, for it is the truth, as it exists in our minds. Here you state that it is truth, and righteousness and holiness. But let us examine the words of the apostle. He asserts, indeed, that the new man is one "which after God is created in righteousness and true holiness." I will not plead the fact that many explain the phrase "after God," as though the apostle would say "by the power of God working in us." I assent to your opinion that the words kata< Qeon mean simply the same as would be implied in the phrase "to the image," or "according to the image of God." Yet do you not perceive that the same order, which we have just indicated, is preserved by Paul; and that the subject, the principle, and the acts or habits, thereby inwrought, are most suitably distinguished? The subject is man, who is the same person, whether as the old; or the new man. The principle is the image of God, which is the same, whether old or new, and purified from corruption. The acts or habits, inwrought by that principle, are righteousness, holiness, and truth. Righteousness, holiness, and truth are not the image, but pertain to the image. Let us return, if you please, to that principle, which the Fathers laid down "natural things are corrupt, supernatural things are removed." You may certainly, hence, deduce with ease this conclusion; -- righteousness, holiness and truth are not removed, therefore, they are not supernatural. Again, they have become corrupt, therefore, they are natural. If they had been removed, none of their elementary principles would exist in us by nature. But they do exist; therefore, they are by nature, and are themselves corrupt, and, with them, whatever originates in them. The same is the fact with the image of God. The image of God is not removed; it is not, therefore, supernatural; and, on the other hand, it has become corrupt; it is, therefore, natural. For it is nowhere, in the Scriptures, said to be bestowed, but only to be renewed. I shall offer proof, on this point, from the Scriptures, when I have made a single remark. Righteousness, holiness, truth, exist only in the image of God; there is, in man, some righteousness, holiness and truth; therefore, there is in man somewhat of the image of God. Moses, in Genesis 1, certainly relates nothing else than the first constitution of nature, as made in reference to every subject and species. But he relates that man was made in the image of God. This, then, was the constitution of human nature. But, if it is of nature, then the image of God pertains universally to the human race, since natural things differ from personal things in this, that they are common. The same is evident from Gen. v. 3. Adam begat Seth "in his own likeness," in his own image; but Adam was made in the image of God; therefore he begat Seth in the image of God. It may be said, however, that the image of God, and the image of Adam differ, and that a distinction is made between them by Moses. They indeed differ, but in mode, not in their essence; for the image of God in Adam was uncorrupted, in Seth it was corrupted through Adam; yet in both cases it was the image. In the same respect, this image, in the rest of the human race, is called according to its corruption, the image of the earthy, according to its renewal, the image of the heavenly. But since the image of God is diverse in mode only, and not in essence, it is said to be renewed, and restored, and not to be implanted or created, as we have before observed, as that which differs not in essence, but in mode or degree. The same thing is taught in Gen. ix. 6. "Whoso sheddeth man's blood, by man shall his blood be shed: for in the image of God made he man." If the image of God did not exist in the descendants of Adam, who are slain, the argument of Moses would be impertinent and absurd. But the argument, either of Moses or of God, is just and conclusive; for if you say, -- "The slayer of him, whom God has made in His own image, ought to be slain by man; God made the man who is slain in his own image; therefore, let the murderer be slain by man." the argument is valid. For since man was made in the image of God, it is just that his murderer should be slain, and indeed that he should be slain by man. But if you explain the passage "for in the image of God made He man," so that "He" shall refer to man, my interpretation of the argument will be even more confirmed. I do not, however, remember that it is affirmed any where in the Scriptures that man made man, nor can it be proved to me. These things, I think will be sufficient that you may see, my brother, that the image of God is naturally in man.

What, then, is the image of God? For it is now time that we pass from destructive to constructive reasoning. I will state it, in the words of the orthodox Fathers. Let Tertullian, of the Latins, first speak (lib. 2 advers. Marcion, cap. 9.) "The distinction is especially to be noticed, which the Greek Scriptures make, when they speak of the afflatus, not of the Spirit, (pnohn non pneu~ma) for some, translating from the Greek, not considering the difference or regarding the proper use of words, substitute Spirit for afflatus, and afford heretics an occasion of charging fault on the Spirit of God, that is, on God Himself; and it is even now a vexed question. Observe, then, that the afflatus is inferior to the Spirit, though it comes from the Spirit, as its breath, yet it is not the Spirit. For the breeze is lighter than the wind, and if the breeze is of the wind, the wind is not therefore, of the breeze. It is usual also, to call the afflatus the image of the Spirit; for thus also, man is the image of God, that is of the Spirit, for God is Spirit, therefore, the image of the Spirit is the afflatus. Moreover the image will never in all respects equal the reality; for to be according to the truth is one thing, to be the truth itself is another. Thus, also, the afflatus cannot, in such a sense, be equal to the Spirit, that, because the truth—that is the Spirit, or God—is without sin, therefore the image, of truth also, must be without sin. In this respect the image will be inferior to the truth, and the afflatus will be inferior to the Spirit, having some lineaments of the Deity, in the fact that the soul is immortal, free, capable of choice, prescient to a considerable degree, rational, and capable of understanding and knowledge. Yet, in these particulars, it is only an image, and does not extend to the full power of divinity, and so, likewise, it does not extend to sinless integrity, since this belongs alone to God, that is to truth, and can not pertain to the mere image; for as the image, while it expresses all the lineaments and outlines of the truth, yet is destitute of force, not having motion, so the soul, the image of the Spirit, is not able to exhibit its full power, that is, the felicity of freedom from sin, otherwise it would be not the soul, but the Spirit, not man, endowed with mind, but God, &c." Ambrose (hexaemeri lib. 6, cap. 7), after many arguments, concludes in this way; "for 'what will a man give in exchange for his soul?' in which there is, not merely a small portion of himself, but the substance of the entire human race. It is this by which thou hast dominion over other living creatures, whether beasts or birds. This is the image of God, but the body is in the likeness of beasts; in one there is the sacred mark of divine resemblance, in the other the vile fellowship with the herds and wild beasts, &c." Also, in Psalm 118, sermon 10, "Likeness to the image of God consists, not in the body, or in the material parts of our nature, but in the rational soul; in respect to which man was made after the likeness and image of God, and in which the form of righteousness, wisdom, and every virtue is found."

To the same purpose are the words of Augustine, in his first Book "De Genes. contra Manich," chap. 17th, and in many other places. I mention also Jerome, because he evidently has the same view, and, in writing against Origen, he uses the same argument with that of Epiphanius and the Greek Fathers. I would refer to Basil, if you did not know that Ambrose quotes from him. Why should I speak of Chrysostom, the two Gregories, Cyril, Theodouret? Damascenus, an epitomist of all those writers, presents this subject, with the greatest accuracy, in the book which he has inscribed "Concerning the respect in which we were made in the image of God." Also, in another, which has reference to "The two wills in Christ," in which he uses the following words, "as to the rational, and intellectual, and voluntary powers, they belong to the mind at birth, and the Spirit is superadded, as having princely prerogative, and in these respects both angels and men are after the image of God, and this is abundantly true of men, &c.," in which passage he has, with the utmost diligence, introduced those things which are essential and those which are adjunct.

I conclude with a single argument from Augustine against the Manichees. "Those men," he says, "do not know that it is not possible that nature should use any action, or produce any effect, the faculty for which has not been received according to nature. For example, no bird can fly, unless it has received the faculty of flying, according to nature, and no beast of the earth can walk, unless it has received the faculty of walking, according to nature. So, likewise, man cannot act or will, unless he has received, according to nature, that faculty, which is called the "voluntary," and the "energetic;" and he cannot understand if he has not received from nature the intellectual faculty, and he cannot see, or perform any other action, and, therefore, in every kind of nature, natural actions find place, and they exist at once and together, but those which depend on the will and activity, do not exist together." From which reasoning he infers that man understands, reasons, wills, and, above other creatures, does many things which savour of divinity; therefore, many faculties exist in man, in respect to which he is said, in the Scriptures, to have been made in the image and likeness of God.

Here then is that image of God, in our soul; its essential parts not only show, of themselves, some resemblance, by nature, to divinity, but are, by nature and grace together, adapted to the perception of supernatural grace, as we shall soon show. You add that "all the fathers, seem, without exception, to be of the sentiment that man was created in a gracious state. So also our Catechism, ques. 6." I have, indeed, known no one among orthodox divines, who holds any different opinion; nor is there any other correct explanation of our catechism.

But you seem to fall into an error from a statement, which is susceptible of a two-fold interpretation, and to unite things really distinct. For it is not meant that the first man was created with grace, that is, that he received, in the act of creation, nature and supernatural grace; but this is their meaning: the man who was first created, received grace, that is, supernatural grace, as an additional gift—which idea we have before presented in this answer. What then? Did he not have supernatural grace in creation? If you understand, by grace, the good will of God, he had grace; if you understand supernatural gifts, bestowed upon him, then he did not have those things, which are supernatural, from creation, or by the force of creation, since creation is the principle of nature, or its first term, but supernatural things entirely differ from it; but he had them in creation, that is, in that first state of creation in which Adam was until he fell into sin. That you may more easily understand the subject, let us use the illustration of the sun and moon, to explain the divine image. The moon has an essential image, and one which is relative and accidental. As its image is essential, it has its own light in some degree; yet it would be darkened, unless it should look towards the sun; as its image is relative, it has light borrowed from the sun, while it is looked upon by it, and looks to it. So, there was, in man, a two-fold relation of the image of God, even from the creation. For man had his own essential light fixed in the soul, which shines as the image of God among created things; he had also a relative light, as he was looked upon by God, and looked back to God. The essential image is natural; the relative image was, so to speak, supernatural, for it looked to God, through nature joined to grace, by a peculiar and free motion of the will; God looked upon it, of grace, (for, what action of God towards us is natural?) We have that essential light, corrupted by sin; it is plain that we have not lost it. We have lost the relative light; but Christ restores this, that we may be renewed, after God, in his own image, and that the essential light may be purified, since natural things are corrupted, the supernatural are lost, as we have previously said.

Your second argument is stated thus: "Since there is found, in the Scriptures, no reference to the love of God according to election, no divine volition, and no act of God, concerning men, referring to them in different respects, until after the entrance of sin into the world, or after it was considered as having entered." If I should concede this, yet the sentiment of those, who say that man is considered, in general, by the Deity, would not, therefore, be confuted, as we have before shown. But I may, perhaps, be able to disprove this assertion by authority, by reason, and by example. You have authority in Romans ix. 11-13. "For the children being not yet born, neither having done any good or evil, that the purpose of God, according to election, might stand, not of works, but of Him that calleth; it was said unto her, The elder shall serve the younger; as it is written, Jacob have I loved, but Esau have I hated." What do those three phrases indicate "the children being not yet born;" again, "neither having done any good or evil;" and "according to election, not of works, but of Him that calleth." You will say, "these expressions are according to truth; but they have reference to fallen and sinful nature." But they exclude, with the utmost care, all reference to sin and refer all blessing to the sole vocation of God, who calleth, as even yourself, my brother, if you are willing to observe it, (and you certainly are thus willing,) may easily deduce from that proposition. To this authority you will certainly submit every semblance of reasoning. (Ephes. i. 4, 5,) "He hath chosen us in Him before the foundation of the world, having predestinated us unto the adoption of children, by Jesus Christ to Himself."

Election originates in special love; and when He is said to have chosen us in Christ, all reference to ourselves is excluded; predestination also precedes both persons and cases relating to them. Indeed this is indicated by the words "foreknow" and "predestinate," (Rom. 8). Christ himself attributes to the blessing of the Father only that they were made possessors of the kingdom, "from the foundation of the world," (Matt. 30). In sin, or previous to sin? In view of sin, or without reference to it? Why should the former be true, I ask, rather than the latter? Why indeed, should not the latter rather, since all things are said to depend on God, who calleth? To these, let the following considerations be added:

1. Whatever absurdity may be connected with this subject, you will perceive, (if you examine it closely,) that it pertains as much to the former interpretation, and rather more to it than to the latter. This absurdity is not to be passed by, but rather to be religiously and suitably removed.

2. I deny that a reference to sin belongs to the matter of filial adoption. I call nature as a witness: Does not a father beget sons, before he investigates or observes what shall be their condition? But this generation, (namely that of the children of God), is of will and not of nature. True: yet it is attributed to the will of God alone, not to any condition in us. Every condition in us is excluded, even that of sin; the will of God, alone, His purpose, alone, is considered in the matter. God distinguishes by His mere will among those equal in nature, equal

in sin; whom, considered in their natural condition simply, not in that of sin, but generally in Christ, He adopts as His children. As in nature, children are begotten without reference to their future condition, so God, of His own will, adopted from eternity His own children.

3. Whatever is more consistent with the wisdom and grace of God, would be performed by the Deity, and is to be believed by us, rather than that which is less consistent. But it is more consistent with His wisdom and grace that He should adopt unto Himself children without any consideration of character, than that He should do so on the supposition of such consideration; otherwise nature would act more perfectly than God, as according to nature, fathers beget children, without such consideration. Therefore, the former view is more consistent with the character of God, and rather to be received with faith by us.

As an example, for the confirmation of this matter, we will take, if you please, that of the Angels. Whoever are the sons of God, are sons by election. Angels are the sons of God, (Job 1, 2, & 37,) therefore, they are such by election, as Paul affirms (1 Tim. v. 21,) when he calls them "the elect." But they are elect without consideration of their sins, as they did not sin, but remained in their original condition.

Therefore, the love of God is with election, without reference to sin, or consideration of it, which you seem to deny in your assertion. Perhaps you will say that your assertion had reference only to men. But I reply, that love and election are spoken of in relation both to angels and men, and in the same manner, since God placed, in both, his own image, in reference to which election is made. The most decisive proof of this is found in the principle that, if any act which apparently exists in reference to two things, which have the same relation, does not really exist in reference to one, it does not exist in reference to the other. In the election of Angels, there is no reference to their condition or their works; therefore, in the election of men there is no such reference. If the condition of Angels and of men is, in some respects, different, it does not follow that the mode of their election is different; especially when the relation of that thing, in reference to which they are chosen, is the same in both cases. This is the image of God, which, preserved or restored according to His own will, he has called and united to Himself, which will remain immutably in Christ, "gathering together in one all things," (Ephes. i. 10,) and which he had placed on the common basis of his own nature, from which, those, who were to be damned according to His judgment, fell of their own will.

It is not possible to adduce any other example; because all other things are created in a different relation. For they are destitute of the image of God, in which consists, with suitable limitations, the object of election. Therefore, the nature of the divine election, made concerning men, can be illustrated by the example of angels, and by no other example. But the divine election was such, not that it separated, at first, the Angels who sinned from those who did not sin, but that, of His own will and grace, he distinguished those who were not about to sin, as previously elected and predestinated to adoption, from others who were about to sin of their own free will. What reason, then, is there that we should think that another mode of the divine election must be devised in reference to men?

REPLY OF ARMINIUS TO THE ANSWER
TO THE TENTH PROPOSITION

I apply the term natural to whatever pertains to the substance and existence of man, without which man cannot exist. Such are the soul and the body, and the whole system compounded of them, with all natural attributes, affections, passions, &c. I apply the term supernatural to whatever God has bestowed on man above and in addition to those natural characteristics, which indeed pertain to the perfection of man, not in respect to his animal nature, but in respect to his spiritual nature, to the acquisition not of natural, but of supernatural good. I apply the phrase "merely natural," in this place, to that which has nothing supernatural added to it. The sense then of my words is that man is not made in a merely natural state, without supernatural endowments.

I do not here contend, with much strenuousness, whether he has those supernatural endowments from the act of creation or from another act of superinfusion, but leave this without decision, as neither useful or injurious to my cause. But I decidedly state and affirm, that God decreed to make man such by nature, as he in fact did make him; but such, that He might add to him some supernatural endowments, as He not only wished that he might be such as he was by nature, but He wished also to advance him further to a happier state, namely, to a participation of Himself, to which he could not attain, unless endowed with supernatural gifts. But when I deny that man was made in a merely natural state, and, therefore, was created with supernatural gifts, I wish not to indicate that the act, by which supernatural endowments are communicated, was creation, (for in my 26th proposition I have called that act superinfused Grace,) but that God was unwilling to cease from the act of communicating His blessing to that part of primitive matter or Nothing from which He created man, and that of His own decree, until he should also have bestowed those supernatural gifts upon him. I thought that I ought to observe the mode of expression, used in the Scripture, which declares that man was created "in the image and likeness of God," which image and likeness of God comprehends in itself also supernatural gifts. If this is true, as I contend, then man was created with supernatural endowments. For he was made in the image of God, and the word "made" is attributed, without distinction, to all parts of the image, without separating that, in the image, which is natural from that which is supernatural to man. I am glad to quote here the words of Jerome Zanchius, who, in his first book concerning the creation of man, chapter 1, speaks concerning this same matter in these terms;" I am pleased with the sentiment of those, who say that with the inbreathing of life, there was also inbreathed and infused by the Deity whatever Adam possessed of celestial light, wisdom, rectitude, and other heavenly gifts; in which he reflects the Deity, as His true image. For he was created such as the Scripture teaches, affirming that he was made in the image of God, and Solomon in Eccl. vii. 29, "God made man upright." But he was not such when his body only was formed. When, with a soul placed in him, he became a living soul, that is a living man, that he was made upright, just, &c., and thus, at the same time with his soul, rays also of divine wisdom, righteousness, and goodness were infused." Thus Zanchius, who clearly decides what I left without decision in either direction, and this for a twofold reason; I knew that it was a matter of dispute among the learned, and I perceived that nothing could be deduced from it either of advantage or disadvantage to my cause.

Those supernatural gifts, which were bestowed on man, he received for transmission to posterity, on the terms, on which he received them, namely, of grace, not as this word denotes the principle of natural endowments, for from grace, understood in its widest sense, we have received even our nature, as that to which we had no claim, but as it is used in contra-distinction to nature, and as it is the principle of supernatural gifts. I can then concede that God had reference to man in nature, as the subject of grace, the natural man as the subject of supernatural gifts; but that He had reference to him, contemplated in the administrative decree of creation, not in the decree of predestination, which we have now under discussion; as the subject of grace sufficient for supernatural felicity, not of effectual grace, of which we now dispute; as the subject of supernatural gifts, to be transmitted to his posterity, without exception, according to the arrangement of grace, and without any condition, not of such gifts as are peculiar to those, who are predestinated, and to be bestowed, with certainty and infallibly, upon them, in reference to which is the controversy between us.

Hence, these things are not opposed to my sentiment, for in them the fallacy of ignoratio elenchi is committed. I wish, however, that you would always remember that I speak constantly concerning the grace, prepared in the decree of predestination, and in no other decree. But I have proved that man was not made in a merely natural state, in the sense, as I have already stated, of a destitution of supernatural endowments, whether he is said to have them by the act of creation, or by the act of superinfusion; and I have proved it by an argument, deduced from the image and likeness of God in which man was created. Which argument is valid, whether the image of God signifies only supernatural gifts, bestowed on man by the Deity, as our Catechism and Confession, and some of our theologians affirm in reference to the image of God, or nature itself, together with those supernatural gifts, which is my opinion; according to which I wish that my affirmation, that "the image of God in man is not nature, but supernatural grace," should be understood, that is, that it is not nature alone, apart from supernatural endowments, which is sufficient for any argument. For the question is not concerning natural qualities, and therefore, the decision of the point whether they belong to the image of God, according to my opinion, or not, does not affect the subject of inquiry. Let supernatural qualities be embraced in the definition of the image of God, in which man was made, and I have obtained what I desire.

I also wish that my subsequent remarks should be understood in the same manner, namely, that the image of God, has respect, not to natural felicity only, but to supernatural, and if that is true, as you seem to concede, I have attained my object. I did not wish to define with accuracy the image of God in which man was made, since this was not necessary to my purpose: it was sufficient to have shown that "knowledge, righteousness, and holiness" pertained also to the image of God, whether that image consisted wholly or only in part in them. For either of these statements would be equally available for my purpose, as I had undertaken to prove that man was not created without supernatural endowments, and therefore that he could not have been considered, in the decree of predestination, as created in a merely natural state, without supernatural endowments. But, before I come to the defense of my argument on this point, I must speak, at somewhat greater length, of three things, in considering which, a considerable part of your answer is occupied. First. I will explain more fully than I have before done, what I call natural, and what, supernatural qualities. Secondly. I will speak of the image of God, and what things, whether natural or supernatural, are embraced in it, and in its definition. Thirdly, by what action of the Deity, man has both the former, and the latter qualities.

First; I call those qualities natural which pertain to the nature of man, without which man cannot be man, and which have their source in the principles of nature, and are prepared, by their own nature, for natural felicity, as their end and limit: such are the body, the soul, the union of both, and that which is made up of both, and their natural attributes, affections, functions,

and passions; under which I also comprehend moral feelings, which are sometimes spoken of in contradistinction to those which are natural. I call those
qualities supernatural which are not a part of man, and do not originate in
natural principles, but are superadded to natural principles, for the increase
and perfection of nature, designed for supernatural felicity, and for a supernatural communion with God, our Creator, in which that felicity consists.

Between these, exists a natural relation of this character, that natural qualities may receive the addition of supernatural, by the arrangement of God, and
that supernatural qualities are adapted for adding to, adorning and perfecting
nature, and are therefore ordained for exalting it above itself. Hence, without
ambiguity, under the term natural, I have comprehended nature both corporeal and spiritual, and that which is composed of both. It is, however, to be
carefully observed—that ambiguities of words are to be noticed and explained,
in a discussion, when, if taken in one sense, they favour any view, and, if in
the other, they do not, when, according to one sense, a statement is true, and,
according to the other, is false. But when the statement is true, and pertinent
to the subject, in whatever sense a word is taken, there is no need of an explanation of the ambiguity. Thus, in this case, you observe that I understand, by
natural qualities, both those which pertain to the inferior nature, that is, to the
body, and those which pertain to the superior nature, that is, to the soul, and in
whatever mode you take it, my argument is equally strong and valid. We shall
hereafter notice examples of equally unnecessary reference to ambiguity.

Secondly; two things must be considered in reference to the image of God
in man, in what things does it consist, and which of them may be called material, and which supernatural?

I affirm that the image of God in man embraces all those things which
represent in man any thing of the divine nature, which are partly essential: yet
God did not wish that the images of all of them should be essential to man,
whom He wished to create, in such a condition, not only that he might be that
which he was, but that he might have the capability of becoming that which
he was not, and of failing to be that which he was. I call essential the soul,
and in it the intellect, and will, and the freedom of the will, and other affections, actions, and passions, which necessarily result from them. I call accidental both the moral virtues, and the knowledge of God, righteousness and
true holiness, and whatever other attributes of the Deity exist, to be considered
in Him as essential to his own nature, but in man as an express image, of which
under the term "divine nature," Peter says, that believers are "partakers." 2. I do
not think that all these things can be comprehended under the term natural,
but I think that "knowledge, righteousness and true holiness," are supernatural,
and are to be called by that name. I am in doubt whether I have your assent to

this affirmation. For in one part of your answer, you say that those are natural qualities, and present arguments in support of that view, and in another place, in the same answer, you acknowledge that Adam had supernatural gifts though not from the act of creation: by which supernatural qualities, I know not what you can understand, except those things which are mentioned by the apostle in Colossians 3, and Ephesians

4. Yet you seem to set forth under the term reflexive image, those very things which you acknowledge to be supernatural. But, whether I rightly understand your sentiment or not, I will speak of those things which, I think, tend to confirm my sentiment, and to refute your view, as I understand it.

I prove, then, that those qualities are supernatural. First, from Colossians 3, and Ephesians 4. Whatever things we have, from regeneration, by the spirit of Christ, are supernatural. But we have, from regeneration, by the Spirit of Christ, "the knowledge of God, righteousness and true holiness." Therefore, they are supernatural. If any one says that we do not have them, in substance, from regeneration, but only a renewal of the same qualities, which had previously been made corrupt, I do not see how that assertion can be proved. For the phrases of the apostle teach another doctrine. For he who must "put on the new man," is not clothed with the "new man," or with any part of him. But to the new man, pertain "righteousness and true holiness." Then, in the case of him, who must be "renewed in knowledge," it is not his knowledge which has become corrupt and must be renewed, but his intelligence, which must be enlightened with new knowledge, which has been utterly expelled by the darkness of the old man. I designed this, only, in my argument, and not to define the image of God in man. But I cannot see that I differ from the view of the apostle in my explanation. For the knowledge of God, in the passage quoted by me, is the "image of God" itself, and "after the image of God." Nor are these expressions at variance with each other, nor are they so absurd as you wish them to appear. You say "the image of God is knowledge, according to the image of God, therefore, the image of God is denied to be either knowledge or image." I deny this sequence if the definition is rightly understood, namely, in the following manner. The image of God, renewed in us by the regenerating Spirit, is the knowledge of God, according to the image of God, in which, at the beginning, we were created. This image has a two-fold relation, in that it is created anew in us by the Spirit of Christ, and that it was formerly created in us by the Spirit of God. That knowledge differs not only in mode, but in its whole nature, from the knowledge of the old man: nor is it said to be renewed, but the man is said to be renewed in it. But I confess that I cannot understand how knowledge is an act of the image of God, and how that image is the fountain or principle of that act, that is of knowledge. For I have hitherto thought that man was said to be created in or to the image of God, that is, because, in mind, will, knowledge of God, righteousness and finally holiness, he refers to God Himself, as the archetype. In the other passage from Ephesians 4, I do not find the three characteristics, "truth, righteousness and holiness," but only two, righteousness and holiness, to which is ascribed truth, that is, sincerity, purity, simplicity. Knowledge, also, is not a member or portion of that truth, but a gift, created in the intellect or mind of man, as righteousness and holiness are ingenerated in the will, or rather the affections of man.

Secondly, I prove that the same qualities are supernatural in this way. Those things, according to which we are, and are said to be, partakers of the divine nature, and the children of God, are supernatural: but we are, and are said to be partakers of the divine nature, and children of God, according to knowledge, righteousness and holiness; therefore, these are supernatural. The Major does not need proof. The Minor is evident from a comparison of the first, second, third, and fourth verses of 2 Peter 1. Thirdly, those things which have their limit in supernatural felicity, are supernatural; but the knowledge of God, righteousness and holiness are such; therefore, they are supernatural.

Fourthly, the immediate causes of supernatural acts are supernatural. But the knowledge of God, righteousness and holiness, are the immediate causes of supernatural acts: therefore they are supernatural. I now come to your arguments, in which you attempt to show that the image of God in man is natural, and that those qualities, knowledge, righteousness and holiness, are natural, not supernatural.

Your first argument is this: Supernatural qualities were removed, natural qualities were corrupted. But truth, righteousness, holiness, were not removed, they were corrupted; therefore, they are not supernatural, but natural. Your first argument is this: Supernatural qualities were removed, natural qualities were corrupted. But truth, righteousness, holiness, were not removed, they were corrupted; therefore, they are not supernatural, but natural. Your Minor is defended thus. The principles of these qualities are in us by nature; they would not be, if they had been removed. I reply—that I admit the Major; but the Minor does not seem at all probable to me, not even by the addition of that reason. For, I affirm that the knowledge which is according to piety, the righteousness and the holiness, of which the apostle speaks, were not corrupted, but removed, and that none of the principles of those qualities remain in us after the fall. I acknowledge that the principles and seeds of the moral virtues, which have some analogy and resemblance to those spiritual virtues, and that, even those moral virtues themselves, though corrupted by sin, remained in us after the fall. It is possible that this resemblance may mislead him who does not accurately discriminate between these moral and those spiritual virtues. In support of this sentiment, in which I state that those gifts were taken away, I have the declaration of the Catechism, in the answer to question nine, in these words:

"Man deprived himself and all his posterity, of those divine gifts." But an explanation of the nature of those divine gifts is given in the sixth question, namely, "righteousness and holiness." I know not but that I have the support of your own declaration on this point. For in the eighteenth of your Theses, Concerning Original Sin, discussed in 1594, are these words: "For, as in Adam the form of human integrity was original righteousness, in which he was made by God, so the form of corruption, or rather of deformity, was a deprivation of that righteousness."

In the nineteenth Thesis, "The Scripture calls the form, first mentioned, the image and likeness of God." In the twentieth Thesis, "The Scripture calls the latter form, the image and likeness of Adam." If I rightly understand these expressions, I think that it plainly follows from them that original righteousness was removed, and that it is, therefore, supernatural, according to the rule "supernatural qualities were removed; natural qualities were corrupted." I have also, in my favour, most, perhaps all, of the Fathers. Ambrose, in reference to Elijah and his fasting, chap. 4th, says, "Adam was clothed with a vesture of virtues before his transgression, but, as if denuded by sin, he saw himself naked, because the clothing, which he previously had, was lost," and again in the seventh book of his commentary on the 10th chapter of that gospel, marking, more clearly, the distinction between the loss of supernatural qualities and the corruption of natural ones, he speaks thus: "Who are thieves if not the angels of night and of darkness? They first despoil us of the garments of spiritual grace, and then inflict on us wounds." Augustine, (De Trinitate, lib. 14, cap. 16,) says, "Man, by sinning, lost righteousness and true holiness, on which account, this image became deformed and discoloured; he receives them again when he is reformed and renewed." Again, (De civit. Dei. lib. 14, cap. 11) he affirms that "free-will was lost." To conclude this part of the discussion, I ask what were those spiritual qualities, which were renewed or lost, if not the knowledge of God, righteousness and holiness.

Another argument, adduced by you, is this: "Whatever belongs to the species is natural; But the image of God belongs to the species; Therefore it is natural." I answer, the Major is not, in every case, true. For a quality may pertain to the species either by a communication through nature or natural principles, or by an arrangement of grace. That, which, in the former, not in the latter, pertains to the species, is natural. In reference to the Minor, I affirm that the image of God pertains to the species, partly through nature, partly of grace; therefore the image of God in man is partly through nature, partly of grace;

therefore, the image of God in man is partly natural, partly supernatural. If you make any other inference, you deduce a general conclusion from a particular proposition, which is not valid. If an addition be made to your Major, so that, in its full form, it should stand thus:

"Whatever is produced in the species, and its individuals, by nature, is natural," I will admit it as a whole. But in that case, the Minor would not be wholly true. For the image of God is not promised in us wholly by nature, for that part of it which is in truth and righteousness, and holiness, is produced in us by nature, but is communicated by an act of grace, according to the arrangement of grace. But it is objected that the image cannot be common, if it is not natural. For natural qualities differ, in that they are common, from those which are personal, (the question refers not to supernatural qualities). I answer a thing is common in a two-fold sense, either absolutely, according to nature, or conditionally, according to the arrangement of grace. The image of God is common in part according to nature and absolutely, in those things which belong to man according to his essence, and which cannot be separated from his nature, and in part conditionally, according to the arrangement of grace, in those things which pertain not to the essence but to the supernatural perfection of man. The former are produced in all men absolutely, the latter conditionally, namely that he should preserve those principles, which are universal to the species, and particular to the individual, uncorrupted. Therefore, the whole image is common, but partly by nature, and partly of the arrangement of grace; by nature, that part, which is called natural; according to the arrangement of grace, that part which I call supernatural. This, also, is according to the declaration of the Scripture that Seth was begotten in the image and likeness of Adam, not in the image of God. He was indeed begotten in the image of God, not as God communicated it, in its integrity, to Adam, but as Adam maintained it for himself. But Adam maintained it for himself not in its integrity, therefore, he communicated it in that condition. But that, which is in its integrity, and that, which is not in its integrity, differ, not only in mode and degree, but also in some of the essential parts of that image, which are possessed by the image, in its integrity, and are wanting to the image, not in its integrity, which Adam had originally, by a complete communication from God, and of which Seth was destitute on account of the defective communication from Adam.

Your third argument is this: "The image of God is not said to be produced or created in us, but to be renewed or restored, therefore, it was not lost or removed, but corrupted."

I answer—Neither part of your assumption is, in a strict sense, true; with suitable explanation, both parts are true, but neither of them is against my sentiment. I will prove the former assertion, namely, that neither part of the assertion is true. We are said to be "new creatures in Christ" and "to be created to good works." David prayed that God would "create" within him "a clean heart." The image of God is nowhere said to be restored and renewed within us, but as we are said to be "renewed in knowledge after the image of God," "to be renewed in the spirit of our mind," and "to be transformed by the renewing of our mind." Yet, with suitable explanation, both parts of the assumption are true, but they are very favourable to my sentiment, as I will show. There are in us, in respect to ourselves, two parts of the image of God, one essential, the other accidental to us. The essential part is the soul, endowed with mind, affection and will. The accidental is the knowledge of God, righteousness, true holiness, and similar gifts of spiritual grace. The former are not said to be produced or created in us, because it was deformed and corrupt. The latter is not said to be restored or renewed in us, because, from a defect in the subject, it has no place in us and not because it was not corrupt and deformed, but it is said to be produced and created in us, (for we are called, on its access, new creatures,) because it resembles a mold, by the use of which, that essential part is restored and renewed. The words of the apostle plainly set forth this idea, in which it is affirmed not that the knowledge, referred to, is renewed, but that we, as partakers of the image of God so far as it is essential to us, are said to be renewed in knowledge, as in a new mold, according to the image of God, so far as it is accidental to us. Both parts, then, of the antecedent are true. For the image of God is restored and renewed in us, namely, our mind and will, and the affections of the soul; and the image of God is produced and created in us, namely, the knowledge of God, righteousness, and true holiness. The former is the subject of the latter; the latter is the form, divinely given to the former. Therefore, also, the argument of Moses in commanding the murderer to be slain, is valid. For in man, even after transgression, the image of God remained, so far as it was essential to him, or that part remained, which pertained to the essence of man, though the part, which was accidental, is removed through sin.

We now discuss the action of the Deity, by which we have both the natural and the supernatural part of the image of God. I have not made any distinction in the act, both because I wished to use the phraseology of Scripture, according to which the word creation signifies the act by which man has in himself, the image and likeness of God, for it speaks thus:

"Let us make man in our image, after our likeness," and "so God created man in his own image," and because both parts equally well answered my purpose. But, if the subject is considered with accuracy, I think that a distinction is to be made in those acts, and that one is rightly termed creation, by which man received natural qualities, the other, superinfusion, by which he received the supernatural. For life in man is two-fold, animal and spiritual; animal, by which he lives according to man, spiritual, by which he lives according to God. Of the former, the principle is the soul in man, endowed with intellect and will; of the latter, the principle is the Spirit of God, communicating to the soul those excellent gifts of knowledge, righteousness, and holiness. It is probable that the principles of these kinds of life, each so diverse from the other, were bestowed on man, not by the same, but by a different act. But it is not important to my sentiment to decide in what mode, whether by a two-fold or a single act of God, man had these qualities, only let it be understood that he had both the former and the latter, before God was employed concerning him in the act of predestination; that is, he had them in respect to the divine consideration. I make the statement in general terms, because those things, both natural and supernatural, were conferred on the whole species, the former absolutely, the latter on the condition that the species should preserve to itself that principle. Hence, I conclude, if it was conferred on the species, then it was conferred by a decree of providence, in contra-distinction to predestination; if it was conferred conditionally, it was not conferred by a decree of predestination, by which no gift is conditionally conferred. It is now evident from this that my argument is valid. For if man was created by God, under this condition, that he should have, not only natural, but also supernatural gifts, either by the same act of creation, or by the additional act of superinfusion, (in reference to which I have never contended,) it follows, then, that God, in the acts of predestination and reprobation, which separate men, could not have reference to men, as considered in a merely natural state. You also seem, afterwards, to concede this, that man had supernatural endowments, even in his primitive state, but as an increment to nature, and not from the act of creation, which is the principle of nature. This I concede, and from it make this inference, since those things, which the first man had, were possessed by all his posterity in him, (for all which he was, we also were in him, according to the 40th Thesis of your disputation concerning Original Sin, previously cited,) the former, of nature, the latter, of the arrangement of grace, it follows that God could not, in the decree under discussion, have reference to man, considered in a merely natural state, nor indeed, to man, considered with supernatural endowments, for a being of such character could not be passed by, or at least was not passed by, except from the fact that it was foreseen that he would lose those supernatural endowments by transgression and sin.

Your assertion that these statements, however true they may be, are not opposed to that sentiment, which considers man in general, is valid, if it is proved that man was, or could be considered universally by God in the act of decree. But I think that my arguments are valid, also, against that sentiment.

For if God could not consider man in a merely natural state, if not with supernatural endowments, if not without sin, regarding him as the object of the acts of predestination and reprobation, then also he could not consider the same being in a general sense. For a general consideration is excluded by the necessary consideration of any particular circumstance, which becomes the formal relation (ratio) of the object, apart from which formal relation God could not consider man, when He was acting in reference to man in that decree. Besides, how can the general consideration yet have place, when a circumstance, which that general consideration comprehends within itself, is excluded.

If what you say concerning "the essential and the relative image" has this meaning, that the essential image comprehends truth and righteousness, and holiness, and yet is entirely natural to man, as may be deduced from some things alleged by you, then I affirm distinctly, that I cannot oppose it; indeed, I think that I can prove the contrary. But if you apply the phrase "essential image" to all which man has, essential to himself, according to the image of God, I admit it. Then the "respective" image will embrace what I call supernatural and accidental. But, as these things, with the premises which I have laid down, do not tend to refute my sentiment, I proceed to the remainder of my argument.

My second argument is this, that no love of God according to election, or divine volition regarding human beings variously, or divine actions varying in reference to them, is found after sin entered into the world, or after it was considered as having entered. But if this argument is valid, it also refutes the sentiment, which states that man was considered "in general." For if there is no divine election and reprobation of men except after the entrance of sin into the world, then man is considered, not "in general," but particularly, in reference to the circumstance of sin. But you plead "authority, reason, and example." You plead "authority" from three passages of Scripture, Romans 9, Ephesians 1, and Matthew 25. Neither of these is opposed to my view, since I do not deny that election and reprobation were made from eternity, and do not say that sin was the cause of the decree, but a condition requisite in its object. The passage in Romans 9, is not adverse to me; first, because Jacob and Esau had been already conceived in sin, when those words were addressed to Rebecca, as is evident from the text. The affirmative, that they had done neither good nor evil, is to be understood in reference to the distinction which might be made between them, as is explained by Augustine in many places. The apostle then denies all reference to sin, namely, to that by which any distinction might be made between them, not to that, of which they were both equally guilty. Secondly, because he attributes all things to the vocation of God, who calleth, which is of mercy, and has reference only to sinners. Thirdly, because the "purpose of God, according to election" which states, "not of works," is a gracious purpose in Christ, to the promise of which reference is made in Romans iv. 16 "it is of fruit, that it might be by grace, to the end the promise might be sure to all the seed," that is, of faith of, or in Christ, which pertains only to sinners, for he, who has not sinned, does not need faith in Christ, since he obtains righteousness, and thereby life, by the laws. Let this, then, be the answer in reference to this passage, if it is to be understood of Esau and Jacob in their own persons, without any typical meaning. But the meaning of that passage is far different, as could be proved, if it were necessary.

I come, now, to the passage cited from Ephesians 1. That passage is so far from being opposed to my sentiment that I shall hereafter use it as a strong argument in my favour. Election is here said to be "from eternity;" I grant it. It is said to have been made "in Christ;" I acknowledge it. It is said to be "unto the adoption of children by Jesus Christ;" I consent to it. I do not, however, see that either of these statements is opposed to the idea, that sin is a condition, requisite in the object of election and reprobation. It is true that any reference to ourselves, as a cause of our own election, is denied. Predestination precedes persons, in respect to their actual existence, not as they are considered by the Deity. It refers to causes, before they actually exist, but not before they are foreseen by God from eternity, though, in the foresight of God, they exist, not as the causes of predestination, but as a condition requisite in the object. In Matthew 25, the blessed of the Father, who shall possess the kingdom prepared for them of the mere benediction of God, are spoken of. But that benediction is in Christ, by which the malediction is removed, which even the blessed themselves had deserved according to the prescience of God, before they were blessed in Christ; and the kingdom, which was prepared for them, by the blood of Christ, is a kingdom, to which they are raised from the ignominy and slavery of sin. If you had thoroughly considered that, which is really in controversy, you would not have thought that those passages could be used effectually against me.

The reasons, adduced by you, are not more adverse to my opinion, for they oppose the sentiment which makes sin the cause of the decree, not that which makes it a condition, requisite in the object. I will examine them. To the first, I answer that my sentiment, either as antecedent or consequent, is not absurd, until it is proved to be so. Your second and third reasons change the state of the question. For they exclude from that decree sin, as a cause, on account of which God adopted children unto Himself, or in view of which He made the decree; in reference to which there is no question. To the second, I say, that the subject of discussion, here, is the adoption made in Christ, which pertains to no one except by faith in Christ, to which we are not begotten but begotten again by God. From this it is proved, that the adoption is of sinners, and of sinners equally involved in sin, not of men equal in nature. To the third, I answer; --

In the first place, we must judge from the word of God, what may be more, and what may be less in accordance with the wisdom and grace of God. In the second place, I affirm that it is equally in accordance with the wisdom and grace of God, that He should adopt unto Himself sons from those who are not sinners as from those who are sinners, and vice versa, if such should be His choice. What you say in reference to "the supposition of such consideration" is aside from the subject. In the third place, the wisdom and grace, according to which God adopted children unto Himself from among men in that "hidden wisdom which God ordained before the world unto our glory, which none of the princes of this world knew," which wisdom is "Christ crucified, unto the Jews a stumbling-block,"—and that grace, is that which is joined with mercy, bestowed on the sinner, and is in Christ. The latter tends far more illustriously to the glory of God than grace, as used in contradistinction to mercy, and so much the more, as he, who has deserved evil, is more unworthy than he, who has deserved nothing, either good or evil. It has been shown before, that the example of angels is not analogous, but the reverse. For God determined to secure the salvation of men and of angels in different modes. The relations, therefore, of predestination, in the former, and in the latter case, are diverse. God stamped His own image on both, but with a different condition, namely, that it should be preserved in none, but restored in some, among men. God so tempered, as Augustine says, the natures of angels and of men, that He might first show, in them, what their own freewill could effect, then what should be the beneficial influence of His grace, preserving in the case of angels, and restoring, in the case of men. He showed in the case of angels, namely, grace in contradistinction to mercy. He showed in men, the power of the latter grace, namely, grace joined to mercy, and both of his own eternal purpose. Since, then, He did, in men, what He did not in angels, and, in angels, what He did not in men, and this from the decree of predestination, I conclude that there is one relation of divine predestination in the case of angels, and another in the case of men. Therefore, there is no love of God towards men, according to election, without the consideration of sin. There was no discussion between us in reference to angels, and, in my argument, express mention was made of men; whatever, then, is proved concerning angels, has no weight in the refutation of my argument.

ELEVENTH PROPOSITION OF ARMINIUS

Secondly, of Election.

1. Election is said to have been made in Christ, who was ordained as mediator for sinners, and was called Jesus, because He should save, not certain individuals, considered merely in their nature, but "His people from their sins." He is said to have been foreordained, and we in Him, and He, in the order of nature and causes, before us. He was ordained as saviour, we, as those to be saved. But in Christ, having such a character, and being considered such as the Scripture describes him to us, man could not be considered in a merely natural state. Much less, therefore, could he be elected in Him.

2. Election is said to have been made of grace, which is distinguished from nature in a two fold manner, both as the latter is pure and considered abstractly, and as it is guilty and corrupt. In the former sense, it signifies the progress of goodness towards supernatural good, to be imparted to a creature naturally capable of it; in the latter sense, it signifies the ulterior progress towards supernatural good to be communicated to man, as corrupt and guilty, which is also, in the Scriptures, called mercy. In my judgment, the term grace is used, in the latter sense, in the writings of the apostles, especially when the subject of discussion is election, justification, sanctification, &c. If this is true, then election of grace was made of men considered, not in a "merely natural state, but in sin."

ANSWER OF JUNIUS TO THE ELEVENTH PROPOSITION

It is true, that election is made by God the Father in Christ the Mediator; but that the Mediator was ordained, only for sinners, is not absolutely true. Therefore, the inference is not valid. Indeed, should its truth be conceded, yet it has no weight against those, who state that, in election, reference was to man in general. But that the Mediator was ordained, not for sinners alone—to say nothing of that Mediation, which is attributed to Christ in creation and nature, "all things were made by Him; and without him was not any thing made that was made. In Him was life; and the life was the light of men." (John i. 3, 4,) "by whom also He made the worlds." (Heb. i. 2, &c.) -- I demonstrate most completely by a single argument.

Christ is Mediator for those, to whom He was, from eternity, given as Head by the Father; -- He was given as Head by the Father to Angels and men;

therefore, he is the Mediator for both the latter and the former. But angels did not sin; he was not, then, ordained Mediator for sinners only. Let us discuss each point, if you please, separately, that we may more fully understand the subject.

When we speak of the Head, we consider three things, according to the analogy of nature; its position, by which, in fact, dignity, and authority, it holds the first place in the whole body; its perfection, by which it contains all the inward and outward senses, in itself, as their fountain and the principle of motion; finally its power, by which all power, feeling, motion and government is accustomed to flow from it to the other members.

According to this idea, Christ is indeed the Head, in common, of all created things; the Head, I say, of superior nature, and of interior nature, and of all those things which are in nature. We transcend this universal relation, when we contemplate the Head, as appointed from eternity. Angels and men are, after God, capable of eternity; and to both Christ was given eternally, by the Father, as the Head, not only that they should exist forever, (which is the attribute of spiritual nature) but also, and this is specially of grace, that they should be forever heirs of eternal glory, as sons of God, heirs of God, and joint-heirs with Christ. The latter were ordained of God, by the adoption of grace in Christ Jesus, all to one end, namely, to the sight, the enjoyment, and announcement of the glory of God, and of them was constituted the mystical body of Christ, the celestial church. Finally, as in all this life, that is the head of a living creature, from which power, feeling and motion flow into the members of the body, so in all that eternal life, the body grows by the influence of Christ, its Head, and each of the members obtain immutability of life, that is, eternity from this fact, that they subsist in Christ, their Head, apart from whom they would be dissolved. But Christ, is the Mediator by the relation in which he is the Head of angels and men, for, as Head, he' joins them to Himself; as Mediator, he joins them to the Father. That Christ is Head and Mediator, is in fact, one and the same thing, only that the divinity intervenes in the relation, since He is called the Head, as to our relation to Himself; and Mediator as to our relation to the Father. "But," it may be said, "he did not redeem the angels as he redeemed us. This indeed is true; but Mediator and Redeemer differ from each other, as genus and species. To angels, Christ is Mediator of preservation and confirmation; but to us, he is Mediator, also, of redemption and of preservation from that from which we have been redeemed. So he is styled Mediator for both, though in a different mode. The Major, then, of my syllogism is true, that "Christ is the Mediator of those to whom he was appointed from eternity as their Head." But that He was appointed, both to angels and men, as their Head, and therefore, as Mediator, is taught by the apostle in Colossians 1, when he affirms of Christ that he "is the image of the invisible God," that is, He represents God the Father, in his word and work, chiefly to those whom the Father has given to him, as their Head and Mediator; "the first born of every creature," namely, every one whom God has, of His grace, predestinated to adoption, and begotten then, that they might be His children; for there is a comparison of things which are homogeneous, and so the passage is to be understood. Then, explaining both those attributes, he subjoins, first, in general terms, "For by Him were all things created that are in heaven, and that are in earth visible, and invisible," (but he explains these things, to take away the plea of the angel worshipers, whom he assails in this epistle,) "whether thrones or dominions, or principalities, or powers; all things were created by Him and for Him, and He is before all things, and by Him all things consist;" and then, with particular reference to the glorious body of which He is precisely the Head and Mediator, "and He is the Head of the body, the church," who, in the confirmation of grace is "the beginning," but in redemption, is "the first-born from the dead," the common end of all, which is "that in all things he might have the pre-eminence." The cause, is the decree of the Father, predestinating His Son for the adoption of His children, "for it pleased the Father that, in Him, should all fullness dwell, and having made peace through the blood of His cross to reconcile all things to Himself;" &c. He sets forth this idea still more clearly, when, warning them from the worship of angels under the pretense of philosophy, he says, "for in Him dwelleth all the fullness of the Godhead bodily. And ye are complete in Him, which is the Head of all principality and power," that is, of angels to the worship of whom, they were solicited. For, of every one soliciting them to the worshipping of angels, he afterwards affirms that they do not hold the "Head, from which all the body, by joints and bands having nourishment ministered and knit together, increaseth with the increase of God." To the same purpose is Ephesians 1.

It is then to be stated, generally, that he was ordained to be Mediator for sinners, but not for them only, since he is also Mediator for the angels, who have maintained their original purity, but he is ordained as Redeemer for sinners only. We may be able to express this very idea in another mode, if we say that he was ordained Mediator, both for those, who could sin, that they might not sin, and for those, who had sinned, that they might be saved from their sins. Both modes of interpretation tend to the same result. The same is the case with the name Jesus. But what need is there of many words? We say that he was ordained as Mediator both for those who stood and for those who fell, as Redeemer only for those who fell; for those who stood, that they might remain, standing, and for those who fell, that they might rise again, and remain standing. From which it follows, a mode of argumentation, plainly the same, being preserved, that when election is said to have been made in Christ, God had reference to man, considered generally, as not yet created as created in a natural state, as standing and as having fallen, but this is the same thing as being considered in a merely natural state, which you deny. The same argument applies to what follows.

I come to your second argument. You say "Election is said to have been made of grace," and further, that "grace is spoken of in a two-fold sense, when it is used in opposition to nature, and that it is to be taken, in the latter sense, in this argument," and you conclude that, "the election of grace was made of men, considered not in a natural state, &c." Do you not see, my brother, that your conclusion is unsound, involving the fallacy of division, and that it is also equivocal? For, in the Major, grace is used collectively or generally, but in the Minor distributively; in the former, it is used simply, as to its essence, in the latter, an accident is taken into account, namely, the different modes of the object, which do not affect the essence of grace. Why shall we not rather argue in this manner? Election is of grace; -- grace has reference to those, whom it establishes in good, and to those whom, saved from evil, it restores to good; election, then, has reference to the same. That, which is stated in general terms, should be applied in general terms, for this, both nature and reason demand, unless there is a positive restriction in the necessity of the subject, or there be some limitation by an adjunct. That election is used in a general sense, is most clearly evident from a comparison of angels and men. You say, that grace is used, in the latter signification, in the writings of the Apostles in this and similar arguments. This may be correct, but this is not affected by a restriction of the term grace, which in God and of God, embraces all things, but by a restriction of the object kata ti the restriction is in the object, that is, in man, not in that which is added or granted to him. What, if a farmer should command his servant to cultivate a field, which field needed first to be cleared, then plowed, and lastly to be sowed, &c., would you, then, restrict the word cultivate to one of these processes? That, which is general or common, remains general or common, and its generality may not be narrowed down by any particular relations of the object. Therefore, as you see, this consequence, deduced from faulty reasoning, is not valid, nor is that, which is stated in general terms, to be restricted to particular circumstances.

REPLY OF ARMINIUS TO THE ANSWER
OF THE ELEVENTH PROPOSITION

The two arguments advanced by me, as they are most conclusive, so they remain unaffected by your answers. I prove this, in reference to the first. Its strength and force consists in this, that the election of men is said to have been made in Christ, as the Mediator between God and sinful men, that is as Reconciler and Redeemer, from which I argued thus: Whoever are elect in Christ, as Mediator between God and sinful men, that is, as Reconciler and Redeemer, they are considered by God, electing them, as sinners; -- But all men, who are elect in Christ, are elect in Christ, as Mediator between God and sinful men, that is, as Reconciler and Redeemer; Therefore, all men, who are elect in Christ, are considered by God, electing them, as sinners.

The Major is plain. For, in the first place, they, who are not sinners, do not need a Reconciler and Redeemer. But election is an act, altogether necessary to those who are elected. In the second place, Christ himself is not considered by God as Mediator of Redemption, unless in view of the fact, that he is ordained as such for those who have sinned. For the divine foresight of sin preceded, in the order of nature, the decree by which its ordained that His Son should be the Mediator, appointed to offer in the presence of God, in behalf of men, a sacrifice for sins. In the third place, the election of men by God is made only in the Mediator, as having obtained, by his own blood, eternal redemption.

The Minor is evident. For since Christ is the Mediator between men and God, only as Reconciler, Redeemer, and the advocate of sinners; Mediator, I say, who, by the act of His Mediation, affords salvation to those, for whom he is Mediator. (1 Tim. ii. 5 & 6; Heb. viii. 6 &c.; ix, 15; xii, 24.) Hence follows the conclusion, since the premises are true, and consist of three terms, and are arranged in a legitimate form.

Let us now examine your arguments in opposition to what I have adduced. You affirm that Christ is not ordained as Mediator for sinners only, and therefore, my conclusion is not valid. Let it be conceded that your antecedent is true, yet it does not follow that my conclusion is not valid. For, in my premises, I did not assert that Christ was ordained Mediator only for sinners, nor are the questions discussed between us, -- of what beings is Christ the Mediator— when spoken of universally—and in what modes. But I spoke of Christ, as ordained a Mediator for men in particular, and affirmed that he was ordained Mediator for them, only as sinners; for he was ordained Mediator to take away the sins of the world. The subject of discussion, then, in the mode in which he is the Mediator for men. Here, you commit two fallacies, that of Irrelevant conclusion [ignoratio elenchi], and that of reasoning from a particular case to a general conclusion, [a dicto secundum quid, ad dictum simpliciter]. I speak of Christ's Mediation as pertaining to a particular case, namely, as undertaken for man, you treat of his Mediation, as simply and generally considered. But you rightly separate the consideration of the mediation, which is attributed to Christ, in creation and nature, for the latter is, entirely, of another kind and mode. According to this, he is the Mediator of God to creatures; according to that, of creatures to God. The one, refers to all creatures, the other, only to those, made in the image of God. The one tends to the communication of all natural and created good to all creatures, the other, to the bestowment, on rational creatures, of a participation in infinite and supernatural good. You, indeed, prove that he was ordained Mediator, not for sinners only, but without any necessity. For this is not the question between us. The point to be proved by you, was that he is the Mediator of men, not of sinners, which I know that you would not wish to attempt, as a different doctrine is taught in the Scriptures. Yet, let us examine the argument. He was ordained as Mediator also for the angels; --

But the angels did not sin; -- Therefore, he was not constituted Mediator only for sinners. I may concede all this, for it weighs nothing against my argument, since I have not said in general terms, that Christ was ordained only for sinners. I restricted his Mediation to men, to the work of their salvation, to the mode in which salvation was obtained for them. Hence, if this be true, I conclude that my argument remains firm and unmoved, in which I proved that, in Christ as the Mediator of men before God, only sinners were elected.

I wish that we might always remember that there is no controversy between us concerning the election of angels or the mediation, by which they are saved, and that we are treating only of the election and reprobation of men, and of the mode of mediation by which they obtain salvation, for it will be perceived that statements, which, taken generally, are not true, may be, in the highest degree, true, when applied to the particular case of mankind. There is, then, no need of considering those things, which are said concerning Christ as the Mediator of angels. If, however, I may be permitted to discuss even this point, I may ask for the proof of your Major, in which you affirm that "Christ is Mediator for those to whom he was given, as Head, by the Father." I think that I have good reason for denying your postulate. For, in Philemon 2, Christ is said to have received "a name which is above every name, that, at the name of Jesus, every knee should bow, of things in heaven, because he, "being in the form of God, humbled himself and became obedient unto death, even the death of the cross." Here we see that the reason of his being constituted the Head, even of heavenly things, was this, that, by his own blood and death, he might perform the functions of Mediator for men before God. If he was the Mediator for angels, then this fact, and not the former reason, should have been alleged, in this passage, for his appointment as Head, even of angels.

These two terms, Head and Mediator, seem to me to have an order and relation, such that the appellation of Mediator pertains to Christ in a prior relation, and that of had in a posterior relation, and the latter, indeed, on account of the former. For, by the act of Mediation, he acquires for himself the right of dominion, the possession of which the Father delivers to him, when He bestows the title of Head upon him. This is implied, also, in the distinction used in schools of Divinity, Christ is Mediator by merit and by efficacy. By merit first, then by efficacy. For by his merit, he prepares for himself a people, the blessings necessary for their happiness, and the right and power of imparting those blessings to his own people; from which are derived the titles Head, saviour, Leader, Prince, and Lord; in accordance with which titles, there flows, of his own efficacy, to his own people, an actual communication of those blessings, which he obtained by the merit of his death. For in Hebrews ii. 16, it is said that Christ: "took not on him the nature of angels; but he took on him the seed of Abraham." Now, if the statement, made by our divines, is true—that this assumption of nature was made that he might be able to perform the functions of Mediator for those whose nature he assumed, you perceive that the conclusion is valid, that since "he took not on him the nature of angels," he did not perform the functions of Mediator for them. To this add, that it is very frequently said, by our Theologians that Christ is Mediator only as he stands between God and men, which assertion they refer to his human nature, taken into a personal union by the Word, that he might, in this way, stand between both, partaking, with the Father, of the Divine nature, and with us, of human nature. Hence, also, he is called Emmanuel in a twofold sense, first, because he is God and man in the unity of his person, and secondly, because, being such, he has united God and men in the office of Mediation. But he does not stand between God and angels. Consider, also, the declaration of Heb. v. 1, "every high priest taken from among men is ordained for men in things pertaining to God." But Christ was not taken from among angels, therefore, he was not ordained for angels in things pertaining to God. Indeed, I affirm, with confidence, that there was nothing to be done, by the way of any mediation for, or in behalf of angels before God. I add, also, that a Mediator should not be inferior in nature to those for whom he acts in that capacity. But Christ, in his human nature, was made "a little lower than the angels, for the suffering of death. (Heb. ii. 9.) Therefore, he is not Mediator for angels. Finally, I remark, angels are "ministering Spirits sent forth to minister for them who shall be heirs of salvation." (Heb. i. 14.) "Unto the angels hath He not put in subjection the world to come," but unto Christ Jesus primarily, and unto all his brethren, secondarily, whose nature he sanctified in himself, and exalted with himself to that dignity. Therefore, Christ is not the Mediator of angels. But the inquiry may be made, Cannot Christ, then, be said in any manner to be Mediator for angels? I answer; --

The term mediator may be applied in a two fold manner, either in behalf of creatures to the Deity, or of the Deity to creatures. I deny that Christ is Mediator in behalf of the angels before God, but I do not deny he is Mediator for God to angels. For this coincides with the appellation of Head, which I confess belong to Christ, in respect to angels, though in a relation different from that, by which he is the Head of believers. For the union, which exists between Christ and believers of the human race, is more strict and close, than that which exists between him and angels, on account of the consubstantiality of his human nature with that of men, from which angels are alien. But enough on these points. Whether they are, as I have stated them, or not, it affects, neither favourably nor unfavourably, my argument, but you entirely agree with me when you say that he was ordained as Redeemer only for the fallen. From this, also, I infer the truth of my sentiment. Men are elected in the Redeemer, only as fallen; for they are not elected that they should remain standing, but that they should rise again, and then remain standing, as you have rightly observed. But how can you infer, that, since election is made in Christ, the election, I say, of men, in Christ, the Redeemer, (for those words are to be supplied), it follows that God had respect to men, in general, considered generally as not yet created, as created in their natural state, as yet standing and as fallen. I think that the contrary can, and must be inferred. Therefore, God, in election, had reference to man, only as fallen. For, in election, He regarded man in the Redeemer, and the Redeemer is such only of the fallen.

As to the latter argument, the form of the answer is the same. I do not use the word grace equivocally; I do not use it at the same time collectively and distributively. I admit that it is used in a two-fold sense, for the grace of preservation and restoration; I admit that it is used collectively, and absolutely, particularly and concretely, that is, the grace of preservation and restoration. But, what then? If I use a word, which has a general and equivocal sense, is equivocation, therefore, at once, to be laid to my charge? But I have used that word, at all times in this discussion, in the same way, namely, as referring to the grace by which some men are elected. It is that grace by which restoration and its means are prepared, not that by which preservation and its means are appointed. For the latter grace was not bestowed on human beings.

From the former grace alone, all they, who are saved, obtain their salvation. In the Major of my syllogism, grace is spoken of in a particular relation, and in the Minor, it is used in the same way, and, neither in the former nor in the latter, is it used in a general sense, as the following syllogism will show.

They who are elected according to the grace of restoration, which is joined with mercy, having place only in reference to sinners, are considered by Him, who elects, as sinners; But all men, who are elected, are elected according to the grace of restoration, which is joined to mercy, having place only in reference to sinners; -

Therefore, all men, who are elected, are considered by Him, who elects, as sinners. Grace is spoken of, throughout, particularly and relatively in respect to men, and in no case, is it used generally or absolutely. Indeed, it cannot be used generally or absolutely when it has reference relatively and particularly to election, whether of angels or of men. For neither these nor those are elected or saved by grace, taken absolutely, but both by grace used relatively, angels by the grace of preservation, men by the grace of restoration.

When, however, we treat of election universally and abstractly, we must discuss the subject of grace, as its cause, universally, absolutely and abstractly; for, to a genus, general attributes are to be ascribed, which may be afterwards applied to the species after their several modes. Your argumentation, then, is aside from our controversy. Election is of grace; grace respects those, whom it establishes, and those whom, saved from evil, it restores to good. Therefore, election has reference to the same persons.

For we do not now discuss election in general, and absolutely, if so, the word grace, according to correct usage, must be understood in a general sense. But we discuss the election of men; therefore, the general term grace must be restricted to that grace, according to which men are elected. It is not, therefore, proper to say that "grace has reference to those whom it establishes in good," for the grace, of which we here treat, does not refer to those whom it establishes in good, for grace established no one of the human race, it only restored those, to whom it had reference. But you say that the grace, which establishes in good, and that, which restores, are one in essence, and only distinguished and restricted in relation to the object. What if I should concede this? My conclusion will still be valid. The question between us has reference to the object and its formal relations by which relation you say that grace is distinguished and restricted. But that restriction of the object has only this force, that the grace, which, according to your assertion, is one in essence, must unfold itself and be applied to a sinner, and to one not a sinner, in a different mode; and indeed must use acts of a different character in the two cases. There is, then, a restriction in "that which is added or granted," but it is a necessary consequence of the restriction of the object. This distinction, then, is sufficient for the conclusion which I desire.

The question is not concerning objects of election, essentially different from each other, but concerning different modes of considering an object, which is one and the same in essence, and concerning a different formal relation. I will illustrate it by a simile. Justice in God is one in essence, namely, giving to each one that which is due to him; to him who is obedient, what pertains to him, according to the divine promise, and to the sinner that which pertains to him, according to the divine threatening. But from the fact that justice renders the retribution of punishment an object, it is necessarily inferred that the object is worthy of punishment, and was, therefore, liable to sin; so likewise with grace. Grace then is one in essence, but varies in its mode; one in principle and end, but varied in its progress, steps and means: one, when taken absolutely and in general, but two-fold, when taken relatively and particularly, at least in respect to opposite and distinct matters. But in the whole of this course of reasoning, I have used the term grace, in a particular relation, as it is varied in mode, progress, steps and means, and as it is taken relatively and distributively. No equivocation, then, has been used in this; there is no reasoning from general to particular, from the abstract to the concrete.

But, though, all these statements be true, they avail nothing, you affirm, against those who state that mankind in general were regarded in election. These arguments, indeed, prove that mankind in general could not have been regarded in election, or at least that such was not the case. For if man was considered in general, then he was elected by grace, taken in a general sense. For a general effect requires a general cause. But man was elected, not by grace considered generally, but by grace considered particularly, relatively, and distributively, with reference to the circumstance of sin. If man was considered in general, then he was elected in the Mediator not considered generally, but considered particularly as Redeemer. Therefore, in election, man was not considered in general, but with restriction to the circumstance of sin, which was to be proved. The illustration of the field to be cultivated, is not against this view, indeed it is in its favour. For if a farmer should command his son to cultivate a field, which was overrun with briars, and, therefore, required culture joined with clearing, then the word cultivate, though, when taken in a general sense, it is not restricted to clearing, yet, when applied to that particular field, it necessarily includes that act. Hence we infer, that, if a field cannot be cultivated without the act of clearing, it is, therefore, overrun with briars and weeds, and, by analogy, if a man can not be saved without the act of restoration, he is, therefore, a sinner; for a sinner only is capable of restoration, and restoring grace is adapted only to his case.

TWELFTH PROPOSITION OF ARMINIUS

Thirdly, of Non-Election or Preterition. Non-election or preterition is an act of the divine pleasure, by which God from eternity determined not to communicate to some men supernatural happiness, but to bestow on them only natural or animal happiness, if they should live agreeably to nature; --

But, in an act of this kind, God has not to do with men considered in a merely natural state; -- Therefore, God does not pass by certain men, considered in a merely natural state. The truth of the Minor is proved; --

1. Because there is no natural happiness of this kind, which is the end of man, and his ultimate neither in fact, for there has not been, and there is not a man happy in this sense, nor in possibility, derived from the decree of God considered, either absolutely, for no man will ever be thus happy naturally, or conditionally, for God did not design happiness of this kind for any man on a condition, as the condition must be that of obedience, which God remunerates by supernatural happiness.

2. Because sin is the meritorious cause of that act of the divine pleasure, by which He determined to deny, to some, spiritual or supernatural happiness, resulting from union with Himself and from His dwelling in man. "Your iniquities have separated between you and your God." (Isa. lix. 2.) Nor can that denial of happiness to man be considered otherwise than as punishment, which is necessarily preceded by the act of sin, and its appointment by the foresight of future sin. These arguments may be useful also in the discussion of other questions.

ANSWER OF JUNIUS TO THE TWELFTH PROPOSITION

Your definition of non-election or preterition, (which Augustine calls also reelection,) is by no means just, -- and this in three respects.

1. Since that, which is made a difference, is not merely an accident. For if the difference of the things defined is only an accident, the definition is not a good one. The essential difference between election and reprobation consists in adoption by Jesus Christ unto God the Father, the accidental consectary of which is supernatural happiness. Ephesians 1, and Romans 8.

2. Because the thing defined is referred, not to its primary end, but to one which is secondary, which is erroneous. The primary end of election is union

with God by adoption, but a secondary, and, as we have said, accidental end, is happiness.

3. Because the definition is redundant; for an addition is made of something positive, when you insert, in parentheses, "but to be bestowed," &c., while the definition itself is purely negative. There is also a fault, and even an error in that which is added. For non-election or preterition does not bestow natural happiness, but rather supposes it; God does not, in that act, bestow a gift on those on whom it already has been bestowed. This we remark concerning the Major.

The Minor is denied. God, in this act, has reference to man in general, therefore also, in this mode, He has respect to the same general reference. Thus you perceive that your whole reasoning is false. To sustain your Minor you use two arguments. The first is designed to confirm that part of the definition, which does not, as we have asserted, belong to definition; therefore, I need not notice it. Yet since you afford the occasion, I shall be permitted to make certain suggestions. The argument denies that there is any "natural happiness of this kind, which is the end of man, and his ultimate." If you speak here of the depraved nature of man, I admit it; for "an evil tree does not bring forth good fruit," much less does it acquire any goodness of itself. If you speak of nature, in its purity, as it was, originally, in Adam, I deny it. For, to undepraved nature, pertained its own future natural happiness, though it was afterwards, so to speak, to be absorbed, by the grace of God, in supernatural happiness. This happiness was the natural design of man and his natural end. Do not all things in nature seek their own good? But since nature seeks not any thing which may not exist, (it is foolish to seek that, which does not exist, even in possibility, and nature, the work of an infinitely wise Architect, is not foolish,) it follows that the good of each thing exists by nature, in possibility, if the thing does not attain to it, and in fact, if the thing does attain to it. But if the condition of natural things is such, consider, I pray you, my brother, how it can be truly said of man that he is deprived of natural felicity, and his natural end, when all things, in nature, are in a different situation. Surely, nature could not be blind, in her most excellent work, and see so clearly in all her other works. But you say that this fact never existed. I admit it, for Adam fell out by the way; but it was to exist in the future. You say that it did not exist "in possibility." This is an error, for God designed it for Adam, on the condition of his remaining in the right way. I prove this from the words of God himself; "in the day that thou eatest thereof thou shalt surely die." (Gen. ii. 17.) What is death? Is it not privation? What is privation? Is it not of some natural attribute or habit? Adam, then, was deprived of natural life, and of that happy constitution of life, which he obtained in Eden, otherwise he would have remained happy in it, if he had continued in the discharge of duty, until God had fulfilled in him the promise of supernatural life, which was adumbrated to him by the tree of life in the garden of Eden. For, on the contrary, it follows that, if he had not eaten the forbidden fruit, he would not have become mortal, but, with life and sight, he would have been prepared for translation to a higher life.

You affirm that God "remunerates obedience by supernatural happiness." He indeed remunerates obedience in that way, but not in that way alone. Conjunctively, it is true; exclusively, it is false. He remunerates obedience in both ways. For even at the present time, when we are very far removed from the natural condition of Adam, godliness has the "promise of the life that now is and of that which is to come." (1 Tim. iv. 8.) I judge that a two-fold idea, namely, of the end and of the mode, has led you into error. You have thought that the only end of man is that which is supernatural. It is very true, that things subordinate are not at variance. There is a natural end. As nature is subordinate to God, so natural ends are subordinate to those which are supernatural and divine. The end of our nature, so far as it is natural, is this, that it should approach very near to the Divine; so far as it is supernatural, it is that man may be united to God. To the former, Adam could attain by nature; to the latter, he could be exalted from the former, by grace. You indeed judged that there could be no mode, in which both kinds of happiness should concur. But two things must be observed in this case, one, that natural happiness is a previous preparation, the other that it is a foundation to the supernatural. It is prepared for and previous to it. Unless he had been already happy in nature, even it he had remained without falling, he would not have attained the other happiness, there must have been in him that natural happiness by which he could approach the supernatural. But when he should have in fact, entered into that supernatural felicity, then natural happiness would be the foundation and upon it the consummation would be in supernatural happiness. If perfection is added to perfection, the less is not destroyed, but the increase is made upon the less, as fire is increased by fire, the vegetative faculty by the sentient, and both by the rational. The less rests in the greater as in its own principle, and is more fully perfected by it, as it more fully ceases to be its own, and partakes of the perfection of another. Thus it will be, in the resurrection of the dead and in eternal life. The nature of man will be both perfected and glorified above the mode of nature. It will so obtain the perfection of nature, as to rest in that divine and supernatural perfection; and nature will not be abolished, but be clothed in a supernatural mode, as the apostle says of the body, in 1 Corinthians 15. These things, however, are merely incidental.

Your second argument may be stated thus: -- Sin is the meritorious cause of that negative act; -- Man, in a merely natural state, has no sin; -- There is not then, in him any meritorious cause. By consequence God has not any cause of that negative act. The whole prosyllogism is admitted, but the inference is denied, because it is made from a particular case. It would indeed be true if the negative act of the Deity resulted only from a meritorious cause, but this position is very far removed from the truth. The cause of every negative act is either in God or in the creature. The same is true of this act. But the cause of this act is not in the creature. Therefore, it is in God. This prosyllogism will be denied by none. In the will of God alone, exists the cause that you are not an apostle, and that you may not live to the age of Adam or Methuselah. Iniquity in man is the cause that he is far from God, and that God is far from him; namely, in that respect, of which Isaiah spoke. (Isa. lix. 2.) For, in other respects, not only is iniquity a cause, but also the will of God; who, if he would, might remove their iniquity as a cloud, and bring man near to Himself: I prove that the cause of this act is not in the creature, as was said before in the 10th proposition; first, by the authority of Christ in Matthew 25, and of Paul in Romans 8 & 9, and Ephesians 1; secondly, by reason, since even that first sin did not take place, except from the negative act of God, of which negative act sin cannot be the cause, for the same thing cannot be both cause and consequence of another thing. But election and non-election were prior even to the first sin, as we have before demonstrated. A positive and a negative act of God also precede every act of the creature, whether good or bad. For there is no evil act which has not been preceded also by a negative act of the Deity, permitting the evil. Adam and Eve sinned, certainly not without a negative act of God, though there had been committed by them no previous sin, deserving that negation. What, then, was the cause of that negative act if it was not the free will of God? In subsequent sins, however, it may be admitted that sin is, indeed, the meritorious cause, and the free will of God is also a cause; for He destroys even sins, when He wills. He has that power, and if He does not destroy them, it is because He does not will to do it. But those sins which He destroys, can not, though a meritorious cause, produce the negative act of God. You see then, my brother, that sin may be indeed a meritorious cause of that negative act, but not singly or alone or always; therefore, it is not the necessary cause.

Thirdly, by the example of the Angels? What has restrained the holy Angels from evil and confirmed them in good? The positive act of God, that is, the manifestation of Himself in election; for they are elect. What did not restrain the fallen Angels from evil, into which they rushed of their own will? The negative act of God, in non-election or preterition which Augustine also calls reelection. It also belongs to this act of election, that the former were confirmed in good against evil, and to reprobation, that the latter were left, who (as Christ says in John 8.) speak a lie of their own, and commit sin. However, I wish that you would always remember, in this case and in subsequent arguments, that it is not suitable to substitute, for the proper and proximate end, a remote consequence, or event (which is also called in its own mode, an end), namely, supernatural happiness. That it is appropriate and proximate to assert that sin is the meritorious cause of that divine negative act, by which He does not adopt certain men as children unto Himself by Christ, the consectary of which adoption is happiness, is denied, my brother, by nature herself. God begets sons unto Himself according to His own will, not according to their character, whether good as in the case of the elect angels, or bad as in our own case. He looks upon all, in Christ, not in themselves, that Christ "might be the first-born among many brethren." (Rom. viii. 29.) In nature, children are begotten by parents, without reference to their future character, and may not God beget his adopted children, without reference to their character? Nature claims the whole for itself in those about to be begotten; may grace claim but a very small part? God forbid.

Of the same nature is the position that "denial of happiness to man cannot be considered otherwise than as punishment." For in the first place, "denial of happiness" is not suitably introduced into the discussion, the subject of which is the denial of adoption, which, as we have said, is the appropriate and proximate end of election. This, then, is not, primarily and per se, the proposition. Again, if the subject of discussion is adoption, the statement is not true; for a denial of adoption is not properly punishment; it is, indeed, previous to punishment, since it is even previous to sin, but it is not, therefore, punishment. Who, indeed, can affirm that the antecedent is the same with its consequent, and that a most remote one? But if, as you think, the statement is made in reference to happiness, it is not, even in that case universally true; for a denial of happiness, on account of sin, is considered as punishment of sin, but a denial of happiness on account of a voluntary arrangement, or of the will only, is not punishment. To Adam, in his primitive state of holiness, God denied supernatural happiness, until he should fulfill his appointed course. That was not punishment to Adam. To a private individual it is not a punishment that he is not an emperor. The denial of happiness, is not punishment, then, of itself alone, but of some accident, as a final consequence, (as they say), of the sin of the creature.

The same consideration is fatal to your statement, that "denial of happiness is necessarily preceded by the act of sin." That is true, indeed, of the denial of final happiness, as they style it; but we are now discussing the denial of the principle of happiness, that is, of grace and gratuitous adoption in Christ Jesus. Therefore, though it may be conceded to you, that sin precedes, in fact, that denial, yet this also should be added, that antecedent to sin is particular reelection by God in the beginning and progress of sin, but that the foundation of that particular reelection is non-election, or preterition and reprobation, which we acknowledge to be, not the cause, but the antecedent of sin. So, likewise, your statement is not universally true, that "the appointment of that act is preceded by the foresight of future sin." For that foresight of future sin is both the consequent, and the antecedent of that divine denial; since the divine negative act, (as they call it), precedes the commission of sin, but, as has been before shown, follows that commission by imposing final unhappiness on the sins of men. These answers may also be adapted, in the most complete manner possible, to the arguments which follow.

REPLY OF ARMINIUS TO THE ANSWER
TO THE TWELFTH PROPOSITION

Definition and demonstration are distinguished by their objects. The former, is used for explanation, the latter, for proof: the former, for the discussion of a single question, the latter, for that of a compound question. But in this case, I did not undertake to explain, but to prove. I therefore, thought I must make use, in my argument, of definition so far as would tend to prove that which I had undertaken to prove, which was the reason that I did not use special effort to adapt my definition of election or preterition to the rules of art. For if what I lay down is on the whole kata< pantov true, even if it do not reach the truth in all respects, kaq o[lou it will be sufficient for me, for the proof which I have proposed to myself. Hence, even with those substitutions, which you have considered important, my proof remains valid, and therefore, that correction does not seem to be necessary for our purpose. Yet, I must say something concerning that matter. In general, I remark, that you could see that I was treating distinctly of that predestination which is unto glory, not of that which is unto grace, and of that preterition, by which glory was not prepared for some, not of that by which God determined not to communicate grace. This is evident from my eighth proposition. I must then abstain from matters which belong in general to grace and glory. Among those general matters is adoption as children, for the beginning and progress of which, grace is prepared, and glory for its consummation. Thus you also remark elsewhere in this answer.

I remark particularly, in reference to your corrections to the first; -- in adoption and non-adoption consists the essential difference of election at once to grace and to glory, and of reprobation from both. Therefore, that the former difference pertains not to election to glory alone, and the latter, is not of reprobation from glory alone. For a difference of genus can not be a difference of species. Therefore, I ought not in this case to have mentioned adoption unless

I wished, in discussing a species, to set forth the genus contrary to the law, referred to above kaq o[lou.

To the second; -- I mentioned no end in my definition of election, or rather in the part of the definition which I presented. I did not, indeed, desire to present it in full. For supernatural happiness or glory is not the end, but the material or subject of election, which material, embraced in your Theses in the term blessing, you divide into grace and glory. I know, indeed, that supernatural happiness is not communicated to us, except by an antecedent union of ourselves with God, which is implied in these words from the same proposition, "to deny supernatural happiness, and resulting from the union with Himself, and from His indwelling in man." But let us notice the definition of preterition contained in your Theses. "Preterition is an act of the divine pleasure by which God determined, from eternity, to leave certain of His creatures in their own natural state, and not to communicate to them supernatural grace, by which their nature, if unfallen, might be confirmed, and, if fallen, might be restored; for the declaration of the freedom of His goodness." In the phrase "to leave in their own natural state," is comprehended, also, exclusion from supernatural happiness, or it is not. If not, the definition is incomplete. I think, however, that you designed to include, also, that idea, otherwise your Theses are imperfect, as they treat of the predestination by which grace and glory are prepared for the elect, but nowhere of the negative act by which God does not appoint glory for the non-elect, if not in those words. Yet, even in those words, according to your idea, that preterition, by which God does not determine to bestow glory on any one, can not be included. For you define preterition (Thesis 14) to be "contrary to the preparation of grace." But the preparation of punishment is an affirmative act, by which He appoints punishment for the sinner, opposed, not negatively, but affirmatively to the preparation of glory. When, therefore, I wished to describe preterition or non-election, so far as it is an act by which God does not determine to bestow glory on some persons, it seemed proper that I should, in some measure, keep in your track, in that, you nowhere, in your definition of preterition, mention exclusion from adoption and union with God.

To the third; -- It is manifest that what is inserted, in parenthesis, was added for the sake of explanation, and does not come within the order or relation of the definition, like the other statements. I do not, however see, that even those statements are false or faulty, though they may be related, in the mode which you consider them, to that definition. For they mark, not an affirmation, but a negative act, and there is emphasis in the word (tantum) which marks the negative. To will the bestowment of natural happiness is an affirmative act, but to will only that bestowment is a negative act, for it excludes all other happiness, which He does not determine to bestow. Also, what is that act by which God determines to bestow only natural happiness, if not preterition or neglect. If to leave in a natural state is a negative act, and otherwise your definition of non-election, which considers it as opposed negatively to predestination, is erroneous, I do not see how those words "to bestow only supernatural happiness," do not designate a negative act. If you explain it so as to distinguish, in this case, the two acts, one, that by which God determined to bestow natural happiness, the other, that by which He determined to bestow only that, and not some other kind of happiness, then I acknowledge that the former, as an affirmative act, does not pertain to this decree of preterition. But we have never discussed that kind of happiness. It might, then, have been easily understood that I used those words so as to note a negative act, that of the non-bestowment of any happiness other than natural. When I was writing those words, I thought of using the phrase "to leave" in imitation of you, but judged that it would be unsuitable as presupposing that the bestowment was already made, and I considered that supernatural happiness was not yet bestowed, but to be bestowed, if man should live in obedience. In which I have also your assent, as is manifest from your answer to my third proposition, at the end. The definition, therefore, remains, and there is nothing in it to be blamed, for which there can not be found apology in the example of your Theses, which I have constantly had before my eyes in this discussion. That this may be made more plain, I will compare your definition with mine. You thus define the preterition by which grace is denied: "Preterition is an act of the divine pleasure, by which God, from eternity, determined to leave some of His creatures in their natural state, and not to communicate to them supernatural grace, by which their nature, if unfallen, may be confirmed, and, if fallen, may be restored, to the declaration of the freedom of His own goodness." If I define the preterition by which glory is denied, analogically according to the form of your definition, it will be like this. "Preterition is an act of the divine pleasure, by which God, from eternity, determined to leave some of His creatures in their natural state and not to communicate to them supernatural happiness, or glory, by which their natural happiness may be absorbed, or into which their ignominy may be changed, to the declaration of the freedom of His own goodness." In this definition, I have proposed that which was sufficient for my purpose; with no evasion, since, the other adjuncts are neither to the advantage, nor to the disadvantage of my argument. Therefore, the Major of my syllogism is true, even if it would not be true, as a complete definition and reciprocally. For a conclusion can be proved from a Major, which is on the whole kata< pantov true.

I come now to the Minor, which I proved by two arguments. The first is not refuted by you, as it is proposed in a mutilated condition, and so it is changed into something else. For I did not deny that natural happiness was prepared for man, but I added "which is, the design and end of man," in which words, I meant not that it alone, but that it also was prepared, but on this condition that it would be absorbed by the supernatural happiness, which should follow. I wish that the explanation, which I add, may be thus understood; namely, that natural happiness, could, neither in fact nor in possibility, occur to man, as the design of man and his end. For God promised to man, on condition of obedience, not only natural but also supernatural happiness. In which, since, I have also your assent, I conclude my proposition thus. God does not will to bestow upon any man, considered in his original natural state, natural happiness alone, as the end and design of man, to the exclusion of supernatural happiness. Therefore, God passed by no one, considered in his original natural state. For whether preterition is the act by which God does not determine to bestow supernatural happiness on any one, or that by which He determines to bestow natural happiness, which I think that you concede, it is equally to my purpose.

I prove the antecedent in this way. All men are considered in Adam, on equal terms, whether in their original natural sate, or in a state of sin, unless some difference is introduced by the will of God. But I deny that any difference was made in respect to man's original state, and you confirm the first reason for that denial, when you say that both kinds of happiness were prepared for man. Again, that, which God, by His providence, has prepared for man, is not denied to him by preterition, the opposite of election, unless from the foresight that he would not attain to it, under the guidance of providence, but would turn aside freely, and of his own accord. But God prepared for the first man, and in him, for all men, supernatural felicity, for He bestowed on him means sufficient for its attainment; with the additional aid of divine grace, (if this was also necessary in that state,) which is not denied to any man unless he first forsakes God.

Your opinion that I have been led into an error, by a two fold idea, namely, that of the end and the mode, and that I thought that a single end only was before mankind, is incorrect, for my words do not, of themselves, imply this. I made a plain distinction between the subordinate ends, when I mentioned natural felicity, which I denied was the end of man and his ultimate. I, therefore, conceded that natural happiness belongs to man, otherwise there would have been no necessity of the addition of the statement that this does not belong to him as the end of man, and his ultimate, that is, as that, beyond which nothing further can happen to man. Does not he, who admits that natural happiness pertains to man, but not as the end of man and his ultimate, acknowledge a two fold end of man, one subordinate, namely, natural happiness, and the other final, which is the end and ultimate of man, namely, supernatural happiness? I do not, however, think that it can be said truly that happiness is the end and ultimate of man. Your additional remarks, concerning the order of natural and supernatural happiness, I approve, as truthful and learned; but they are, as you admit, "merely incidental," and do not affect the substance of my argument.

My second argument is also valid, but it should be arranged correctly, thus; -- An act of the divine pleasure by which God determined to deny to any man spiritual or supernatural blessedness, depends on a meritorious cause, which is sin;

Preterition is such an act; -- Therefore preterition depends on sin as its meritorious cause. The reason for the Major is contained in these words, "that denial of happiness can not be considered otherwise than as punishment," but it is necessarily preceded by sin, as its proper cause, according to the mode of merit. From this it follows that God can not have reference in that act to men, considered in a merely natural state, without reference to sin.

I will briefly sustain the Major, and the reason assigned for it, and then examine your answer. I prove the Major thus:

That which the Providence of God has prepared for man, under a condition, is not denied to him, except on the non-performance or the violation of the condition. But God, by His Providence, prepared supernatural happiness for man, &c. Again, the passage from Isaiah plainly shows that God would not have deserted the Jews, if they had not merited it by their "iniquities." The reason, assigned for the Major, I sustain in this manner: Whatever is contrary to the blessing of happiness, prepared, promised, and therefore conditionally due to man, as made in the image of God, cannot be considered otherwise than as punishment. A denial of supernatural happiness is contrary to the blessing of happiness, prepared for man, as such, for even supernatural happiness was prepared for him as such. Therefore its denial is punishment. Again, there is no passage of Scripture, I assert it confidently, from which it can be shown that such denial is or can be considered otherwise than in the relation of punishment, than as it is prepared only for sinners. For we have stated, with truth, that punitive justice has place only in reference to sinners.

I proceed to examine your answer. In my syllogism the inference is not "made from a particular case." For that negative act of God, now under discussion, only exists in view of a meritorious cause, that is, it does not exist except in view of that cause, and that act of God would not exist, if that cause did not exist. The particle "only" does not amount to an exclusion of the will of God. For it is certain that sin is not, in fact the cause of punishment, except as the will of God, who wills to punish sin according to its merit, otherwise he can remove sin, and remit its punishment. How indeed could you suppose that he, who made sin the meritorious cause of punishment, wished to exclude the will of God, when the very nature of meritorious cause requires another cause also, which may estimate merit, and inflict punishment in proportion as it is merited. I acknowledge that the cause of every negative act does not exist in man, nor have I made that statement, for why should I needlessly enter into the general discussion of this matter. My subject is the act of preterition or non-election, by which God denies supernatural happiness to man, and I affirm that the cause of this is in and of man, so far, that without the existence of this cause, that act would never be performed. But you argue that the cause of this act does not exist in man. First, by authority, then by reason, finally by example. I deny that proof is contained in the passages, cited as authority. Let it be shown in what sense, these are the antecedents, from which this consequence may be deduced. We have previously examined those passages, so far as the necessity of the subject required.

Your argument from reason is not more conclusive. You say that the "first sin did not take place, except from the negative act of God," also "a positive and a negative act of God also precede every act of the creature," and "there is no evil act, which has not been preceded also by a negative act of the Deity, permitting the evil. I concede all those points, if rightly understood. But an affirmative statement, reasoning from the general to the specific, is not valid, unless a mark of universality is added. Many negative acts of the Deity precede the act of sin; therefore, also the negative act of preterition precedes sin. I deny the sequence. The controversy concerns that very act. The first sin results from a negative act of God, but not from the act of preterition. A positive and a negative act precede every act of the creature, but not the act of election and that of preterition. You affirm that election and non-election are prior to sin. To sin, as existing in fact, I admit, but not to sin, as foreseen. That point, however, has been previously discussed. But you affirm that the free will of God is the cause also of this negative act. Who denies it? It is indeed within the scope of God's free will, either to punish or to remit sin, but neither is necessary, even though sin has been committed, (that is, since God is "in Christ reconciling the world unto Himself,") but neither is possible unless sin has been committed. The will of God is, in the most complete sense, free, as the cause of creation, the cause of glorification, the cause of condemnation. But He creates those non-existing; He glorifies those created and existing, and, indeed, called and justified; He condemns only sinners, and those, who die in their sins. There is, then, no limitation placed on the freedom of God, even if we consider sin as antecedent, and necessarily so, to that negative act of God. You see, then, that sin is the meritorious, cause, which necessarily precedes that negative act of God; and that I have reasoned correctly from that cause, necessarily antecedent, that God, in that negative act of preterition, has reference only to sinners.

That the example of the angels, in this case, is not analogous, I show in a word. You say that "the negative act of God, in non-election or preterition, which Augustine also calls reelection, did not restrain the fallen angels from evil." But I affirm that the negative act of God, by which man is not restrained from evil, but permitted to fall into sin, is not the act of preterition, but a negative act of providence, and I prove, by two arguments, that this is distinguished from predestination. If it is by the negative act of preterition, then all are passed by, for all have sinned. Also, if it is the negative act of preterition, then all men have sinned irretrievably, and without hope of pardon and remission, as in the case of the angels who sinned. I add a third consideration, that an act of election, opposed at the same time to preterition, must have place here, in respect to certain individuals; but there is not and can not be such an act, in this case, since all men are comprehended under that preterition. There is a great difference between the negative act, by which God left man to his own counsel, and the negative act of preterition, which is to be here considered. Nor do I think that it is of much importance to this subject that, for non-adoption, as the proper and proximate end, I have substituted, the remote consequence, the absence of supernatural happiness. For, in addition to the fact that adoption, in your Theses already often cited, occupies the place of form not of end, I affirm that, in the negative act, by which He did not will adoption for any man, God could not, or, at least, did not have reference to any except sinners.

But you say that "God begets sons unto Himself according to His own will." He does this, however, from among sinful men. "He looks," you say, "upon all in Christ, not in themselves."

Therefore, I affirm, He considers them as sinners, not in themselves, as having, in themselves, any reason that He should regard them, but in themselves, as in need of being considered in Christ as Mediator of such character. "May not God," you ask, "beget His adopted children without reference to their character?" I admit that He may, without such reference to them as may influence God to beget them, not without such reference to them, that, not generation, but regeneration may be necessary to them. Grace claims for itself the whole in generation, but more strongly claims the whole in regeneration. But that God begets sons to Himself from among men, the word generation being used in any other sense than that of regeneration, I consider contrary both to theology and to Scripture. The subject, however, of discussion is adoption according to the decree of God.

Let us now consider the position, by which I strengthened my argument. I said that the "denial of happiness to man can not be considered otherwise than as punishment. I said "denial of happiness" not "of adoption." For I am, here, discussing the denial of glory, not of grace; but non-adoption, either alone or also, pertains to the latter. I wish, however, that it might be shown in what mode a denial of adoption to a man, made in the image of God, has not the nature of punishment, and is not caused by sin. You indeed affirm that it is previous to punishment, since it is previous even to sin. I deny both parts of the assertion. It belongs to him, who makes an assertion, to prove it, but I, though denying the assertion, will give the reason of my denial, to show the strength of my cause. He, who is made in the image of God, as Luke says of Adam, "which was the Son of God," (chap. iii, 38,) is, by the grace of creation, the son of God. But Adam was, not begotten, but created, "the son of God," as said in the marginal note of Beza's Testament. That, which any one has by the gift of creation, is not taken from him, unless the demerit of sin precedes, according to the justice of God. Supernatural happiness, whether it is bestowed on condition of obedience to law, or according to the condition of the covenant of grace, is always to be considered in the relation of an inheritance; but it was promised to Adam, on the condition of obedience; therefore, Adam was then considered as the Son of God. Filiation, then, could not be denied to him except on account of sin and disobedience. But the subject, of which I was treating, was denial of happiness.

You assert, that denial of happiness, considered in general, is not punishment, since that, which exists on account of a voluntary arrangement of God, is not punishment. I wish that you would show that any denial of supernatural happiness is according to voluntary arrangement of God, apart from the consideration of sin. You remark, in proof of your assertion, that "to Adam God denied supernatural happiness, until he should fulfill his appointed course. That was not punishment to Adam." I reply, the term, denial of supernatural happiness is ambiguous; it may be either final or temporary. The former is peremptory, the latter is conditional. That, of which we treat, is final and peremptory. The decree of predestination and preterition is peremptory, and that, which is prepared for or denied to any one, according to that decree, he will finally enjoy, or want. But you treat of temporary denial, "until he should fulfill his appointed course," according to the rule of divine justice, and of denial, on the consideration that he should not live according to the requirement of God, -- which denial belongs to the just providence of God, in contra-distinction to predestination and preterition. Indeed what you call a denial, can not be so called except in catachrestic sense. For how shall he be said to deny happiness to any one, who has promised it on a certain condition? You concede, however, that sin is antecedent to the denial of final happiness. But preterition or non-election is a denial of final happiness. Therefore, sin is antecedent to preterition. You say that it should be stated in addition "that antecedent to sin is particular abandonment by God, in the beginning and progress of sin, the foundation of which abandonment is non-election, or preterition and reprobation." I concede that abandonment by God was antecedent to sin, so far that God left man in the power of his own purposes; but it is not particular, but universal, in respect to the beginning of sin, for in that abandonment he left Adam, and, in him, all men; hence preterition can not be the foundation of that abandonment. For all mankind were left, in the beginning of sin. In respect to its progress, it may be called particular, for He freed some from sin and left others in sin; and non-election or preterition may be called the foundation of this abandonment, since some were left in the progress of sin, others being freed from sin by the gratuitous election of God, which is the direct opposite of preterition. Hence it follows that it can not be rightly said that preterition or non-election is the antecedent of sin, since it is only the antecedent of the progress of that which has already been perpetrated, and, indeed, its cause, by a denial of that which prevents the progress of sin, namely, grace. I affirm that it is universally true that the foresight of sin precedes the appointment of that negative act by which he does not determine to bestow felicity on an individual. For the act of preterition does not precede commission of sin, as has been already frequently shown. Sin, which is common to all men, does not result from that negative act which discriminates among men, but from a negative act common to all men. Preterition is a negative act, not common to all men, but discriminating among them. Therefore, preterition is not an act antecedent to sin. So my arguments are confirmed against your answers; they may, therefore, also be available for the decision of the other questions.

THIRTEENTH PROPOSITION OF ARMINIUS

The second question, referring to the preparation of grace, and its opposite, preterition, is not, whether God designed to bestow saving grace only on some persons, and those considered in certain relations, and did not design to bestow it on others, for this is very manifest from the Scriptures, in many passages. But the question is, whether God, in the act of predestination and its opposite, preterition, had reference to men, considered in a natural condition. I have not been able to persuade myself, either from the writings of Thomas Aquinas, or from those of the advocates of his views, that this question is to be answered affirmatively. My reasons for answering it negatively, are these: --

ANSWER OF JUNIUS TO THE
THIRTEENTH PROPOSITION

I have previously stated that divine election and non-election have reference to men in general, and this is very true. The phrase, "merely natural state," is ambiguous. The question before us, then, is not, whether election has reference only to men, considered in a natural condition, (as you understand that phrase,) if one attends closely to the subject. This is rather the question, whether it also has reference to men, so considered. We answer this affirmatively. Indeed, though it differs, in phraseology, from the first theory, yet we think that, in fact, it is very much in harmony with it, since this particular relation was added neither by Thomas Aquinas, nor by others, that the relations, previously noticed, might be excluded, but only that, in this argument, a consideration of sin, as a cause, might be excluded. Yet, let us examine your arguments as they are presented.

THE REPLY OF ARMINIUS TO THE ANSWER
TO THE THIRTEENTH PROPOSITION

That man, considered in general, is the object of the decree of which we treat, has not yet been made clear to me from your answers. Indeed I have proved from many arguments, adduced, as opportunity has been offered, that a general consideration of man has no place in that decree, and I shall prove the same by other arguments, as there may be occasion. Concerning the state of the question, as you propose it, I will not contend with you. Let the question be as you state it, whether God, in the decree of predestination and reprobation, has reference also to men, considered in a merely natural state. I maintain the negative. Not only does the affirmative of this question please you, but, from your Theses and other writings, you seem to me to incline to it so strongly that you seem even to have proposed the affirmative of the former theory. For if He, who predestinates and passes by, did not consider man as a sinner, then He did consider him as created among those things, on which He imposed certain conditions, or as not created, or as to be created. But let these remarks suffice. I have every where denied, and still deny, that God, in the act of predestination and of preterition, had reference also to men, considered in a merely natural state; but I assert that He had reference only to men, as considered in their sins. Concerning the difference between the first and second theory, we have already spoken.

FOURTEENTH PROPOSITION OF ARMINIUS

First, because Adam and, in him, all men were created in a state of supernatural grace, hence no one could be considered in a merely natural state. The antecedent is proved, because all were created in Adam after the image and likeness of God; but that is supernatural grace, as has been said: secondly, the law, which was given to Adam, was enacted for all, which is evident from the fact that all sinned in Adam, and became guilty of transgression. But that law could not be obeyed without supernatural grace, which I prove from the subject of the law, from the appendix of the law, from the instigator of transaction, and from the mode of instigation. The law required obedience towards God, that man should live, not according to man, but according to God, which life is not animal, but spiritual, and its cause in man is supernatural grace. The appendix of the law consisted in the threatening of temporal and spiritual death, that of the body and of the soul. Punishment, which is spiritual and opposed, not only to animal, but also to spiritual good, ought not to be annexed, in equity, to a law which can be observed without supernatural grace; especially when the same law, if observed, could not afford supernatural or spiritual good, since it can be observed without supernatural grace. It seems unjust that the transgression of a law should deserve eternal and spiritual death, but its observance could not obtain eternal and spiritual life from God, on the terms of divine goodness and justice. The instigator was Satan, whose design was to cast down man, by transgression, to death, not only of the body, but of the soul, and when man could only resist through supernatural grace. The mode of temptation was such that it could not be successfully resisted by man, if destitute of supernatural grace.

ANSWER OF JUNIUS TO THE FOURTEENTH PROPOSITION

Your antecedent, namely, "Adam and in him all men were created in a state of supernatural grace," is ambiguous. Again, it can not be proved, as we have shown, in answer to the tenth proposition. The consequent is denied, and is also ambiguous. Since I have previously discussed both of these points, I come now to the arguments. The proof from the image of God, was related in the same answer, and it was shown that it was not supernatural of itself; but that it had relation and adjustment to supernatural grace, not of nature or its own essence, but by the arrangement of grace. This argument, therefore, now, as before, is denied. The first position in the second argument, is not to be admitted without some distinction, for one law, given to Adam, was general;

the other particular. The general law, namely, that which is natural and joined to the natural, was enacted for all. This was by no means true of the particular law. The latter was that he should not eat of the tree of knowledge of good and evil. It is not credible that this law, which was one of particular requisition should have been enacted for all; it is not credible that, if all had remained unfallen, they would have come into Eden to that tree, that their obedience should be tested.

The Scripture, also, does not make this statement. We concede the second position in reference to the universal law, not in that the law was natural, but in that the nature of man itself and the natural law, was adjusted to grace. The natural, as such, was within the capability of man; as it was related and adjusted to grace, it could not be observed without supernatural grace. In reference to the special law, the second position is erroneous. For the mere act of eating or not eating of any fruit, is natural. The power to eat or abstain from that fruit, was, in fact, possessed by man, though these acts were not both left with him by the requisition and arrangement of the special law declared by God. Therefore the second point is, in this case, erroneous, for it was possible for him not to choose, not to touch, not to eat the fruit, as it was to do the contrary. This was of natural power (which possessed full vigour) in a natural subject. To establish this point, you adduce four arguments, all pertaining to the mode of general law. I will briefly examine each in order. The first argument pertains to general law, both as it is natural and as it is adjusted to grace. We concede, then, that the affirmative is true of general law, but deny it as to the particular law, by which God required obedience in a particular matter, and in one merely natural or animal. It pertained to natural power to abstain from or to eat that fruit; it pertained to natural will to avoid the experiment of sin and death, of which God had forewarned them. God tested the obedience of man in a matter merely natural, and in the same thing he miserably renounced obedience to God, of his own will, not by any necessity. He had then no just ground of complaint that God should hold him responsible, because, in a matter of no difficulty, and according to nature, he did not willingly render due obedience unto the Lord, but preferred, to His word, the word of the serpent in the case of Eve, and that of his wife in the case of Adam.

You will perhaps say that he would not have committed that transgression, if grace had been bestowed upon him. Must you, then, always require grace, and make it ground of accusation, if it is not bestowed, even in a matter which is natural, and, indeed, merely natural? God bestowed a natural constitution on Adam, for this very reason, that in a matter merely natural, he might use his natural powers. He gave that which was sufficient. Do you demand more? I quote, on this point, the words of Tertullian (lib. 2 advers. Marcion, cap. 7.) "If God bestowed upon man the freedom of the will and power to act, and bestowed it suitably, He undoubtedly, according to His authority as Creator, bestowed them to be enjoyed, but to be enjoyed, so far as depended upon Himself; in accordance with His own character, that is 'after God,' that is according to goodness, (for who would grant any permission against himself,); but so far as depended upon man, according to the motions of his freedom. Who, indeed, bestowing on a person any thing to be enjoyed, does not so bestow it, that it may be enjoyed according to his mind and will? It was, therefore, a consequence that God should not interfere with the liberty once granted to man, that is, that He should retain in Himself the action of His prescience and prepotency, by which He could have intervened, so that man should not fall into danger, in attempting to enjoy his own freedom, in an evil mode. For had He thus intervened, He would have rescinded the freedom of the will, which, in reason and goodness, He had bestowed. Then let it be supposed that he had intervened, that He had destroyed the freedom of the will, by calling him back from the tree by not permitting the tempting serpent to converse with the woman, would not Marcion exclaim, O futile, unstable, unfaithful Lord, rescinding that which He had established! Why did he bestow the freedom of the will, if He must interfere with it? Why did He interfere, if He bestowed it? Let Him then choose the point in which He shall charge Himself with error, whether in its bestowment, or in its rescision, &c."

Your statement, that "supernatural grace is the cause of spiritual life in man," we believe to be most certainly true, and we avow the same thing. Yet there was one mode of spiritual life in Adam, and there is another mode in us, in whom supernatural grace alone produces this life, while Adam had, together with this grace, the image of God unimpaired and uncorrupted, and therefore had spiritual life in both modes, the natural and supernatural. But these things will be introduced, appropriately, in another place.

Your second argument, from the appendix of the law, is plainly in the same condition. This seems to be its scope. If God, in the case of election and reprobation, had reference to men considered in a merely natural state, (that is, with the same ambiguity, and on the supposition which we have denied above,) He would not have ordained spiritual punishment, opposed not only to animal, but is spiritual good, for transgression of a law, which might be observed without supernatural grace; for it is in accordance with equity (which point was also regarded in the law of the twelve tables) that the punishment should be adapted to the crime; -- But God ordained punishment of this kind; --

Therefore, He did not have reference to men, considered in a natural condition. In reference to the antecedent of the Major, I will say nothing; I have already spoken often on that point. The consequent is denied. It would be true, if both sins or evil deeds and their punishments were estimated only from the deed (which the law forbids), and according to its kind. But there are many other things, by which the gravity of offenses is usually, and most justly estimated; the author of the law, the author of the crime, its object, end, and circumstances. We must consider the author of the law, for the authority of a law, enacted by an emperor, is greater than that of one, enacted by a tribune, of one imposed by God, than of one imposed by man. The author of the crime, whether he commands it, or personally commits it. For a crime is greater which is committed through the persuasion of an enemy, than one committed through that of a master or father. The same distinction may be applied to the personal commission of sin. The object, for an offense, against a parent, is more heinous than against a stranger, against one's self and family, than against a person not thus connected, against God than against man. The end, for it is a greater sin, if you transgress a law with an unimportant end or no end in view, than if the same thing is done of necessity, if with all unworthy and wicked design than if with a worthy and good design.

What shall I say in reference to circumstances? What I have already said is, in my judgment, sufficient. But he, who transgresses the law of God, is guilty of these aggravating particulars, of which even the first, alone, is sufficient for the infliction, with the utmost justice, of spiritual punishment. Should he regard lightly the legislator, God? Adding the second, should he listen to an enemy, the enemy of God, and of his race, and of the universe, Should he, the recent workmanship of God, and the tenant of Paradise, transgress the recent commandment of God, Adding the third particular, should he rush forward against himself, his family, and God, not ignorantly, but with due warning? Do not these, my brother, seem to you to be cases of the greatest aggravation? Are they not worthy of bodily and spiritual punishment? As in general, so in special or particular law, the same rule is to be observed. The law was particular, and that in a natural requirement, which man could perform naturally, as we have before said. Here perhaps, you will say, that it is improper that supernatural punishment should be imposed in reference to a natural offense. But consider all those things which I have just said. Man transgressed the law of God, from which he has just received the blessings of nature and of grace, and to whom he owed all things as his Supreme Ruler. He transgressed by the persuasion of the Devil, the public and sworn enemy of God, of the universe, and of the human race, to listen to whom, once only, is to renounce God. At the time of his transgression, he was the recent work of God, the heir of all natural and supernatural good, the inhabitant of Paradise, the foster-child of heaven, the lord of all things, servant of God alone. Man transgressed, using violence against himself, and bringing sin and death, and all evils upon himself and his posterity, dishonouring God in himself, though forewarned by the God of truth, and prescient, in his own mind, of coming evil. He transgressed in a matter, most trivial, entirely unnecessary, of the least importance, when he really abounded in the blessings of the whole world, and this with a most unworthy and plainly impious design, that he might be like God, "knowing good and evil." How could he, who was not faithful and obedient in a matter of the least importance, be faithful in one of great importance, He transgressed in a beastly manner, served his belly and appetite, blind to all things belonging to heaven and earth, except the flame of lust, wickedly placed before his eyes, deaf to all things except the voice of the devil. Here, if we please to glance at other circumstances, how many and how strong arguments exist for most just though most severe damnation! Truly, was that, in many respects, an infinite fall, which brought infinite ruin. But should any one affirm, that it was an unworthy thing that man should be condemned for so small a matter, let him consider these two things; first, it was an unworthy thing that man, in "so small a matter," should disobey the mandate of his Supreme Ruler, of the author of nature, of grace, and of his salvation; secondly, it is not a small matter, which was ordained for the manifestation of due obedience in natural things, and as a just method of the perception of supernatural blessings. God willed that Adam should, by this sign, manifest his religious and voluntary obedience in natural things, and in this way suitably exert himself to attain supernatural blessings. Does this seem a small matter, when he acted contrary to the will of God, and to all natural and supernatural blessings in a thing of so little importance? But, to proceed; do you think, my brother, that this punishment can be inflicted on man more justly, if considered in his fallen state, than if considered in his natural condition, This is the amount of your argument. I have not indeed hesitated to affirm the contrary. I say that the sin of Adam was more heinous, because he sinned when unfallen, than if he had sinned, as a fallen being. Consider the simple fact in the case of man. You will, I know, declare that it was a more unworthy thing that man, in a state of integrity, should become the slave of sin, than if, in a sinful state, he should fall into sin. It is, therefore, more just that Adam, at the time of that transgression, should be considered as unfallen, than in reference to the fall which afterwards supervened. This illustrates the truth of the righteousness of God. As to your statement, "it seems unjust that the transgression could deserve eternal and spiritual death, &c." I wonder, indeed, that it could have been made by you. For you are not ignorant that the law of God, whether general or particular, is the appointment of the present course according to which we both worship God in the discharge of duty, and reach the goal of supernatural grace. As a traveler, to whom his Lord has prescribed the mode of his journey, if he departs from the prescribed path, by the same act renounces both his journey and its goal, by his own sin, but if he remains in the path, he performs his duty, thus I judge that it was necessary that Adam should be treated. The unhappy traveler left the right path. Did he not, therefore, also renounce the good which God had graciously set before him? If he had remained in the path he certainly would have attained the goal, of grace, not of merit. How, not of merit? Because, by not keeping the path, the servant loses both his way and his life, as the proper cause of his own evil, but by keeping the way, he obtains life, as the result of his journey. Life is proposed, of grace, not of merit, both to the obedient and to the disobedient, as the result of pursuing the right path. In this way the obedient obtains grace, and the disobedient is the cause to himself that he does not obtain grace, and, by his own act, forfeit the life, which depends on that grace.

The third argument, from the instigator of the transgression, and the fourth, from the mode of temptation, are disposed of in the same answer. The third argument is this; "man could resist the Devil only through supernatural grace; therefore the law could not be observed without supernatural grace"— and the fourth; "the mode of temptation was such that it could not be successfully resisted by man, if destitute of supernatural grace; therefore, the law could not be observed without supernatural grace."

In the first place, though I should admit both arguments, in reference to general law according to our previous distinction, yet we might, with propriety, deny their validity in reference to that particular law, which enjoined a natural act, situated properly and absolutely within the capability of nature, for it is as truly natural not to eat that which is bad in its nature or effect, as it is to eat that which is good. It was then within the capability of man not to sin, for the refusal or neglect to eat was in the capability of man, of his own natural power.

In the second place, we must make a distinction in reference to both those arguments, even when referred to the general law of God, concerning that which is called supernatural grace. For, as in nature, the work of Providence is threefold, to sustain a thing as to its existence, to govern it as to its action, and to protect or preserve it as it may be liable to destruction, so also in the pious, the work of grace is threefold, for it is accustomed to sustain, and to govern, and to protect them. It always sustains, because inherent and common grace is permanent, but it rules and protects, or preserves when and as it chooses; for this act, as it is assisting and not inherent, is particular, and the free act of variable grace. This distinction having been stated, we thus judge concerning these arguments. Man was never without supernatural grace, either inherent or habitual: he was not without assisting grace, except in that particular act, in which God did not govern, did not preserve, because it was an act of nature, which must be tested in its own mode, which has been allotted to it by the infinite wisdom of God. For, as Tertullian says—God retired, from the administration not of all grace, but of supernatural grace from the time when he said to man, "Of every tree of the garden thou mayest freely eat. But of the tree of knowledge of good and evil thou shalt not eat of it," (Gen. ii. 16 and 17,) and committed the whole matter, of compact and solely, to the nature of man." Indeed he wholly transferred to the will of man, according to the law of his nature, the power to render or not to render obedience in all matters pertaining to nature. But "he could not resist the devil, and the mode of the temptation was irresistible." This is denied; for if he could, according to his nature, refrain from eating of the forbidden fruit, he could, in this, resist the devil, and the mode of the temptation was not irresistible. He could refrain from eating, because that was, in the simplest sense, natural, and, by compact, as we have just said, was placed in the power of man. But he did not refrain from eating, certainly, because he did not wish to do so, but he willingly consented to the temptation, concerning which point, we have already under Prop. 9 noticed the opinion of Augustine.

In the observance of general law, the case is different, cause, as we have before said, the law operates on nature and adjusts nature to the supernatural, and it could not be observed, nor indeed could the devil be resisted, without supernatural grace.

REPLY OF ARMINIUS TO THE ANSWER OF JUNIUS TO THE FOURTEENTH PROPOSITION

My object, in the arguments which I now present, is to prove that Adam, and in him, all the human race, were created in a state of supernatural grace, that is, that in their original condition they had, not only natural attributes, but also supernatural grace, either by the act of creation or superinfusion. From which I conclude, that God, in the act of predestination, and preterition or reprobation, could consider no one in a merely natural state. My first argument is taken from the nature of the divine image, to which or in which man was created. Another argument is deduced from the law, which was imposed on Adam, and on all men in him, which I assert, was not to be observed without supernatural grace. The former argument was discussed in my reply to the answer to the tenth Proposition, and I refer to what was then stated.

We will now consider the latter, and, in the first place, its Major, which supposes that the law, given to Adam, was enacted for all men, with the addition, as proof, of the fact that all men have sinned in Adam, and become partakers of his transgression. You discuss this Major Proposition, without reference to the proof. I notice the mode in which you assail the former, and what force is possessed by the latter for its confirmation. You make a distinction in the law, imposed on Adam, and regard it as having a two-fold relation, first, as common and natural; second, as particular. You say that the former was enacted for all men, the latter, not for all men. I agree with what you say concerning common or general law, and shall hereafter make use of it to confirm my own proposition. I do not, in all respects, assent to what you say concerning particular law. The law, concerning the forbidden tree, had, in part, a particular reference, and in part, a general one. For it is symbolical, and consists, therefore, of two parts, the symbol and that signified by it. The symbol was abstinence from the forbidden tree; the thing signified was abstinence from disobedience and evil, and the trial of obedience. So far as abstinence from disobedience and evil was prescribed by that law, it was a general law. But as the law required an observance of a symbolical character, it must be considered in a two fold light, either as prescribing symbolical observance in general, or the observance of that particular symbol. So far as the law should prescribe the observance of any symbol, in general, to test the obedience of man, it would, to that extent, be general. For God would have determined to test the obedience of all men by some symbol, either this one or some other, if it had been their lot to be born in a state of integrity. I prove this first from the fact that He purposed that the condition of all men should be the same with that of Adam, if they should be born in the state in which Adam was created, in respect to the image of God. Secondly, it was most suitable that the experiment of obedience should be made in a matter which was indifferent; but a law, which commands or forbids any thing indifferent is symbolical and ceremonial.

But, so far as the observance, prescribed by the law, had reference to that particular symbol, namely, abstinence from

the fruit of the forbidden tree, it can, in one sense, be called general, and in another, it may be particular. It was general as prescribed to Adam and Eve, the parents and social head of the human race, in whom, as in its origin and root, was then contained the whole human race. It was particular, as prescribed to the same persons as individuals, and as it, perhaps, would not have been imposed on other human beings, if they had, at that time, been born, and considered in themselves, and not in their first parents. I say perhaps; for you know that there are those who think, that if the first human beings had maintained their integrity, that their descendants would have been born and would have dwelt in Paradise, and this idea has some probability. For if that earthly paradise was a symbol of the heavenly kingdom, as seems probable from the fact that the third heaven, the residence of the blessed, is called, in the Scripture, paradise, it is most probable that no one of the human race would have been excluded from that paradise on earth, if he had not first rendered himself worthy of the heavenly paradise. This point may, however, be left without decision.

That the law (to come to the argument of my Major) which Adam transgressed, was enacted for all men, I proved by an irrefragable argument, which you passed by. "Sin is the transgression of the law." (1 John iii. 4.) The law can not be transgressed by him for whom it was not enacted. Hence that law, which Adam transgressed, was enacted for all who are said to have sinned in him. But that law was the same which is called particular by you. More briefly; the law, which all men transgressed in Adam was enacted for all men. But all men transgressed, in Adam, the law concerning the forbidden tree. For against no other law is Adam said to have sinned, and, indeed, we are all said to be guilty of the sin committed against that law. Therefore that law was enacted for all men. In whatever respect, then, it is considered, it is equally in my favour, and is equally adapted to sustain my sentiment.

I come now to the Minor. "But that law could not be obeyed without supernatural grace." You grant this in reference to the general law, you deny it concerning that in which the eating of the fruit of that tree was forbidden. I may assent to your position for the sake of the argument, and from that position sustain my proposition. A law which can not be observed without supernatural grace, should be imposed only on those to whom supernatural grace has been given by God; --

But that general law could not be observed without supernatural grace; -- Therefore, it should be imposed only on those to whom supernatural grace was given by God. It was imposed on Adam, and, in him, upon all men. Therefore, Adam, and, in him, all men, had supernatural grace. Therefore, they could not be considered in their natural condition by God in the act of predestination and reprobation. This might suffice for my purpose. I affirm, however, that even the particular law concerning the forbidden tree could not be obeyed without supernatural grace, not indeed so far as the external act of abstinence from the fruit of that tree was prescribed, but as, under that symbol, obedience was commanded, and it was enjoined on man to live not according to man, but according to God. This you acknowledge when you say that "these acts" (eating and abstaining), "were not both left with him by the requisition and arrangement of the special law declared by God, though the power to eat is to abstain from that fruit was in fact absolutely possessed by man. That law, however, was to be observed, not according to fact only, but according to the arrangement of that particular law. You say that my argument "pertains to the mode of general law." Let that be admitted, and still sustain my proposition, as I have before demonstrated, and I have also shown that, in the law which you call particular, there is something of the nature of general law. Those arguments are, therefore, in this respect valid. The first also is sustained, as is apparent from our previous statements. For as the law required obedience which should consist, not only in the external deed, but in the external disposition of the mind, for that reason it could not be obeyed without supernatural grace.

My second argument does not seem to have been understood by you in accordance with my meaning. The design of the argument was—and in this consists its force—that spiritual punishment could not be inflicted for the transgression of that law, to the observance of which spiritual good was not promised. But spiritual good was not promised to the observance of this law, if, indeed, it could be observed without supernatural grace. For supernatural grace and supernatural happiness are analogous. Hence it follows, that if spiritual punishment was the penalty of the transgression of that law, then, also spiritual good was promised to the observance of the same, and, therefore, it could be observed only by supernatural grace; otherwise nature could, by its own fact, obtain supernatural good. Here we must consider a three-fold distinction in the transgression and observance of law. First, a single transgression of law deserves punishment, but reward pertains only to those who observe the law even to the end; secondly, the violation of one precept deserves punishment, but reward is bestowed only on those who have kept all its precepts; thirdly, the violation of a precept may be estimated from the omission either of an external act or of an internal feeling, or of both at once, also, from the intention, so that he, who fails in one of these points, may be considered a transgressor, but observance is judged of from all these united, nor can it be regarded as perfect if it is not complete in all these points. I acknowledge that what you say concerning the heinousness of the sin perpetrated by our first parents is very true, nor do I think that its heinousness can be declared in words. But how do you infer that my argument is designed to set forth that punishment would be inflicted more justly, on a man, if he should violate the law, when he was corrupt and sinful by nature, than if he should do the same thing, when he was pure by nature, These states of human nature were placed in opposition by me, but I contrasted man in a natural condition with one endued with supernatural grace. Punishment is inflicted with greater justice on the latter than on the former; indeed it would be inflicted unjustly on the former, if the law could not be observed without supernatural grace; and if the observance of the law had not the promise of spiritual good, spiritual punishment is inflicted unjustly on the transgression of that law.

I will not now speak of my last two arguments and your answers to them, both because so much has been said on the preceding points, and because you concede to me that man was not without habitual, supernatural grace. I conclude then that man could not be considered in a merely natural condition by God in the act of predestination, since he was not in that state. In this, then, we agree. But you say, "these arguments have no weight against the opinion which considers man in general." I answer, that these arguments prove that man could not have been considered in general, for he could not have been considered in a merely natural condition. But in the state of supernatural grace, he was not considered as reprobate or passed by. For, in reprobation or preterition, man is left in the state of nature, which can have nothing supernatural or divine, as is stated in your Theses. Also, that state of supernatural grace has its measure and proportion to supernatural felicity according to the providence of God. Moreover as to those, on whom God wills to bestow supernatural happiness, by the affirmative act of His providence, on them he cannot, by the negative act of preterition, will not to bestow the same happiness, unless he has considered them as failing to attain, by those supernatural means, to that happiness, but as either about to sin, or as having already in fact transgressed, of their own free will. Otherwise there would be two contrary acts of God in reference to one subject, considered in the same relation, and performed at the same time.

FIFTEENTH PROPOSITION OF ARMINIUS

Secondly, because the grace of predestination, or that prepared for man in predestination, is Evangelical, not Legal; but that grace was prepared only for man considered as a sinner. That it is Evangelical is clear, because the decree of predestination is peremptory. It has reference, then, not to Legal grace, of which a man may not make use, as in the case of transgression of law, and yet be saved, but to Evangelical grace, by which he must be saved, or excluded from salvation.

Again, the grace, prepared in predestination, is that of the remission of sins, and of regeneration, that is, of the turning of sin and to God, by the mortification of the old, and the vivification of the new man.

ANSWER OF JUNIUS TO THE FIFTEENTH PROPOSITION

I accede to your first statement, if it be correctly understood, but some explanation may be necessary concerning the second. In the assumption which you make, there should be a distinction, for it is false, if referred to Evangelical grace, understood with a general reference to nature; if that grace be understood with reference to ourselves, it is very true. But, as you know, it is fallacious to argue from the concrete to the abstract. I will explain the subject in a few words. In supernatural Evangelical grace there are two parts, one to preserve those who are now in a state of grace; the other to gain those who are not in that state. The order of this grace, considered according to nature, is one thing; considered according to ourselves it is another. The order of nature is that they, who are in a state of grace, should be preserved (as in the election and predestination of angels), and afterwards that they, who are not in that state, should be brought into it, as is done for men. Considered according to ourselves, who have fallen from grace, the order is different. It is necessary that they, who have fallen, should first be raised up, as Christ does in the gospel, and then be kept, as He will do for us eternally, in heaven, when we shall be like the angels. Your second statement, then, is false in the abstract, if you say that Evangelical grace, in general, is not prepared for man, except as he is considered sinful, for it was prepared for man in the abstract and in common, as God also testified to man, in the symbol of the tree of life, placed in Eden. But if you speak of Evangelical grace, in the latter sense, that is considered in this mode and order, then indeed I accede to your statement. But then the conclusion will not be valid, as we have just said. For the Evangelical grace of God is one in its substance, but two-fold in its mode and order, which mode and order does not change the substance of the thing. Hence it was not at all to the purpose that your first statement might be sustained, which we also, if it is rightly understood, strongly affirm.

Your statement that "a man may not make use of Legal grace and yet be saved," is a doubtful one, unless it be fully explained, and as I know that you understand it; but this does not relate to the question. Finally, Evangelical grace, by your limitation to the remission of sins, regeneration, &c., is, as you also, my brother, perceive from what we have now said, rendered incomplete, because you pass over preservation, which is one essential part of it. In other respects we accede to your proposition.

REPLY OF ARMINIUS TO THE ANSWER
TO THE FIFTEENTH PROPOSITION

My argument may be stated thus: -- Evangelical grace is prepared only for man, considered as a sinner; -- But the grace of predestination, or that prepared for man in predestination, is Evangelical; -- Therefore, the grace of predestination is prepared only for man, considered as a sinner. This is a syllogism in form, mode, and its three terms. Hence it includes nothing else and nothing more than is in the premises. Though Evangelical grace, considered in general, might have two parts, yet I have restricted the Evangelical grace, which was prepared for man. But grace, considered in the abstract, was not prepared for man, but only one part of it; that is, the acquisition of those who are not in a state of grace, not the preservation of those who are in a state of grace, for no one of men has been kept in that state of grace, which he obtained at his creation, all have fallen. There is, therefore, in this case no fallacy from the concrete to the abstract. I use the term Evangelical grace in my first and second statements in entirely the same manner; not in one case "according to nature" and, in the other, "according to ourselves" or vice versa, but in both cases "according to ourselves," namely, as that which was prepared, for men, not angels. Therefore, by your own acknowledgment, both my statements are true. You say that "it is false, in the abstract, that Evangelical grace is not prepared for man, except as he is considered as sinful, for it was prepared for man in the abstract and in common, as God also testified to man in the symbol of the tree of life placed in Eden." I reply—there is an equivocation in the word "prepared," and when that is removed, the truth of my view will be manifest. The preparation of grace is either that of predestination or of providence, as used in contra-distinction to the former. In providence, sufficient grace is prepared, and if it is efficacious, as some think, it is not finally efficacious. In predestination, grace, which is efficacious, and indeed finally efficacious, is prepared. Predestination superadds to providence, as the School-men say, fire certainty of the event. In providence is prepared that general grace, which pertains promiscuously to all men; in predestination is prepared that particular grace, which is peculiar to the elect. In providence is prepared both Legal and Evangelical grace; in predestination only Evangelical grace. In providence is prepared grace communicable both in and out of paradise; in predestination is prepared grace, communicable only out of paradise. It is true that God symbolized, by the tree of life, general not particular grace, Legal not Evangelical grace, grace communicable in paradise, and, finally, sufficient, not efficacious, grace. Therefore, the grace, which God symbolized by the tree of life, is that of providence, not of predestination. But Evangelical grace, which is finally efficacious, particular not general, only communicable out of paradise, and which is prepared for man in predestination, is no other than that which is adapted only to man considered as a sinner. I refer, then, in my first and second statement, to Evangelical grace, in this mode and order. Therefore, my conclusion is valid. And, though grace is the same, in substance, and varies only in its mode and relation, yet that variation of mode, is a reason that grace, constituted in that mode and order, can certainly be prepared only for the sinner. The whole matter will be more manifestly evident, if I conclude by the addition of proofs of the Minor of the preceding syllogism. Evangelical grace, by which man is in fact saved, which consists in the remission of sins and in regeneration, belongs only to man considered as a sinner;

-- But the grace, prepared in predestination for man, is Evangelical grace, by which man is in fact saved, consisting in remission of sins and in regeneration; -- Therefore, the grace, prepared for man in predestination, does not belong to man except as he is considered as a sinner. Consequently man was not considered by God, in the act of predestination, in his natural condition.

If any one should argue thus, "Evangelical grace was prepared for man in the abstract and in common; -- But the grace, prepared for man in predestination, is Evangelical grace;

Therefore, grace was prepared in predestination for man, considered in the abstract and in common," he will, on more than one account, be chargeable with fallacy. In the first place, the Major, considered in the abstract, is false. For that grace, which preserves its subjects in their primitive state, which you call, also, Evangelical in respect to the angels, was not prepared for man. Again, there are four terms in the syllogism. For, in the Major, Evangelical grace is spoken of in the abstract; in the Minor, it is spoken of in the concrete. If it be said that it is understood in the Minor in the same manner as in the Major, then the Minor, also, is false. For the grace prepared for man in predestination is Evangelical grace, in the concrete, and understood in respect to us. I use your phraseology. But what if I should deny that the grace which is bestowed on angels, in election and predestination can be called Evangelical, and should ask for the proof of your statement? This I could do with propriety and justice. For it is certain, especially as the gospel is explained to us in the Holy Scriptures, that the grace bestowed on angels can not be called Evangelical. The sum of the gospel is this, "Repent and believe the gospel" or "believe in Jesus Christ, the Son of God, and your sins shall be remitted unto you, and ye shall receive the gift of the Holy Ghost, and afterwards, eternal life." These expressions are by no means adapted to the elect angels.

If you say that it is not Evangelical in the mode in which the gospel is adapted to sinful men, yet, it can be called Evangelical as, according to it, they are preserved in their own state, you will permit me to ask the proof of that statement. In the weakness of my capacity, I can conceive of no other reason for that sentiment than that Christ is also called the Mediator of angels, and that they are said to be elect in him. You know, however, that this is in controversy among the learned, and we have already presented some thoughts concerning it. But, even with the concession that Christ can be called the Mediator of angels, I can not persuade myself that the grace, which was bestowed on the angels, was prepared or obtained for them by any merit of Christ, or any work which he performed, in their behalf, before God. Grace, which Christ did not obtain, can not, in my opinion, be called Evangelical. Again, I think that, in general, there is a two-fold mode and way of obtaining supernatural and eternal happiness. One of strict justice and Legal, the other of mercy and Evangelical, as there is, also, a two-fold covenant with God, of works and of faith, of justice and of grace, Legal and Evangelical. In the former mode and relation, happiness is obtained by perfect obedience to the law, given to the creature by God; in the latter, happiness is obtained by remission of disobedience and the imputation of righteousness. The human mind can not conceive any other mode; at least, no other is revealed in the Scriptures. These two modes have, to each other, this relation, that the former precedes, as is required by the justice of God, by the condition presented to the creature, and by the very nature of the case; the other follows, if, in the former way, happiness can not be allotted to the creature, and it seems good to the Deity, also, to propose the latter, which depends on the mere will of God. For He can punish or pardon disobedience. Both modes are used in reference to man, as the Scriptures declare in many places, and briefly in Rom. viii. 3. "For what the Law could not do, in that it was weak through the flesh, God, sending his own Son in the likeness of sinful flesh, and for sin, condemned sin in the flesh."

I think that the former mode only was used in reference to the angels, and that God determined to treat the angels according to the Legal covenant strictly of justice and works; but to display all His goodness in the salvation of men. This is apparent from the fact that the angels, who fell, sinned irremediably and without hope of pardon, and the other angels did not obtain pardon for sins, for they had not committed them, but were preserved and confirmed in their own state, through the grace, it may be, which they received through the mediation of Christ, and which he communicated to them, not, in a correct sense, by that which Christ either merited or obtained for them by any work performed in their behalf, before God. These things, however, are irrelevant.

In my statement that it is possible for man not to use Legal grace, and yet be saved, I intended to convey the same idea which you also have expressed, that God can, if he will, move iniquity "as a cloud;" and I think that the apostle says the same in Romans iv. 5. "To him that worketh not," (that is, who does not fulfill the law, and therefore, does not use Legal grace,) "but believeth on Him that justifieth the ungodly, his faith is counted for righteousness."

In limiting Evangelical grace to the remission of sins and regeneration, I committed no fault. For I explained it, not in the abstract, (if it is ever so used), but in the concrete. But, thus explained, it excludes that part which you call "the grace of preservation" (unless that phrase is applied to perseverance in a state of restoration). We were not saved, in the primitive state, by that grace, for it was not prepared for in that state, by predestination. For we all fell and sinned. Here, again, there is need of the admonition that we are not now treating of angels, therefore those things which may be common to angels and men, are here, according to the law of general and specific relations kaq o[lou, to be so restricted as to apply only to men, otherwise, in discussing the species, we shall treat of the genus.

SIXTEENTH PROPOSITION OF ARMINIUS

Thirdly, because the reelection of a creature, in his natural state, of a creature, on whom is imposed a law only to be performed by grace, is a cause of sin by the removal or the non-bestowment of that which alone can restrain from sin. This is grace. According to which view this sentiment is equivalent to the former, which ascribes the ordination of sin to a decree, from which sin necessarily exists.

ANSWER OF JUNIUS TO THE SIXTEENTH PROPOSITION

The proposition can not be predicated of man in his primitive integrity, for the law, to Adam in his integrity, was not only his glory, but it was to be performed both by nature and grace, since his nature was rightly adjusted to grace, but he fell in a matter pertaining to nature, and capable of performance by nature, which did not belong to general law, which is here the subject of discussion, but to that particular law, which had reference only to nature, and absolutely pertained to it, and was to be observed by its power alone, as was declared to Adam by God, as shown in the answer to the fourteenth proposition. In reference to ourselves, however, as we now are, it can be stated, with the utmost propriety, that the law can be observed only by grace. Indeed, it can not be observed at all by us, but its observance is imputed of grace and is apprehended by faith in Christ. The statement, also, is erroneous that "the reelection of a creature, in his natural state, is a cause of sin by the removal or non-bestowment of restraining grace," if it is understood in a universal sense. It is a partial cause of sin, when removed or not bestowed, if there was obligation to bestow it, but if there was no such obligation, it can not, with propriety, be called a partial cause of sin. If there was obligation to bestow it, there is responsibility, it there was no such obligation, there is no responsibility for the sin, even if that grace should be wanting. This is taught by nature itself, and it is very fitly illustrated by Clemens Alexandrinus, in two places. But, in the law, there was something natural, which Adam could perform by nature, and something adjusted to grace, for which he could not, by nature alone, be sufficient.

Therefore, though Adam sinned against natural law, if he did sin in a matter pertaining to nature, (in which grace was not due), his own will alone was in fault, not destitution of grace, as evidently happened to him in the particular law, given to him in Adam. The conclusion, then, is unsound.

Of the ordination of sin, and the decree of God, and what is signified by ordination, properly understood, we have spoken, in answer to the sixth proposition. Your argument, that sin, therefore, necessarily exists, is inconclusive; since the Divine ordination would perform nothing unobligatory upon it, but that is done by him who commits sin; and it omits nothing obligatory upon it, but must perform and most wisely perfect all thing. But there has been, in the answer to the sixth proposition, a sufficient discussion of this whole subject.

THE REPLY OF ARMINIUS TO THE ANSWER TO THE SIXTEENTH PROPOSITION

When I speak of grace, I do not exclude nature, for the former presupposes the latter. The phrase "only to be performed by grace" is equivalent to this, "not to be performed without grace," the word "only" referring, not to the exclusion of nature, but to the necessary inclusion of grace. But these antecedents being supposed—a law was given to man, which he could not perform without grace—and grace was not bestowed—the conclusion follows that the cause of sin was not man, but he, who imposed such a law and did not give the means of its observance, or, to speak more correctly, a transgression of a law cannot be called sin, when the law is unjust, as that of God, reaping where He has not sown, which is far from a good and a just God, and its transgression is necessary, not voluntary, on account of an inability not to transgress. It is, then, in all respects, true, that he, who does not bestow that without which sin can not be avoided, or removes that without which the law can not be observed, is truly the author of sin, or rather the cause that the law is not observed, which non-observance, can not have the relation of sin. The condition, "if there was obligation to bestow restraining grace," is added, in this case, in vain. For God is, necessarily, under obligation to bestow on man the power to keep that law, which He imposes on him, unless, indeed, man has deprived himself of that power, by his own fault, in which case, God is not under obligation to restore it. That, however, was not the case in the primitive state of man, before his sin. In this sense, I grant that he, who is not under obligation to bestow the power, to observe the law and to avoid sin, is not the author of sin, if he does not bestow it; but this statement should be added, that God is under obligation to give that power, if He gave the law, the observance of which necessarily implies the power. God does not, indeed, owe any thing to any person, in an absolute sense, for no one has given that to Him which should be repaid, but God can, by His own act, place Himself under obligation to man, either by promise, or by requiring an act of him. By promise, if He has made it absolutely or on a condition, then He is a debtor, absolutely or conditionally; "God is not unrighteous to forget your work." (Heb. vii. 10.) By requiring an act, He is placed under obligation to bestow the power necessary for the performance of the act. If He does not bestow it, and yet, by an enactment of a law, requires the performance of the act, then He, not man, is the cause of the transgression of that law.

In reference to those antecedents, whether a law was imposed on man, to be observed without grace, or not, and whether man received, in his primitive state, supernatural grace, there has been sufficient discussion under propositions tenth and fourteenth. Nor is it to the purpose to say that "if he sinned in a matter pertaining to nature, (in which grace was not due,) his own will alone was in fault, not destitution of grace"; who denies that statement, if that law could be observed by the powers of nature? But I deny that such was the case in that particular law given to Adam, and the reasons for this denial have been already given in my review of your answer to the fourteenth proposition. We have also remarked, at sufficient length, in the sixth proposition, concerning the ordination of sin, and how it is made, according to the view of Calvin and Beza, the basis of the divine decree. I grant that the ordination of God does nothing unduly, but as an ordination of sin, such as they attribute to the Deity, is not in harmony with the character of God, it is not wonderful that, from it, something undue should he attributed to God.

SEVENTEENTH PROPOSITION OF ARMINIUS

In reference to the third question, it is not in controversy whether God, foreseeing the sins of some, prepared for their deserved punishment, but whether, foreseeing the sins of those thus passed by and left in their natural state, He prepared punishment for them from eternity. The latter does not seem to me to be true.

REPLY OF JUNIUS TO THE SEVENTEENTH PROPOSITION

They, for whose sins God prepared merited punishment, are not the elect: therefore they are passed by and reprobate. It has been before demonstrated that they were passed by, in a mode in harmony with the wisdom of God.

REPLY OF ARMINIUS TO THE ANSWER TO
THE SEVENTEENTH PROPOSITION

It is not true, universally, that "they, for whose sins God prepared merited punishment, are not the elect," for He prepared merited punishment even for the sins of the elect, both by laying them upon Christ, that he might expiate them, and by sometimes inflicting the consequences of sin even on the elect, that they may learn how they have deserved to be treated forever, and how they would have been treated, if God had not determined to have mercy upon them. It is true, however, if it is understood with reference to the preparation of punishment by the decree now under discussion. For by that decree, the merited punishment of sin, is not only prepared, but it is, in fact and forever, inflicted on sinners. It is indeed true, rather, that, by the decree, punishment is prepared for sin, not as merited and due, but as not remitted by mercy, which forgives the debt to some. This distinction is required by the order of election, and of predamnation, its opposite. For election remits merited and due punishment. Its opposite, preordination, does not remit merited and due punishment. This then is inflicted, by damnation, which is the execution of predamnation, not as merited or due, but as not remitted.

Again, a distinction is to be made between the preparation of punishment, made by the just Providence of God, and that made by the decree of divine predamnation, which is the opposite of election. For the former is avoided by all who repent and believe in the Son. The latter is avoided by none, since the decree of predamnation is irrevocable and peremptory. The question is not whether God prepared punishment for those passed by in a mode in harmony with the wisdom of God"; for who denies that, if any are passed by, they are passed by in a manner in harmony with the wisdom of God? But the question is, whether God, foreseeing the sin of those, so passed by and left in their natural state, as has been explained, prepared punishment for them by the decree of predamnation, which does not seem very probable to me. I have presented arguments for this opinion, which we will now consider.

EIGHTEENTH PROPOSITION
OF ARMINIUS

In the first place, from what has been already stated: since punishment can not be justly prepared, of the mere act of the divine pleasure, for those passed by on account of foreseen sin, which must be committed, as the necessary result of that preterition and reelection in a state of nature. Secondly, the punishment ordained for them is spiritual, but spiritual punishment can not be ordained for those falling from their original state, if spiritual reward, on the contrary, is not prepared for those who should remain in their original state. But a reward of this kind was not prepared for such, since they could, by mere natural power, remain in their original state, and spiritual happiness could not be acquired by them.

ANSWER OF JUNIUS TO THE
EIGHTEENTH PROPOSITION

In reference to the first argument, I deny:

1. that Adam was, to speak in general terms, passed by and left in a state of nature by God, but, according to the mode of nature, he was left to himself only in reference to a particular and natural act, which was in the power of mere nature, and that he was carefully forewarned by God, and that he received information from God, as by compact.

2. It is denied that sin was committed by him, of necessity, in view of that preterition. For, if it was necessarily committed, it would have been a habit, or passive quality in the nature of man; but it pertained to capability, his will being free, and borne contingently in this or that direction. It was not then perpetrated necessarily; therefore he committed it contingently, (as the Scripture and the agreement of the church have always declared,) according to the free natural power, which is that of the will. The wise man rightly says in Eccl. vii. 27, "Lo, this only have I found, that God hath made man upright; but they have sought out many inventions."

Concerning the second argument, I remark that the word "also" should be added to your proposition in this manner: "the punishment ordained for them is also spiritual." For punishment of both kinds, of the body and of the spirit, was ordained for them, by the testimony of Scripture. Your assumption is denied, which states that a reward of this kind was not prepared for them, in general, if they had remained in their original state. For it is entirely evident that it was proposed to them in the covenant of nature, and in the ordination to grace, if they should remain in their original state, as was also signified in the symbol of the tree of life, and declared in the denunciation of death. For what is death but the privation of this and of the future life? What privation could there be, if man did not possess life, on the one hand by nature, and on the other by the ordination of grace to be consummated after the natural course of this life. But to prove this statement, you add, "for they could, by mere natural power, remain in their original state." This also is denied. They could do so only in natural things, but by no means in things pertaining to grace, as we have already frequently showed. The whole argumentation, then, is erroneous. "But," you will say, "my reasoning is valid on the hypothesis of Aquinas, who held that man, in the matter of election, was considered in his natural condition." I reply in this manner:

1. This does not affect us, who affirm that God, in election, has reference to man in general.

2. Though Aquinas uses that form of expression, yet it must be correctly understood, since there may be ambiguity here, for the relation of election: concerning which we have already presented the sentiment of Aquinas, in my answer to the sixth proposition, is one thing, and that of the condition of Adam, when he fell into sin, is another. It is evident from all his writings, that it did not, even in a dream, enter into his mind, that Adam was then merely in his natural condition. Could he, indeed, entertain such an idea, who every where openly avows that man was made in a state of supernatural grace, and expressly asserts this in his controversy with the Master of Sentences. Therefore the hypothesis is false, and is erroneously ascribed to Aquinas. If that is false, the argument also is without force. Man also could not, by natural power alone, continue in his primitive condition and state, (for I prefer these expressions to "origin," as more clearly conveying the idea,) or by its means acquire spiritual happiness. For that happiness is not the reward of labourers, but the inheritance of children in Christ, bestowed by grace, not obtained by labour.

REPLY OF ARMINIUS TO THE ANSWER TO THE EIGHTEENTH PROPOSITION

My first argument rests on the hypothesis of the definition by which preterition is described in your Theses. That definition is in these words: "Preterition is the act of the divine pleasure, by which God, from eternity, determined to leave certain of His creatures in their natural state, and not to communicate to them the supernatural grace by which their pure nature might be strengthened, or their corrupt nature might be restored, to the declaration of the freedom of His own goodness, but a natural state is that in which there can be nothing supernatural or divine," according to Thesis 10, of the same disputation. For those, who are passed by, are left in the same natural state and condition in the same manner, as that from which they, who are predestinated, are raised up. Being left in such a natural state, "in which there can be nothing supernatural or divine," they can not keep the law, which is not to be kept without supernatural grace. Hence punishment can not be justly prepared for them on account of sin, committed against a law which can not be kept by them. Therefore your first negation seems to me to be irrelevant.

We are not treating of the mode in which Adam was left to his own nature and given up to his own direction. The reelection of Adam to himself belongs, not to the decree of predestination, but to that providence, in which God, without the distinction of predestinate and reprobate, had reference to man, newly created, and this, indeed, of necessity, according to the hypothesis that He purposed to create man free. But we are treating of his reelection in a natural state, which belongs to the decree of preterition. If you should say that they who are passed by are considered by the Deity in Adam, as partakers of the same things, which Adam had in his primitive state, I answer that, thus considered, they were not left in that natural state, which can effect nothing supernatural or divine. Hence the hypothesis will be false, which seems only to rest on the definition of preterition given in your Theses.

To your second negation, I reply—from the reelection in a natural state "which can effect nothing supernatural or divine," (that is, neither of itself, as I admit, nor by any thing superinfused, so that nothing supernatural may be added to it, according to the hypothesis of your definition,) sin must of necessity be committed by the person left, and it can not be avoided without supernatural grace. The will is, indeed, free, but not in respect to that act which can not be performed or omitted without supernatural grace, just as it is not free in respect to that act by which it wills the good of the universe and of itself. The reason of this is—there is in man a passive quality, inclining him to that forbidden act, and impelling the will to a consent to and commission of that act; and necessarily impelling it, unless the will is endued with some power to resist that motion, which power is supernatural grace, according to our hypothesis. To explain this subject more fully, I add a few thoughts. The negative act of the Deity, which preceded the sin of man, pertained either to providence, or to reprobation, or to preterition, as distinct from providence. In the first place, it did not pertain to reprobation.

1. Because the act of reprobation has reference to some men, not to all, for not all are reprobates.

2. If sin exists from the act of reprobation, or not without it, then only some men commit sin, and the rest do not commit it, that is, they sin, to whom God had reference in the negative act of preterition, and they do not sin, to whom He had no such reference. But all have sinned. It is not then from that act.

3. If sin exists from the negative act of reprobation, it then follows that Adam and all men in him are reprobates, for Adam, and, in him, all men have sinned. This consequence is false, therefore the antecedent is also false.

4. By converse reasoning, if the sin of man resulted from the negative act of preterition, then, from the affirmative act of predestination, which exists at the same moment with the opposite of the act previously referred to, for neither of these acts exists without the other, and they are oppositely spoken of, results the perseverance of man in goodness, at least in reference to this single act. But no man perseveres in the good in which he was created, according to the affirmative act of predestination. Therefore, also, the sin of man is not from the negative act of reprobation or preterition.

5. To those, to whom God once, by the negative act of reprobation, denies efficacious aid, He finally denies efficacious aid, otherwise the reprobate are not reprobate. He does not deny, finally, to all men, efficacious aid, for then all would be reprobate. Therefore, that act, by which efficacious aid was denied once to all men, is not an act of reprobation. But some negative act of the Deity preceded the sin of man, for otherwise man would not have sinned. Therefore that is an act of providence.

Here, however, two things are to be considered. First, sin did not exist of necessity from that negative act, but, in view of that act, it might or might not be committed. For providence ordained man to eternal life, and conferred means sufficient and necessary for the attainment of that life, leaving, (as was suitable at the beginning), to the choice of man, the free use of those means, and refusing to impede that liberty, lest it might rescind that which it had established, as Tertullian happily remarks in the passage quoted by you, (Advers. Marcion, lib. 2, resp. 14). From which act of God, refusing to prevent sin efficaciously, (the opposite of which, the affirmative act of determining to prevent it efficaciously, would be inconsistent with the first institution of the human race, and the affirmative act of determining to prevent a sin, finally, would have pertained to predestination,) results the fact that man could commit sin, not that he did commit it, but because God, in His infinite wisdom, saw, from eternity, that man would fall at a certain time, that fall occurred infallibly, only in respect to His prescience, not in respect to any act of the divine will, either affirmative or negative. Whatever happens infallibly in respect to an act of the divine will, the same also happens necessarily, not only by the necessity of consequence but by that, also, of the consequent. It may be proper, here, to mark the difference between what is done infallibly and what is done necessarily. The former depends on the infinity of the knowledge of God, the latter on the act of His will. The former has respect only to the knowledge of God, to which it pertains to know, infallibly and with certainty, contingent things; the latter belong to the existence of the thing itself, the necessity for which resulted from the will of God.

In the second place, the providence of God does not discriminate definitely between the classes of men, as elect and reprobate. Therefore, that negative act of God has reference to all men in general, and universally, without any distinction of elect and reprobate. From these thing, I conclude, since that negative act, which preceded sin, was not of reprobation or preterition, but of providence as distinct from the former, it follows that God, in the act of preterition, had not reference to men apart from sin or considered as not yet sinners. For no negative act of preterition preceded, either in order or in time, this negative act of providence. Likewise no other act of preterition intervened between this act of providence and sin. If any act of preterition intervened, an act of predestination also intervened. There was no intervention of the latter, and, therefore, there was not of the former. This act of predestination would be the preservation of some in goodness, and their deliverance from possible sin. No one of mankind has been preserved in goodness and delivered from possible sin, for all have sinned. It was not, however, necessary to prove here that man sinned, not necessarily but freely, for that point is not in controversy, but it was to be shown, that, if preterition is supposed, man, nevertheless, sinned freely, and not of necessity.

My second argument is also based on a hypothesis, which, in my opinion, whether incorrect or correct your wisdom will decide, I have taken from your Theses. The hypothesis consists of two parts; -- first, supernatural happiness cannot be acquired by the powers of nature alone; secondly, the law, given to Adam, could be observed by the powers of nature alone. The first part is true. The second is contained in your Theses. Man is left in a state of nature, which can effect nothing supernatural or divine. But yet he was able to keep the law, otherwise God is unjust, who imposes a law, which cannot be obeyed by the creature. Hence I concluded that spiritual punishment ought not to be inflicted for the transgression of that law, to the observance of which spiritual or supernatural reward is not promised. But supernatural reward is not promised to the observance of a law, which can be obeyed by the powers of nature alone, otherwise nature could acquire that which is supernatural, therefore, spiritual punishment ought not to be the penalty of the violation of the same law. Further, the law, imposed on Adam, could be performed by the powers of nature alone, according to your view, as I have understood it; therefore, spiritual punishment ought not to be its penalty. But its penalty is spiritual; therefore it is unjust.

I will not, at this time, inquire whether such may or may not be the consequence of your Theses, since you now say distinctly that a supernatural reward was prepared for our first parents, if they should remain in their original integrity. Therefore, I claim that my reasoning is valid, though the hypothesis, on which it was based, is removed. From your own statement, indeed, I deduced an inference in favour of my sentiment. That which was prepared for all men on condition of the obedience, which they could render the gift of divine grace, bestowed or to be bestowed on them, could not be denied to some men by the sure and definite decree of God, except on account of their foreseen disobedience. Eternal life was prepared for all men, on condition of that obedience which they could render. Therefore, eternal life could not be denied to some men, by the sure and definite decree of God, that is, by preterition, except on account of their foreseen disobedience. Therefore, also, men are considered by God, in the act of preterition, as sinners; they are not, then, considered in general.

I do not touch the sentiment of Aquinas, except as it is explained in your Theses. I might, however, require him to prove that God passed by man, considered in a state of integrity, in which he had, not only natural, but also supernatural endowments. I grant that supernatural happiness is that inheritance of the children of God, but it would have been given to those, who should remain in their primitive integrity, though in a different mode from that in which it is bestowed on believers in Christ. It would have been given to the former "of the works of the law;" it is given to the latter "of faith;" to the former the reward would have been reckoned not "of grace, but of debt;" (Rom. iv. 4), to the latter, as believers, it is "reckoned of grace;" to the former, it would have been given by "the righteousness which is of the law," which saith "that the man which doeth these things shall live by them," to the latter by "the righteousness of faith, which speaketh in this wise, if thou shalt believe in thine heart," &c. (Rom. x. 6, 9.) We have already spoken in reference to that primitive state, and to perseverance in it.

NINETEENTH PROPOSITION OF ARMINIUS

In addition to all that has been said, it is proper to consider that, since predestination, preterition, and reprobation, really produce no effect on the predestinate, passed by, and reprobate, the subject of the actual execution, and that of the decree in the divine mind, are entirely the same and are considered in the same mode. Hence, since God does not, in fact, communicate grace, except to one who is a sinner, that is, the grace prepared in predestination, since he does not, in fact, pass by, does not condemn or punish any one, unless he is a sinner, it seems to follow that God did not decree to impart grace, to pass by, to reprobate any one, unless considered as a sinner.

ANSWER OF JUNIUS TO THE
NINETEENTH PROPOSITION

Before I treat of the subject itself, it is necessary to refer to the ambiguity which was alluded to, in my answer to the second proposition. In the whole of your letter, to reprobate is to damn, and reprobation is damnation. But in my usage, reprobation, and preterition or non-election are the same. Hence that the subject may be made more plain, you will not complain if I should substitute the word damnation for the word reprobation. You say that "predestination, preterition and damnation, have no reference to action in the predestinate etc.," that is, that the predestinate or elect, the passed by, and the damned, are elected, passed by, and damned by God without any consideration of quality which exists in the individual. I think, indeed, that the relation of these things is different according to the Scriptures. Election and non-election have reference to nothing in the elect and the passed-by: but damnation supposes sin, in view of which the sinner is damned, otherwise the entire work of predestination, is limited to eternity.

I readily acknowledge that, in these matters, the subject must be considered in the same light whether existing in fact or only in the mind. For the elect is elected, and the reprobate is passed by as a man; he is damned as a sinner. He, who is, in fact, elected or passed by as a man, is so elected or passed by in the mind of the Deity. He who is damned as a sinner, is so predamned. Else, the internal and the external acts of God would be at variance, which is never to be admitted. This being fully understood, you see, my brother, that whatever things you construct on this foundation, they can, in no way, be consistent.

You say that" God does not, in fact, communicate the grace prepared in predestination," that is, saving grace, "except to one who is a sinner, he does not, in fact, pass by any one, unless he is a sinner." If you affirm this of saving grace, in an absolute and universal sense, it is shown to be false by the salvation of the elect angels, and the preterition of others. Did God elect and pass by the angels as sinners. Origen may hold this view. We hold an entirely different one. If, however, you say that you are speaking of grace towards man, then it follows, from this statement, that the first man, in that primitive integrity, had not the communication of saving grace. This, indeed, I think that you will not affirm. Therefore, this grace is communicated to man as man, though not as a sinner, and not to man only, but to the angels. If you say that it was communicated to man, in his present sinful character, we do not deny it. Indeed, we believe that it is now communicated to none except he is a sinner, since no one of the human race is not a sinner. We readily concede to you that no one is damned or punished unless he is a sinner. Thus, a part of your conclusion is denied, namely, that which has reference to election, and a part is conceded, namely, that which refers to damnation.

REPLY OF ARMINIUS TO THE ANSWER TO
THE NINETEENTH PROPOSITION

I used the word reprobation in the sense in which you use it, as I have several times already stated and proved. I do not, however, object to your substitution, in its place, of the word damnation. But you do not take my argument in its true sense. I do not, indeed, consider that the predestinate, the passed-by, the damned are elected, passed by, damned by the Deity without reference to any quality, which may exist in them. Is it possible that I should do so, when I, always and every where, endeavour to prove that sin is a condition or quality requisite in the object of the divine decree, My real meaning is this. Predestination, preterition, pre-damnation, as acts remaining in the agent, or as internal acts, produce no feeling in an external object, but the execution of those internal acts, which consists in external acts, passes over to external things, and produces an effect on them, as is explained by Thomas Aquinas (Summa prima quaest. 23, artic. 2), from which passage it is apparent that, in the scholastic phraseology, it is one thing to produce an effect and another thing to suppose or have reference to something in the elect, the passed-by, the damned. But if those internal acts have no effect on the object, then it follows that the object is the same in every respect, and is considered in the same mode by the Deity, both in the act of decree and in that of execution. Hence, I conclude that, since it is certain that God, in the external act, communicates the grace, which is prepared in predestination, to man, only as a sinner, and, in the external act, passes by man only as a sinner, and, in the external act, damns man only as a sinner, it follows that God, in the internal act, prepared grace only for a sinner, determined to pass by only the sinner, and predamned only the sinner, that is, in the internal acts of predestination, preterition, and predamnation, had reference only to man considered as a sinner. That God communicates the grace, prepared in predestination, only to the sinner, passes by only the sinner, (concerning damnation, we agree), is, I think, most evident. Your two-fold argument does not at all affect this truth. To the first part, I make the answer, which your foresight has anticipated that we are discussing, not the predestination and reprobation of angels, but those of men, the term grace being restricted to that which was prepared for man, in the act of predestination.

To the second part of your argument, which charges my proposition with absurdity, I reply, that there is an ambiguity in the phrase, saving grace. It may refer to that grace which is sufficient and able to confer salvation, or to that which is efficacious, and does, certainly, and in fact, bestow salvation. Again, it may refer to the grace, which God bestowed on man in his primitive state, or to that which is now bestowed in his sinful state, that, being made free in Christ, he may, through Him, obtain life from the dead. My proposition concedes that man possessed the former in his state of innocence, and so avoids absurdity. It also denies that he possessed the latter before the fall, and, at the same time, denies that this is absurd. This latter grace, and not the former, was prepared in predestination, and so my argument remains firm and immovable.

For these reasons, Reverend Sir, I can not yet persuade myself that man, considered as a sinner by the Deity, is not the adequate object of predestination, preterition and predamnation.

TWENTIETH PROPOSITION OF ARMINIUS

It does not seem to me that this sentiment is established by the argument from the necessary declaration of the freedom of grace and of the divine goodness. For though I might concede that the declaration of that freedom was necessary, yet I might say that it is declared in the very creation and arrangement of things, and moreover that it could, and indeed ought to be declared in another way.

The argument, from the necessary declaration of the divine justice, has no more weight with me, both because justice in God, as His nature, is equally directed towards the whole object and all its parts, unless, there be some diversity, dependent on His will, and because God has declared Himself, in Scripture, to be of such character that it was not necessary for Him to punish the sinner, according to strict legal justice, in order to the manifestation of His justice, but that He knew another, more noble, way for the revelation of His own justice. Nor, does the argument, deduced from the nature of providence, seem to have weight, since it pertains to providence to permit that some should fail of the highest good, and of a supernatural end, and that permission, understood in harmony with this sentiment, is to be attributed not so much to a sustaining and governing, as to a creating providence.

ANSWER OF JUNIUS TO THE TWENTIETH PROPOSITION

After the discussion of election and reprobation, we come in this place to the consideration of the design, according to which, the good or evil of an action is often to be decided. But here a three-fold design is presented; having reference to the divine freedom in grace and goodness, and to the divine justice, and to the divine providence. Other attributes, might indeed, be considered, but from these a decision may be made concerning others. In reference to the first design, you present two arguments.

1. You affirm that this freedom "is declared in the very creation and arrangement of things." You would infer then, that it was unnecessary that it should be also declared in this way. This inference is denial. For it was not sufficient that such declaration should be made in the creation and arrangement of things, if it should not be declared also in their progress and result. Nor, indeed, if it has been sufficiently declared in our present nature and life, does it follow, of consequence, that there is no necessity of any declaration in the life of the future world. For, on the contrary, if God should have declared His liberty in matters of an inferior nature only, and not in those, which are superior and pertain to the future world, it would seem that he, through want either of knowledge or of power, had omitted the more worthy declaration of His own freedom. For the nobler manifestation of that freedom is made in things of a nobler nature; and that good is better and more noble, the consequences of which are better and more noble. Who can believe that God lacked either knowledge, power, or will in this matter.

2. You affirm that this liberty "could, and indeed ought to be, declared in another way." I grant it. It could and ought to be, declared in this, and in other modes, as has been done by the Deity. But if you use the phrase another, in an exclusive sense, as having reference to some particular mode and not to this one, it is denied, and, in the preceding argument, is sufficiently confuted.

The second design is, in like manner, opposed by two arguments. Your first argument, contained in these words, "because justice in God, as His nature is equally directed, &c.," is, in the very same sentence, refuted by the addition of the words, "unless there be some diversity, dependent on His will." For justice in us is regarded in two aspects, as a habit and as an act proceeding from that habit, and diffusing itself first inwardly and then outwardly. In God, it is also, considered in two modes, as nature, and as an act of nature through the will, flowing from the nature and according to the nature of God. In the former mode, it is the very essence of God; in the latter, it is the work of that essence. Of theformer, you rightly affirm that "justice in God as nature is equally directed towards the whole object, and all its parts." The phrase "as nature" is susceptible of a two-fold reference, as equivalent either to w[sper fusiv and imply a similarity of operation to that of nature, (in which sense I understand you to use it), or to kaqw<v fusiv and implying that the nature of God or His essence is justice itself. For since the essence of God is entirely simple, justice, nature, essence, and His other attributes are, in fact, one, though a distinction is made in them in our usage. In reference to the latter mode of justices the expression "unless there be some diversity dependent on His will," is subjoined most suitably, and yet with some ambiguity. For in the justice of God, as His nature, there is never diversity, not even as the result of His will. What? Can a change in His essence, in His own nature result from the will of God, whose attribute, I do not say in all respects, yet absolutely, and pertaining to Him alone, and always, is immutability? But that justice, which is the work of the divine essence, emanating from that will, whether outwardly or inwardly, may indeed be diversified in an infinite number of modes, according to His wisdom and will.

Your second argument, to speak in a few words and with directness, is faulty in two respects. First, though your statement is true, if properly understood, namely, "God has declared Himself, in Scripture, to be of such character that it is not necessary for Him to punish the sinner, according to strict legal justice, in order to the manifestation of His justice," since His justice, in all respects and infinitely, surpasses legal justice, as, in the nature of things, the reality exceeds the type, and the substance exceeds the shade. Yet it, by no means, follows from this, that God must not so punish the sinner for the manifestation of His own justice, or that it is from legal justice that He so punishes him. But, on the contrary, it follows rather that God must so punish the sinner for the manifestation of His own justice, and that the fact of such punishment is dependent on His justice, which exceeds and in a most excellent, that is, in a divine method, surpasses legal justice, and which, in His word, to us, according to our measure, takes the form of legal justice, as the shadow of that most excellent justice. There is no element of justice, expressed to us in the law, which does not exist in the justice of God, and flow from it in a most excellent manner. In the law, He has both expressed the justice due from us, and shadowed forth His own. Consider only this, that God is justice in an absolute sense, or (if you prefer), that He is the absolute principle and cause of all justice, as of all good, you at once destroy your own argument. For if He is, absolutely, justice, or the absolute principle and cause of all justice, then He is the principle of this justice also, and the cause and effector of it, as not only mediately shadowed forth in the law, but also, immediately effected by His own work. For whence is that legal justice, if not from God, expressing by His own infinitely wise will, what He is, and what He does, as it is? Besides, if God is, absolutely, justice, and the principle of justice, he punishes not according to the justice of the law, but according to His own justice, which the law adumbrates to human comprehension, and which He cannot but set forth in His creatures, both in the present and the future worlds as he has declared in His word. I am still less satisfied with your second statement, in which you affirm that "He knew another, more noble way for the revelation of His own justice." God certainly knew and thoroughly understood both that and the other, and every possible way, according to the divine mode. But it is necessary, my brother, that you should, in this case, consider that God always contemplates all things, according to their individual relations, and according to their relations to the universe, over which He presides. If it should be denied that God, in respect to its individual relation, knew another more noble way for the manifestation of His justice, how, I pray, would you prove it? Would it not, indeed, on the contrary, seem, to the pious to be altogether more probable, since God is infinitely wise, that He most wisely adopted the noblest way to manifest (which is the work of the divine wisdom) His justice, to His own glory, to our instruction, and to the perfection of the universe, Let it, however, be conceded that God, since He has all knowledge, knew another more noble way for accomplishing this thing, yet I deny, that with reference to the relations of the universe there existed another more noble way, in which God could obtain this object, since it would have been better that He should use that other nobler way. For it concerns the wisdom of God, that every variety of way should be adopted in manifesting His justice, and should be set forth before the eyes of all in the universe. For example, let the more noble way of displaying that wonderful justice of God, be that which has punished and shall forever punish the wicked angels. Should I grant this, do you not see that it would pertain to divine wisdom to vary in this case also, the mode of the divine justice? This is sufficient in reference to the second argument. The third design, which has reference to the Providence of God, is excluded in your argument, in a peculiar manner, by limitation, as it is called, "since that permission is to be attributed, not so much to a sustaining and governing, as to a creating Providence." By your permission, this whole limitation is denied. It is indeed destroyed by the very definition of the terms, without any argument on my part. Describe the course of the divine Providence. Its principle, or first step, is called creation, that is the production of existence from non-existence. Its middle step is government, containing ordination and sustainment. Its third or last step is consummation. Consider, now, to which part permission shall be ascribed. Creation is an act of God alone, the glory of which He, by no means, communicates to the creature, for it is created, not creating. In the act of creation, existence is bestowed on some thing, that it may become what it is not, essentially, in nature. By creation, then, it is given to man that he should be a man, and that there should be in him whatever belongs to him as a creature. Thus freedom of the will was bestowed on man.

What is permission? Not an act of God, but a cessation of action. It does not bestow existence, but gives to that, which already exists, power over its own life. Nature itself affirms that creation differs in kind and characteristic from permission. Creation is not a part of ordination, but it is the principle, point, first term. Permission belongs to ordination, consequent on that principle. It does not then pertain to creation.

It is true, that freedom of the will in man pertains to creation, but as an essential faculty, not as developed in action; which action, without doubt, after the creation of the faculty and its endowment with its qualities, depends on the divine ordination, and that ordination on providence. I do not, indeed, see how that permission could be bestowed on our first parents at their creation, which, in our case, must be referred to ordination. It is necessary that there should be correspondence in both cases. But, finally, though I should concede that permission pertains to creation, this also, even on your authority, would be the work of providence, since you say that providence is creating, as well as sustaining and governing. Permission, then, by your consent, belongs to providence. It belong, according to our argument, and, as I hope, with your assent, to governing or ordaining providence. Therefore, whatever may be said concerning the relation of providence, permission, by necessary consequence, pertains to it.

REPLY OF ARMINIUS TO THE ANSWER OF JUNIUS TO THE TWENTIETH PROPOSITION

I have now discussed the theory, which considers man as the object of predestination and preterition, either in a purely natural state, or also with some supernatural endowments, yet apart from the consideration of sin as a condition requisite in the object. And I think that I have proved that man is considered by God, in His decree, not otherwise than as a sinner. I proceed to answer the three arguments usually urged in favour of this theory; and I only show that a theory, like this, is not sustained by those arguments. It seems, therefore, to be requisite, not only that my reasoning should be refuted, but also that the force of those arguments should be established. The latter has been entirely neglected by you. We will now consider in what respects my reasoning has been invalidated.

The first argument from the necessary declaration of the freedom of grace and of the divine goodness, I answer, first, by simply denying that such necessity exists, and then, if that necessity is conceded, by denying that mode, which is preterition, such as is described in the theory which I oppose. This denial is confirmed, partly from the fact that God has declared the liberty of His own goodness in the creation and various circumstances of material things; partly because he could, and indeed must declare that same liberty also in a mode other than that of preterition. For the better understanding of these things, I will make a few illustrative remarks.

First, since no external act of the Deity is absolutely necessary, no declaration of the freedom of the divine goodness is absolutely necessary. For God is happy by the internal and essential knowledge of Himself, and is glorious in Himself. Secondly, since, nevertheless, it seemed good to the Deity, to communicate, by the free act of His will, His own good, to the declaration of His goodness, it was suitable that there should be a declaration, not only of His goodness, but also of the freedom of that goodness, that it might be manifest that God communicated good to His creatures, not by any necessity, but of His mere will; not to the increase of His own good, which was already perfect, but to the perfection of Nothing, and of the beings created out of it, according to the mode of communication, adopted by the internal act of His will, both to the single parts of Nothing, and to the individual creatures. The good which God purposed to communicate, is two-fold in respect to the subject, on which He determined to bestow it, natural and supernatural. In the communication of both, it was just that He should declare, not only His goodness, but also the liberty of His goodness and grace. In the communication of natural good, He declared the freedom of His goodness in the creation and various condition of material things. For when He communicated to that part of original nature, which is purely nothing or chaos, this entity and form, He declared His own liberty to communicate an entity and form which should be different.

In the communication of supernatural good, He manifested the same freedom, when He made a great part of His creatures without a capacity to receive supernatural blessings, and made angels and men alone capable of those blessings, and actually partakers of some of them. In respect to those blessings of which He made all the angels, and the first human beings, and in them all, conditionally, who should be born from them, partakers, there is no place for preterition of this kind, as this pertains to a portion either of angels or of men, but only for that preterition, which has reference to other creatures, who were passed by, in the communication of supernatural blessings. But in the communication of blessings, of which he made angels and men not actual partakers, but only capable, the freedom of the divine goodness and grace was also to be declared, that it might, in this way, be evident both that those things, which they all received, were bestowed, and that those things, of which they were made capable, would be bestowed on angels and men, not according to the excellence of their nature and of merit, but of grace.

I thus acknowledge and concede this, but I deny that the mode of declaring the divine freedom in the communication of these blessings is the preterition now under discussion; and I deny that this preterition was used by the Deity for the display of that freedom, and this was my meaning when I said "it could and indeed ought to be declared in another way," by the word "another," excluding that mode which is contained in that preterition.

If it should be asked in what other way the freedom of the divine goodness "could and indeed ought to be declared," I reply that, in reference to men, (I have always excluded angels from the discussion), it was possible to declare that freedom, if God should prescribe the condition on which He would communicate good; that it was declared by his eternal decree, when he prescribed to man the condition on which he might obtain eternal life, and those gifts of grace, which, in addition to what had already been bestowed, might be necessary for its attainment. I reply also that it ought to be declared in some other way, if declared at all, since it ought not to be in that way, for that one is in accordance neither with the wisdom of God nor with His justice, since, by it, to creatures, capable of certain blessing from the divine goodness and grace, the same blessings are, absolutely and apart from any condition, denied. Therefore, it ought to be declared in some other way, and, indeed, in that way of which I have spoken. For God can not decree not to give to any creature that of which it is capable and for which it was made, except on condition that it has made itself incapable of receiving the blessings of which it was made capable by its Creator. But whatever may be true in reference to this, you should have shown in what manner the argument from the freedom of the divine goodness and grace proves the preterition or non-election which is described in your Theses. The second argument is from the necessary display of the divine justice. I impugn it in two ways. That it may be seen how my reasoning avails against this argument, it is to be considered that I design to assail it, in the form in which it is presented in your Theses. These are your words: - - (Thesis 17.) "The preparation of punishment is an act of the divine good-pleasure, in which God purposed, from eternity, for the display of His grace, to punish His creatures, who should not continue in their original integrity," &c., and (Thesis 18) "God prepares punishment for His creatures, who, sin contrary to His law, to be reprobated on account of sin, according to the necessity of His justice." Since reprobation and preparation of punishment, which are here used as synonymous, are in these words said to have originated in "the necessity of the divine justice," I wished to confute it, as, for two reasons, not in harmony with the truth. The first reason is this; -- If God prepares punishment for sinners from the necessity of His own justice, then He prepares punishment for all sinners universally, that is, by the decree of predamnation. But the consequent is false; therefore, the antecedent is also false. The reasoning is certainly valid. For, since justice in God is considered as a natural attribute, it acts in the same manner towards its whole object and all its parts. Sinners are the objects of justice in this case. Therefore, it acts equally on all sinners, that is, it prepares punishment for all. This is plainly signified in the word "necessity" in connection with "justice." For, if He necessarily prepares punishment for sinners or for those about to sin, He prepares it for all without distinction, and that word added to "justice" indicates that justice is to be considered as a natural attribute in God, and it can not, for the reason already mentioned, superintend predamnation. I added, however, the qualifying remark "unless there be some diversity dependent on His will," my meaning, in which, was that it is dependent on the will of God whether that attribute should act in an absolute manner or respectively, in reference to all sinners, or in reference only to some. In this way I refute not that which I previously said, but that necessity, which is considered as laid on predamning justice. For if, by the will of God directing that justice, it occurs that God prepares punishment for some sinners, and does not prepare it for others but remits it to them, then that predamnation, or reprobation (as it is here called), was decreed by God, not by the necessity of His justice.

Let me more briefly state this idea. Justice in God tends to the punishment of sin, as mercy or grace tends to its remission, without any distinction in those who have committed sin. If justice should administer its own act, all sinners would be punished; if mercy should administer its own act, all sinners would be pardoned. These acts could not be performed at the same time, and, in this case, the one would oppose the manifestation of the other, which could not with propriety occur.

Therefore, the wisdom, appointed over them, for the direction of both, judged that its own sphere of action should be assigned to each. In accordance with this decision, the will of God directs His justice in such manner, that there can be opportunity for mercy, and His mercy, that the honour of His justice may also, in the mean time, be maintained. But it can not, in my opinion, be affirmed that what is decreed by the divine will, was done by the necessity either of justice or of mercy.

The second reason is this. If God knew a more noble way for the manifestation of His justice than that by which, according to the law, punishment was prepared for those who should sin, then the display of justice, according to the law, was not necessary. But the former is true, therefore the latter is also true. The reasoning is conclusive. If two ways were open for the illustration of the divine justice, then it is not absolutely necessary that God should make use of one to the complete conclusion of the other. The justice of God may be displayed in the exaction of punishment from the individuals who have sinned; the same justice may also be displayed in the exaction of the same punishment from him, who has, according to the will of God, offered himself as the pledge and surety for those sinners. He is "the Lamb of God, which taketh away the sin of the world," (John i. 29.) "He hath made him to be sin for us, who knew no sin," (2 Cor. v. 21). This is that "other more noble and more excellent way." In it there is a more vivid display of the Divine execration of sin, than in that, which demands punishment from the sinners, in their own persons, both from the fact that, in the latter case, the infliction of punishment could be ascribed, by His enemies, to the vindictive passion of the Deity, and not to His justice, alone, which would be impossible in the former case, since the punishment is inflicted on one, who has not personally sinned, and from the fact that in this way, the inflexible rigor of divine justice is displayed, which could not grant, even to the intercession of His Son, the pardon of sin: unless punishment had been inflicted; according to which, indeed, that Son could not even intercede, if his own blood had not been shed, and atonement had not, by it, been made for sin. I conclude, then, that the display of justice, according to the law, was not necessary, and consequently that punishment was not, from any necessity of the divine justice, prepared for these, who should sin, since God was free to impose on His own Son, to be received and suffered, their due punishment, removed from the individual sinners.

That, which you adduce in opposition to these ideas, does not seem to me to be valid. For God, of His own justice, punishes either sinners or their surety. The former mode of its manifestation is according to the law, the latter mode transcends, the former is revealed to us in the gospel. It may be said, however, that both modes were necessary. I deny it. The latter, depended on the mere good pleasure of God; the former could be changed to it. Otherwise it would have been necessary, for "without shedding of blood there is no remission." (Heb. ix. 22.) These things which are said concerning the justice of God, as exceeding the justice of the law, are not to the purpose; for it was not my meaning that the justice, which actuates God in the punishment of sin, and by which He punishes sin, is legal justice, but that He should punish it according to the letter of the law, "In the day that thou eatest thereof, thou shalt surely die," (Gen. ii. 17) and "Cursed is every one that continueth not in all things which are written in the book of the law to do them." (Gal. iii. 10.) It should also have been shown in this place how this argument, from the necessary display of the divine justice, proves this preparation of punishment.

The third argument, deduced from the nature of providence, is of this nature, in the view of Thomas Aquinas, (summa prima, quæs. 23, act 3.) "To permit some to come short of the highest good, pertains to the providence of God;"—"But to reprobate is to permit some to come short of the highest good; -- Therefore, the reprobation of some pertains to the providence of God." I affirmed that this argument possessed no weight in favour of the theory, which I now oppose; against that which makes sin a requisite condition in the object of reprobation or preterition. I proved it from the fact that permission, understood in accordance with that theory, is to be attributed not so much to sustaining and governing providence, as to creating providence. I will first explain my meaning, and then show the force of that argument.

I make three sets of providence—creation, sustainment, or preservation of the creature, and its government, and according to those acts, I say that providence is creating, sustaining and governing, and I attribute to each of these modes its own particular acts, which are appropriate to each of them. I also say that there are some acts, which so pertain to one of these, as, at the same time, to depend on another preceding act, so that they may not be entirely under the control of that providence from which they proceed, but may be limited and determined by the act of some preceding providence. These acts, being mixed in their nature, can be referred both to this and to that providence, to one as immediately flowing from it, to the other as determined by it, and necessarily dependent on its previous set. Such acts seem to be attributed not so justly to that providence from which they immediately flow, as to that, which prescribed their form and mode, to which mode and form that immediate providence was bound, and in reference to those acts was a servant to the other as principal. I now apply these thoughts. The permission, by which God left man to his own counsels, pertains immediately to governing providence, but it is government uncontrolled, determined by a preceding act of creation. For it could not choose between leaving and not leaving man to himself, for then, that, which had been already divinely instituted, would be rescinded; it was bound by that condition of creation, by which freedom of the will was bestowed on man, and he was left to his own counsel.

This was my meaning, when I said that this permission pertained, not so much to governing or sustaining, as, to creating providence. We may now consider the validity of my argument in sustaining my view. We must here consider a two-fold permission, that by which man is left to his own counsel and permitted to sin, and that by which the sinner is left in his sins and permitted finally to fail of the highest good. The former, pertains to governing providence as was said, but determined by the act of creation; the latter, pertains to governing and uncontrolled providence. The former, pertains to providence, the latter, to preterition in contradistinction to providence. For all men, represented in Adam, have been left to themselves, and to their own counsel, yet all are not reprobates or passed-by. But all, who are finally left in their sins, and given up to their own counsel, after the commission of sin, are reprobate and passed by, and they who are passed by, are all left finally in their sins, and are permitted to fail of the highest good. Now I grant that, if by permission is understood a final reelection in sin, the whole syllogism is sound and valid, but, in that case, it sustains the theory, which makes sin a requisite condition in the object of reprobation or preterition. For that permission has reference to sinners.

But, if it is referred to the leaving of men to their own choice before the commission of sin, I deny that reprobation can be defined by that kind of permission. It is apparent, then, that no conclusion can be drawn from that syllogism in favour of the second theory, and against the view which I advocate. For the second theory presents man, apart from any reference to sin, as the object of preterition and reelection. That syllogism, however, is unintelligible, if it does not refer to permission and reprobation of sinners. For, in the permission by which the first men were permitted to sin, no one failed of the highest good, unless there was also a dereliction in sin; and reprobation is not that permission by which men were permitted to sin. It should also have been shown, in this place, how that argument from providence and permission is adapted to the confirmation of the second theory.

This might be sufficient for my purpose, but I am disposed to add some thoughts concerning providence, in view of your remarks in reference to it. Far be it from me, indeed, to disapprove them. They, however, omit the mutual arrangement and connection of the particular parts of providence. I made the distinction of providence into creating, sustaining and governing, not so much from my own idea, as from that of Dr. Francis Gomarus, who, in many passages of his writings, comprehends creation in the term providence. In the Theses on The Providence of God, discussed under his direction as the presiding professor, by Hadrian Cornelius Drogius, in the year 1596, it is said (Thesis nine) "The parts of this execution" (that, by which God executes the decree of providence) "are two, creation and government, &c., under which government are comprehended continuation, and preservation, and legitimate ordination." (Libre de provdentia Dei. cap. 1, ex Cicerone) "I affirm, then, that the world and all its parts were constituted at the beginning, and are administered through all time by the providence of God." (Ex Lactantio) "There is, then, a providence, by the force and energy of which, all things, which we see, were made, and are ruled." (Ejusdem, libro 7) "That execution is distributed into the creation and the government of this world. The parts of this government are two, the preservation and ordination of the world, thus constituted." Your view is also the same, as presented in your disputation. On the providence of God, discussed in the year 1598, for, in the first Thesis, are these words: "The word providence, taken in a wider sense, embraces the eternal decree of creation, government, and ordination, and its execution." I am not very solicitous in reference to the distinction of these words, government, preservation, ordination; whether government embraces both preservation and ordination, or only the latter, and there is a contradistinction between it and the former.

As to the arrangement and mutual connection of those parts, I affirm that it is possible that the act of the latter should depend on some act of the former, and in such a manner that the act of the latter should be determined to one direction by the former. I showed this in the example of the permission, by which God let, man to his own counsel. That act originated in the government of God, or in His governing providence, but it was determined by His creating providence, which made man free and self controlling, so far as pertained to that freedom, but, in other respects, responsible to the law of God. I here do no injustice to the providence of God, nor do I deny to Him universal liberty in His own action. I acknowledge that the providence of God is absolutely free. In the creation of man, He acted freely; in bestowing free will on man, He acted freely. But, if one action of the Deity, through the providence of God itself, be supposed, the necessity of another act of the divine providence can be deduced from it, which necessity is dependent on the free dispensation of the antecedent act of providence.

I will present another example, by which the same may be demonstrated. God has created angels with this condition, that they, who should not continue in their original innocence, should be punished forever without pardon. Some sinned. God, in the act of his governing providence, inflicted punishment on them by an act determined by previous creation, so that, if he did not wish to change that which was established in creation, he could not remit their punishment. This was my meaning in what I presented in answer to the third argument, which you do not refute, even though it be conceded that permission pertains to governing or ordaining providence, which I freely concede to you in the sense in which I have explained it. It should have been proved that the permission, by which man was left to his own control, pertains to reprobation or preterition, or that the permission, by which he was permitted to fail of the highest good, has place in reference to man, not a sinner, or considered as a sinner. Hence, also, those words of Thomas Aquinas (prima sum, quaes. 23, art. 3, in respons.

generali), "For as predestination includes the purpose to bestow grace and glory, so reprobation includes the purpose to permit some to fall into transgression, and to inflict the punishment of damnation for that transgression," if diligently examined, are not accurately true. For the purpose to permit some to fall into transgression, does not belong to reprobation, since God permitted all men to fall into transgression. This is also susceptible of proof from the acts which he attributes to predestination. The purpose of bestowing grace and glory is attributed to predestination. What grace? That by which some are not permitted to fall into transgression, but are preserved in their original state of integrity? By no means; but that grace by which some are delivered from that sin into which all were permitted to fall. The act of reprobation, then, should have been directly opposed to that act of predestination. But that is a permission to remain in sin, or an abandonment in sin, which is a negative act, and a purpose to inflict punishment for the sin, which is an affirmative act. The former is the opposite of grace, the latter, of glory. But it is not strange that a man who has written so many most erudite volumes, should not have been able to examine accurately each and every subject.

TWENTY-FIRST PROPOSITION OF ARMINIUS

In a comparison of these two theories, the latter seems not more probable than the former, since it involves the same absurd consequence. This I will briefly prove. In the former theory, the following order may be observed. God decreed to illustrate His own glory by mercy and punitive justice. He could not effect this without the introduction of sin. Hence, sin must, of necessity, and with certainty, have been committed. It could only be committed by him who, being accountable to the law, was able to fulfill its requirements, but it could not be committed, of necessity and with certainty, by a free and contingent cause, (which could commit sin or refrain from it,) if it was not circumscribed and determined by a more powerful agent, surely and with certainty moving or impelling the cause, in its own nature, free and contingent, to the act of sin, or else withholding or withdrawing that which was necessary to the avoidance of sin, on which conditions the necessity and certain existence of sin, committed by the creature, depend. The chief advocates of the first theory disapprove of the former mode of action in the more powerful agent (that which moves and impels), and incline to the latter mode (that which withholds or withdraws). This mode is also stated in the second theory. For the creature, left to his own nature, necessarily sins, if a law is imposed upon him, which can not be observed by the natural powers alone. God determined to leave the creature in his natural state. He, therefore, determined also that the creature should sin, since that was the necessary sequence. But the reason of that determination can not be given, if it is not that which is proposed in the former theory. Indeed the former theory seems even more probable than the latter.

ANSWER OF JULIUS TO THE
TWENTY-FIRST PROPOSITION

We have previously shown that those, which are called two theories, are not, in fact or substance, two, but differ only in their relations and mode of explanations; that there is, therefore, one, I say not probable, but true theory, founded on the truth of God, and the authority of the Scriptures. We have, also, in the appropriate place, shown that the charge of absurdity which is made against this theory is futile. Since, however, this objection is repeated, we may also briefly repeat in what respects and on what grounds we demur to it. The first position—"God decreed to illustrate His own glory by mercy and punitive justice," we have, in answer to the third proposition, shown to be expressed in too narrow terms.

The second, "He could not effect this without the introduction of sin," we thus proved to be an erroneous statement; for if the creature had remained righteous, there would have been an opportunity for mercy and justice, though the latter would not have been punitive in its character. Punitive justice, even, might have been displayed in respect to those things, which were unsuitable, on account, not of guilt, but of imprudence, for any just person is liable to this without sin or guilt.

In the third place, we deny that" sin must of necessity have been committed," as dependent on the energy of a cause, universally or in some measure, efficient. That it must certainly have been committed, we acknowledge, since it existed certainly in the knowledge of God, as knowledge, not as a cause of sin. If, then, the word certainly is explanatory of the word necessarily, and the latter word means no more than the former, we assent to its use; but if otherwise, we deny the latter (necessity), and assent to the former (certainty). The first man was not under the necessity of committing sin, either from an internal, or an external cause. He did it of his own free-will, not of any necessity. Again, this conclusion is not valid, since it is deduced from incomplete and erroneous antecedents, as we have just shown. Therefore, it is true, that sin could have been committed with certainty, by a free and contingent cause, which sinned (as was the case in the will of devils and of men), and could have been avoided with certainty by a free and contingent cause, which did not sin, (as in the case of the good and elect angels), and, on the contrary, it is false, that it could have been committed of necessity, if you refer to the necessity of any sufficient cause, that is, an external and internal cause, for the will was the cause or rather the principle—the attribute of which is freedom at that time free from all necessity, now bound by its own necessity, but nevertheless free, and thus producing contingent, not absolutely necessary effects as is the case in nature. When it is said that it could have been committed necessarily, there is an opposition in terms. For the word "could," which in this sentence is used in its legal sense, supposes contingency, to which the adverb necessarily is directly opposed.

In the fourth place, two conditions, are presented for the existence of sin, neither of which is probable. The former is that "sin could not be committed by a contingent cause, if it was not circumscribed and determined by a more powerful agent, surely and with certainty, moving or impelling the cause, in its own nature, free and contingent to the act of sin." This condition is denied; for, in the first place, it is contrary to nature, which per se can do or not do; otherwise it indeed has no power. Reference may, perhaps be made to partial power. This, certainly, is inapplicable to the human will, for it is a principle of action, and no wise man would ever place principles of action among partial powers. Again, if it is limited and determined by a more powerful agent, that agent must hold the relation of principle or cause. If the latter, the will must cease to be a principle, for principle pertains to the cause, it does not originate in the cause, of which it is the principle; the same thing can not at the same time, be the cause and the effect of itself. If the former is true, and the will is determined by a superior principle, there is this difficulty, that no superior principle so acts on an inferior one as to take away its peculiar mode of action, as we have before quoted from Augustine. But freedom is the peculiar mode of the will, and its appropriate adjunct is contingency, since it is freely per se inclinable in this or that direction. Besides, if it is "circumscribed and determined by a more powerful agent," that agent, either acts efficiently in each particular case, or ordains generally according to an established order in the universe. We have before, in answer to the sixth proposition, admitted that such an ordination occurred. You say that it is affirmed that the will is determined by an agent, absolutely efficient in particular cases. I deny that this can, with propriety, be attributed to our writers, whom it is unjust to charge so abruptly with that sentiment, if some of their expressions seem to savour of this, since it is contrary to their view, as they explain themselves in other passages. I will not argue this point further, but repeat the simple denial that it can be absolutely effected by a more powerful agent, operating efficiently, that a principle and contingent cause should sin. Here, my brother, you present two modes, one efficient, the other deficient, yet each, in its own way, efficient. For that which acts efficiently, is present with the work, and effects it; that, which is deficient, abstains from the work, and in itself effects that abstinence. You refer to the former mode in these words, "by a more powerful agent, surely and with certainty moving or impelling the cause in its own nature, free and contingent, to the act of sin." This we deny, and you, indeed, acknowledge that it is denied by our writers.

Let us, then, consider the other mode which you express, in these words, "or else withholding or withdrawing that which was necessary to the avoidance of sin, on which conditions the necessity and certain existence of sin, committed by the creature, depend." Here, also, the mode is two-fold, namely, that the "more powerful agent" withholds that which is necessary to the cause, if it is absent, and removes it if it is present; either of which would be a cause for the production of sin. Here three things are to be considered, the necessity of the avoidance of sin; -- the withholding or even the removal of what is necessary; -- and the consequence.

Concerning the first, it may be observed that every sin, that is, every inordinate act contrary to law, whether it is regarded in a universal or particular relation, is a habit or act of the individual, for genera or species do not act per se. It is, therefore, primarily and per se inordinate in the individual agent, and pertains, in a secondary sense, to that which is common and universal. Indeed, it does not at all concern the constitution of the universe that sin should be prevented, not only because sin could not disturb the relations of the universe, and the Ruler of the universe maintains its order, but also, because sin might, incidentally, be of advantage even to the constitution of the universe, and illustrate the wisdom, goodness, grace, mercy, justice, patience, power, and all the beneficent attributes of the Ruler of the universe. It was, then, plainly not necessary, in the abstract, to the constitution of the universe that sin should be avoided, and, therefore, nothing was necessary for the avoidance of sin. If it had been necessary to the constitution of the universe, God would have provided for it, in the most complete manner, as Augustine (Enchiridio ad Laurentium) proves.

It may be said that it was necessary to the constitution of the individual agent. It is true that if we regard the good of the individual only, the avoidance of sin seems to be necessary. But since the common good of the universe must be preferred to the good of the individual, and even sin itself, though incidentally, may be to the advantage of the constitution of the universe, and sin is committed only by the individual, it should be stated that the constitution of the universe does not allow the assertion that it is necessary that sin should not occur. If, however, the creature knows that it is necessary, not for the universe, but for himself, that he should not commit sin, the prevention of sin must be sought, neither from the universe, nor from its ruler, but from the individual agent, especially when the ruler of the universe bestowed on that same agent the unrestrained power to sin or not to sin, publicly and in the very condition of his nature, and when He made him the master of his own course, informed him of his power in that respect, and most carefully admonished him of the necessary result of his conduct in view of his individual end, with the addition, even, of threatening. What then? Should God resume that which He had bestowed. That would have been the act of an imprudent, inconstant or impotent being, neither of which qualities can be attributed to the Deity. Should He not have made the original bestowment. In that case He would not have displayed all the modes of His own wisdom, and man would have desired that, which had not been bestowed upon him, for he desired that which was far higher, and indeed impossible—to be like God. If we have suitably considered these points, which Tertullian discussed at length in his second book against Marcion, we see, at once, that it was necessary, neither to the constitution of the universe nor to the relations of the individual agent, that sin should be prevented by an external influence, since man himself possessed, within his own power, the means of preventing it, and had in the strongest possible mode, received from the Deity, the knowledge of the necessity existing in his case in view of his end. God infused into him the principle of freedom. We, forsooth, wise in view of the result, judge that that this was badly done by the Lord, that it would have been better that He had not infused that principle, or, at least, that it would have been better to have restrained that freedom.

Concerning the second, we have shown that it was not necessary that sin should be prevented. It belonged to man to avoid it, not to another being to prevent man. This being proved, we need not refer to the withholding and the removal of that which was necessary for the avoidance of sin. But that the truth may be presented, we remark, further, that it did not pertain to the Deity to bestow that, which was necessary to the avoidance of sin, in that particular act of Adam; first, because He had already bestowed it; secondly, because He could not bestow it, unless He should resume what He had already bestowed. That He had already bestowed it is evident from the gift of the free-will to man, which was a principle, in the highest sense, free, and sufficient for either course, either for the commission or the avoidance of that sin. Nor, indeed, could He bestow any other hindrance, unless He should resume that which He had already bestowed; for that was a natural principle, namely, the free-will, constituted, by the Deity, without any exception or modification, the pure and absolute mistress in natural things. If He had prevented it, either the will must have wholly ceased to be a principle of action, or, in that particular act, the condition of that principle, which God had given to man by nature, and which He had, in that very act, pledged to keep unviolated by Himself, would have been violated. Why should God use such precaution with the man to whom He had given full power over himself, and whom He had already cautioned by an admonitory precept. Then, you will say, He should, at least, not have withdrawn that which He had bestowed; for He bestowed grace, and then withdrew it. I deny that He withdrew any thing, previously bestowed, except on account of sin, when man rejected it. Grace, that is, the gift of grace, had been bestowed on man for the work of grace, that is, according to which nature was ordained to supernatural glory. For the work of nature, He bestowed, not grace, but nature and the will. It was the office of nature that the man should eat or not eat; it was the office of the will, according to the command of God, that he should not eat of the forbidden fruit. This was purely and merely the office of the will, to which it was not necessary that grace should be added, since it was bestowed in reference to things of a gracious, not of a natural character.

Concerning the third, it may be observed that the remark "on which conditions the necessity and certain existence of sin, committed by the creature, depend," is wholly erroneous in reference to the act of Adam. For Adam was under no necessity, from any source, of committing sin; he was endowed with pure freedom, as we have now, and frequently at other times, affirmed. Indeed that assertion is not absolutely and properly true in the present condition of the human race. For, on the will of the creature, that is, on our will, depends the necessity of the commission of sin, which necessity the infinitely wise will of God permits and ordains; but, on the contrary, the necessity of the non-commission of sin, by the communication of grace, depends on that infinitely wise will of God. It is hardly correct to say that the necessity of the commission of sin depends on the will of God, withholding or withdrawing His grace. Yet that statement, in a certain sense, may be allowed.

In the fifth place, we admit your proposition "the creature, left to his own nature, necessarily sins, if a law is imposed on him, which cannot be observed by the natural powers alone." But that particular law, imposed on Adam, was observable by the natural powers alone, as we have proved in answer to the fourteenth and sixteenth propositions. This whole argument, therefore, and whatever depends on it, is destroyed. Adam was prepared, by nature and grace, for the observance of natural law. He was prepared for the observance of this particular command, because the requisition was only of a natural character, and of the utmost facility. Your assumption is ambiguous and improper. The proper form would be "God placed the creature in his natural state." It is improperly affirmed that He "determined to leave the creature, &c." Man left God, before God left man, as we have before shown. The conclusion is, therefore, false. Your assumption is ambiguous on account of the various use of the verb, statuit, which is used in this place. We referred to that ambiguity in our answer to the sixth proposition.

Finally, it is unsuitably affirmed that "the former theory seems more probable than the latter." Since in fact or substance and in their relation they are but one theory, differing only in the mode of discussion and language. Let us, however, see wherein one is more probable than the other.

REPLY OF ARMINIUS TO THE ANSWER TO
THE TWENTY-FIRST *PROPOSITION*

The respects, in which those theories differ, have been already stated in the reply to your answer to the first proposition. We now inquire whether the first or the second theory is founded on the truth of God and the authority of the Scripture. I have already showed that the absurdity, which I alleged against the first theory, is its necessary consequence. You have not vindicated it, as it is explained by those authors, from that charge, but have explained it differently from the view of its authors, and have proved that, so explained, it can be, in various ways, defended from the allegation of absurdity, but this is irrelevant to our present discussion. There has never been any question between us concerning that theory, explained, as you think that it ought to be explained. In this proposition, however, I do not repeat this allegation, but show that the second theory is liable to the same objection, and prove it by a comparison of the first and second theories. This is the plan and scope of the twenty first proposition. It will, therefore, be necessary that we consider, first, the grounds of the correct and deserved allegation of absurdity against the first theory; secondly, the same allegation against the second theory, and, at the same time, what you have said in defense of both.

As to the first theory, I will show by certain syllogisms, that it is a legitimate inference from it that God is the author of sin. Then I will examine what you say in its behalf.

The declaration of mercy, saving from actual misery, and of justice, punishing sin is necessary, according to the decree of God; -- But such mercy and justice cannot be declared without the existence of sin and misery; -- Therefore, the existence of sin and misery is necessary from the decree of God, or—therefore, sin must necessarily be committed from the decree of God. All the points of this syllogism are taken from the first theory, rightly understood according to the sentiments of the authors themselves, as I proved in my reply to your answers to propositions third and sixth.

Again; -- Sin cannot be committed necessarily by a free and contingent cause, unless it be circumscribed and determined by a more powerful cause, which it can not resist; -- But the will of man is a free and contingent cause; -- Therefore, sin cannot be necessarily committed by the will of man (which must be the proximate cause of sin,) unless it be circumscribed and determined by a more powerful cause which it cannot resist. I add, that the mode of that determination is two-fold.

Lastly; -- the cause, which determines the will, in its own nature free and contingent, to the commission of sin, is, by that determination, the cause of sin; -- But, according to the first theory, God is the cause, which determines the will to the necessary commission of sin; -- Therefore, God is, by that determination, the cause of sin.

Now let us proceed to those things which you adduce in apology and defense of that first theory. First, you affirm that "the first position, 'God decreed to illustrate His own glory by mercy and punitive justice,' we have, in answer to the third proposition, shown to be expressed in too narrow terms." I reply that the question is not whether the position is true or false, or whether it is expressed in too wide or too narrow terms, but whether it is assumed by those against whose theory I have alleged absurdity, as its consequence. And I showed in my reply to that answer that they, in so many words, assume this position.

In the second place, you say that "the second, -- 'He could not effect this without the introduction of sin' we thus proved to be an erroneous statement." I reply, that it is not the question whether the statement is erroneous or not, but whether it is made by those, whose theory I charge with absurdity. That they do assert this, and in plain language, I proved in the reply just mentioned. The error is, then, to be charged on them, not on me. Their assertion, however, is true, that "mercy and justice—as understood by them—could only be declared by the entrance of sin into the world." For sin is the formal cause in the object of that justice, and of that mercy, as having consequent misery, as its adjunct.

In the third place you "deny that 'sin must, of necessity and with certainty, have been committed.'" This is not the point in controversy. For I, also, admit that it is not true that sin must necessarily be committed, and affirm that they, who take the opposite ground, blaspheme the goodness and justice of God, though I grant that the advocates of this theory do not perceive this consequence, and the concession is due to them, that in other places they teach that which is precisely the contrary. But if those two premises are granted, I affirm that it is a legitimate consequence that sin must of necessity have been committed. You concede that it "must certainly have been committed," but "certainly" in the knowledge of God, not "certainly" in the relation of the divine decree, which is dependent on the will of God, with foreknowledge, as its antecedent. Those authors of the first theory, of whom I have spoken, say that sin "must have been committed certainly and necessarily in the relation of the decree, and that it could only have been a subject of certain foreknowledge, because it was decreed and ordained by God to be committed." But I denied and still deny that sin could necessarily have been committed by a free and contingent cause. The cause of a necessary effect is necessary, that of a contingent effect is contingent.

But the will of man is a free and contingent cause. Sin, therefore, could not have been committed necessarily by it.

The "opposition in terms" is in your words, not in mine. I did not say that sin "could have been committed necessarily" but that it "could not have been committed necessarily." There is here no contradiction in terms, as will be evident by an examination of the statement in the following form; --

It could not occur that sin should be committed necessarily by a free and contingent cause. Is it an absurd statement that it can occur that a necessary cause should produce a necessary effect, or its effect necessarily? Indeed it must occur. I admit that the distinction which you make between the words certainly and necessarily, is founded in truth; certainty pertains to the knowledge of God; the necessity of an event, to the will and decree of God. If this distinction had been correctly observed by many, it might serve greatly to the solution of many grave questions connected with this matter; this you have illustrated, in a very learned manner, in your book Concerning the fall of Adam.

In the fourth place you say that "two conditions, neither of which is probable, are presented for the existence of sin." Let us examine both. The former is not fully stated by you, for the word which is the whole subject of controversy, is omitted. Its insertion strengthens what I have affirmed; if it is taken away, my statement is weakened. That word is necessarily, and the condition should have been stated thus, "The former is 'that sin could not have been committed necessarily by a contingent cause, &c.'" Those things, which you adduce, do not affect this condition. You indeed proved that the will of man, as principle and complete power, could have, freely and contingently, committed sin, but who denies that statement? I add that if it did not freely sin, it did not, at all, sin; and there is a contradiction in terms, if it is asserted that the will sins necessarily, and this, not in a single, but in a two-fold mode. For it pertains to the will to do freely that which it does, and sin, if it is necessary, is no longer sin. We are here speaking on the hypothesis of the first theory, which we have undertaken to refute.

You deny that the will is determined by a more powerful agent; since it is not determined by a cause for then "the will must cease to be a principle;" not by a principle, for, as opposed to partial power, a superior principle so acts on an inferior one as not to take away its peculiar mode of action." I readily concede that this is truly and learnedly affirmed. But did I say that the will was determined by a more powerful agent? By no means. I affirmed that it could not occur that the will should sin necessarily, unless it was determined by a more powerful agent. That conclusion was to be refuted by you, if, indeed, you wished to speak against me in these things, not the antecedent or the consequent, concerning which there is no controversy between us. I grant that if the

will is determined by a cause, it ceases to be a principle; if by a principle, there
is, in fact, no determination, for, if its peculiar mode, which is freedom, is not
taken away, then it is not determined. If, then, it is determined, it is by a cause;
-- But it is determined, for thence results the necessity of sin; -- Therefore, it is
determined by a cause. But if it is determined by a cause, then, you say, the will
must cease to be a principle, which is absurd. I assent to this, and, therefore,
affirm that the first theory which involves this absurdity, is deservedly disapproved. In your addition that in that determination, the superior agent "either
acts efficiently in each particular case, or ordains generally," you do not, in my
opinion, correctly separate and distinguish between these two things, if you
do not previously show how that, which acts efficiently, can be separated from
that which ordains, (the latter word being used, in the sense of Calvin and Beza
in the first theory, for the ordination, not of a thing already done for a certain
end, but of a thing to be done to secure a fixed and prescribed result). If the
same word is used according to your idea, and as it should be used, I admit that
the distinction is a valid one, but this is not the point in controversy, for it is in
reference to the theory of Calvin and Beza, who do not, at any time, so speak,
but whose meaning and sentiment is, invariably, that which I have presented.

I concur, then, in your denial that it can be absolutely effected, by a superior,
efficient cause, that a principle and a contingent cause should sin. Your denial,
however, should have been that the necessity of sin is a legitimate sequence of
that theory, and this denial should have been sustained. Indeed, you should
not have said that it can not "be absolutely effected by a more powerful agent,
operating efficiently, that a principle and a contingent cause should sin," but
that it can not be so effected that a man should necessarily sin, for, in the case
supposed, a man ceases to be a principle and contingent cause. I stated that
"the chief advocates of the first theory disapprove of the former mode of action
in the more powerful agent (that which moves or impels) &c.," but they do this
only in word, and do not show how that mode has not an appropriate place in
their theory.

Let us now examine the second mode, which I did not lay down as absolutely necessary; but because I saw that the necessity of the commission of
sin could only be made out in one of these two modes, therefore, I separately
presented both. It seems, however, to have belonged to your duty in this case,
in the first place, to show that it was possible that sin should be committed,
apart from either of these modes; in the second place, set forth that other mode
in which this could be, and, in fact, was done; and in the third place, to prove
that this mode was such as not to make God the author of sin. You do neither
of these things: and I could, therefore, have passed over all these things, as

not within the scope of our discussion, and as having no weight against my arguments. We will, however, consider your answer.

In the first place, you show, by prolix argument, "that it was necessary, neither to the constitution of the universe, nor to the relations of the individual agent, that sin should be prevented." No one denies this; no one affirms the contrary. In that case, sin would not have been committed; but it was committed. How could you have supposed that I had any affinity for that sentiment, when I have at all times contended that God made man of free-will, and of self control that he might be able, of his own accord, and freely, to avoid sin, or to commit it of his own choice, to which divine constitution is directly opposed this idea of the necessary prevention of sin. I, therefore, concede that it was not absolutely necessary that sin should be prevented, that is, that sin should not occur. If, however, I may be permitted briefly to consider this point, though it may be a digression, I will note some things which do not seem to me to be said, with sufficient correctness. You say that it was not necessary to the universe that sin should be prevented, that is, as I interpret your meaning, it did not pertain to the good of the universe that sin should be prevented. I may, with your permission, deny this. For it pertained to the good of the universe that the creature should remain in the perfection of that state, in which the universe was created, and established in the economy of the creation, by the Deity. But by sin, it fell from that perfection of the universe, and "was made subject to vanity" (Rom. viii. 20), whence results the desire of deliverance from that vanity (v, 21 and 22). If this does not pertain to the good of the universe, it would not desire it. If it were not necessary, the whole universe would not desire it. For its desire is for every good thing, and its natural desire is for necessary good.

You prove your affirmation by a two-fold argument, first, "because sin could not disturb the relations of the universe," and secondly, "because sin might, incidentally, be of advantage even to the constitution of the universe, and illustrate the wisdom, goodness, grace, mercy, justice, patience, power, and all the beneficent attributes of the Ruler of the universe." To the first, I reply that it does not seem to me to be very probable. The constitution of the universe was such, by the creation and ordination of God, that man was made in the image and likeness of God, and other creatures were made subject to man, and subservient to his use and advantage, because he was made in the image of God. Sin has very greatly disturbed this relation and order. By it, man became a rebel against God, and the whole creation was not only removed from under his authority, but armed for his destruction, except so far as there has been a restoration in Christ. (See Heb. ii, 6-9.) There are those who explain the word ajnakefalaiwsasqai used in Ephes. i. 10, as referring to the restoration of all things to that original condition from which they had fallen, on account of human sin. The relation of divine providence in which it sustains and governs all things, is far different from that which would have existed, if sin had not entered into the world, as may be very clearly proved from many passages of the Bible. "But," you will say, "sin could not so disturb the constitution of this universe, that God could not reduce it to order." This, I acknowledge; but that order is not one, which prevented that disturbance, but followed and corrected it.

In the second argument, I think that there are two things to be observed and corrected. First, that you say that "sin might incidentally be of advantage, even to the constitution of the universe," for neither per se nor incidentally, could sin be of advantage to the constitution of the universe. Not per se, for it resulted not from the intention of the Creator of the universe, but from the disobedience of the rational creature. Not incidentally, for, since this whole universe is finite, its constitution is also finite; and, therefore, the good, which pertains to its natural perfection, is finite; the opposite of which finite good, that is, evil or defect, erring from it, could be incidentally to the advantage of the universe, that is, could be reduced to the good of the universe. But sin is an evil, opposed not to finite but to infinite good, to the justice and will of God. Hence, it could not, incidentally, be to the advantage of the constitution of the universe, determined and circumscribed by its own limits. It could contribute, incidentally, to the glory of the infinite good, because that infinite good, more powerful than it, could, according to its own choice, turn it out of its natural course, and, in this way, reduce to order that, which is most disorderly; to the order, not of this universe, but to one far transcending this whole universe, and only circumscribed by the limits of infinite good. It can not occur that any creature should so pass out of its own appropriate order, or that of the whole universe, as not to be under the control of the Infinite Author. I know, indeed, that sin is, in a certain respect, opposed to finite good, namely, to man, with whose happiness it interferes, but it does not primarily prevent it, unless it is previously regarded as opposed to the justice and will of God.

Secondly, I think that your statement, -- "Sin might, incidentally, illustrate the wisdom, goodness, etc, of the Ruler of the universe," is worthy of notice. This illustration of the divine attributes is not the effect of sin, but of the action of God, which makes use of sin to the illustration of those divine attributes. Sin, in itself, or abstractly, disgraces and dishonours God. Sin is said to do this incidentally, for this is the common phraseology, but, in my opinion, it will be more correctly affirmed of sin that it is, incidentally, an occasion of illustrating the divine glory by the exercise of those attributes. Indeed, if God had not been able to triumph over sin, and to reduce it to order, He would, by no means, have permitted it to be committed.

To return from this digression, I affirm that the subject of discussion is not the necessity of avoiding sin, but what is necessary for such avoidance, namely, that without which sin can not be avoided by a man on whom the law is imposed. Concerning this, indeed, you acknowledge that God gave to man those things, which were necessary to the avoidance of sin, which He neither resumed nor withdrew until man had, by his own sin, rejected them. In this, I agree with you. This, however, was not the point in controversy. It was to be explained how, if a man could, avoid sin, the same man must necessarily sin, which is the inference from the hypothesis of the theory, which I impugn. It has been, previously, discussed, at sufficient length, to what extent and in what respects, grace was necessary for the observance of this or that law. I readily admit that, with the explanation, which you make, the inference is that Adam was under no necessity to commit sin; but this is irrelevant to the controversy, and indeed, is contrary to the view of Calvin and Beza. As we have just affirmed, it was to be explained how it could be true that Adam was under no necessity to commit sin, and yet that he did necessarily commit sin, and how, if there was imposed on him any necessity, either in this or that mode, or in any mode whatever, God is not made the author of sin. Far be it from me to make such a charge against the Deity, but I affirm that it is a legitimate inference from that first theory, and that the theory is, therefore, to be disapproved.

I come, now, to the second theory, of which I affirm that the same absurdity can be inferred from it, in the following way. My argument may be stated in the following syllogism, -- That creature sins necessarily, on whom, left to his own nature, a law is imposed, to the observance of which, the powers of that nature are not adequate; -- But on man, left to his own nature, a law was imposed, to the observance of which, the powers of that nature were not adequate; -- Therefore, man, left to his own nature, necessarily sinned. By consequence, God, who imposed that law, and determined to leave man in a state of nature, is the cause of the sin of man.

You admit the truth of the Major, but deny that of the Minor, and then refer to your answer to the fourteenth and sixteenth propositions. To these answers, we replied, -- We remark further that if man has the ability to observe that law, and God neither takes it away, nor prevents its free use, then it must be conceded that it does not follow that man necessarily commits sin. The phrase, which I use in the Minor, if improper and ambiguous, is not to be imputed to me, who, in explaining and impugning the theory of others, have used their phraseology. For, in your disputation, already frequently cited, Thesis fifteen, I find the following statement. "Preterition is an act of the divine pleasure, by which God, from eternity, determined to leave some of His creatures in their natural condition." But, though I may not be able to prove by that syllogism,

the Minor of which I have thought to be laid down by yourself in your Thesis—
in view of the denial of that Minor—that the necessity of sin may be deduced
from that theory, and that God is, therefore, as a consequence of the same
theory, made the author of sin, yet I do not see how that denial of the Minor is
consistent with the sentiment set forth in your thesis, and how the necessity of
sin is not deducible from the same sentiment, and I will give the reasons of my
difficulty in both cases.

In the former case, you affirm that man could, by those powers, which he
has received from God, whether of nature or of grace, observe the law which
was enacted for them. Also, in your Theses, you affirm that God passed by men,
of such character and capability, without the condition of sin, or any foresight
of the same. I deny that these two things are mutually consistent, and prove it
thus; -- "To him who is made, from the condition of his nature, capable of any
grace, that is, of grace without which he can not obtain the end for which he
was made, that grace can be considered to be denied only in view of the foresight of some act by which he may have made himself incapable and unworthy
of receiving it. But such an act could only be sinful." In proof of this Major,
I remark that, otherwise God in vain bestowed on man the capacity for that
grace, which is absurd. I add that, if nature does not fail to bestow that which is
necessary, much less is this true of God, the author and finisher of nature. But
God does not fail in things which are necessary, if He denies to man that grace,
without which he is unable to attain the end for which he was made, which
is also absurd. I proceed with the syllogism: "But all men, not only the first
pair, but, in them, their posterity, considered in respect to the primitive state,
were capable of that grace, and were created for an end, which was attainable
only through that grace; -- Therefore, that grace could be denied, or could be
considered as denied to man apart from the fact that he was considered as a
sinner." I sustain this consequent, namely, that all men were capable of that
grace, first, because all men were created in the image of God. Secondly, if
they were not thus capable, they, who are to receive that grace, must be made
capable by some act on His part, which act could not be that of predestination.
For it is reasoning in a circle, to argue that any act of predestination should
make a person capable of receiving the grace of predestination. Again, it does
not pertain to predestination to render any one capable of receiving grace, but
simply to bestow grace. The act must, then, be one common to all men. If it
is such, then by it all men were made capable of that grace, which coincides
with my assertion that all were capable. I wish, on this account, that it might
be shown, in this place, how God could justly deny, by a mere act of His pleasure, to any man that grace, the capability of which He bestowed on him, and
without which he could not attain the end for which he was made, unless the

man had made himself, by his own demerit, unworthy of that grace, and unable to receive it.

In the latter case, namely, that the necessity of sin is not excluded from the theory, which is set forth in your Theses, but may be fairly deduced from them, I show in the following manner; -- The denial of grace, necessary to confirm the pure nature of man, is a cause of the fall of man, that is, of his sin, by the withdrawal or the non-bestowment of the necessary preventive; -- But preterition, as defined in your Theses, is a denial of grace, necessary to confirm the pure nature of man; -- Therefore, preterition, thus defined, is a cause of the fall of man, that is, of his sin, by the non-bestowment of the necessary preventive. The truth of the Major is self-evident; nor is it affected by the exception, "if that grace was due to man, for it was due to him, if it was necessary to the confirmation of his nature, without which he could not attain the end for which he was made. The Minor is sustained by your Thesis. "Preterition is an act of the divine pleasure, by which God determined not to communicate to some of His creatures that supernatural grace, by which their pure nature might be confirmed, &c." But that grace is either necessary or not necessary for the confirmation of the pure nature of man. If it was not necessary, that pure nature could have remained unfallen, without that grace. If it could have remained unfallen without that grace, then those who maintained their integrity, would have been partakers of eternal life, and then, those, to whom, He had determined to deny His grace, could have been among those not passed-by. This is at variance with the definition, considered both in itself and in relation to the other Theses. The necessity of that grace, therefore, follows from that definition, and consequently the denial of the same is the cause of the fall by the non-bestowment of the necessary preventive.

Again, the final denial of supernatural happiness, of necessity, either supposes or induces sin, for supernatural happiness is denied, and can be denied only to sinners. Preterition is the denial of final supernatural happiness.

Therefore, it necessarily either presupposes or induces sin. But preterition, as defined in your Theses, does not presuppose sin; it must then induce it. I do not see how it can do this in any way, other than that of which I have spoken. Let another way be presented, and one which may not charge the Deity with the responsibility of sin, and this theory may be freed from the allegation of absurdity.

You say that the Minor is improper and ambiguous. If this is true, the responsibility is not on me, but on yourself, who have thus spoken in the Theses so frequently cited, for in them are the words "God determined to leave, &c." This phraseology, however, is neither improper nor ambiguous. It is not improper; for if He forsakes either the men who have not already forsaken

Him, or those who have forsaken Him, the words "determined to leave" are properly used. It is not ambiguous, since the word "determined" is used in the same sense, in all parts of the syllogism, as we demonstrated concerning the word "ordain" in the sixth proposition. We spoke of the difference between this theory and the first, in reply to your answer to the first proposition.

TWENTY-SECOND PROPOSITION OF ARMINIUS

First, it presents to the Deity, in the act of election, of non-election, of predestination, and of preterition, man as created, and created of such a character as did not in fact pertain to him, while the first theory presents to the Deity, in the act of predestination and of reprobation, man as to be created, and to be created such as he was, in fact, afterwards created.

ANSWER OF JUNIUS TO THE TWENTY-SECOND PROPOSITION

That this difference is not real, we have sufficiently demonstrated in answering the sixth and tenth propositions. The decree has reference to man to be created, considered generally; and its execution to man as created according to his various relations.

REPLY OF ARMINIUS TO THE ANSWER TO THE TWENTY-SECOND *PROPOSITION*

I affirmed that the second theory was less probable than the first, and proved it by five reasons. We proceed to a more extended consideration of them, and, in the first place, we examine the first, that is, the one presented in this proposition.

The theory of Calvin regards the Deity, as engaged, in the decree of predestination, with an object identical with the object of the execution of that decree, but the second theory regards the Deity as having reference, in the decree of predestination, to man as he is considered in a purely natural state, which can effect nothing supernatural or divine, while, in its execution, He can not have reference to man in such a condition, since no man ever existed wholly without a participation of supernatural endowments, either by creation or superinfusion. It should be observed that predestination does not intervene between creation and superinfusion, and that superinfusion is not the work of predestination, as was previously demonstrated. The answer which you present does not seem to be relevant. For though the decree was made before the creation of man, yet predestination, explained according to the second theory, had reference only to man considered as created. Creation is not a result of the execution of the decree of predestination, understood in that sense, and though the execution of the decree may, according to this theory, refer only to man as created, yet the question is to be answered—whence did the first act of execution take its origin? Let those things be examined which are said in reply to your answer to the 6th and 8th propositions.

TWENTY-THIRD PROPOSITION OF ARMINIUS

Secondly, because it does not unite decrees between which there is a just coherence. For it unites the decree in reference to leaving some in their natural state with the decree of reprobation by the mode of the foresight of sin, which foresight, or which sin it considers as contingent; while from the decree of preterition sin results of necessity, and therefore, the reprobation, according to the justice of God, of those on whom He has determined not to have mercy, should have been united to that decree, not by a conditional, but by a necessary copula. Those things, which have, to each other the relation of necessary sequence, are decreed, by the Deity, in decrees which necessarily cohere; -Preterition and sin necessarily cohere; -- Therefore, decrees concerning them should be conjoined by a closer bond.

ANSWER OF JUNIUS TO THE TWENTY-THIRD PROPOSITION

We affirm, on the contrary, that, according to this theory, there is a just copula of the decrees which mutually cohere. For it is necessary that any transition from one decree to the other must be in harmony with its own execution. But the transition has not reference properly and per se to the necessity of that decree, but it pertains to contingency. As in the predestination of the saints, the decree is two-fold, first, that of election and the preparation of grace, secondly, that of glory; and the transition of the former to the latter, is by death which is contingent, as the wages of sin, so also in the predestination of the reprobate is contained a two-fold decree, first, that of non-election, or preterition, or reprobation and alienation from grace, secondly, that of damnation; and the transition from the former to the latter, is by sin and death, the consectary of sin, between which God graciously leaves a space that there may be even in sinners and the reprobate themselves, a proof of the divine forbearance, calling them to repentance. In this case, then, the copula should have been stated to be not necessary, but contingent. For everywhere in the Scriptures God disavows sin, and the saints commit it, "for the righteous Lord loveth righteousness; His countenance doth behold the upright." (Psalm xi. 7.)

We concede that "from the decree of preterition sin results of necessity," that is, certainly; since the inference from that which is true is necessarily true? But we most firmly deny that sin is, universally or in part, of necessity, in an efficient sense, the result of that decree, by the necessity of the consequent or the conclusion. We by no means deny that sin is the consequent of that decree, though not as caused by it, or as its necessary effect.

A syllogistic argument is added for the proof of assertion, but we can not absolutely or simply approve the Minor. We deny that "preterition and sin necessarily cohere," per se, for if they necessarily cohere, it would be as true that all are passed by who have sinned, as that some are passed by who have sinned; that is, all sinners would be passed by as all the passed by are sinners. But the consequent is false, therefore, the antecedent is also false. It is not necessary, indeed, that there should be a reciprocal coherence between those things, which differ in mode, one being necessary and the other contingent; if it were so, nothing would be contingent. There are many things which are necessary; yet without a cohering contingency. But on the contrary, nothing is so contingent, as not to have, with it, something of a necessary character. Such is the connection of preterition and sin, in relation to themselves. But, in relation to man, in the case of those who are descended from Adam, and involved in his corruption and fall, and who are passed by of God, we confess that preterition and sin cohere necessarily, that is immutably, since, though it is committed contingently, yet that necessity of the connection of sin with preterition and reprobation becomes absolute and immutable, as he who contracts a debt, if he is not able to pay, necessarily remains a debtor. The other points have been previously discussed.

THE REPLY OF ARMINIUS TO THE ANSWER TO THE TWENTY THIRD PROPOSITION

Those decrees, neither of which can exist or not exist without the other, are said to be united by a necessary copula. By this copula the decree of the preparation of grace should be connected with the decree of the preparation of glory. For neither exists without the other, and neither can exist without the other. If preterition and predamnation are to be connected by the same copula,

I have already obtained what I desired. But the transition by which one passes from grace to glory is not the copula by which one decree is united to the other, but that copula is the will of God, which wills to bestow, upon no person, one without the other, and which wills to bestow both where it wills to bestow either. The transition to glory is death; to which sin does not hold a corresponding relation in the decree of preterition and predamnation. For predamnation is on account of sin; glory is not account of death. With reference to sin and its merit, God determined to damn some, for sin alone is the meritorious cause on account of which God can damn a person. Death has no such relation to glory, which, after death, follows of the divine predestination and grace. That death is not the copula is apparent from the fact that it is the transition both from grace to glory, and from non-grace to damnation or punishment by the intervention of sin. For the copula of those opposite decrees can not be the same, and without any modification.

I accede to what is said concerning death and transition, and I wish that the consequence may be considered. If death is the transition from the decree of the preparation of grace to glory, it follows that the decree of preparation of grace and glory has reference to sinners. For death can not be the transition from one decree to another, or from execution to execution, apart from the relation of sin, as a condition requisite in the object. I concede that death, as a transition, depends not, per se and properly, on the necessity of the decree, by which God determined to bestow grace and glory on any creature. It does, however, depend on the necessity of that decree by which God ordained to lead man to glory only by the intervention of death. This decree supposes sin. It has been proved that sin necessarily results from the decree of preterition, that is, of preterition, defined according your Theses.

In the Minor of my syllogism there was a verbal mistake, and the word reprobation should be substituted for the word sin, and the syllogism should be read with this correction. Preterition and reprobation (the latter referring to preparation of punishment,) necessarily cohere, as is apparent from the previous statement, in which I said that "it unites the decree in reference to leaving some in their natural state, with the decree of reprobation by the mode of the foresight of sin, &c." The Minor, thus corrected, is true, and, when I wrote it, I satisfied myself of its truth by that very argument, which you use. For all the passed-by are predamned (to substitute that word according to the view which you have set forth in this answer,) and all the predamned are passed by. Therefore, the decree concerning the passing-by of some must be connected, by a necessary copula, with the decree concerning the damnation of some. But, in this case, they are united, not by a necessary, but by a contingent copula; for they are connected by the mode of the prevision of sin, which is made contingent. But preterition and predamnation have a necessary mutual coherence; preterition and sin also necessarily cohere. For predamnation is decreed only on account of sin.

Let us now consider your answer to my Minor as it was erroneously stated by me. You "deny that preterition and sin necessarily cohere," as asserted in my Minor. Your reason for denying it, is that "all sinners would be passed by, as all the passed-by are sinners," and this is not true, for all the passed-by are indeed sinners, but not all sinners are passed-by. I concede the antecedent, and yet deny the consequent. It is not, of necessity, true that every case in which a copula is necessary, that it should be so in a reciprocal sense. Sin and preterition can cohere by a necessary copula, even if this is not reciprocally true. Man and animal are connected by a necessary copula, but this is not reciprocally true. We may say that every man is necessarily an animal, but we may not say, reciprocally, that every animal is a man. Here let us consider the reason on account of which it can be truly said that all the passed-by are sinners, but it cannot be truly said that all sinners are passed by. It is not this, that sin is a wider term than preterition, and sinners a wider term than the passed-by, whence also it seems to me to be a very probable conclusion that sin was prior to preterition, since things, which are generic in their character, are naturally prior to those which are specific. It also seems to me to be deducible from this reciprocation and inversion, (namely, all the passed-by are damned, and all the damned are passed by, and all the passed-by and damned are sinners, and, indeed, only sinners are passed by and damned), that, consequently, preterition and predamnation pertain to sinners, and, therefore, to men considered in their sins, which I designed to argue, and have especially undertaken to prove. In this way also, sin precedes both preterition and predamnation, and if its natural efficiency is considered, all sinners, not some merely, will be passed by and damned. But since the natural efficiency of sin is hindered in some, by the force of a superior cause, which is the will of God, it hence occurs that those sinners are passed by and damned on whom God has determined not to have mercy, those are not passed by or predamned, on whom He has determined to have mercy.

Your observations concerning the mode of coherence between the necessary and the contingent, are not opposed to my view, even if they are true, which I do not think to be beyond controversy. The necessary and the contingent differ in their entire essence, so that no thing, whatever it may be, can be said, at the same time, to be necessary and contingent, that is, (to preserve the phraseology,) to be done necessarily and contingently. Yet I think that it can not, without an exception necessary to be considered in this place, be said that he necessarily remains a debtor, who has contracted a debt, and is not able to pay it. There should have been the addition of the exception "unless a remission of the debt is granted by the creditor," for without that exception, there would be a reciprocal relation between sin and damnation, so that all sinners would be damned, and all the damned would be sinners. For sin is a debt in which all sinners are involved, and not only does it deserve punishment, but it will also be certainly punished, unless it shall be pardoned and remitted.

From what you here say, I think that it is possible to deduce an argument in favour of my theory. For you make an analogy between the contingent act of sin and the contraction of debt; also between the being necessarily a sinner, the being necessarily passed by, and the remaining necessarily in debt, unless there is ability to pay. There is between the first terms in each, an analogy, and also, between the second terms, such a relation that in each case the former naturally precedes the latter; hence sin was committed contingently by man before he was necessarily constituted a sinner, also, before he was passed by of God. And who does not know that man, since he freely sinned, made himself the bond-slave of sin, and, therefore, is necessarily subject to sin, until his deliverance is effected through Christ, the Mediator, according to the words of Scripture, "Whosoever committeth sin, is the servant of sin. If the Son, therefore, shall make you free, ye shall be free indeed." (John viii. 34-36.)

TWENTY-FOURTH PROPOSITION OF ARMINIUS

Thirdly, because it leaves a hiatus in the decrees, not introducing, between the decree of preterition and that of reprobation, the decree concerning the certain and necessary existence of sin; for, sin, in my judgment, necessarily results from preterition itself, by the removal, as they say, of the hindrance

ANSWER OF JUNIUS TO THE TWENTY-FOURTH PROPOSITION

We deny that any intermediate decree is necessary between the decree of preterition and that of damnation, (for so you understand the word reprobation), or that any decree is interposed, and claim that this is so from the very nature of the decrees. For these decrees are of the divine efficiency, and they are effected by the Deity, immediately of His own will, and justly of His own wisdom. But the decree concerning the existence of sin pertains to the mediate work of nature, and is effected in that mode, in which God decreed, that is, contingently, from a contingent cause, for the will is, in this case, the principle of contingent causes, and that particular motion of Adam towards the fall was the contingent cause of the fall and of sin, which befell our race.

Therefore, it is necessary that a distinction should be made, in this mode, in what is said concerning the certain and necessary existence of sin. The existence of sin, if you regard its origin, was certain in the knowledge of God, but not necessary by the power of the decree as a cause, because God, as absolutely as possible and without any exception, by the order of nature in natural things, bestowed on the will of Adam, the free power of committing or avoiding sin. Thus, by the power of that decree, it was necessary that man should sin or should not sin; by the power of the will, it was contingent that man should sin; finally sin was committed contingently by the motion of the will, because it was decreed contingently.

But the existence of sin, if you have respect to the act in which our first parents fell, though contingent in its origin, is yet certain and necessary in the order of nature, by which it occurs that the leprosy of that sin, which infected them, is transmitted to their posterity. For an evil cause produces an evil effect, "a corrupt tree bringeth forth evil fruit," (Matt. vii. 17), a serpent begets a serpent, a leper begets a leper. That, which pertains to nature, can, with no probable reason, be ascribed to a decree concerning supernatural things. The existence is, in every mode, of nature. It can not then be ascribed to supernatural decrees. You present, as the reason of your affirmation, that sin necessarily results from preterition itself, by the removal of the hindrance. This was, in my judgment, refuted with sufficient clearness, in the answer to your twenty-second proposition.

REPLY OF ARMINIUS TO THE ANSWER TO THE TWENTY-FOURTH PROPOSITION

The mode should have been pointed out here, in which it could occur that the decree of preterition should necessarily cohere with the decree of predamnation, without a necessary copula. The foresight of contingent sin is not a necessary copula. That they may necessarily cohere, since the decree of preterition considers man, not as a sinner, and that of predamnation considers him only as a sinner, there must, of necessity, be the necessary existence of sin, either by the force of the decree of preterition, or of some other divine decree, such, for example, as Beza describes. We speak here of the existence of sin, in respect to the act of Adam, not of its necessary existence in respect to our corrupt conception and birth. For the latter is the effect of the former, by the mode of merit, by the intervention of the judgment and sentence of God, imputing the guilt of the first sin to all the posterity of Adam, not less than to Adam himself and to Eve, because they also sinned in Adam.

I concede the truth of what you say, at the end of your answer, that those things, which are natural, are not to be ascribed to supernatural decrees. But sin, if it is necessary, that is, if it is necessarily committed, and is not a natural act, namely, an act dependent on the will of man, as the principle of his own action; and if sin is natural, then its necessity would not have been ascribed, by Calvin and Beza, to the decree of predestination. We do not here discuss the thing considered in itself, but considered on the hypothesis of that theory which unites preterition with predamnation, by a necessary copula, not by sin, existing previously both to preterition and predamnation. Whether that, which I said concerning the necessary existence of sin as a result of the decree of preterition, by the mode of the removal of the hindrance, was refuted by you, may, perhaps, be decided by a reference to my reply to your answer to the twenty-second proposition.

TWENTY-FIFTH PROPOSITION OF ARMINIUS

Fourthly, because it is not consistent with the condition of the creation and perpetuation of the human race, which was that all should be considered in one, and that all should come from one. It regards men, either as not considered in Adam, or as considered in various modes in Adam, that is, in him as just created, not yet fallen.

REPLY OF JUNIUS TO THE TWENTY-FIFTH PROPOSITION

Those things, which are distinct in their whole genus, are distinct also in their mode. The condition of the creation and the perpetuation of the human race, is natural (for creation is natural by reduction, as unity is ascribed to number, a point to a line,) but the condition of election and predestination is wholly supernatural. They differ, therefore, in mode. A consequence, from things which lack analogy and equality, is not valid. All things, indeed, in nature are considered in one thing, and all come from one, but in the case of predestination, all are not considered in one, but each is considered in himself, nor do all come naturally from one, but all are supernaturally distinguished, by God, in Christ. Man, according to nature, is considered universally and individually in Adam; according to grace, he is considered only individually in Christ, for this is not the order of nature, but the benefit of grace. Therefore, the predestinate are considered, not in nature and according to nature, but of nature according to grace, which is personal and not natural. Law pertains to nature; privilege to grace. Consequently, what is presented in reference to the consideration of men in Adam, is irrelevant.

REPLY OF ARMINIUS TO THE ANSWER TO
THE TWENTY-FIFTH PROPOSITION

The force of my argument is sustained. For though creation and predestination differ in mode and genus, as natural and supernatural, yet predestination and reprobation, which impinge on the conditions of creation, can not be true. I should have used a more correct phraseology, if I had said inconsistent instead of not consistent. For a supernatural action can add something to created nature, and exceed the order of nature, but can do nothing contrary to creation. But predestination and reprobation, as set forth in your Theses, ordain something contrary to the conditions of creation; they cannot, then, have place among true doctrines. I will prove my assumption. You state that some are passed by apart from the consideration of sin. But a man can be considered apart from sin, only as he was in his primitive state, but the theory under consideration regards some as passed-by, considered in their primitive state, which can not be true, because, in their primitive state, they had the power to persevere in good, and in the avoidance of sin, and, therefore, they could be saved by obedience to the law, and, by consequence, they were not passed by, considered in that state, since the passed-by, according to the definition of your Theses, necessarily fail of salvation, and are even necessarily damned, though with the intervention of sin. If you say that they were necessarily damned after they were foreseen as sinners, I reply that they were also passed by after they were foreseen as about to sin, indeed, seen as sinners. We notice, also, your two-fold distinction in that consideration. Men are considered in one, and they are considered also, each in himself, but all are considered in one such as they are in him, and each is considered in himself, such as he is in himself, else the distinction is false. This consideration is two-fold in reference to a two-fold condition. They are considered in the condition of primitive integrity, and in that of fallen, sinful creatures. In the primitive state, all are considered in one, as in their origin and stock, and while this stands, they stand. Each is considered in himself as standing, and as having, from the arrangement of nature and grace, every thing which the original stock had, whether of nature or of grace—the term grace being used in contradistinction to nature, otherwise whatever a man has may be regarded as of gracious bestowal. Therefore, all are considered as true, just, and holy. In the state of sin, all are considered in one who sinned, and all are considered to have sinned in him. Each is considered in himself as deficient in those things, which he would have had of grace, if the first man had remained pure, and as involved in sin and in the demerit of sin. Now, so far as all are considered in one, whether as a pure or as a fallen being, there is no predestination, no preterition or reprobation, no predamnation. For then all would be predestinate and none reprobate, or all would be reprobate and none predestinate. Therefore, predestination and reprobation have place in reference to them, as they are each considered in themselves. Concerning this, then, there is no question between us. But the point at issue, is this—In what state are they each considered by God, in the act of predestination and of preterition? You answer, that they are considered in the primitive state, or rather that they are considered in general; I affirm that they are considered, individually and definitely, in the state of sin. Otherwise, I say that this decree impinges on the conditions of creation, as I have demonstrated. This is absurd, for supernatural things can and indeed must be superior to natural, but by no means contrary to them.

TWENTY-SIXTH PROPOSITION OF ARMINIUS

Fifthly, because, according to it, the decree is equivocal, and true only on condition of a distribution of its terms. It is equivocal because glory and grace, which are prepared in election and reprobation, are equivocal; for it is the glory which follows the ignominy of sin through the grace of remission and regeneration, or it is glory bestowed on nature, as originally created, by supernatural grace superinfused into that nature. It is true only on the condition of a distribution of its terms, because it absolutely ordains neither kind of grace to its subject; not the grace, superinfused upon nature, and glory by means of it, because it is not that grace by which a man is saved and glorified; not the grace of remission and removal, because it can ordain that grace only to the sinner. The decree must, then, be understood with this distribution; -- I will to this man glory and grace, certainly indeed, yet of the former or latter kind, as one or the other may be necessary for him, according to the diversity of his condition.

REPLY OF JUNIUS TO THE
TWENTY-SIXTH PROPOSITION

We deny that "the decree is equivocal and true only on condition of a distribution of the terms." It is not equivocal for it is expressed in general terms and refers to grace and glory in a general sense. That which is thus stated is not equivocal. Neither grace nor glory, in the decree, is two-fold, but both are one in substance, in fact, and in relation, but different in degrees in relation to their object. As life in man is not two-fold in its nature, though it may increase of itself, by the law of nature, so neither grace nor glory is two-fold, though each may progress in us by its own degrees. Grace, in both cases, is supernatural, both when it graciously renews nature, and when it raises a person above the mode of nature. Whatever may be said of it, it is supernatural and in fact one. Glory, also, in both cases, is universally supernatural, both that which is adequate to the mode of nature, and that which is above nature. The latter embraces and absorbs the former, as the greater light does the less; yet, in both cases, it is light, and is supernatural, since nature lost and grace may restore it. Nor, indeed, is that decree to be considered as certain only on condition of a distribution of terms; for God absolutely ordains His whole grace, that is, every mode of it, to His own elect, without modification or any exception. Therefore, also, He ordains and bestows upon them the grace of remission and renewal, as its antecedent mode, and the grace of that celestial glory, as its consequent mode. Indeed, if it was possible that any thing of a supernatural character, in addition to the antecedent grace or consequent glory pertaining to nature, should be desired, and if there is any thing else to which I might wish to refer, God will fully bestow it, because He has universally decreed to His own, that grace and glory which is, indeed, communicable. But God can ordain the grace of remission and renewal only to the sinner and in relation to sin, but He had respect to the whole man, generally, on whom He could bestow His whole grace and apply it in a supernatural mode. The decree, then, of grace and of glory is to be understood absolutely, because it was ordained absolutely and generally, without restriction, exception or modification of the grace and glory which God communicates to His own. There is variety in the object and in its mode, but the fact that grace and glory is absolutely and generally decreed and bestowed on various objects, does not evince that the grace and glory are diverse in themselves; as the light of the Sun is not various, if it comes to us variously, or is variously perceived by us.

REPLY OF ARMINIUS TO THE ANSWER TO
THE TWENTY-SIXTH PROPOSITION

You seem not to have fully understood my proposition.—That you may understand it according to my meaning, I will, so far as I am able, state it in phraseology, used by yourself in this matter. I say that this decree is equivocal, because grace and glory, prepared in this decree, are equivocal, that is each of them is equivocal. For the grace, which preserves and confirms in original integrity, is one thing; that, which restores from a sinful state is another. Also, glory, in respect to the mode of the object, which, being above nature, is superadded to that which is adequate to the mode of nature, is one thing, and that, which is bestowed on nature, freed from the ignominy of sin and misery, is another.

This decree is true only on condition of a distribution of its terms, because it does not ordain to man either this grace or that, or glory of this or that mode, absolutely, but one only, in the case of grace or of glory, and on a certain condition. It does not ordain to man, absolutely, the grace of preservation in his original integrity, and glory from or through that grace, because that is not the grace and glory, by which man is saved and glorified. It does not ordain to man, absolutely, the grace of restoration from a state of sin, and of glory from a state of ignominy, because it can absolutely ordain that grace and glory only to a sinner. Therefore the decree must be understood with the following distribution of its terms: -I ordained to this man grace or glory, certainly indeed, but either of this or of that mode as the former or the latter shall be necessary for him, according to his different state of integrity or of sin.

I will now consider your answer. You deny that this decree is equivocal: I affirm it. To sustain your denial, you add, "it is expressed in general terms, and refers to grace and glory in a general sense. That, which is thus stated, is not equivocal." I concede the latter, and deny the former. I affirm that grace and glory are spoken of, indeed in general terms, but they are not understood in a general sense, which is equivocation. I prove that they are not understood in a general sense, because grace and glory are prepared for man, in predestination, not understood in a general sense, but as they are spoken of particularly. Examine your remarks in answer to Proposition 11th. That cannot be said to be prepared generally, which is not prepared in some particular part or species. Much less can that be said to be so prepared, which is of a nature, such that, if it is prepared, in one part or species, of itself, it can not be prepared in another. But this is the state of the case. Grace, taken generally, comprehends the grace of preservation in the state of integrity, and of restoration from the state of sin. Glory, taken generally, comprehends glory superadded to primitive nature and glory bestowed on fallen nature, raised from a state of ignominy. Neither grace nor glory, generally, is prepared for man. If, indeed, the grace of preservation in a state of integrity, and glory, superadded to nature, was prepared for man, then the grace of restoration from a state of sin, and glory, from a state of ignominy, could not be prepared for him, since he did not need this latter grace and glory, if he obtained the former, and there could be no place for the latter, if the former had a place. But, if there is any place for the grace of restoration from a state of sin and of glory from one of ignominy, a place was not made, in the predestination of God, for the grace of preservation and for glory by means of that grace. Hence it is apparent that my proposition was not clearly understood by you, who have thought that there is such a relation of two-fold grace and glory, that one grace embraces and absorbs the other, and one glory has the same relation to the other, according to the illustration of light. Grace, renewing the nature, and grace, exalting, above the mode of nature, the same renewed nature, sustain this relation, for one embraces and perfects the other. I did not, however, refer to that two-fold grace, but to the grace of preservation in the primitive state, and to that of restoration from a state of sin. These are not mutually dependent; one does not comprehend the other, but one excludes the other. But glory, adequate to the mode of nature, and glory, above nature, sustain such a relation, that one perfects and embraces the other. I did not, however, refer to this two-fold glory, but to glory, in both modes supernatural, in one superadded to primitive nature, in the other bestowed on fallen nature, restored from its ignominy. In this sense, therefore, that decree is equivocal, since, in it, the words, grace and glory, are spoken of, generally and in a universal sense, but they are not prepared, generally and in a universal sense, in predestination, but separately, distinctly and particularly.

You also deny that "this decree is true only on condition of a distribution of its terms," but you deny it in the sense, which was really intended by them. Your denial is true in the former sense. For the grace of remission and that of renovation, as an antecedent mode, are simply and truly prepared for man. But that was not my meaning, as is most clearly apparent from the words themselves. For I placed the grace of remission and of renewal in contrast not to the grace of celestial glory, but to the grace of preservation in a state of integrity. God, in predestination, did not absolutely ordain grace in those two modes, or those two parts or species of grace for man, or either of them absolutely; but one only, and that on the condition of distribution, according to the decree of which we treat. He did not ordain both parts absolutely, since both parts can not have place at the same time. The former excludes the latter as unnecessary, and, indeed, as not being able to have place at the same time; the latter excludes the former, as not having been applied, from which want of application in the case of the former, namely, the grace of preservation in the primitive state, the latter, namely, that of restoration from a sinful state, became necessary, if indeed man was to be saved of grace. He did not ordain either of these, simply and absolutely without any condition; not that of preservation, for it was not bestowed on man, and it would have been bestowed, if it had been prepared absolutely and of predestination; not that of remission of sins and of renewal, that is, of renewal from a state of sin, because He could ordain that grace absolutely only to a sinner, and that decree did not regard man as a sinner. But it ordained, on condition of the distribution of the terms, either this or that, as the condition of man demanded one or the other.

That a decree of this kind is true only on condition of the distribution of its terms is clear from the terms, if correctly understood. I will illustrate it by an example. Every statement is necessarily true or false; -- But this is a statement; Therefore it is necessarily true or necessarily false. This does not follow. For on condition of a distribution of the terms, it is true that every statement is necessarily true or false, and neither part is, abstractly and separately, necessary. The nature of the decree of predestination demands that it should be absolutely certain and true that God ordained for a man the grace of preservation in a state of integrity, or absolutely certain and true that God ordained for a man the grace of renewal from a state of sin. But God does not ordain, on condition of the distribution of terms, for a man either the grace of preservation or the grace of renewal.

But since predestination, as it is defined by you, refers to the last mode, I affirmed correctly that it is only certain on condition of the distribution of terms. I conclude, by a fair deduction, that it is, therefore, not predestination. If it truly pertains to predestination to ordain, absolutely and definitely, the grace of preservation and, if it does not ordain that, to ordain, absolutely and definitely, the grace of restoration, then it follows that God did not and could not regard man in general. For the ordination of the former grace definitely excludes sin, that of the latter definitely includes the consideration of sin, and, in both modes, that general consideration is equally refuted. For the general consideration of an object neither excludes any circumstance, nor is united to any certain and special circumstance. That predestination of grace, however, which preserves in a state of integrity, excludes the circumstance of sin, and this predestination of grace restoring from a state of sin, is definitely united to the circumstance of sin. Therefore the decree of predestination was not made abstractly and universally or generally, without any restriction or modification of grace and glory, but it was, and necessarily must have been, made with a restriction and modification of grace and glory. For the decree of predestination is that, by which is prepared the grace, through which a man is certainly saved, not that, by which salvation would be possible, if indeed any state of man might require the application of such grace, nor that, by which he would be saved, if it should be applied to any state of man. But that grace, by which a man is certainly saved, must be modified and restricted. For he is saved either by the grace of preservation, or by that of restoration, by one or the other, of necessity. If he is saved by one, he does not need to be saved and he can not be saved, by the other; if he is not saved by one, he must be saved by the other, or excluded from salvation, and that, by which he is saved, is prepared in predestination, and the other, by which he is not saved, is absolutely excluded.

You affirm that "there is variety in the object and in its mode." But we here treat of that variety in the object and its mode, which variety is so great that grace and glory must be modified and restricted to this or that variety of the object; the grace of preservation in the state of integrity and glory, by means of it, are suitable to the object, considered in its original state; the grace of restoration and glory, by means of it, are suitable to the object, considered in sin and misery. Grace and glory, considered absolutely and universally, can not be decreed or bestowed, in predestination, upon various objects. For predestination has reference, necessarily, to a uniform and univocal object, that is either to one absolutely not a sinner, or to a sinner, and it bestows grace only on a subject, of one mode and univocal. It saves one, absolutely not a sinner or absolutely a sinner; it does not adapt itself to this one or that one, of this or of that character, but it adapts itself absolutely to an object of this character, and not otherwise considered. The grace of preservation saves, absolutely, the angels, for the grace of restoration was never ordained concerning them or bestowed upon them. The grace of restoration absolutely saves human beings, for the grace of preservation, in their original state of integrity, was never ordained for them or bestowed upon them. Grace is, indeed, as you say, one in itself, and in its essence, as, also, is glory, but each is variously applied according to the mode and relation of the object; and, between the application of grace and the mode and relation of the object, there is this reciprocity that, from the application of grace, the relation of the object may be inferred, and from the mode of the object, reciprocally may be deduced what grace it may be necessary to apply to that object. The same is true of glory.

The illustration of the light of the Sun, introduced at the end of your answer, may also serve my purpose. The light of the Sun is one and the same, whether it is shed upon and renders more luminous a body already illuminated, or it is shed on a dark body and drives away the darkness, and renders that light which was before dark. If only the same difference existed between an illuminated and a dark body, as exists between a man in his original state and a sinner, then rays of the Sun, sufficient to illuminate the body already light, would not suffice to illuminate the dark body, unless they were greatly increased and multiplied.

TWENTY-SEVENTH PROPOSITION OF ARMINIUS

I will not now touch the theory of Augustine, because that would be a futile task, if the theory of Aquinas, of prior consideration, can be sustained to my satisfaction. These, then, are the matters which I would present to your consideration.

ANSWER OF JUNIUS TO THE TWENTY-SEVENTH PROPOSITION

I have always thought, and yet think, that the theory of Augustine was substantially consistent with the two theories which have been considered. You will see that this is the fact, if you make allowance for certain modes of expression used by him, and for a single diverse circumstance.

I have thus, my brother, in this subject, used the diligence and promptitude which was possible, in view of the duties which have, not rarely, interrupted me. Receive my effort with kindness, if it may not answer your expectation. May the God of truth and peace seal on your mind that saving peace, more and more, and graciously guide both of us and all His servants in the way of truth to His own glory, and to the edification of His church in Christ Jesus our saviour. Amen.

REPLY OF ARMINIUS TO THE ANSWER TO THE TWENTY-SEVENTH *PROPOSITION*

The theory of Augustine is very different from both the preceding theories, as may be seen from this whole discussion, on account of the circumstance, added by him to the object of the decree, concerning which we treat. For, if the circumstance of sin was, of necessity, to be considered by the Deity, in the act of decree, and was definitely considered in that very act, then it must be true that those discussions and explanations of the same decree, err greatly from the truth, which state that there was no necessity of the consideration of sin, and no actual consideration of it by God, when He ordained the decree. The remark may be added, with propriety, that, by the mere addition to the object of the decree and right explanation of the circumstance of sin, all the absurdities and blasphemies, which are usually alleged against the decree of predestination and reprobation may be repelled and clearly refuted, not being logical consequences of that decree.

I have thus presented my objections to your answers to my propositions, not so much with the thought of refuting them, as with a desire to elicit from you more extended answers and explanations, by which I might perhaps be satisfied and my mind might be freed from its difficulties on this subject. I, therefore, beseech God, that, if I have written any thing contrary to the truth, He may pardon me concerning it, and may reveal the truth unto me; if I have advanced any thing agreeable to the truth, that He will confirm me in it, and that he will grant to me yourself, assenting to my views, and aiding me, that, by means of you, the truth may daily gain greater authority, and may be more and more propagated to the glory of the divine name, to the advantage and increase of the church, in our Lord Jesus Christ. Amen.

APPENDIX

THESES OF DR. FRANCIS JUNIUS

Concerning Divine Predestination,

Composed, In These Very Words, By Himself, And Publicly Discussed, Under His Direction, By William Coddaeus, In The University Of Leyden, In The Year 1593 -- Also Some Brief Annotations Of James Arminius.

Appendix: 20 Theses Of Dr. Junius: Predestination & Arminius: Annotations

Appendix: 20 Theses And Brief Annotations

As We Have Frequently Referred To The Theses Of Doctor Francis Junias Concerning Predestination, We Will Here Insert Them, And Make Some Brief Annotations Upon Them.

THESIS 1

Predestination is properly, according to the etymology of the word, a determination to an end, but in common usage, it is equivalent to the Greek word protagh and signifies the relation of the whole arrangement to the end, and thus we use it.

Destination is a determination of an existing object to its end; the particle prae, prefixed to the word, denotes that the act of destination is antecedent to the actual existence of the object.

THESIS 2

Predestination, therefore, is an act of the divine good-pleasure, by which God, from eternity, prepared the plenitude of His blessings, in Christ, for those, who should be heirs of salvation, to the praise of His glorious grace. The word eujokia or good-pleasure, is here used, correctly, according to the Scriptural sense, for the particle eu+ refers to the favourable and benevolent inclination of God towards its object, not to the precise and determinate will of God in reference to any of His own purposes, as the word good-pleasure is used by the school-men, when they distinguish the will of God into his revealed will and the will of His good-pleasure. Prepared in Christ.] No blessings are prepared in Christ for men, except those which are adapted to sinners. Christ himself; the saviour of men, is called Jesus only because "He shall save His people from their sins," (Matt. i. 21). No one is blessed in Christ, if he is not a believer;

"So then, they, which be of faith, are blessed with faithful Abraham" (Gal. iii. 9.)

For those who should be heirs of salvation]. Salvation itself; and the inheritance of eternal life, are comprehended in the fullness of those blessings, which God has prepared in Christ. Therefore those, for whom that fullness was prepared, should have been otherwise described. For there is an absurdity in the statement, -- "predestination is an act, by which God has prepared salvation for those who shall be heirs of salvation." For they are made heirs of salvation according to which, the inheritance, comprehended in the fullness of those blessings, was prepared. Persons, as one part of the material or object of predestination, are not to be described by the divine things, which were prepared for them in that predestination, and which constitute the other part of the material or object of predestination. The persons are more correctly described by Sohnius, thus: "Predestination unto life, or election, is that by which God decreed, from eternity, to justify and to accept unto eternal life, believers, or the faithful, to whom he decreed to teach faith." To the praise of His glorious grace]. The Scriptures recognize the grace of God as the cause and end of predestination, only as mercy is united with it, and as it is exercised towards sinners and the miserable.

THESIS 3

It is an act (for God is simple energy) proceeding not from any external cause, but purely from Him who predestinates; otherwise it would not be, purely, predestination, preceding all things and causes.

The divine predestination, indeed, precedes all things and causes, so far as their actual existence is considered; or it was decreed from eternity. It, however, follows, in the mind and prescience of God, the pre-existence of some things and causes; that of sin, for example, without which neither grace, as it is described above, nor Christ, in his true character, nor those blessings could have any adaptation to men. Therefore, although this predestination may not depend on an extrinsic cause, yet it was occasioned, as they say, by sin.

THESIS 4

Its cause is eujdokia good-pleasure, by which He was favourably disposed towards those, whom He pleased to adopt as sons, through Jesus Christ, according to the purpose of His election.

By that same good pleasure, by which God was favourably disposed towards some. He also was pleased to adopt the same persons as sons. Therefore, this is not a correct description of the persons towards whom God was favourably disposed. Indeed, it was because He was favourably disposed towards them, that He adopted them as sons.

To adopt as sons]. Observe here that adoption is not placed among the prepared blessing, but that it is used to describe the persons for whom blessings are prepared. Compare this with your answer to my first proposition.

But, that the inappropriateness of that definition may be more manifest, let it be put in this form; -- Predestination is an act of the divine good-pleasure, by which God, from eternity, prepared filial adoption, and its consequent, eternal life, in Christ, for those whom He pleased to adopt as sons, and who should be heirs of salvation.

To adopt as sons through Jesus Christ]. Christ Jesus is here to be considered not only as the foundation on which is based the execution of the decree, but also as the foundation on which the decree itself is based. For we are adopted in him as in our head, therefore he is, in the order of causes, first constituted and predestinated to be our head, then we are predestinated in him as his members. This admonition I present, not because I think that you understand that expression differently, but because I perceive that Beza on the first chapter to the Ephesians, adopts an order entirely different, and which seems to me to invert the correct order of predestination.

According to the purpose of his election]. This purpose of election is nothing else than the good-pleasure of God, by which he is favourably disposed towards some, and by which He pleases to adopt some, in Christ, as sons. But your words are so arranged as to convey the idea that this purpose is something different from that good-pleasure.

THESIS 5

It is, therefore, God alone, who predestinates, the cause of His own predestination, and of that preparation which He proposed to Himself, according to that good pleasure of His will.

THESIS 6

Therefore, this act is said to be from eternity, that is, before all things and causes, in things or of things, which He predestinated to exist.

If this Thesis excludes also the sin of man as a condition requisite in the object of that predestination, it is not correctly said that predestination precedes the provision of sin; for, though sin did not move God to the act of predestination, (for it is the appropriate effect of sin to move the wrath of God), yet this predestination was made in view of sin, the occurrence of which in time, God foresaw in the infinity of His knowledge.

THESIS 7

The material of predestination is twofold; divine things, and persons to be partakers of them.

Divine things and persons, to be partakers of them, have a mutual relation to each other, so that a conclusion concerning the character of the persons can be formed from the nature of those things, and conversely, the nature of those divine things may be inferred from the character of the persons. The things are adapted to the persons, and such persons need such things for salvation. Thus, from the grace of the remission of sins and the renewal of the Holy Ghost, we infer that the men, for whom those things are prepared, are sinners; also, if men are sinners, it is inferred that such grace is necessary for them.

THESIS 8

The genus of the divine things, which are communicable through Predestination, is blessing, which the Apostle circumscribes within these modes; it is complete, not partial; spiritual, not carnal; "in heavenly places," not natural, but surpassing all nature; finally, in Christ, that is, divine in its principle and foundation, that Christ may be the eternal head of the predestinate.

The expression, in which divine things are said to be communicable through predestination, does not seem to me to be in harmony with the nature of predestination. For predestination does not cause that those things should be communicable, but does in fact communicate them. They are made communicable by the blood and death and resurrection of Christ, by which those blessings were acquired and obtained from the Father. Since any thing is communicable before it is, in fact, communicated, it follows that predestination is posterior, in the prescience and preordination of God, to the death and resurrection of Christ. I leave the inference for the consideration of the intelligent.

Spiritual, not carnal]. spiritual is contrasted in the Scriptures not only with carnal, but, also, with natural; as in 1 Corinthians ii. 14, also, in 1 Corinthians xv. 44, 45, 46. Carnal, however, may sometimes also comprehend in itself the natural.

"In heavenly places," not natural]. Heavenly things are, in the Scriptures, contrasted with mundane and earthly good, adapted to nature as such, and, thus, heavenly and natural are indirectly opposed.

Finally, in Christ]. Christ obtained those blessings by his death; he has received the same from his Father to be communicated to his followers; in him believers are predestinated to a participation in the same.

Divine in principle and foundation]. Blessing is divine in principle, for its principle is God, the Father, who confers it; but it is not said, in the same sense to be divine in its foundation. For Christ is the foundation of that blessing, not as he is God, but as he is God-man, Qeanqrwpov Mediator, saviour and Head of the church. This consideration of Christ is, everywhere in the Scriptures, distinguished from that, in which Christ is regarded as God, as in John xvii, 3; xiv, 1;

1 Tim. ii. 5, 6; 1 Pet. i. 18, 19, 20, 21; 1 Cor. v. 19, &c.

That Christ might be the eternal head of the Predestinate]. Whether Christ was constituted the head of those who were to be predestinated, or of those who had been already predestinated, has been a point in dispute among Theologians. It is my opinion that, in the order of nature, the decree by which Christ was constituted the head of those to be saved, was prior to that decree by which some are ordained in Christ to a participation in salvation. For Christ, as our mediator before God and our High Priest, merited those blessings, which were to be communicated by predestination, and, at the same time, the dignity of head, and the power to communicate those blessings. Then he actually received those blessings from the Father, and obtained the titles of Head, King and Prince. "Having been made perfect, or consecrated, he became the author of eternal salvation to all who obey him."

Finally, in him believers are predestinated, that they should be partakers of those blessings, by union with him. For God loves, in Christ, those whom He has determined to make partakers of eternal life, but this love is the cause of predestination. It was, indeed, in Christ born, dead, raised again, and constituted the head of the church. "But," some will say, "God so loved the world that He gave His only-begotten Son."—I answer, that the love, referred to in this passage, differs in degree from that which is the cause of predestination, and is prior to it. For that love, which sent His Son, did not, with certainty, ordain eternal life to any one, and, indeed, it could not do so, for Christ had not merited it by his death. Indeed, by making Christ the foundation and Head of the predestinate, you seem to declare that Christ was made the Head of them who were to be predestinated in him unto life.

THESIS 9

Of these blessings, the chief points are two, grace and glory; the former, acting on men in the present life, the latter to be consummated in them in the future life.

THESIS 10

Human beings are creatures, in a condition of nature—which can effect nothing supernatural or divine—to be exalted above nature, and to be transferred to a participation of divine things by the supernatural energy of the Deity.

It is here most manifestly evident that the object of predestination is considered by you to be men in their natural state, which can effect nothing supernatural or divine, that is, as I have said, considered, in a merely natural state, apart from supernatural endowments, and from the corruption which afterwards supervened. But this is not an adequate object of this decree. For the exaltation, which is according to predestination, is not from nature, but from sin beginning. The divine things, a participation in which is prepared by predestination, are not adapted to man in his natural state, but to man involved in sin and misery. That supernatural power belongs to God, which He exercises in Christ, "the power of God and the wisdom of God," 1 Corinthians i. 24, the Jews and Gentiles being called to salvation. Therefore, it was applied to man, considered not in his primitive natural state, but in sin and misery.

THESIS 11

The form is adoption, as sons, through Jesus Christ, that is, that real relation and ordination, in which we are blessed of God, by the communication of "all spiritual blessings in heavenly places" in Christ. Predestination is unto adoption, therefore adoption is not the form of predestination. For "the form gives being to the thing," and adoption does not give being to predestination, but receives its own being from predestination; and it is the first per se and immediate work of divine predestination, and its consequent is life and the heavenly inheritance. Nor is that real relation and ordination, in which we are blessed, "the form of predestination;" for that ordination, in which we are blessed; is the execution of the divine predestination. But the preparation of those blessings is the form of predestination, for, by it, predestination has its being. That preparation is internal and eternal, and that is true also of predestination. Or—to speak with greater accuracy -- the preparation of those blessings is not the form of predestination, for that preparation was made by the death of Christ, the Mediator, but the form consists in the preparation of the communication of those blessings to believers in Christ. We might add that the preparation is certain, and that, according to it, a communion in the benefits of Christ is certainly bestowed on those for whom the participation is prepared.

THESIS 12

The order of this form is placed in the preparation, of persons, by election, vocation, and "gathering together in Christ" (Ephes. i. 10); but of things, by a gracious beginning, progress, and glorious consummation of blessings, in a perfect union with Christ.

The order of that preparation, as the form, can, indeed, be declared, in respect both to persons and to things. Persons are prepared in the minds of God, when election from the world, vocation to a union with Christ, and the gathering together in Christ, are ordained for them. Things are prepared in this order, that their gracious communication should he ordained, in reference to its beginning, progress, and final consummation; the beginning, in Christ; the progress, in the same; but the consummation, in the perfect union with God. For this is the consummation of a supernatural felicity "that God may be all in all." If, however, the subject of discussion be the mediatorial consummation, I concede that this is effected in Christ, but this tends to that chief consummation, which is union with God, to which we come by a perfect union with Christ. For Christ shall deliver up his own kingdom "to God even the Father, that God may be all in all." (1 Cor. xv. 24, 28.)

THESIS 13

The end is the praise of the glorious grace of God, by which He has freely made us acceptable unto Himself, in the Son of His love.

The grace, by which God "has freely made us acceptable unto Himself, in the Son of His love, is grace only adapted to sinners." The praise of that grace is sung to God and the Lamb, who died and lives again, "who was delivered for our offenses, and was raised again for our justification." (Rom. iv. 25.) That praise is ascribed to God by sinners, whom God has redeemed by the blood of His Son, "out of every kindred, tongue, and people, and nation." (Rev. v. 9.)

THESIS 14

What is contrary to this predestination can not, with propriety, be expressed in a single term, since the relation of predestination is single, that of its contraries is various. For preterition is contrary to the preparation of grace, and reprobation or preparation of punishment is contrary to the preparation of glory.

Grace and glory are prepared in predestination. To this preparation, as an affirmative act, is opposed the negative act of the non-preparation of grace and glory, and the affirmative act of the preparation of those things, which are affirmatively contrary to grace and glory. But here, to the preparation of grace, is opposed only the negative act of preterition, and, to the preparation of glory, only the affirmative act of reprobation or the preparation of punishment. Hence it seems to me to be a correct conclusion that this discussion is not absolutely consistent in all its parts, unless, perhaps, there is no affirmative act, which can be opposed to the preparation of grace. There is, however, such an act, namely, hardening, blinding, and the delivering to a reprobate mind, which can be fitly and fully explained only by negative acts. Also, the denial of celestial glory is a negative act opposed to the preparation of glory. It is to be observed, here, that the word reprobation is used for the preparation of punishment, while, in your answers to my propositions, you affirm that it properly signifies non-election or preterition.

THESIS 15

Preterition is the act of the divine will, by which God, from eternity, determined to leave some of His creatures in their natural state, and not to communicate to them that supernatural grace, by which their nature might be preserved uncorrupt, or, having become corrupt, might be restored, to the declaration of the freedom of His own goodness.

Preterition is defined to be a denial of grace only, not of glory, while, nevertheless, glory is denied to the same persons. It is rightly called an act of the divine pleasure, not good-pleasure; for pleasure is the general term, applied to any purpose or decree of God; good-pleasure, as has been remarked, includes a favourable and benevolent disposition in the Deity. To leave in their natural condition]. From this also it is evident that the object of predestination is, in your view, men considered in a merely natural state.

Supernatural grace, by which their nature might be preserved uncorrupt, or, having become corrupt, might be restored]. If the e words are to be understood to have reference to the particular predestination of men, then that distinction is not correctly used. For the grace by which nature is "preserved uncorrupt," is not denied by the decree of preterition. For that grace was denied to all men without distinction. But the denial of grace, by which nature, having become corrupt, is restored, is peculiar to the decree of preterition, and, therefore the object of preterition is fallen man, and to one who needs renewing grace.

To the declaration of the freedom of His own goodness.] The freedom of the goodness of God is declared not only when God communicates to one, and denies to another, His own goodness, but also when He communicates it only on the condition, which He has been pleased to impose; I concede, however, that the freedom of the divine goodness is also declared in the former mode.

But there is a declaration in preterition, as described to us in the Scriptures, not only of the freedom of the goodness of God, but of His justice. For God, according to justice also, uses preterition, by which He determines to deny His grace to some on account of their sins. Sin, indeed, is the only meritorious cause of the denial of grace, which is here discussed. Therefore, the statement of the end of that preterition was not sufficiently complete.

THESIS 16

This preterition is without blame: for God bestowed on man the perfection of human nature, He was not under obligation to bestow grace upon any one. It is grace; therefore, there is no obligation.

God, in the abstract and absolutely, was not under obligation to bestow grace on any one, but He could place Himself under that obligation in two ways, by promise, and by making certain requisitions. By promise, if He should promise to bestow grace, either with or without condition. By requisition, if He should require, from a man, an act, such that it could not be performed. without His grace, for then He would be under obligation to bestow it, otherwise He would reap where He had not sowed.

THESIS 17

The preparation of punishment is the act of the divine pleasure, by which God, from eternity, determined, for the declaration of His own justice, to punish His creatures, who should not continue in their original state, but should depart from God, the author of their origin, by their own deed and depravity, You call the preparation of punishment an affirmative act, opposed to predestination; but it is opposed, affirmatively, to the preparation of glory. That, which is opposed affirmatively, to the communication of grace is not here stated. I think that it should be called hardening and blinding, and that it should have been also treated in this Thesis.

To punish His creatures who should not maintain their original integrity]. This decree was ordained by God, not until after the certain foresight of future sin, lest any one should think that sin is necessarily inferred from that decree, as some of our Doctors believe.

Should full away from God by their own act and transgression]. It should be explained how he can, by his own act, fall away from God, who has, already, been passed by of God, in the communication of that grace, which is necessary for the avoidance of defection from God. And since all the passed-by are also predamned, I could wish that it might be explained how preterition and predamnation necessarily cohere, if preterition existed apart from any consideration of sin, but predamnation, only on account of sin.

The declaration of the justice of God, also, as has been previously remarked, has a place in preterition.

THESIS 18

Therefore, in the predestinate, God does all things according to the good-pleasure of His own predestination. In those who are not predestinate, He uses preterition according to the pleasure of His will, and prepares punishment for His creatures who transgress against His order, and who must be reprobated, on account of their sins, from the necessity of His justice.

In predestination, God provides only for the salvation of the elect; yet, in such a manner, that many acts of the divine Providence concur to the same effect, which acts are so administered by the Deity, that from them salvation certainly results, which is the proper work of predestination. God uses many acts of His providence towards those, who are not predestinated, sufficient, indeed, for salvation, yet not efficacious, since this pertains to predestination. It is not absurd nor irrelevant, then, to observe, here, this distinction between providence and predestination. Who must be reprobated on account of their sins]. You here, also, use the word reprobation for the preparation of punishment.

THESIS 19

If reprobation is made the opposite of predestination, the statement is figurative, and synecdochical: wherefore, it either should not be made, because it is improper, dangerous, and liable to give offense, or it should be distinctly explained, as pious and learned men have done.

In your answer to my second proposition, you use this language: "Reprobation is used in three senses, one common and two special. In its common use, it comprehends preterition and damnation. Its second mode is special, when it is opposed to election, and signifies non-election or preterition. The third is also special, when it is used for pre-damnation. The first mode is by synecdoche, the second proper, the third metonymical, and it may also be called catachrestic." Here, you call that meaning of reprobation common, which, in your Theses, and elsewhere, you call figurative. We are not to abstain from the use of the term, for it is Scriptural, but we are to be careful that it be also used in the sense in which it is used in the Scriptures.

THESIS 20

The presentation of this doctrine is especially necessary, if it is treated skillfully, soberly, and reverently, that is, that not any thing else be treated, not otherwise, not to another end than as the Holy Scriptures teach, both in explanation and in application, according to the advice of St. Paul: "not to think of himself more highly than he ought to think, but to think soberly." Rom. xii. 3.

That, which is taught, and inculcated in the Holy Scriptures, can not but be esteemed useful and necessary for salvation, though there may be different degrees of necessity. But the doctrine of predestination, and its opposite, that of reprobation, is taught and inculcated in the Scriptures; it is, therefore, also necessary. It should, however, be considered what that predestination is, and what is its character, which is discussed in the Scriptures as necessary, and which is called the foundation of our salvation. Your admonition is altogether proper and necessary, by which you enjoin that the doctrine should be set forth entirely in accordance with the Scriptures—"not any thing else, not otherwise, not to another end than as the Holy Scriptures teach." But there is a practical difficulty in this matter, because each one desires to appear to present his own doctrines according to the Scripture. I am satisfied that, in your discussion of this doctrine, you are not, in every case, sustained by the Scripture, but in some parts you err, and I have treated this more fully in the discussion held between us.

An Examination

**BY REV. JAMES ARMINIUS, D. D. OF A TREATISE;
CONCERNING THE ORDER AND MODE OF
PREDESTINATION
AND THE AMPLITUDE OF DIVINE GRACE**

**BY REV. WILLIAM PERKINS, D.D.,
A THEOLOGICAL WRITER IN ENGLAND ALSO,
AN ANALYSIS OF THE NINTH CHAPTER
OF THE EPISTLE TO THE ROMANS**

CONTENTS

- An Examination Of The Treatise Of William Perkins Concerning The Order And Mode Of Predestination
- Rev. William Perkins Views On Predestination & Grace
- Allegation 1
- Allegation 2
- Allegation 3
- DISCUSSION OF THE SUBJECT OF PERMISSION
- ALLEGATION 4

PART 1

William Perkins,. D. D., Fellow of Christ' s College, Cambridge, was a Theological writer at the close of the sixteenth century. As will be seen from the following strictures on one of his treatises, he advocated views highly Calvinistic. The following "Examination, etc," was written by Arminius, in 1602.

Reverend Sir, and Beloved Brother in Christ, -- While I was lately, and with eagerness, examining a certain library, abundantly supplied with recently published books, a pamphlet presented itself to me, entitled "A Christian and Perspicuous Discourse concerning the Order and Mode of Predestination, and the extent of Divine Grace." When I observed that it bore your name, which was already well known to me by previously published works of a high character, I thought that I must diligently read and consider it, and see whether you, who are devoted to the most accurate learning, could remove, in that work, the difficulties which have long disquieted my mind. I, therefore, read it once and again, with impartiality, as far as I could, and with candour, as you desire. But, in reading, I perceived that all my difficulties were not removed by your work, while I thought that some things, written by you, deserved to be examined in the light of truth. Accordingly, I judged it not improper to commence a friendly discussion with you concerning your treatise. This I do, with the greater freedom and confidence, because, in the second page of your pamphlet, you say, to the encouragement of my mind, that you "have written these things, that, by those devoted to theological investigation"—among whom I willingly reckon myself—"they may be read without prejudice or acerbity of mind, duly weighed, and judged by the pure word of God." This I undertake, and pledge myself to do according to my ability; asking of you that in return, you will, with the same disposition, read my remarks, weigh them, and examine and judge them by the rule of the same Scriptures. May God grant that we all may fully agree, in those things which are necessary to His glory, and to the salvation of the church; and that, in other things, if there can not be harmony of opinions, there may at least be harmony of feelings, and that we may "keep the unity of the Spirit in the bond of peace."

With this desire, then, expressed at the beginning of our discussion, I enter on the subject itself, following in the track, which, in your writing, you have pursued before me. I will commence with your "Epistle to the Reader," and then proceed, with the divine help, to the treatise itself.

EXAMINATION OF THE EPISTLE

In your Epistle to the Reader, you lay down two fundamental principles, on which this doctrine of Predestination and Divine Grace, can and must be built. The first is "the written word of God;" the second "the common ideas, and the principles which God has infused into the minds of men," I have no opposition to make at this point, only let this be added, that, when, on account of the darkness of our minds, and the weakness and diversity of the human judgment (which you regret), it is not possible for us to agree concerning these matters, we must recur, for definite and final decision, to that which is first and equivalent to all other things—the word of God.

Of the first principle, laid down by you, I remark that it is true; but care must be used, lest any thing, which is not in accordance with human judgment, should be attributed to God, and defended as just, on the consideration that it is declared to be unjust by corrupt human judgment; unless it can be made clear, by a conclusive argument, that it is suitably ascribed to the Deity. For, it is sufficient, for the sake of referring any action or work to God, to say that He has justly performed it; though, from the antecedent, God has done this, will follow, of necessity, the consequent, therefore, it is just.

Of the second; -- I concede that it is true. For He is the first cause, and the cause of causes, who, from the foreseen free act of rational creatures, takes occasion to make any decree, and to establish a certain order in events; which decree He would not have made, and which order He would not have established, if the free second causes had acted otherwise. The Apostle says, "the creature was made subject to vanity, not willingly, but by reason of Him who hath subjected the same," (Rom. viii. 20.) To this vanity the creature would not have been subjected, if he, for whose sake it was created by God, had remained in his original integrity. The decree, in reference to sending Christ into the world, depends on the foresight of the fall; for he is "the Lamb of God, which taketh away the sin of the world," (John i. 29.) He "was made a little lower than the angels, for the suffering of death," (Heb. ii. 9); "as the children are partakers of flesh and blood, he also himself likewise took part of the same; that through death he might destroy him that had the power of death, that is, the devil," (Heb. ii. 14.) He was constituted a "high priest, ordained for men, that he might offer both gifts and sacrifices for sins," (Heb. v. 1.) The decrees of God, by which He ordains to punish His creatures, are universally on this principle, according to the Scriptures: "That be far from thee to do after this manner, to slay the righteous with the wicked: shall not the Judge of all the earth do right?" (Gen. xviii. 25.) "Whosoever hath sinned against me, him will I blot out of my book," (Exod. xxxii. 33.) "I said, indeed, that thy house, and the house of thy father, should walk before me forever, but now the Lord saith, be it far from me; for them that honour me I will honour, and they that despise me shall be lightly esteemed," (1 Sam. ii. 30.)

But it is not therefore to be supposed that the imposing of penalties depends on second causes; so far from it, they would put forth every effort to escape punishment, if they could do so either by reason or force. I could wish also that the word "ordaining" were used in its proper sense: from which they seem to me to depart, who interpret it—to decree that something shall be done. For its true meaning is to establish the order of things done, not to appoint things to be done that they may be done; though it is used sometimes by the fathers in the latter sense. But then God is denied, by the fathers, to be the ordainer of evils. Thus says Augustine: "God knows how to ordain, not crime, but the punishment of crimes."

Of the third; -- It is characteristic of a wise being to do nothing in vain. But he does something in vain, who does it not to attain some end. But God is infinitely wise. Let me caution you, then, not to extend the phrase, "to regard with indifference," farther, or to interpret it otherwise than is suitable. There is a real distinction between doing and permitting. He, who permits any thing, that he may attain some end, does not regard it with indifference. From this it is clear that not to regard with indifference is not the same as to do or to make. Of this also I remind you for a certain reason. Then consider whether the phrase, which you use, is correct. The word "prudently" seems to be too feeble to be applied to so great wisdom. And it is not a usual form of expression to say that an action is performed "in view of a certain end," but for the sake of that end. The statement, He does not will or decree that which He can not, is ambiguous, and not sufficiently full. It is ambiguous, because it may be understood to mean that He can not will or decree, or that He can not do. It is not sufficiently full, because there should be an addition, so that the statement would be this: "He does not will or decree to do or permit that which He can not do or permit." For which reason also your conclusion is likewise imperfect, and, to the expression, "He has decreed thus to do," add, "or permit."

Of the fourth; -- The decree of God is two-fold; that of efficacious action and that of permission. Both are immutable. The creature, however free, can not change himself by his own act, or receive any change from another, contrary to either of these decrees, and without the certain and fixed determination of the former or the latter. But it is not merely necessary that God should fix these, and not other, limits of the change, as if the creature—if this was possible without the divine superintendence of the change—might be able either to change himself, or to receive change from another, to such an extent that God could not bring it into order, and have occasion for the illustration of his glory. For to Him even NOTHING ought to be material for the declaration of His glory: and any change from Nothing to Something, produced by Him, ought to serve the same purpose.

Of the fifth; -- All the judgments of God, "whatever they may be, whether hidden or partly known to us, are to be honoured, and to be adorned with the praise of righteousness, provided, however, that it be manifest that they are the judgments of God. But under this pretense, no judgments are to be attributed to God which the Scripture does not assign to Him; much less those which are contrary to the righteousness of God revealed in the Scriptures. Thus Augustine says: "As man becomes more like God, so the more does the damnation of perishing men move him: it moves also our saviour himself, and caused his tears, not once only, to flow. It moves also God Himself; who says: "What could have been done more to my vineyard that I have not done in it?" (Isa. v. 4.) "O that my people had hearkened unto me." (Psalm lxxxi. 13.) "Have I any pleasure at all that the wicked should die," (Ezek. xviii. 23.) But it so moves God, that He is yet delighted in the destruction of His enemies, who are refractory and refuse to repent. For His righteousness demands this. It moves Him, I say, because they are unwilling to be saved, not because, when they are unwilling to be saved, He may devote them to just destruction. It so moves Christ, the saviour, that he shall yet, willingly, banish, from his presence, unbelievers and evil doers, and adjudge them to eternal fire. For this is demanded by the office of Judge. It so moves a pious man, that he may not utter any objection against God in reference to His various decrees, and the execrations of His righteous judgments on the obstinate. This is required by the obedience which the creature owes to his Creator and Redeemer."

Concerning that objection, I may be allowed, with the leave of Augustine, to say that it is not the offspring of infirm and weak human nature, but of the refractory disposition of the Jews and of those like them, of whom the apostle speaks, (Rom. ix. 20.) It is indeed true that we, when compared with God, "are as grass-hoppers," yea, and "are counted to Him as less than nothing," (Isa. xl. 17, 22.) But, in such exaggerations of human insignificance, we are to be careful not to do injustice to the creation of God. For man was made in the image of God, and therefore, even to God Himself, man, not any beast, is the noblest creature, with whom, as the wisdom of God declares, are His delights, (Prov. viii. 31.)

Of the sixth; -- The concurrence of God with second causes to perform any act, or produce any work, is two-fold, of the general, and the special aid of His grace. It is most certain that nothing good can be performed by any rational creature without this special aid of His grace. But whether it is the province of the divine will, absolutely willing it, to communicate this gracious aid, and by this communication, to absolutely work good in us, is in controversy among Theologians. This is not improperly so, since the word absolutely can not be found in the Scriptures, and it has not yet been proved that its equivalent is found in the Scriptures.

Of the seventh; -- So also it is certain that "no evil can be avoided if God does not prevent it." But there is dispute concerning the mode of prevention; -- whether it is by the omnipotent action of the Deity operating on the human will according to the mode of nature, from which there exists a necessity of prevention, or by such an action as operates on the will, according to the mode of the will as respects its freedom, from which the certainty of prevention exists.

Of the eighth; -- It can not be concluded from an event that God has willed something, but we may know either this fact, that He was unwilling to hinder an event which He foresaw would occur.—Otherwise the distinction, which exists between the action and the permission of God, is destroyed. For some things occur, because God produces them, but others, because He permits them to occur, according to Augustine and to truth itself. But to will that any thing should occur, and to be unwilling to prevent its occurrence, are not the same things. For, in the former case, the event is resolved into the will of God as its first and special cause; in the latter, it is resolved affirmatively into a second cause, and negatively into the divine will, which has not prevented it, which prevention also is produced either by power according to the mode of nature, or by persuasion according to the mode of free-will. But concerning permission and prevention we shall treat more fully hereafter in their own place. Of the ninth; -- But let us examine this idea; "to be able to perform," "to will to do," and "actually to do," are divine gifts and effects on men. But there should be this additional remark, that God gives to no one the power of doing right, unless He is ready also to give the will and the act itself, that is, by the further aid of grace, to concur with man in willing and in actually doing that good, for which

He has received sufficient strength, unless the man on his part may interpose, or, as the school-men say, may have interposed some obstacle. "For unto every one that hath shall be given; but from him that hath not shall be taken away even that which he hath." (Matt. xxv. 29). Were this not so, the power would have been given in vain. But the all-wise God doth nothing in vain. Thus He gave to Adam the faculty of observing the law which He had enacted, and He was prepared to give him whatever else was needed, in addition to that faculty, for actual obedience, namely, both to will and to do, unless Adam willingly and by voluntary motion turned himself away from God, and from His grace. I see here a labyrinth which I will not now enter, because I should not be permitted to make my egress from it, except by the thread and guidance of an accurate explication of the mode of the concurrence of God with man in the performance of any good thing; which explication does not belong to this place, or, as I indeed, acknowledge, to my abilities.

Of the tenth; -- That "God presides over the whole world, and all things created by Himself, and administers and governs all and each of them" is certain. But this is not only in justice, but also in mercy, even so far as He, in His infinite wisdom, knows what place ought to be assigned to each. But, indeed, do all those axioms seem to you to be natural and common notions, They, indeed, belong to nature, as it was when it come from the hand of its Creator, surely not to it, as it has been darkened by sin. For to few among men is it given to know and understand those things. The whole troop of Pelagians and Semi-Pelagians in the church itself, do not know them. What the opinion of many of the Greek and Latin philosophers was concerning most of them, is apparent from an expression used by not one of them only:

"What we are, is given to us by the Gods; what of good we are, we have from ourselves." To this notorious falsity, Augustine in more than one passage, sharply opposes himself.

On these principles in part, as a foundation, you build up a doctrine of Predestination, which is, indeed, beset with difficulties. This is caused by the fact, that men do not fear to add to the Scriptures, whatever they think proper, and are accustomed to attribute as much as possible to their own conceptions, which they style natural ideas. I can not but praise your effort. For light ought, by all means, to be thrown upon truth by all, to the utmost of their ability. Calumnies and accusations, by which the truth is assailed and beset, are to be refuted. Minds, embittered against it, are not only to be softened and soothed, but also, to be induced to embrace it. It can not be made an objection against you, that you adduce the opinions of the ancient Theologians, especially those whom you quote, some caution being observed, lest we go too far in that direction. For the Fathers are themselves also liable to diverse interpretations, and, indeed, more than the divine and inspired writers, as they were endued with knowledge of the truth, which was less in degree and in clearness, and they could express the thoughts of their minds only with less accuracy and fitness. When I consider this, I doubt whether they have consulted the best interests of the church, who have thought that, in this age, the opinions of the Fathers are to be considered by them as authority in matters of religion. But the die is cast, and we must advance, whithersoever the fates of the Church bear us. In reference to your declaration, that you present the testimony of the ancient Doctors and School-men, for the sake of exhibiting an agreement in that part of doctrine, I do not see how that is so. For I am quite persuaded that nothing can be thought of, more adapted to bring that whole doctrine of Predestination and the grace of God into confusion, and to overwhelm it with darkness, than the effort on the part of any one to bring forward and unite together all the opinions of the Fathers and the School-men, in reference to it. But I desire that you may not at once pronounce him an unjust estimator or judge, who dares to assert that the dogmas, which you present in this treatise, are found neither in the Scriptures nor in the Fathers. For if you shall, after reasons have been adduced by that estimator, arbiter or judge, be able to sustain your statement, you will find him not struggling against it, with an unfair and obstinate mind, but ready to yield to what is proved to be the truth with becoming equanimity. Nor will it be an easier matter to persuade me that the dogmas of which you here treat, are, in that same mode and sense, proposed and set forth in all the Reformed Churches. I say this, lest you should think that you can bear down one thinking differently by the prejudgment of those churches.

EXAMINATION OF THE TREATISE

I come now to the treatise itself, which I will examine with somewhat more care and diligence. You will not complain if, in some places, I may with the closest criticism also subject some of the nicer points to the most rigid scrutiny. For who would not consent that a serious and solid discussion should be, as it were, spiced by a friendly diversity and a pleasant contest concerning the more accurate handling of a subject.

You begin and rightly with a definition of Predestination. But that definition does not seem to be adapted to the Predestination, which is set forth in the Scriptures. For the Predestination, of which the Scriptures treat, is of men in their relation as sinners; it is made in Christ; it is to blessings which concern, not this animal life, but the spiritual life, of which a part also are communicated in this animal life, as is clearly evident from Ephesians 1, where, among the spiritual blessings to which we have been predestinated in Christ are enumerated "adoption of children (verse 5), "redemption through his blood, the forgiveness of sins," (verse 7th), "having made known unto us the mystery of his will," (verse 9th), which blessings are given to the predestinated in this life. The apostle well say "the life, which I now live in the flesh, I live by the faith of the Son of God," (Gal. ii. 20)

signifying that he, in this animal life, was a partaker of spiritual gifts, and from them lived a spiritual life. But perhaps you did not wish to give an accurate definition, but only by some description to give us an idea of predestination. I may concede this, yet in that description there seem to be many things which ought to be noticed. For the word "counsel," by which you have desired to explain one kind of Predestination is not a kind of Predestination, but pertains to its efficient cause; for a decree is made by "counsel," which decree can be fitly considered a kind of Predestination—if indeed counsel can be attributed to God, by which He may decree anything, as in the Scripture, -- e.g. Acts iv. 28, and Ephes. i. 11. This I say, is apparent from the passages quoted. For in the former (Acts iv. 28), "counsel" is said to determine before or predestinate things to be done; in the latter (Ephes. i. 11), it is said that God "worketh all things,"—even institutes predestination-after the counsel of His own will.

There is, in this life, an equality of the pious and the wicked as to external blessings, but they are to be considered generally. For in individual cases there is a great difference both among the pious and the wicked, and so great indeed is it that, to those, who are dissatisfied with that inequality, it may need a defense by an argument for reducing it, hereafter, to an equality. Indeed it is said of the pious and the faithful "if in this life, only, we have hope in Christ, we are, of all men, most miserable." (1 Cor. xv. 19.)

I approve what you say concerning "the final cause of Predestination," when rightly understood, that is, if a declaration of the glory of God through mercy and justice is attributed to Predestination, so long as it is the foreordination of sinners who shall believe in Christ to eternal life, and on the contrary, the predamnation of sinners who shall persevere in sins to eternal death; who shall believe, through the gracious gift of God, and who shall persevere in sins through their own wickedness and the just desertion of God. But if you think that God, from eternity, without any pre-existence of sin, in His prescience, determined to illustrate His own glory by mercy and punitive justice, and, that He might be able to secure this object, decreed to create man good but mutable, and ordained farther that he should fall, that in this way there might be a place for that decree, I say that such an opinion can, in my judgment, be established by no passage of the word of God.

That this may be made plainer, a few things must be said concerning the glory of God and the modes of its manifestation. No one can doubt that God, since He is the first and Supreme Efficient Cause of all His own acts and works, and the single and sole cause of many of them, has always the manifestation of His own perfection, that is, His own glory, proposed to Himself, as His chief and highest object. For the first and supreme cause is moved to produce any effect, by nothing, out of itself otherwise it would not be the first and supreme cause. Therefore, not only the act of Predestination, but also every other divine act has "the illustration of the glory of God" as its final cause. Now it is equally certain and known to all, who have even approached the threshold of sacred letters, that the manifestation of the divine perfection and the illustration of his glory consists in the unfolding of His essential attributes by acts and works comparable to them: but an inquiry is necessary concerning those attributes, by the unfolding of which He determined to illustrate His own glory, first, by which, in the second place, and so on, by successive steps. It is certain that He could not, first of all, have done this by means of mercy and punitive justice. For the former could be exercised only towards the miserable, the latter only towards sinners. But since, first of all, the external action of God both was and must be taken up, so to speak, with Nothing, it is, therefore, evident that goodness, wisdom, and omnipotence were, first of all, to be unfolded, and that by them the glory of God was to be illustrated. These, therefore, were unfolded in the creation, by which God appeared to be supremely good and wise, and omnipotent.

But, as God made all His creatures with this difference that some were capable of nothing more than they were at their creation, and others were capable of greater perfection, He was concerned, as to the former, only with their preservation and government, accomplished by goodness, wisdom and power of the same kind and measure, since preservation is only a continuance of creation, as the latter is the beginning of the former, and government may not go beyond the natural condition of the creatures, unless when it seems good to God to use them, for the sake of men for supernatural purposes, as in the bread and wine used, in the Lord's Supper, to signify and seal unto us the communion of the body and the blood of Christ; as to the latter, which He made capable of greater perfection, as angels and men, the same attributes were to be unfolded, but in a far greater measure. In the former case, the good communicated is limited, as each creature receives that which is appropriate to itself, according to the diversity of their natures, but, in the latter, there is a communication of supreme and infinite good, which is God, in the union with whom consists the happiness of rational creatures. Reason demanded that this communication should be made contrary to justice, wherefore He gave a law to His creatures, obedience to which was made the condition on which that communication should be made. Therefore, this was the first decree concerning the final cause of rational creatures, and the glory of God to be illustrated by justice and the highest goodness—highest as to the good to be communicated, not absolutely; by goodness joined to justice, in the case of those who should be made partakers of the highest good, through steadfastness in the truth; by punitive justice, in the case of those who should make themselves unworthy of it by their disobedience. Then we see that justice, rewarding obedience, which was its office, according to the gracious promise of God, and punishing disobedience as it deserves, according to the just threatenings of God, holds the first place; in the former case, justice joined to goodness, in the latter, punitive justice opposed to the gracious communication of the highest good, without any mention of mercy, unless it may be considered as preserving the creature from possible misery, which could, by its own fault, fall into misery; as mercy is not considered when it is predetermined by the decree of Predestination. That decree was peremptory in respect to the angels, as in accordance with it, they are condemned: wherefore the predestination and reprobation of angels was comprehended in this. But what grace was prepared for the former in Predestination and was denied to the latter in Reprobation, and in what respects, I do not now argue. But it was not peremptory in reference to men, whom God did not decree to treat according to that highest rigor of the law, but in the salvation of whom He decreed to exhibit all His goodness, which Jehovah showed to Moses in these, His attributes, "The Lord, Lord God, merciful and gracious, long-suffering, and abundant in goodness and truth" (Exod. xxvi. 6). Therefore, the Predestination and Reprobation of men were not considered in that decree. For since Adam sinned, and in him all who were to be his descendants by natural propagation, all would have been devoted to eternal condemnation without hope of pardon. For the decree of Predestination and Reprobation is peremptory. So far, then, no predestination of men unto life, and no reprobation unto death had any place. And since there could be no Predestination and Reprobation, except in accordance with those attributes by which men are at once saved or damned—but the predestinated may be saved at once by mercy, and the reprobate may be damned at once by justice opposed to that mercy—it follows that there was no fixed predestination and reprobation of men, in reference to whom there could be no place for mercy and justice opposed to it. But there could be no place for them in reference to men who were not miserable, and not sinners. Then, since Predestination includes the means by which the predestinated will certainly and infallibly come to salvation, and Reprobation includes the denial of those same means, but those means are the remission of sins and the renewing of the Holy Ghost, and its perpetual assistance even to the end, which are necessary and communicable to none, except sinners, I conclude that there was no Predestination and Reprobation in reference to men, in whose case these means were neither necessary nor communicable.

Finally, since God can love no sinner unto salvation, unless he be reconciled to Himself in Christ, hence it is, that there could be no place for Predestination, except in Christ. And since Christ was ordained and given for sinners, it is certain that Predestination and its opposite, Reprobation, could have no place before human sin—its existence as foreseen by God—and the appointment of Christ as Mediator, and indeed his performance, in the prescience of God, of the functions of the office of Mediator, which pertains to reconciliation. Nor does it follow from this, that God either made man with an uncertain design, or failed of the end at which He aimed. For He prescribed to Himself, both in the act of creation, and in that of glorification, and its opposite, condemnation, the illustration of His own glory as an end, and He obtained it; by goodness, wisdom and power in creation, and He obtained it; by the same, but in a greater measure, and joined with justice in glorification and condemnation, and He obtained it. But, though the mode of illustrating His glory by mercy, which is a certain method of communicating goodness and the approach of the same to a miserable creature, and by justice, opposed to that mercy, could have no place except from the occasion of human sin, yet the decree of God is not, therefore, dependent on the man, for He foresaw from eternity what would be in the future, and in ordaining, concerning the future, to that end, He freely arranged it according to His own choice, not compelled by any necessity as if He could not, in some other way, have secured glory to Himself from the sin of man. But that the glory of God does not consist merely in the illustration of mercy and, its opposite justice, is evident from the fact that, then, He would not have obtained glory from the act of creation, nor from the predestination and reprobation of angels. It is to be understood, that mercy is not an essential attribute of the Deity distinct from goodness itself, as in the womb and the offspring of goodness; indeed, it is goodness itself extending to the sinful creature and to misery. It can for this reason be said, in simple terms, that, in all His eternal acts, God determined to declare His own glory by goodness, wisdom, and omnipotence, with the addition of justice when equity demanded it at the prescription of wisdom, but that He adapted the mode to the state, or rather to the change of the object, in reference to which He had determined to unfold those attributes. In reference to this thing Tertullian says, in a beautiful and erudite manner, "God must, of necessity use all things in reference to all being, He must have as many feelings, as there are causes of them; anger for the wicked. and wrath for the ungrateful, and jealousy for the proud, and whatever else would not be for the advantage of the evil; so also, mercy for the erring, and patience for those not yet repentant, and honour for the deserving, and whatever is necessary for the good. All these feelings He has in His own mode, in which it is fit that He should feel them, just as man has the same, equally after his own manner." (Adversus Marcion, Lib. 2, cap 16.)

Predestination does not arise merely from goodness simply considered, the province of which is, indeed, to communicate itself to the creature, but also from that mode of mercy, which goes out from that goodness to the miserable to remove their misery, of grace in Christ, which goes out from it to sinners to pardon their sins, of patience and long-suffering, going forth from the same goodness towards those who, for a long time, struggle against it, and do not at once obey the call, thus prolonging the delay of conversion. So also reprobation is not merely fixed by justice, the opposite of that goodness, simply considered, but by justice tempered by some mercy and patience. For God "endured with much long-suffering the vessels of wrath fitted for destruction." (Rom. ix. 22.)

From these things, thus considered, I may be allowed, with your kind permission, to conclude that Predestination has not been sufficiently well defined or described by you. If any one is inclined to consider the series and order of the objects of the knowledge and the will of God, he will be more and more confirmed in the truth of the things briefly set forth by me. The passage from Augustine, is in agreement with these views, if one wishes to gather his complete opinion from other passages. Fulgentius and Gregory most clearly support me in the passages quoted by you. For, if the act of predestination is the preparation for the remission of sins or the punishment of the same, then it is certain that there is place for predestination only in reference to sinners. If also the act of Predestination is the pre-election of some who are to be redeemed from their depravity, and the leaving of others in their depravity, from this also it is evident that predestination has to do with men considered as sinners.

That sentiment of the School-men agrees most fully with the same views. For it openly declares that Predestination depends on the foresight of the fall, when they say that the perfection and goodness of God, who predestinates, is represented by the mode of mercy and punitive justice, which mode, as I have now frequently said, can have place only in reference to sinners. If any one acknowledges that this is indeed true, but says that God has arranged this, as an occasion for Himself, by decreeing that man should fall, and by carrying forward that decree to its end or limit, we ask the proof of that assertion, which, in my judgment, he will be unable to give. For that sentiment is at variance with the justice of God, as it makes God the author of sin, and introduces an inevitable necessity for sin. This I will prove. For if that decree existed, man could not abstain from sin, otherwise the decree would have been made in vain, which is an impious supposition. For "the counsel of the Lord standeth forever." (Psalm xxxiii. 11). We remark also that the human will would have been circumscribed and determined by that decree, so that it could not turn itself except in one direction, in which there would be sin; by that act its freedom would be lost, because it would move the will, not according to the mode of free-will, but according to the mode of nature. Such an act it could not resist, nor would there be any volition in that direction, indeed, there would not be the power to put forth that volition on account of the determination of the decree. Consider, also, that, by that sentiment, mercy and justice are considered as means resulting from Predestination, while they are the primary causes of Predestination, as is evident from the fact that the final cause of Predestination may be resolved into the manifestation of mercy and justice.

Here, observe, also, in what way you make the creation and the fall of man the means in common lying at the foundation of the counsel, or rather the decree of predestination, I think, indeed, that both the creation, and the fall preceded every external act of predestination, as also the decree concerning the creation of man, and the permission of his fall preceded, in the Divine mind, the decree of Predestination. I think, also, that I have partly proved this, in my preceding remarks. But it will be well to look at this with a little more diligence.

Every act, which has reference to an object, is posterior in nature, to its object. It is called an object relatively. Therefore, it has an absolute existence prior to the existence of its relation to the act. The object, then, exists in itself, before it can be under the influence of the act which tends towards it. But man is the object of Predestination. Therefore, man is prior to the act of Predestination. But man is what he is by creation. therefore, creation is prior to Predestination—that is, in the divine mind, or the decree concerning the creation of man is prior to the decree of Predestination, and the act of creation is prior to the execution of the decree of Predestination. If any one should reply that God, in the internal act of Predestination, is employed with man considered as not created, but as to be made, I answer that this could neither take place, nor be so understood by a mind judging rightly. For Predestination is a decree, not only to illustrate the divine glory, but to illustrate it in man, by the mode of mercy and justice. From this, it follows that man must also exist in the divine mind before the act of Predestination, and the fall of man must itself, also, be previously foreseen. The attributes of God, by which creation is affected, are, therefore, considered as prior, in the divine nature, to those in which predestination originates. Goodness, simply considered, wisdom, and power, operating upon Nothing, are, therefore, prior to mercy and punitive justice. Add, also, that since predestination originates, on the one hand, in mercy, and on the other, in justice, in the former case having reference to salvation—in the latter, to damnation—it cannot be that any means exist pertaining, in common, to the execution of election and of reprobation. For they are provided neither in mercy nor in justice. There exist, then, no means of Predestination, common to both parts of the decree.

Whether the definition of the creation of man is correct. If you wished to define the creation of man that should have been done with greater accuracy. But if you wished only to describe it, there is yet, in that description, something which I may note. "Man was made mutable," as was demanded by the very condition of that Nothing from which he was made, and of the creature itself. which neither could nor ought to be raised, by creation, to the state of the Creator, which is immutability. But he was made mutable in such a sense that actual change from good to evil would follow that possible mutability, only by the voluntary and free act of man. But the act of the creature does not remain free when it is so determined in one direction, that, if that determination continues, there cannot but be a change.

Whether the permission of the fall, is rightly defined. But of the "permission of the fall," we must treat at somewhat greater length: for very much depends on this for the expediting of this whole matter. It is certain that God can by the act of His own absolute power prevent all things whatever, which can be done by the creature, and it is equally certain that He is not absolutely under obligation to any one to hinder him from evil. But He can not, in His justice, do all that He can in His absolute power. He cannot, in His justice (or righteousness), forget the "work and labour of love" of the pious (Heb. vi. 10). The absolute power of God is limited by the decree of God, by which He determined to do any thing in a particular direction, And though God is not absolutely under obligation to any one, He can yet obligate Himself by His own act, as, for instance, by a promise, or by requiring some act from man. He is obligated to perform what He promises, for He owes to Himself the immutability of His own truth, whether He has promised it absolutely or conditionally. By requiring an act, He places Himself under obligation to give ability and the strength without which that act can not be performed; otherwise, He would reap where He had not sown. It is plain, from these positions, that God, since He conceded the freedom of the will, and the use of that freedom, ought not, and indeed could not, prevent the fall in any mode which would infringe on the use of that freedom; and farther, that He was not obligated to prevent it in any other way than by the bestowment of the ability which should be necessary and sufficient to the avoidance of the fall. Permission is not, therefore, a "cessation from the act of illuminating and that of inclining" to such an extent that, without those acts, a man could not avoid sin. For, in that case, the fault could be justly and deservedly charged upon God, who would be the cause of sin, by way of removing or not bestowing that which is necessary for the performance of an act which Himself has prescribed by His own law. From which it also follows that the law is unjust, as it is not in proportion to the strength of the creature on which it is imposed, whether that deficiency of strength arises from the nonbestowal or the removal of it before any fault has been committed by the creature.

Permission is, indeed, a cessation of the act of hindrance, but that cessation is to be so explained that it may not be reduced to an efficient cause of sin, either directly, or by way of the denial or removal of that, without which sin can not be avoided. In reference to this permission, if it be fitly explained, it can be doubtless said that "God not only foreknows it, but He even wills it by an act of volition" affirmatively and immediately directed to the permission itself, not to that which is permitted. As it can not be said concerning this, that God wills that it should not be done, for He permits it, and not unwillingly, so, also, it can not be truly said that God wills it. For permission is an act intermediate between volition and nolition, the will being inactive.

But the cause, in view of which He permits sin, is to be found, not only in the consequent, but in the antecedent. In the antecedent, because God constituted man so that he might have a free will, and might, according to the freedom of his will, either accord obedience or refuse it. He could not rescind this constitution, which Himself had established, in view of His own immutability, as Tertullian clearly shows, in his argument against Marcion (Lib. 2, cap. 5, 6 and 7). In the consequent, because He saw that He could use sin as an occasion for demonstrating the glory of His own grace and justice. But this consequent does not naturally result from that sin. From this, it follows that even from the highest evil, (if there be any highest,) evil, only, could result per se, or there would be an injury to the divine majesty, opposed to the divine good; but that consequent is an incidental result of sin, because God knows and wills to elicit, by His wisdom, goodness and power, His own glory from it, as light from darkness. As, then, evil is not good, per se, so it is not absolutely good that evil should occur. For if this be true. then God not only permits it, but is its author and effector. But it is incidentally good that evil should occur, in view of that wisdom, goodness, and power of God, of which I have spoken, by which God takes from sin the material for illustrating his own glory. Therefore, sin is not, in this respect, the means per se, for illustrating the glory of God, but only the occasion not made for this purpose, nor adapted to it by its own nature, but seized by God and used in this direction with wonderful skill, and praiseworthy perversion. No absolute good in the universe would be prevented, even if God should prevent evil, provided that prevention should not be affected in a manner not adapted to the primitive constitution of man; and God is free to prevent sin, but in a way not at variance with the freedom of the will. Any other method of prevention would be absolutely contrary to the good of the universe, inasmuch as one good of the universe consists even in this, that there should be a creature endued with free will, and that the use of his own free will should be conceded to the creature without any divine interference. But if the existence of evil or sin should absolutely contribute to the good and the perfection of the universe, then God ought not only not to hinder sin, but even to promote it, else He would fail in His duty to His own work, and do injury to His own perfection. I admit that, without the existence of sin, there would not be that place for the patience of the martyrs, or for the sacrifice of Christ; but the patience of the martyrs and the sacrifice of Christ are not necessary results of the existence of sin. Indeed we shall see, by considering the natural effect of sin, that from it would result impatience in those who are afflicted, and by it the wrath, of God would be kindled, which not only could, but in fact, would, prevent the bestowment of any good, even the least, and much more that of his Son, unless God should be, at the same time, merciful, and could, in His wisdom, find a way by which He might prevent the natural effect of sin, and using sin as the occasion, might promote other effects, contrary to the very nature of sin.

The passages cited from Augustine and Gregory, are not only not opposed to, but actually in favour of this opinion. For they do not say that it would have been good absolutely that evils should occur, but that God judged it better to bring good out of evils than to prevent them; thus comparing two acts of the Deity, and esteeming the one better than the other. I may be allowed to observe, in reference to the remark of Gregory, that he is not sufficiently accurate, when he compares the evils which we suffer on account of sins with the blessing of redemption as something greater: for he ought to compare our sins and faults, not the evils which we suffer on their account, with the blessing of redemption. If he had done this, and had carefully considered the words of the apostle, "and not rather (as we be slanderously reported, and as some affirm that we say), Let us do evil that good may come," (Rom. iii. 8), he would have judged otherwise, or, at least, would have expressed his views more fitly, without making such a transition, and without substituting the punishment of sin for sin itself. It is indeed right, for men and for any believer, to say with entire confidence, that there can be no redemption so excellent and no method of redemption so glorious that, for the sake of obtaining either, any sin, however small, is to be committed. For the Redeemer "was manifested that he might destroy the works of the devil," (1 John iii. 8,) i.e., sins; they are not, therefore, to be committed in order that the Son of God, the Redeemer, might come. For that circular form of reasoning, the Son of God came that he might destroy the works of the devil, and sin was committed that it might be destroyed by the Son, is not only contrary to the Scriptures, but also hostile to all truth, as it leads infinitely astray.

From this it is also easily proved that the fall can not be called a happy transgression, except by a catachrestic hyperbole, which, while it may be adapted to declamations, panegyric orations, and rhetorical embellishments, should be far removed from the solid investigation of truth. To these is always to be added the remark, which I have made, frequently and with reiteration, that redemption could not have resulted from transgression, except as the latter might afford an occasion for it, by the arrangement of God, in accordance with His will, that the transgression should be expiated, and washed away by a Redeemer of such character and dignity.

But the distinction which you make between "the permission of the fall" and "the permitted fall" seems to me to be of no force. For the permission of the fall is not less by the Divine arrangement than the permitted fall. For God ordained His own permission for a certain end. But consider whether it is not absurd to distinguish between "the permission of the fall" and "the permitted fall." In the latter case, I speak of the fall, not considered in that it is a fall, but in that it is a permitted fall: as you must, of necessity, consider, when you style it "the means of the decree," which appellation is not appropriate to the fall except on account of the adjunct "permitted." For not the fall but the permission of the fall, tended to the glory of God; not the act of many which is the fall, but the act of God, which is permission, having immediate reference to that act of man according to the prescript of the Divine arrangement, tended to His glory. But I acknowledge that permission is the means of the decree, not of predestination, but of providence, as the latter is distinguished from the former. I speak now of providence, as governing and administrative, which is not only not prior, in nature and order, to predestination, but is also the cause of the mission of the Son as the Redeemer, who is our head, in whom predestination is made, as the apostle teaches, (Ephes. 1.)

But how can it be true that the fall is permitted by God, and yet that "it would not have occurred unless God had willed it" I wish that it might be explained how God could, at once, will that the fall should occur, and permit the same; how God could be concerned, by His volition, with the fall both mediately and immediately—mediately by willing the permission, and immediately by willing the fall itself. I wish also that these things may be harmonized, how the fall could occur by the will of God, and yet the will of God not be the cause of the fall, which is contrary to the express declaration of God's word, "Our God is in the heavens; He hath done whatever He pleased," (Psalm cxv. 3.) Also, in what way could God will the fall, and yet be "a God that hath no pleasure in wickedness," (Psalm v. 4,) since the fall was wickedness. The distinctions which are presented are not sufficient to untie the knot, as I shall show in the case of each of them separately. For they distinguish between the fall and the event of the fall; between the will of open intimation and that of His good-pleasure, revealed or hidden; between the fall as it was sin, and as it was the means of illustrating the divine glory. They say that God willed that the fall should occur, but did not will the fall; that He willed the fall according to His good-pleasure and His hidden will, not according to His will, of open intimation, revealed and approving; that He willed the fall, not as it was sin, but as it was the means of illustrating His own glory.

The first distinction is verbal, and not real. He, who willed that the fall should occur, willed also the fall. He who willed that the fall should occur, willed the event of the fall, and He, who willed the event of the fall, willed the fall. For the event of the fall is the fall, as the event of an action is the action itself. But if He willed the fall, He was the cause of the fall. For "He hath done whatsoever He pleased," (Psalm cxv. 3.) If any one replies, that He willed that the fall should occur by the act of another, not by His own act, I answer—it could not be that God should will that the fall should occur by the act of another, and not by His own act: for it would not happen by the act of another, unless He should interpose with His own act, and, indeed, with an act, such that, from it, the act of another should necessarily exist; otherwise that, which He wished should occur by the act of another, would not be effected or occur by that act of another. The force of the argument is not increased: whether God willed that the fall should occur, mediately, by the act of another, or, immediately, by His own act. These are mediately connected—the act of God and the act of another, that is, of man, or the fall. The fall proceeded from the act of man, but that depends of necessity on the act of God; otherwise it could happen that the act of another should not be performed, and thus it could happen that the fall should not occur, which, nevertheless, God willed should occur. It is not, therefore, denied that God is the cause of the fall, except immediately; it is conceded that He is so, mediately. No one, indeed, ever wished to deduce, from the declaration of any one, that God is the immediate cause of the sin perpetrated by man, for he would deduce a contradiction in terms, as they say in the schools, unless, indeed, the subject might be the general concurrence of God with man, in producing an act which can not be produced by man without sin.

The distinction of the will into that of hidden and revealed, while it may have place elsewhere, can not avail here. For the hidden will of God is said to be efficacious; but if, in its exercise, God willed that the fall should occur, it is certainly a necessary conclusion, also, that He effected the fall, that is, He must be the cause of the fall; for whatever God wills, even by His hidden will, the same, also, He does both in heaven and on the earth; and no one can resist His will, namely, that which is hidden. But I may remark concerning that distinction in the will, that I think that it may be said, that neither of these can be so contrary, or opposed to the other, that God, by one, wills that to be done, which, by the other, He wills not to be done, and vice versa. God wills by His revealed and approving will, that man should not fall, it can not, therefore, be true that God, by any will, considered in any way whatever, can will that man should fall; for though there may be distinction in the will of God, yet no contradiction can exist in it. But it is a contradiction, if God, by any act of His own will, should tend towards an object, and at the same time towards its contrary.

The third distinction, in which it is said that God wills sin, not as such, but as the means of illustrating His own glory, defends God from the charge of efficiency in sin no more than the two preceding. For that assertion remains true God doeth whatsoever He wills, but He wills sin, therefore, He effects sin, not indeed as it is such, but as it is the means of illustrating His own glory. But if God effects sin, as it is the means to such an end, it can not be effected, unless man commits sin as such. For sin can not be made a means, unless it is committed. There exists, indeed, that distinction of sin into separate and diverse respects, not really, and in fact, but in the mode of considering it. But that we may make that distinction correctly, as it is indeed of some use, it must be said that God permits sin as such, but for this reason, because He had the knowledge and the power to make it the means, yea, rather, to use it as the means of illustrating His own glory. So that the consideration of sin as such was presented to the Divine permission, the permission itself being, in the mean time, caused both by the consideration that the sin could be the means of illustrating the Divine glory, and by the arrangement that the sin, permitted, should be, in fact, the means for illustrating that same glory.

The simile, which you present, of the mutable decaying house is not apposite for many reasons. For in the first place, in its fall, the house is passive; but in the fall of man he is active, for he sins. Secondly, that house is, not only mutable, that is, capable of decay, but subject to decay; but man, though capable of sinning, was still not subject to sin. Thirdly, that house could not stand if attacked by the winds; but man could preserve his position, even though tempted by Satan. Fourthly, the necessary props were not placed under that house; but man received strength from God, sufficient for steadfastness against the onset of Satan, and was supported by the assistance of divinity itself. Fifthly, the builder anticipated the ruin of the house, and in part willed it, because he was unwilling to prevent the fall when he could have done it; God, indeed, foresaw sin, but He did not will it; indeed, He endeavoured to prevent it by precept and the bestowment of grace, necessary and sufficient for the avoidance of sin. Farther than this, He must not prevent, lest He should destroy the constitution which He had established. The ideas, I will the ruin, and I will it, so far as I will not to prevent it, do not agree. For the ruin and the permission of the ruin can not be at the same time the immediate object of the will. For God can not be concerned in the fall, at the same time, both by an affirmative and by a negative act of the will. The act of willing the fall was affirmative, the act of not willing to prevent is negative, intermediate between two opposite affirmative acts, namely, between the act of volition and that of nolition concerning the fall. It is altogether true, that so much causality or efficiency is to be attributed to the builder as there is of will, directed to the ruin of the house, attributed to him. Let us now consider the application of the similitude. God left Adam to himself, but yet Adam was not deserted by God; for He placed under him as it were a triple prop, lest he might sin or fall. He gave him a precept, that he might, in obedience, not choose to sin; He added a threat that he might fear to sin on account of the annexed and following punishment; He bestowed grace that he might be able in fact to fulfill the precept, and avoid the threatened punishment. It may be lawful, also, to call the promise, which was placed in opposition to the threatening, and which was sealed by the symbol of the tree of life, a fourth prop. The reason, in view of which, God left man to himself, was not that his ability might be tested by temptation, for from the actual occurrence of the fall, his inability to stand could be neither proved nor disproved; but because it was suitable that there should be such a trial of the obedience of him whom God had made the ruler of his own will, the lord and the head of his own voluntary sets. Nor was permission instituted to this end, that it might be seen what the creature could do, if the Divine aid and government over him, should cease for a time, both because the Divine aid and government was not deficient, and because it was already certain that man could do nothing without the government and general aid of God, and nothing good without the special aid of His grace.

That "God was not the cause of that defection" is a Theological axiom. But you, by removing those acts, do not remove the cause of the defection from the Deity. For God can be regarded as the cause of sin, either by affirmative or negative acts. You, indeed, take from Him the affirmative acts, namely, the inclining of the mind to sin, the infusion of wickedness, and the deprivation of the gift, already bestowed, but you attributed to Him a negative act, the denial or non-bestowal of strengthening grace. If this strengthening grace was necessary to the avoidance of sin, then, by that act of denial, God became the Author of sin and of Adam's fall. But if you attribute the denial or the non-bestowal of strengthening grace to God, not absolutely, but on account of the transgression of Adam, because he did not seek the Divine aid, I approve what you say, if you concede that it was in the power of Adam to seek that aid; otherwise it was denied to him to seek that also, and so we go on without end.

You say—"There are two parts or species of predestination, the decree of Election and that of Reprobation," concerning which it must be stated that one can not exist without the other, and that, one being supposed, the other must be also. This is signified by the word election, otherwise, predestination may be considered per se and without an opposite, and so all men universally would be predestinated unto life. In that case, there would be no election, which includes the idea of reprobation, as united to it by a necessary consequence and copula. Election and Reprobation are opposed to each other both affirmatively and negatively. Negatively, because election refers to the act of the will by which grace and glory are conferred, reprobation, that by which they are not conferred. Affirmatively, since reprobation refers to the act of the will, which inflicts punishment on account of sin.

It is worthy of consideration that God, both in the decree of Election and in that of Reprobation, was concerned with men considered as sinners. For the grace which was provided by election or predestination, is the grace of the remission of sins, and the renewal of the Holy Ghost; and the glory which He has prepared by the same decree, is out of the ignominy to which man was liable on account of sin. Reprobation, also, is a denial of that grace and a preparation of the punishment due to sin, not in that it was due, but that it was, through mercy, not taken away. Isidorus and Angelomus, quoted by you, express this condition of the object both of Election and Reprobation. The former, when be says—"the reprobate are left, and predestinated to death," the latter, when he says that—of "the unbelieving people some are predestinated to everlasting freedom, but others are left in their own impiety, and condemned to perpetual death by occult dispensation, and occult judgment."

Your definition of Election is obscure from the want of some word. It seems that the phrase to be illustrated ought to have been added, thus: "The decree of election is that by which God destines certain men to His glorious grace to be illustrated in their salvation and heavenly life, obtained through Christ," otherwise the phraseology is not sufficiently complete. But the definition, even when completed, in that way, seems to me to have been, ineptly arranged, as the parts are not arranged according to their mutual relations. For "salvation" and "heavenly life" hold the relation of the material prepared for the decree of election; "certain men" hold the place of the object or subject for which that salvation is prepared; the "illustration of His glorious grace" is the end of election;

"Christ" is here made the means of obtaining that salvation and life. The order of all these in the definition according to their mutual relations, ought to be, -- "The decree of election is that, by which God destined certain men to salvation and heavenly life, to be obtained through Christ, to the praise of His glorious grace." In this definition, however, Christ does not seem to me to obtain that place, which he deserves, and which the Apostle assigns to him. For Christ according to the Apostle is not only the means by which the salvation, already prepared by election, but, so to speak, the meritorious cause, in respect to which the election was made, and on whose account that grace was prepared. For the apostle says that we are chosen in Christ (Ephes. i. 4), as in a mediator, in whose blood salvation and life is obtained for us, and as in our "head," (Ephes. i. 22) from whom those blessings flow to us. For God chooses no one unto eternal life except in Christ, who prepared it by his own blood for them who should believe on his name. From this it seems to follow that, since God regards no one in Christ unless they are engrafted in him by faith, election is peculiar to believers, and the phrase "certain men," in the definition, refers to believers. For Christ is a means of salvation to no one unless he is apprehended by faith. Therefore, that phrase "in Christ" marks the meritorious cause by which grace and glory are prepared, and the existence of the elect in him, without which they could not be elected in him. The definition, then, is susceptible of this form. "Election is the decree of God, by which, of Himself, from eternity, He decreed to justify in (or through) Christ, believers, and to accept them unto eternal life, to the praise of His glorious grace." But you will say, "Then faith is made dependent on the human will, and is not a gift of divine grace." I deny that sequence, for there was no such statement in the definition. I acknowledge that the cause of faith was not expressed, but that was unnecessary. If any one denies it, there may be added after "believers" the phrase "to whom He determined to give faith." But we should observe whether, in our method of consideration, the decree, by which God determined to justify believers and adopt them as sons, is the same with that by which He determined to bestow faith on some, but to deny the same to others. This seems to me not very probable. For there are, here, two purposes, each determined by the certain decree of God; their subjects are also diverse, and different attributes are assigned to them. I think that this ought to have been noticed in treating correctly of the Order and Mode of Predestination. I do not much object to your statement that "the act of the divine mind is two-fold, regarding the end, and the means to the end, or to salvation," but that remark does not seem correct to me, in which you say that "the former is commonly called the decree, and the latter the execution of the decree"—for such is your marginal annotation—each of these is an act of the decree, as you acknowledge; but an act of the decree is internal, and precedes its execution whether it is in reference to the end or the means. The passage in Romans 9, does not favour your idea as you claim. For it not distinguish the purpose from election, nor does it make the election prior to the purpose of damning of conferring salvation, but it says that the purpose is "according to election," not without election or apart from election, as is clearly evident from the words of the apostle. For they are as follows—"i[na hJ kat ejklogh<n tou~ Qeou~ proqesiv menh| " that the purpose of God according to election might stand," from which it is apparent that, by these words, is described the purpose of God, which is "according to election."

But that this may be more plainly understood, we may examine briefly the design and the scope of the apostle. The Jews objected that they, by virtue of the covenant and the divine word, committed to them, were the peculiar people of God, and, therefore, that honour could not be taken away from them, without the disgrace and the violation of the divine decree. They asserted, however, that the honour referred to, and the title of the people of God was taken from them by the Apostle Paul, when he made those only, who should believe in the Christ whom he preached, partakers of the righteousness of God, and of eternal salvation. Since they had not believed in that Christ, it followed, according to the doctrine of the apostle, that they were strangers to the righteousness of God and eternal salvation, and unworthy to be longer considered the people of God. But since they considered this to be contrary to the decree and the covenant of God, they concluded that it was, at the same time, absurd and foreign to the truth. The apostle answers that the covenant, decree, or word of God hath not "taken none effect," (verse 6), but remains firm, even if many of the Jews should not be reckoned among the people of God, because that decree or covenant did not comprehend all Israelites, universally without election and distinction; for that decree was "according to election," as set forth in those words of God announcing his purpose. For God said "In Isaac," not in Ishmael, "shall thy seed be called." Also "The elder," Esau, "shall serve the younger," Jacob. The apostle asserts that God declared most clearly in these words, that He did not regard the whole progeny of Abraham, or that of Isaac, or of Jacob, or all of their individual descendants, as His people, but only those who were "the children of the promise" to the exclusion of "the children of the flesh." The Apostle reasons, most conclusively from those words of God, that the purpose of God is according to election, and that it, therefore, embraces, in itself, not all the Israelites, but, while it claims some, it rejects others. From which it follows that it is not wonderful or contrary to the purpose or covenant of God, that some of the Jews are rejected by God, and those indeed, who are specially excluded by that decree according to those words of God, as "the children of the flesh," i.e. those who were seeking to be justified "by the works of the law" and according to the flesh. Compare Rom. ix. 7-11 and 30-32, also x, 3-5 with ch. iv, 1-3.

In Romans viii. 29, those acts—I refer now to the decree and the execution of the decree—are clearly distinguished. In the decree two things are mentioned, foreknowledge and predestination, "for whom He did foreknow, He also did predestinate to be conformed to the image of His Son." It is inquired—what is the import of this foreknowledge or prescience? Some explain it thus: -- "whom He foreknew," i.e. whom He previously loved, and affectionately regarded as His own, as indeed the simple word "to know" is sometimes used, as "I know you not." (Matt. xxv. 12.) "The Lord knoweth the way of the righteous." (Psalm i. 6.) Others say that foreknowledge, or prescience of faith in Christ, is here signified. You assent to the former, and reject the latter, and with good reason, if it has the meaning, which you ascribe to it. But it is worthy of consideration whether the latter meaning of the work "foreknow" may not be so explained, as not only not to impinge upon the former, but also to harmonize with it most completely so that the former cannot be true without the latter. This will be evident, if it shall be demonstrated that God can "previously love and affectionately regard as His own" no sinner unless He has foreknown him in Christ, and looked upon him as a believer in Christ.

To prove this I proceed thus: -- God acknowledges, as His own, no sinner, and He chooses no one to eternal life except in Christ, and for the sake of Christ. "He hath chosen us in Him," (Ephes. i. 4); "wherein He hath made us accepted in the Beloved," (verse 6). "Nor any other creature shall be able to separate us from the love of God which is in Christ Jesus our Lord." (Rom. viii. 39). "God was in Christ reconciling the world unto Himself." (2 Cor. v. 19).

For, if God could will to any one eternal life, without respect to the Mediator, He could also give eternal life, without the satisfaction made by the Mediator. The actual bestowment of eternal life is not more limited, than the purpose to bestow it. God truly loved the world, and, on account of that love, gave His own Son as its Redeemer. (John iii. 16). But the love, here spoken of, is not that by which He wills eternal life, as appears from the very expression of John—for he interposes faith in Christ between that love and eternal life. Hence God acknowledges no one, in Christ and for Christ's sake, as His own, unless that person is in Christ. He who is not in Christ, can not be loved in Christ. But no one is in Christ, except by faith; for Christ dwells in our hearts by faith, and we are engrafted and incorporated in him by faith. It follows then that God acknowledges His own, and chooses to eternal life no sinner, unless He considers him as a believer in Christ, and as made one with him by faith. This is proved by the following testimonies:

"As many as received him, to them gave He power to become the sons of God, even to them that believe on his name." (John i. 12.) But to those, to whom He gave this power, and to them, considered in one and the same manner, He also decreed to give this power, since the decree of Predestination effects nothing in him who is predestinated, and there is, therefore, no internal change in him, intervening between the decree and the actual bestowment of the thing, destined and prepared by the decree. "God so loved the world that He gave His only begotten Son that whosoever believeth in him shall not perish, but have everlasting life." (John iii. 16). "They which be of faith are blessed with faithful Abraham." (Gal. iii. 9.) "Without faith it is impossible to please him." (Heb. xi. 6.) Hence he is not in error who says that foreknowledge or prescience of faith in Christ is signified in Rom. viii. 29, unless he adds the assertion that the faith, referred to, results from our own strength and is not produced in us by the free gift of God.

The same explanation is proved true from the following member: "whom He did foreknow, He also did predestinate to be conformed to the image of He Son." No one is conformed to the image of the Son of God if he does not believe on him.

Therefore, no one is predestinated by God to that conformity, unless he is considered as a believer, unless one may claim that faith itself is included in that conformity which believers have with Christ—which would be absurd, because that faith can by no means be attributed to Christ, for it is faith in him, and in God through him; it is faith in reference to reconciliation, redemption, and the remission of sins. It is true, also, since it is the means of attaining that conformity. But you say, -- "They, who are predestinated to be justified and to become the sons of God, are also predestinated to believe, since adoption and justification are received by faith." I deny that consequence; indeed I assert that just the contrary can be concluded from that argument, if the act of predestination is one and the same. This I will prove: -- If adoption and justification is received by faith, then they, who are predestinated to be justified and to become the sons of God, are, of necessity, considered as believers. For that, which is destined to any one by Predestination, will certainly be received by him. And as he is when he receives it, such he was considered to be, when he was predestinated to receive it. Therefore, the believer alone was predestinated to receive it. From which I again conclude, that no one is chosen by God to adoption and the communication of the gift of righteousness, unless he is considered by Him as a believer. You add—"It cannot be said correctly, that God foreknew that men would believe, and then predestinated them to faith, since those, whom He foreknew to believe, He thus foreknew because He decreed that they should believe. But what relation has this to the matter. Such an affirmation is not made by the defenders of the sentiment to which I have referred. You confound two kinds of Predestination, and unite together acts of a different character. The Predestination in which God decreed to justify and adopt as sons believers in Christ, is not the same with that, in which He decreed, by certain means, to give faith to these and not to those. For the decree, is in this case, concerning the bestowment of faith in that, concerning the justification and adoption of believers; which, can not, indeed, be the same decree, on account of the diversity of the subject and the attribute. Otherwise it is true, that "God first foreknew that men would believe, and then predestinated them to faith." For He foreknew that they would believe by His own gift, which decree was prepared by Predestination. These things, having been thus plainly set forth, may throw some light on this whole discussion, in reference to Predestination. This we will do, at greater extent, hereafter, when we shall subjoin our own view of the mode and order of Predestination.

Those testimonies, which you cite from the Fathers and School-men, can be very easily harmonized with what has been said by us, yet to avoid prolixity, I will dispense with that labour. One thing, however, I will observe; namely, that the explanation of Peter Lombardus, however true it may be elsewhere, it is not adapted to the passage in Rom. viii. 29. For the Apostle has there presented the object of Predestination, (conformity to the image of Christ,) in a different light from that in which it is set forth or presented by Lombardus, namely, "that they should believe the word preached unto them." I will add, also, that you do not rightly conclude, because the word foreknowledge is used elsewhere by the Holy Spirit for the purpose of God, that, in the passage under discussion, it can not signify prescience of faith.

Further, in the decree of election, you refer to two acts, one "the purpose of choosing certain men to His love and grace, by which choice, men are made vessels of mercy and honour;" the other, "the purpose of saving, or of the bestowment of glory. This is not an unimportant distinction, if all things are correctly understood. For those things, which God prepares in election, are contained in grace and glory. But your statement—"Some, by the divine purpose, were chosen to the eternal love of God," must be explained to refer to that communication of love, by which God determined to communicate Himself to some.

If you regard, in a different light, that love of God which embraces us, it must be considered as preceding, in the order of nature, that decree or the Divine purpose by which grace and glory are prepared for us, grace, I say, which is the means of attaining to glory. Otherwise if you understand, by that word, the gracious disposition of God towards us, it coincides with the love of God, and is to be placed above the purpose or decree of God as its cause. This also is indicated by the order of the predicaments (in the logical sense of that word). For the purpose or decree is placed in the predicament of Action, the gracious affection and love, in the preceding predicament of Quality. This is evident from Ephes. i. 5-6, where God is said to have predestinated and adopted us "to the praise of the glory of His grace." If grace, then, is to receive praise from those acts, it must be placed before them as their cause.

Your position that "men to be created," are the object of the former purpose is not correct. For we are now treating of the subject, not as it is, in itself—for we know that the eternal purpose of God is antecedent to the actual existence of man—but as it is presented to the divine mind, in the act of decree, and in that of Predestination. If the object of that purpose is considered with that limitation, it is certain that men, not" to be created," but "already created, and sinners,"—that is, in the divine mind—are the object of the divine purpose and Predestination. This is evident, from the love and gracious affection from which, and the grace to which he chose them. For that love is in Christ; in him is that gracious affection of God towards us; the grace which is prepared for us as a saving means, has place in Christ, and not elsewhere. This you have, with sufficient clearness, signified, when you said that men, in that grace to which He chose them, were made vessels of mercy;" which word is misplaced, except when wretchedness and sin have preceded it.

But if you think of the love and gracious affection of God, as in God apart from any consideration of Christ, I shall deny that the purpose and decree of Predestination was instituted and established by God, according to those things, so considered, and I shall claim from you the proof, which, in my judg-ment, you will not be able to give, both because the love of God towards those "to be created" is uniform towards all, for in Adam all were created without any difference, and because that love and gracious affection, by which the purpose of Predestination was executed, saves with certainty, the predestinated; but the predestinated are not saved by that love and affection, considered out of Christ. If you say that the love and gracious affection in God is the same, whether considered in Christ or out of Christ, I admit it: but man, "to be created," and man "having been created, and a sinner," are the same man. Created, and continuing in the condition of creation, he could be saved, by obedience, of the love and gracious affection of God, considered out of Christ. As a sinner, he could not be saved, except by the same feelings, considered in Christ. If you make the sinner the object of Predestination, you ought to add to predesti-nating grace, a mode adapted to the sinner who is to be saved. If you do not add this, will grace, considered without that mode, be sufficient? I do not think that you will urge that the grace and love, by which a man, who is not a sinner, can be saved, and which is separate from mercy, is to be considered in Christ, and affects us on account of, and in respect to, him. If, however, you do this, I shall ask the proof. And, after all the proof which you may be able to present, it will be proper to say that Christ himself is to be here considered in different rela-tions; in the former case, as Mediator, preserving and confirming the predes-tinated in the integrity of their state; in the latter, as Mediator, redeeming and renewing the same persons from the state of sin and corruption; and I will add that grace and salvation come to us, not by the former, but by the latter mediation. For he is "Jesus, for he shall save his people from their sins." (Matt. i. 21.) He is "the Lamb of God, which taketh away the sin of the world" (John i. 29). He is the Redeemer of the world by his flesh given "for the life of the world" (John vi. 51); by the destruction of "the works of the devil" (1 John iii. 8, and Heb. ii. 14); and by that reconciliation, which consists "in imputing their trespasses unto them, and hath committed unto us the word of reconciliation." (2 Cor. v. 19).

That act, indeed, is "of the mere will of God," but not "without respect to sin in the creatures;" of sin, which is considered, not as the cause moving God to election, but as a condition, which must exist in the object of that act. And, in this sense, He does injury. to no one, if He does not elect all, since He is not under obligation to bestow mercy on any one. But He can ordain no one to punishment, without the prevision of sin, in view of any right which He possesses over His creatures. For that right is not unlimited, as many think—unlimited, I say, in such a sense that God can rightly inflict any act, possible to His omniscience, upon any creature considered in any respect, and without injustice bring upon the creature all things which the creature can suffer from his omnipotent Creator. This can be made plain by the following demonstration: Every right of God, over His creatures, depends either on the goodness of God towards His creatures, or on their wickedness towards Him, or on some contract entered into between God and His creatures. Without considering the right, which depends on contract, let us discuss the others. The right, which depends on the goodness of God, or on the wickedness of men, can not exceed the magnitude of those things severally. Man received from God, by His goodness in creation, his existence, both that of nature, and that of supernatural grace, in the latter of which is also included the power of attaining to the highest felicity, and that of a supernatural nature, which God promised to man on the condition of obedience. The opposite of this highest felicity is the deepest misery into which the same man would fall, justly and according to divine right, if he should transgress that law. Hence, exists the right of God over man, in that he is a creature, according to which He can take from him that very being which He has given, and reduce it to its pristine Nothing. Hence, also, He can not have the right to condemn to eternal punishment a man unless he has become a sinner. For these four things—existence, non-existence, happiness, misery—are so mutually connected, that, as happiness is better than existence, so misery is worse than non-existence. This, Christ signified when he said "good were it for man if he had never been born" (Mark xiv. 21). Therefore, the divine right does not permit that He should inflict misery on man, to whom He has given existence, except on the commission of that, by the opposite of which he could obtain felicity, the opposite of that wretchedness. Hence, if He should not elect all, He would do injustice to no one, if the non-elect should be only deprived of the good to which they had no claim; but injustice would be done to them, if, by non-election or reprobation, they must suffer evil which they had not deserved. The right of God does not so far extend itself over them.

There seems to have been need of this explanation, otherwise, we must, of necessity, far into many absurdities, and impinge on the righteousness of God. This, Augustine also, admits, in many passages. I will quote one or two: "God is good, God is just; He can deliver some without merit, because He is good;

He can not damn any one without demerit, because He is just." (In Julian, lib. 3, cap. 18.) "If it is believed that God damns any one, who does not deserve it, and is chargeable with no sin, it is not believed that He is far from iniquity." (Epistola 106, ad Paulinum.)

I may be permitted, with your leave, to note some things in the explanation of the second act, which seem to have been propounded by you with too little accuracy. For, when you, here, change the formal relation of the object, and consider men, under this act, as "about to fall," whom, under the first act, you presented as "about to be created," you seem to do it with no good reason. For, in your mode of considering the subject, men "to be created" are the object of both acts. But if all things are duly weighed, the object in both is, in fact, men as sinners, neither more in the former than in the latter, nor more in the latter than in the former act. Nor was it necessary to use the participle of future time, since the discussion is, here, concerning the act of the divine mind to which all things are present. I pass over the fact that the ordination to salvation depends on the fall, as the occasion of making that decree, wherefore, you should have said "fallen," not "about to fall." I could wish, also, that there might be an explanation how that act, which is the purpose of saving and of bestowing of glory, is the same with the act under which they are ordained, on whom that glory is bestowed, and to whom it is manifested; also, how the second act, namely, the purpose of saving, pertains to the execution and completion of the former purpose, namely, that by which He chooses some to His own love and grace.

That "the act referred to has no preparative cause, out of the good-pleasure of God," is true, only let Christ be duly included in that divine good-pleasure. To this, you seem, indeed, to assent, when you say "that act is in respect to Christ, the Mediator, in whom we are all elected to grace and salvation."

But when you so explain your meaning that we are said to be elected, in Christ, to grace and salvation, "because he is the foundation of the execution of election," you again destroy what you have said. For, if Christ is only the foundation of the execution of election, the election itself is made without respect to Christ in the decree of God, preceding, in fact, the execution of it. It can not be said, then, that we are elected in him to grace and salvation, but only that we, having, out of Christ, been previously elected to grace and salvation, are by Christ made partakers of them. But the Scriptures make Christ the foundation not only of the execution, but of the act of election. For He is, according to the Scriptures, Mediator, not only in the efficacy of the application, but in the merit of obtainment; wherefore, also, when they speak of Christ, the Scriptures affirm that grace and eternal life are bestowed upon us, not only through him, but on account of him, and in him. The direct relation is first presented, because God can not love the sinner unto eternal life, except in Christ, and on account of Christ, since the justice of God requires that reconciliation should be made by the blood of Christ.

The sum of the whole is, that both acts, that of choosing to grace and the love of God, as well as that of the bestowment of glory and the preparation of the means necessary to salvation, depends upon Christ as their only foundation—upon Christ, ordained by God to be High Priest and Mediator by the blood of his cross, the saviour from sins, the Redeemer from the bondage of sin and Satan, the Author and Giver of eternal salvation. Therefore, neither of those acts is in reference to men as "to be created," but both of them in reference to them, as "fallen sinners, and needing the grace of the remission of sins and the renewing of the Holy Spirit."

Those "five degrees" are well considered as mutually dependent, but they can not all be attributed, nor are they all subordinate to the "second act;" nor yet, indeed, to the first act. For the first three, namely, the "appointment of the Mediator, the promise of him, as appointed, and the presentation of him, as promised" are in the order of nature and of causes antecedent to all predestination of men to grace and glory. For Christ, appointed, promised, presented, yet more, having accomplished the work of reconciliation, having obtained eternal redemption, and having procured the Holy Spirit, is the head of all those who are predestinated in him unto salvation, not yet, in the order of nature, predestinated, but to be predestinated. For Christ is the head; we are the members. He was, first, in the order of nature, predestinated to be the head, then we to be the members. He was first, ordained to be the saviour, then we were ordained, in him, to be saved for his sake and in him. He inverts the order laid down in the Scripture, who says "God first predestinated men, and then ordained Christ to be the head of those predestinated." It need not be inquired, with much prolixity, why many have conceived that the order should be inverted, yet I think that some passages of the Scripture, in which the love of God towards men is said to be the cause of the mission of his Son, on the one hand, and on the other, that, other passages, in which Christ is said to gather together and to bring to salvation the children of God, and the elect, have given occasion for a conception of this kind—an occasion, not a just cause. For that love is not the cause of predestination, and it has no necessary connection with predestination, and Christ is not only the saviour of those, who have been elected and adopted as Sons by God, but he is also the Mediator and head in whom the election and adoption were made. This I have already often said. Your definition of the "appointment of the Mediator" was not sufficiently complete, for the condition of men was omitted, in reference to which the whole matter of Mediation was arranged. The passage which you have cited from 1 Peter i. 18-20, might admonish you of this. For Christ is there said to be the foreordained Mediator who redeemed us by his own "precious blood, as of a lamb without blemish, from vain conversation." The word "sinners" ought to have been added. For Christ was ordained to be Mediator, not between God and men absolutely considered, but between God and men considered as sinners. From this, I may also deduce a proof of what I have already argued in reference to the object of predestination. For if Christ is Mediator for sinners, then it follows that no one is loved, in Christ the Mediator, unless he is a sinner. Therefore, no one is predestinated in Christ, unless he is a sinner.

It seems to me that there is, also, some confusion in your discussion of "the promise of the Mediator". For the promise is considered either as the pure revelation of the decree to give and send the Mediator, or as having, united with it, the offering of the Mediator, who was to be given, with all his benefits. The former is a mere prediction of the advent of the Messiah himself, antecedent to his mission. The latter is the offering of the Messiah, in reality to come at a future time, but, in the decree of God, having already discharged the office of Mediator, pertaining, with the gifts obtained by the discharge of the office, to the application of its benefits. In this latter respect, it is made subordinate to predestination. Considered in the former respect, it precedes, not predestination, it is true, for that is from eternity, but the execution of predestination. The revelation, without the offering, consists in these words, "I will give a Mediator to the world;" but the offering in these words "Believe in the Mediator, whom I will give unto the world, and you shall obtain salvation in him." By that revelation and prediction, God binds Himself to offer the Mediator to the world, whether it should believe or not; but by that offering He demands faith, and by the internal persuasion of the Holy Spirit, added thereto, He effects faith and binds Himself to give salvation to the believer. It appears from this, that the promise is to be considered with this distinction, that in the former part, only, it is antecedent to the mission of the Messiah, but in the latter part it pertains to the execution of predestination.

Let us now, passing over that distinction of the promise and the offering, consider the universality of the promise, and the offering, taken jointly and in connection. Its universality is not to be measured by the degree of faith. For faith is posterior to the promise and the offering, as it marks the apprehension and embraces the application of the promise. But a distinction must be made between the promise and offering made by God, with the act of man which apprehends the promise, which is faith, and that act of God which applies, to the believer, that which is promised and offered. The promise and the offering extends itself to all who are called, -- called by the external preaching of the gospel, whether they obey its call or not. For even they received an invitation, who "would not come" to the marriage, and were, therefore, judged unworthy by God, (Matt. xxii. 2-8), since they "rejected the counsel of God against themselves," (Luke vii. 30), and by the rejection of the promise, made themselves unworthy (Acts xiii. 46). It is not that unworthiness, in accordance with which all sinners are alike unworthy, as the Centurion, and the publican, who are, nevertheless, said to have had faith, and to have obtained the remission of their sins from Christ; from which they are, in the Scripture, called "worthy" (Rev. iii. 4). But the passages of Scripture which are cited by you, do not limit the promise made, but the application by faith of the promised thing, with the exception of the second, Matt. xi. 28, which contains only an invitation to Christ, with the added promise of rest, as an inducement to come, but in reality not to be given, unless they should come to Christ.

You say also, that" an exhortation or command to believe is joined with the promise, and that this is more general than the promise." In this last assertion you are, in my judgment, in an error. For the promise, as made, and the command to believe are equally extensive in their relation. If the promise does not refer to all, to whom the command to believe is given, the command is unjust, vain, and useless. It is unjust, Since it demands that a man should have faith in the promise, not generally, that it pertains to some persons, but specially, that it was made for himself. But the promise was not made for him, if the command is more extensive than the promise. This command is vain, since it is in reference to nothing. It commands one to believe, but presents no object of faith, that promise which is the only object of faith, having been taken away. For which reason, also, the command is useless. It can in no way be performed by him, to whom the promise, as made, does not pertain. Indeed, should he attempt to obey the command to believe, he would effect nothing else than the conception in his mind of a false opinion of a falsity. For since the promise was not made to him, he can not believe that it was made for him, but only think so, and that falsely. The Scripture, however, every where represents the promise and the command to believe as of equal extent. "Repent and be baptized every one of you in the name of Jesus Christ, for the remission of sins; and ye shall receive the gift of the Holy Ghost. For the promise is unto you and to your children, &c." (Acts ii. 38, 39.) "Come unto me all ye that labour" the command; "and I will give you rest," the promise, made to all who are commanded to come (Matt. xi. 28). "If any man thirst, let him come unto me and drink," the command; "He that believeth on me, as the Scripture hath said, out of his belly shall flow rivers of living water," the promise, made to all who are commanded to come to Christ and drink (John vii. 37, 38). Perhaps some may prefer to join the phrase "drink" to the promise, in this way, "if any one thirst, let him come unto me; if he shall do this, he shall drink so abundantly that out of his belly shall flow rivers of living water." But explained in this way, it equally answers my present purpose.

You may say that you make the promise, in respect, not to its presentation, but to its application, of narrower extent than the command to believe. This, indeed, is correct. But the comparison is then incongruous. As, in the promise, three things are to be considered, as we said before, the promise made. faith exercised in the promise made, and the gift or application of the promised good, so, also, in the command, three things are included, the command itself, the obedience yielded to the command, and the reward bestowed on obedience. These three things, in each, answer severally to their corresponding opposites; the promise, as made, to the command; faith exercised in the promise, to the obedience yielded to the command; the gift or application of the promised good, to the reward bestowed on obedience. It was suitable that you should have instituted the comparison in this way. If you had done so, you would not have made the command more general than the promise; unless in this way, that the command is to be considered more general than the remuneration, which is bestowed on obedience. But who does not know that the promise is made to many, by whom it is not apprehended by faith, and that the command is addressed to many, by whom it is not obeyed? Hence you can perceive that it was not fitly said—"the promise relates to believers, (that is, the promise, not as merely made, but as applied, for the promise in the latter sense is antecedent to faith); and "the command relates to believers and to non-believers." It belongs to neither. The command is prior to faith, demands faith, and prohibits unbelief.

But what are those things which follow? You seem, most learned Perkins, to be forgetful of yourself, and to be entirely a different person from him whom you have displayed in other of your published works. Again and again I intreat you to be patient with me, as I shall discuss these points with candour and mildness.

First, observe the coherence of that, which follows, with that, which precedes. "For the elect are mingled with the wicked in the same assemblies." What then? Is the promise, as made, therefore, less extensive than the command to believe? You answer affirmatively, for the reason that the promise relates to the elect only, the command pertains to the elect and to the wicked. I reply, that the promise, as made and proposed by God, relates not to the elect only, but to the wicked, whom you place in opposition to the elect: and that the command, is not imposed either on the elect or on those opposed to them, except with the promise joined. I think that I see what you mean, namely, that, as the promise is not applied except to the elect, so also the same is not proposed except to the elect, that is: according to the divine mind and purpose. How this may be, we shall see hereafter. Meanwhile, I make the same remark in reference to the command. As the command, by which faith is not obeyed except by the elect, so, also, it is not proposed except to the elect, that is, according to the divine mind and purpose. For as, in the former case, the promise is proposed to the non-elect, without the divine purpose of applying the promise; so in the latter case, the command is proposed to the non-elect, without the divine purpose that they should fulfill or obey the command. If, on account of the absence of the divine efficacy, you think that the promise is not made to the non-elect, on account of the absence of the divine efficacy, I affirm, also, that the command is not imposed on the non-elect. The fact is the same in reference to both. We will, hereafter, more filly discuss that matter.

Secondly, the phrases "elect" and "wicked" are unsuitably placed in opposition to each other, since with the former, "reprobate," and with the latter, "pious," should have been contrasted, according to the rule of opposition. But here the opposition of the two things is unsuitable, since, in one of the opposites, the other is also comprehended. For the wicked, in this case, may comprehend also the elect. For it refers to those who are commanded, in the exhortation of the ministers of the word, to repent. But repentance is prescribed only to the wicked and to sinners, whether they are elect or reprobate, though with a contrary result in each case. I now speak of the call to repentance.

Thirdly, you seem to me to limit the office of ministers to the mere calling of sinners to repentance, excluding the presentation of the promise, which is another part of the message entrusted to them. For they say—"Repent and believe the gospel, for the kingdom of heaven is at hand." Finally, of what importance is it, whether they know, or do not know, "who, and how many are elect and to be converted"? "Then," you will say, "they might arrange their sermons, and present them to each person with an adaptation to his state." This I deny. For Christ knew and understood that Judas was a reprobate, and yet he did not arrange his sermons differently on his account. The preachers of the word must not desist from the functions of their office in any assembly, as long as they may be permitted to discharge them, and there are those who are willing to hear. But when they are cast out, and none whatever listen to their word, they are commanded by Christ to depart, and to shake off the very dust from their feet as a testimony against them. From this it appears, that their rule of teaching and exhorting is not an internal knowledge, which they can have, of the election of some and the reprobation of others, but the external obedience or contumacy of those whom they teach, whether they be elect or reprobate.

You add, moreover, the cause, in view of which, "God wills that they should be admonished to repent, who, as He sees, never will repent, namely, that they may be left without excuse." But this, I say, is neither the only object, nor the chief object, nor the object per se, but incidentally, and the event rather than the object, except in a certain respect, as we shall see. It is not the only object, since there is another, that they should be admonished of their duty, and invited and incited to faith and conversion, "not knowing that the goodness of God leadeth them to repentance" (Rom. ii. 4); also that God may satisfy Himself, and His own love towards His own creatures also, by that exercise of long suffering and patience. "What more could have been done to my vineyard, that I have not done in it?" (Isa. v. 4.) "God endured with much long-suffering the vessels of wrath fitted to destruction," (Rom. ix. 22.)

These two objects are, also, of far greater importance than that of rendering the impenitent inexcusable; therefore that is not the chief object. It is not the object per se, because the admonition does not render them inexcusable, unless it is despised and rejected, but this result of the admonition depends on the wickedness of those called. God does not will this result, unless He also foreknows that future admonition will be useless through the wickedness, not through the infirmity, of those who are admonished, and unless He has already frequently invited them in vain to repentance, as in Isa. vi. 10, "Make the heart of this people fat, and make their ears heavy," &c. For a distinction should be made between the admonition, as first addressed to a person, and as repeated the second or third time, and the final presentation of the same, after long contumacy. For the former is done through grace and mercy to miserable sinners, the latter through wrath against the obstinate, who, having hardened themselves by their own sin, have made themselves worthy of divine hardening. Therefore the rendering them inexcusable is rather the event of the admonition than an object proposed to the Deity, except against the obstinate, and those who are incorrigible through their own voluntary wickedness. This event deservedly, indeed, results from that rejected admonition, as the admonition becomes a savour of death unto death to those who were unwilling that it should be to themselves a savour of life unto life, that it might become against them a testimony of contumacy, as they refused to have the remedy of repentance, that they might endure the just and punitive will of God, who refused to obey His merciful and benevolent will.

But some one may reply that no other end was proposed to the Deity, in the exhortation, than that they should be indeed inexcusable, both because God, in the decree of reprobation, determined not to give the repentance and faith, which they could not have, except by His gift, and because God obtained no other end than that of rendering them inexcusable, and yet He is never frustrated in His design. These arguments seem, indeed, to be of some value, and to present no little difficulty, and if they can be fitly answered, by the use of necessary analysis and explanation, there is no doubt but that much light and clearness may in this way be thrown upon the whole subject of which we treat. I will endeavour to do what I may be able, trusting in divine grace, and depending on the aid of the Holy Spirit. Do you, my friend Perkins, assist me, and if you shall desire any thing, which may not be presented by me in the discussion, kindly mention it. I pledge myself that you will find me susceptible of admonition and correction, and ready to give my hand to the truth, when proved to be so. It will facilitate the discussion, if I arrange both the arguments with the parts of the subject under discussion in the form of a syllogism, and then examine the parts of the syllogism by the rule of the truth. That which belongs to the former argument may, in my judgment, be arranged thus: Those to whom God by a fixed decree has determined not to give repentance and faith, He does not admonish to repent and believe with any other object, than that they should be rendered inexcusable; -- But God has determined, in the decree of reprobation, not to give repentance and faith to the reprobate; -- Therefore, when God admonishes the reprobate to repent and believe, He does it with no other object than that they should be rendered inexcusable.

I reply to the Major; -- It seems to depend on a false hypothesis. For it presupposes that "God, by the external preaching of the gospel, admonishes some to repent and believe, to whom He has determined by a fixed decree not to give repentance and faith." This proposition seems to me to disagree with the truth.

In the first place, because it inverts the order of the divine decrees and acts. For the decree, by which God determined to exhort some to repentance and faith, by the external preaching of the gospel, precedes the decree of the non-bestowment of repentance and faith. For the former pertains to the will of God, in the relation of antecedent, the latter, in that of consequent. This can be proved from many, and very clear passages of the Scripture. In Isaiah 6, hardening and blinding is denounced against those who refuse to obey "the calling of God," as appears from the fifth chapter. The Apostle Paul manifestly agrees with this in Acts xxviii. 26, 27, citing the declaration of Isaiah against those Jews who did not believe. Again, it is said, "My people would not hearken to my voice; and Israel would none of me. So I gave them up unto their own heart's lust; and they walked in their own counsels" (Psalm lxxx. 11-12). In Hosea i. 6, the Israelites are called "not beloved," or "not having obtained mercy," "and not the people of God," only, after they had merited that rejection by the foul crime of unbelief and idolatry. "The Pharisees and lawyers rejected the counsel of God against themselves, being not baptized of him" (Luke vii. 30. "Paul and Barnabas waxed bold, and said, It was necessary that the word of God should first have been spoken to you; but seeing ye put it from you, and judge yourselves unworthy of everlasting life, lo, we turn to the Gentiles" (Acts xiii. 46).

The Jews are said in Romans ix. 22, to have "stumbled at that stumbling stone," because they had not sought to be justified by faith in Christ, but by the works of the law. In 1 Peter ii. 7, 8, Christ is said to be "a rock of offense, even them which stumble at the word, being disobedient." From this it appears that the decree of blinding and hardening, of the non-bestowment of the grace of repentance and faith, pertain to the decree of God, in the relation of consequent, depending on the foresight of incredulity, disobedience and contumacy. This proposition, then, ought to be enunciated thus, the subject being changed into the attribute, and vice versa; -- "God determined, by a fixed decree, not to give repentance and faith to those who, as He foresaw, would reject, in their wickedness and contumacy, the preaching of the gospel, by which they should be called to repentance and faith." It does not, indeed, follow from this, that God decreed to give faith to those whom He foresaw to be obedient. For there is a wide difference between the acts of divine mercy and divine justice. For the latter have their cause in men, the former have their occasion, indeed, from men, but their cause from God alone. This is the purport of that passage from Augustine, (Book 1, to Simplicianus, Ques. 2), "Esau did not will or run; but if he had willed or run, he would have found God to be his helper, who would even have effected that he should will and run by calling him, unless he had become reprobate by the rejection of the call." In the second place, because it charges God with hypocrisy, as if He would demand, by an admonition to faith made to such persons, from them, that they should believe in Christ, whom He had, nevertheless, made to them, not a saviour, not a savour of life unto life, unto the resurrection, but a savour of death unto death, a rock of offense, which charge must be contradicted both in its statement and proof.

If any assert that God demands faith not of them, but of the elect, who are mingled with the reprobates, but that this admonition, being presented by the ministers of the world, ignorant who may be the elect, and who reprobate, is to be presented also, to them, I shall reply that such can not be called "disobedient," because they do not obey an admonition, not made to themselves. If, however, that hypothesis is false, then the argument which follows is of no weight, since it is presupposed on both sides, that God does exhort to repentance and faith, those to whom He has determined not to give repentance and faith. For if He does not exhort such to repentance, He does not exhort them to any end, either that they may be rendered inexcusable, or any other.

It is in no way unfavourable to my reply, that the decree of reprobation was made from eternity. For we must consider what is the first external act, either negative or affirmative, towards, or in reference to a man, reprobate from eternity by the internal act of God. For the first external act, towards, or in reference to a man, when really existing, makes him reprobate in fact, as the internal act of God makes him reprobate in the mind and counsel of God, that is, as is commonly said, a distinction is to be made between the decree and its execution. It is certain that a man can not be called a reprobate in fact, in reference to whom God has not yet, by an external act, begun to execute the decree of reprobation.

I also remark, that the Major seems to me to be at variance with the truth, because it regards those who are reprobate, as being rendered inexcusable, while the order should be inverted, and those who are inexcusable should be made reprobates. For reprobation is just, and therefore, the reprobate must have been inexcusable before the act of reprobation; inexcusable in fact, before the external act of reprobation, and, foreseen or foreknown as inexcusable before the decree of reprobation. If they were reprobate on account of original sin, they were inexcusable on this account; if reprobate on account of their unbelief and rejection of Christ, they were inexcusable on account of that unbelief, &c.

I reply to the same Major that it is not possible that the exhortation is made, only to this end, that it might render one, who should hear it, inexcusable, and should, in fact and of right, render him inexcusable. For the exhortation renders its hearer inexcusable, not as it is heard, but as it is rejected. Moreover a rejection, which must render the person, who rejects, inexcusable, ought not to be inevitable. But the rejection of the exhortation, which is here discussed, is inevitable. First, because the exhortation is addressed to one in reference to whom God has already been employed in the external act of reprobation. But such a man can not avoid disobedience, according to the sayings of Christ. "Therefore, they could not believe, because that Esaias saith again, He hath blinded their eyes, and hardened their hearts, &c. (John xii. 39-40.) Secondly, since it is only presented to the end that it may be rejected. But this presentation is of the will of God, in the relation of consequent, which is always fulfilled, and attains its end.

Therefore, that rejection is inevitable. As then the Major is false in these three respects, it follows that the conclusion from the syllogism is not legitimate. But let us look at the Minor. For in reference to this also, and by occasion of it, there will be some things to be said which will be, in no small degree, adapted to our purposes.

The Minor was this, -- "But God has determined, in the decree of reprobation, not to give repentance and faith to the reprobate." I willingly agree to that statement, but let it be correctly understood. That it may be correctly understood, it is necessary to explain the non-bestowment or denial of repentance and faith, which is established by the decree of reprobation. For there is another denial of repentance and faith, which is administered by the decree of providence, inasmuch as this is distinguished from the decree of reprobation. If there is not an accurate distinction between these, error can not be avoided. I say, then, that it is very plain, from the Scriptures, that repentance and faith can not be exercised except by the gift of God. But the same Scripture and the nature of both gifts very clearly teach that this bestowment is by the mode of persuasion. This is effected by the word of God. But persuasion is effected, externally by the preaching of the word, internally by the operation, or rather the co-operation, of the Holy Spirit, tending to this result, that the word may be understood and apprehended by true faith. These two are almost always joined. For God has determined to save them, who believe by the preaching of the word, and the preaching of the word, without the co-operation of the Holy Spirit, is useless, and can effect nothing, as it is said "Neither is he that planteth anything, neither he that watereth, but God that giveth the increase" (1 Cor. iii. 7). But God does not will that His word should be preached in vain, as it is said, "So shall my word be that goeth forth out of my mouth: it shall not return unto me void; but shall accomplish that which I please, and it shall prosper in the thing whereto I sent it" (Isa. lv. 11).

It is in vain without the co-operation of the Holy Spirit; and it has, always joined with it, the cooperation of the Holy Spirit. For which reason, the gospel is called "the ministration of the Spirit" (2 Cor. iii. 8), and they who resist it are said "to resist the Holy Spirit," (Acts 7 & 13, and Matthew 12), not only because they oppose the external preaching administered by the command and the guidance of the Holy Spirit, but also because they strive against the cooperation of the Holy Spirit. Whence, also, some are said to sin against the Holy Ghost, in that they wickedly deny, and, through their hate, persecute and blaspheme the truth of which they are persuaded in their own minds, by the persuasion of the Holy Ghost. This internal persuasion of the Holy Spirit is two-fold. It is sufficient and efficacious. In the former sense, since he, with whom it is employed, is able to consent, believe, and be converted. In the latter, because he, to whom it is applied, does consent and believe, and is converted. The former is employed, by the decree of providence, with a sure prescience that it will be rejected by the free will of man; the latter is administered by the decree of Predestination, with a sure prescience that he, to whom it is applied and addressed, will in fact consent, believe, and be converted, -- because it is applied in a way such as God knows to be adapted to the persuasion and conversion of him to whom it is applied. These remarks are made in accordance with the sentiments of Augustine. Hence also there is a two-fold denial of grace, namely, of that which is sufficient, without which he can not believe and repent, and of that which is efficacious, without which he will not repent or be converted. In the decree of reprobation, sufficient grace is not, with propriety, said to be denied, since it is bestowed on many, who are reprobate, namely, on those, who by the external preaching of the gospel, are called to faith and repentance, but efficacious grace is denied to them, namely, that grace by which they not only can believe and be converted, if they consent, but by which they also will consent, believe, and be converted, and certainly and infallibly do so.

The Minor has this meaning, -- God has determined by a sure decree of reprobation not to give to some persons repentance and faith, that is, by using with them efficacious grace, by which they will surely believe and be converted. But has not by that decree denied the grace, by which they may be able, if they will, to believe and to be converted. Indeed by another decree, namely, that of Providence, in distinction from Predestination, He has determined to give to them faith and repentance by sufficient grace, -- that is, to bestow upon them those gifts in a manner in which they may be able to receive them, by the strength given to them by God, which is necessary and sufficient for their reception. God has, therefore, ordained, by the decree of Providence, by which external preaching is addressed to those whom God foreknew as persons who would not repent or believe, to give to them, having this character, sufficient grace and the strength necessary to their faith and conversion to God. Upon this determination, also, depends the fact that they are without excuse, who are all called by sufficient grace to repentance and faith. But He further decreed not to give efficacious grace to the same persons, and this by the decree of reprobation. But their inexcusableness does not depend upon this denial of efficacious grace. If, indeed, sufficient grace should be withheld, they, who do not believe and are not converted, are deservedly excused, for the reason that, without it, they could neither believe nor be converted. But if these things are explained in this way, according to the view of Augustine, and, perhaps also, in accordance with the sense of the Scriptures, it follows that it can not be concluded that God admonishes the reprobate to repentance and faith with no other design than that they may be left without excuse. For according to the decree of providence, by which He gives to them grace sufficient to faith, and exhortation to repentance and faith is addressed and it is to this end, that they may be led to repentance and faith, and that God may satisfy His own goodness and grace, and be clear from the responsibility of their perdition. The exhortation, then, is not made according to the decree of reprobation, therefore, its design is not to be measured by the decree of reprobation.

The second can also be arranged and disposed in the form of a syllogism; God proposes to Himself in His acts, no end, without attaining it, for He never fails of His purpose; --

But God, in the admonition which He addresses to the reprobate, attains no other end than that they should be left without excuse; -- Therefore God, in that admonition, proposes no other end to Himself.

To the Major I reply that it seems to me to be simply untrue. For God has not determined all His own deeds in accordance with His own will, in the relation of consequent, which is always fulfilled, but He administers many things according to His will, in the relation of antecedent, which is not always fulfilled. Legislation, the promulgation of the Gospel, promise, threatening, admonition, rebuke are all instituted, according to the will of God, as antecedents, and by these acts He requires obedience, faith, repentance, conversion, and those acts were instituted to this end; yet God does not always attain those ends. The falsity of this proposition can be proved by the clearest passages of Scripture; "Wherefore, when I looked that it should bring forth grapes, brought it forth wild grapes" (Isa. v. 4); "How often would I have gathered thy children together, and ye would not" (Matt. xxiii. 37); "The Lord is long suffering to us-ward, not willing that any should perish, but that all should come to repentance" (2 Pet. iii. 9).

The Pharisees are said to have "rejected the counsel of God against themselves" (Luke vii. 30), when they might have been brought, by the preaching of John and baptism to a participation in his kingdom. But though God might fail of any particular end, yet He can not fail in His universal purpose. For, if any person should not consent to be converted and saved, God has still added, and proposed to Himself, another design, according to His will as consequent, that He should be glorified in their just condemnation.

Therefore, that this proposition may be freed from its falsity, it must be amended thus, -- God proposes to His will, as consequent, no end which He does not attain. If any one should say that it follows from this that God is either unwise and not prescient of future events, or impotent, I reply that it does not follow. For God does not always propose an end to Himself from His prescience—and further God does not always please to use His own omnipotence, to accomplish any purpose which He has proposed to Himself.

As to the Minor, it also seems to me to be chargeable with falsity. For God, by that admonition, attains another end than that they should be rendered inexcusable, namely, He satisfies His own goodness and love towards us. Add to this that, as the fact of their being without excuse arises, not from the presentment, but from the rejection of the admonition, God has not proposed to Himself their inexcusableness as an end, except after the foresight that the admonition would come to them in vain. In this view, then, their inexcusableness does not arise from the antecedent will of God, administering the admonition, but from the consequent will, furnishing the rejection of the admonition.

It follows, therefore, that a true conclusion can not be deduced from these false propositions. The words of the Abbot Joachim must be understood according to this explanation, or they will labour under the error, which we have now noticed in your words.

The command of God by which He exacts repentance and faith from those, to whom the gospel is preached, can, in no way, be at variance from the decree of God. For no will or volition of God, whatever may be its character, can be contrary to any other volition. But it may be possible that a decree may be ignorant]y assigned to God, which is at variance with His command; also, a decree of God, which is assigned to Him in the Scriptures, may be so explained, as to be necessarily at variance with the command of God. The command by which God exacts faith of any one, declares that God wills that he, on whom the command is imposed, should believe. If, now, any one ascribes any decree to God, by which He wills that the same person should not believe, then the decree is contrary to the command. For it cannot be that God should, at the same time, will things contradictory, in whatever way or with whatever distinction the will may be considered. But to believe, and not to believe are contradictory, and to will that one should believe, and to will that he, the same person, and considered in the same light, should not believe, are contradictory. The decree is of such a character, that God is said to have determined, according to it, to deny the concurrence of His general government or of His special grace, without which, as He knew, the act of faith could not be performed by him, whom, by His command, He admonishes to believe. For He, who wills to deny to any person the aid necessary to the performance of an act of faith, wills that the same person should not believe. For he, who wills in the cause, is rightly said to will, also, in the effect, resulting, of necessity, from that cause. For, as it can not be said that God wills that a person should exist longer, to whom He denies the act of preservation, so, also, it can not be said that He wills that an act should be performed by any one, to whom He denies His own concurrence and the aid, which are necessary for the performance of the act. For the act of the divine preservation is not more necessary to a man, that he may continue to exist, than the concurrence of the divine aid, in order that he may be able to exercise faith in the gospel. If, then, that purpose not to do a thing, of which you speak, marks a denial of the concurrence of God, which is necessary to the exercise of faith in the promise, it certainly impinges upon the command, and can, in no way, be harmonized with it. For that denial, being of this character, holds the relation of most general and most efficacious hindrance, as that, which is not, is hindered, that it may not become something, most efficaciously by the purpose of creation, (i.e., by a denial of its exercise), and that which is, that it may not longer exist, by the will of preservation (not being exercised). If you understand the "purpose not to do a thing," in such a sense, then, truly, you do not free the will of God from contradiction by either of your answers.

You say that "God, in His commands and promises, does not speak of all which He has decreed, but only in part manifests His own will." I grant it. But I say that whatever God says in His commands and promises, is such in its nature that He can not, without contradiction, be said to will or determine any thing, contrary to it, by any decree; for it is one thing to be silent concerning certain things which He wills, and another thing to will that which is contrary to those things which He has previously willed. It is certain, from the most general idea of command, that the whole will of God is not set forth in a command, but only that which He approves and wills to be done by us. There is no decree of God by which He wills any thing contradictory to that command.

I wish, also, that you would consider how ineptly you express what follows—What are these expressions? "God does not will the same thing alike in all. He wills conversion in some, only in respect to their trial and exhortation, and the means of conversion; in others, also: in respect to the purpose of effecting it." If you say those things in reference to the will of God as it requires conversion, they ought to have been differently expressed; if in reference to His will as it effects conversion, they ought, in that case, also, to have been differently expressed. Understood in either sense, the phraseology is not correct. But I think that you are here speaking of the will in the latter sense, according to which God does not will to effect conversion equally in all, for whom He does equally, and of the same right, require it. For, in some, He wills to effect it only by external preaching, admonition, and sufficient means, for so I explain your meaning. If this is in accordance with your views, it is well, but if not, I would wish that you would inform us what you have understood by the word "means." In others, He wills to effect it, by efficacious means, administered according to the decree of Predestination. There is here, indeed, no conflict of wills, but only different degrees of will, as far as we are concerned, or rather different volitions of God in reference to different objects, according to which God can not be said to will and not to will the same object, that is, to will the conversion, and not to will the conversion of the same man—the laws of just opposition being here observed. I could wish that it might be explained how "God sincerely wills that the man should believe in Christ, whom He wills to be alien from Christ, and to whom He has decreed to deny the aid necessary to faith," for this is equivalent to not willing the conversion of any one.

To your second answer, I say, that it is not sufficient that you should say that "the revealed will of God is not adverse to the will of good-pleasure, but the matter of predestination is to be so treated that the will of good-pleasure is not to be opposed to the revealed will; for I think that the limits of that opposition ought to have been thus expressed. For the will which you call that of "good-pleasure," ought to be investigated by means of the revealed will; hence the latter is to be brought into agreement with the former, not the former to be reconciled with the latter. I desire, also, that it should be considered by what right the revealed will is usually considered as distinguished from the will of good pleasure, since the good-pleasure of God is frequently revealed. It is the good-pleasure of God that he who beholds the Son and believes on him, should have everlasting life. The word eujdokia is often used in the Scriptures, for that will of God, which is inclined towards any one, which is called "good-pleasure" in distinction from the pleasure of God, considered in a general sense.

Reprobation can not be referred to good-pleasure; for every exercise of good-pleasure towards men is in Jesus Christ, as the angels sung "good will toward men" (Luke ii. 14). In reference to the passage in Matt. xi. 25, 26, in which the word eujdokia is used in reference to the pleasure of God by which He has hidden the mysteries of the kingdom of heaven from the wise, and revealed them unto babes. I remark that the word eujdokia is properly to be referred to that, concerning which Christ gives thanks to his Father, that is, the revelation of the heavenly mysteries to babes. For it is to be understood in this way: "I give thanks unto thee, O Father, that thou hast revealed unto babes the mysteries which thou hast hidden from the wise." Christ does not give thanks to the Father that He has hidden the mysteries from the wise, for he prayed for the wise men of this world who crucified him. For the "princes of this world" are said to have crucified the Lord of glory" (1 Cor. ii. 8), and he is said to have prayed for his persecutors, and particularly for those who crucified him. In what respect is it true that the revealed will "always agrees, in its beginning, end and scope," with the good-pleasure, in the ordinary acceptation of that phrase, since the revealed will has often a different object from that of the will of good-pleasure? Also, if both are in reference to the same object, there can not be the same beginning, and the same end and scope to both except it be also true that God wills by His good-pleasure, that which, in His revealed will, He declares that He wills, unless, indeed, that same beginning is considered universally to be God, and the same end to be the glory of God. But that "the revealed will of God seems often to be diverse, and, indeed, in appearance, to be contrary to the decree of God, and also in reference to the mode of proposing it," is true, if you mean that this "seems" so to ignorant men, and to those who do not rightly distinguish between the different modes and the various objects of volition. These two wills of God, however diverse, never seem contrary to those, who rightly look into these things, and so judge of them. As to the death of Hezekiah, and the destruction of Nineveh, God knew that it belonged to His justice, unless it should be attempered with mercy, to take away the life of Hezekiah, and to send destruction on the Ninevites; for the law of His justice claimed that these things should be denounced against them by Isaiah and Jonah. But God was not willing to satisfy the demands of justice, unless with the intervention of the decree of mercy, by which He determined that neither death should come on Hezekiah, nor destruction upon the Ninevites, unless they should be forewarned to seek the face of God by prayers, and, in this manner, to turn away the evil from themselves; and, if they should do this, they should be spared. But He knew that they would do this, being, indeed, assisted by grace and the divine aid, by which He had determined to co-operate with the external preaching; and so He determined to prolong the life of Hezekiah and to preserve the city of the Ninevites from destruction. Here, then, there seems to be not even apparent contrariety.

What you observe concerning "the human and the divine will of Christ," does not affect our present subject of discussion. It is true that there was such a difference; but this is not strange, since those wills belonged not to one origin, though they did belong to one person, embracing, in himself two natures and two wills. I may add, also, that Christ willed both to be freed and not to be freed from death. For as a man, he said, "O, my Father, let this cup pass from me," and as a man, also, he corrected himself, "nevertheless, not as I will, but as thou wilt" (Matt. xxvi. 39). That this is to be understood of the human will, is apparent, because there is one and the same will, as there is one nature to the Father and to the Son, as divine. I may say, in a word, that Christ, as to the outward man, willed to be freed from immediate death, but according to the inward man, he subjected himself to the divine will. And, if you will permit, I will say, that there was, in him, a feeling and a desire to be freed, not a volition. For volition results from the final decision of the reason and of wisdom, but desire follows the antecedent decision of the senses or the feelings.

That "Abraham was favourably inclined towards the Sodomites, who were devoted, by the decree of God, to destruction," the Scripture does not assert. It also does not seem to me to be very probable that "he could pray in faith" for those whom he knew to be devoted, by the decree of God, to irrevocable destruction. For prayer was not to be offered in behalf of such persons. God commands Jeremiah not to pray for the people, which He had, by an irrevocable decree, and by His will as its consequent, destined and devoted to captivity and destruction. For although it may not be requisite in prayers, offered for any thing whatever, that one should certainly believe that the thing, which he seeks, shall be granted, it is necessary that the mind of him, who prays, should certainly believe that God, in His omnipotence and mercy, is both able and willing to do that which is asked, if He knows that it will be in accordance with His own grace. But that, which God has decreed not to do, and what He has signified, absolutely, that He will not do, He neither can do, nor will He ever will to do, so long as the decree stands, and it is not right for a believer to intercede with God in his prayers for that thing, if the decree of God has been known to him.

Your third answer is, that "God, as a creditor, can require what Himself may not will to effect." But there is an equivocation or ambiguity in the words, "what Himself may not will to effect." They may be understood, either in reference to that concurrence of God, which is necessary to the doing of that, which He commands, or in reference to that efficacious concurrence by which that, which He commands, is certainly done. If in reference to the latter, it is true.

There is no kind of conflict or contrariety between these two

"demand or command that any thing should be done," and "yet not to do it efficaciously." If in reference to the former, it is not true. For God does not command that, in reference to which He denies the aid necessary to effect it,

unless any one, of his own fault, deprives himself of that grace, and makes himself unworthy of that aid. The right of creditor remains, if he, who is in debt, is not able to pay by his own fault. But it is not so with the command, in which faith is prescribed; for faith in Christ is not included in the debt which a man was bound to pay according to his primitive creation in the image of God, and the primitive economy under which he lived. For it began to be necessary, after God changed the condition of salvation from legal obedience to faith in Christ.

We come now to "the presentation of the Mediator." consisted both in the fact that the Mediator presented himself to God, the Father, as a victim for the sin of the world, and that the Father, by the word and His spirit, presents the Mediator, having performed the functions of that office, and having obtained remission of sins and eternal redemption to the world, reconciled through him. The former pertains to the provision of salvation, the latter to its application by faith in the same Mediator. The former is the execution of the act of appointment and promise, the latter coincides with the actual offering, which we have previously considered in discussing the promise. But the presentation, as it is defined by you, not immediately antecedent to the application, for between that presentation, and the application, there intervenes the offering of the Mediator by the word and the Holy Spirit.

What you say concerning the virtue and efficacy of the price, paid by Christ, needs a more careful consideration. You say, that "the efficacy of that price, as far as merit is concerned, is infinite"; but you make a distinction between "actual and potential efficacy." You also define "potential efficacy" as synonymous with a sufficiency of price for the whole world. This, however, is a phrase, hitherto unknown among Theologians, who have merely made a distinction between the efficacy and the sufficiency of the merit of Christ. I am not sure, also, but that there is an absurdity in styling efficacy "potential," since there is a contradiction in terms. For all efficacy is actual, as that word has been, hitherto, used by Theologians. But, laying aside phrases, let us consider the thing itself. The ransom or price of the death of Christ, is said to be universal in its sufficiency, but particular in its efficacy, i.e. sufficient for the redemption of the whole world, and for the expiation of all sins, but its efficacy pertains not to all universally, which efficacy consists in actual application by faith and the sacrament of regeneration, as Augustine and Prosper, the Aquitanian, say. If you think so, it is well, and I shall not very much oppose it. But if I rightly understand you, it seems to me that you do not acknowledge the absolute sufficiency of that price, but with the added condition, if God had willed that it should be offered for the sins of the whole world. So then, that, which the School-men declare categorically, namely, that Christ's death was sufficient for all and for each, is, according to your view, to be expressed hypothetically, that is, in this sense—the death of Christ would be a sufficient price for the sins of the whole world, if God had willed that it should be offered for all men. In this sense, indeed, its sufficiency is absolutely taken away. For if it is not a ransom offered and paid for all, it is, indeed, not a ransom sufficient for all. For the ransom is that, which is offered and paid. Therefore the death of Christ can be said to be sufficient for the redemption of the sins of all men, if God had wished that he should die for all; but it can not be said to be a sufficient ransom, unless it has, in fact, been paid for all. Hence, also, Beza notes an incorrect phraseology, in that distinction, because the sin-offering is said to be absolutely sufficient, which is not such, except on the supposition already set forth. But, indeed, my friend Perkins, the Scripture says, most clearly, in many places, that Christ died for all, for the life of the world, and that by the command and grace of God.

The decree of Predestination prescribes nothing to the universality of the price paid for all by the death of Christ. It is posterior, in the order of nature, to the death of Christ and to its peculiar efficacy. For that decree pertains to the application of the benefits obtained for us by the death of Christ: but his death is the price by which those benefits were prepared. Therefore the assertion is incorrect, and the order is inverted, when it is said that "Christ died only for the elect, and the predestinate." For predestination depends, not only on the death of Christ, but also on the merit of Christ's death; and hence Christ did not die for those who were predestinated, but they, for whom Christ died; were predestinated, though not all of them. For the universality of the death of Christ extends itself more widely than the object of Predestination. From which it is also concluded that the death of Christ and its merit is antecedent, in nature and order, to Predestination. What else, indeed, is predestination than the preparation of the grace, obtained and provided for us by the death of Christ, and a preparation pertaining to the application, not to the acquisition or provision of grace, not yet existing? For the decree of God, by which He determined to give Christ as a Redeemer to the world, and to appoint him the head only of believers, is prior to the decree, by which He determined to really apply to some, by faith, the grace obtained by the death of Christ.

You allege these reasons in favour of your views, concerning the death of Christ. "Christ did not sacrifice for those for whom also he does not pray, because intercession and sacrifice are conjoined; -- But he prays, not for all, but only for elect and for believers, (John xvii. 9,) and, in his prayer, he offers himself to the Father; -- Therefore he sacrifices not for all, and, consequently, his death is not a ransom for all men.

I reply that the Major does not seem to me to be, in all respects, true. The sacrifice is prior to the intercession. For he could not enter into the heavens that he might intercede for us in the presence of God, except by the blood of his own flesh. It is also prior, as sacrifice has reference to merit, intercession to the application of merit.

For he is called the Mediator by merit and the efficacy of its application. He acquired merit by sacrifice; he intercedes for its application. He does both, as Priest; but he makes that application as King and Head of His church. It is indeed true that Christ, in the days of his flesh, offered up prayers with tears to God, the Father. But those prayers were not offered to obtain the application of merited blessing, but for the assistance of the Spirit, that he might stand firm in the conflict. If, indeed, he then offered up prayers to obtain the application referred to, they depended on the sacrifice, which was to be offered, as though it were already offered. In this order, sacrifice and intercession are related to each other.

In reference to the Minor, I assert, that Christ prayed also for the non-elect. He prayed for those who crucified him, for his enemies, among whom also were non-elect persons. For "the princes of this world" crucified him, and to most of them the wisdom and power of God, which is Christ, was not revealed (1 Cor. 2). Secondly, the prayer of Christ, which is contained in the 17th chapter of John, was offered, particularly for those who had believed, and those who should afterwards believe, and, indeed, to obtain and apply to them the blessings merited by the sacrifice of his death. He asks that they may be one with the Father and the Son, as the Father and the Son are one; which He could not ask unless reconciliation had actually been made, or was considered, by God, as having been made. But such is not the character of all the prayers of Christ. Thirdly, I remark that the word "world," in John xvii. 9, properly signifies those who rejected Christ, as preached to them in the word of the gospel, and those who should afterwards reject him. This is apparent from the contrast—"I pray not for the world, but for them which thou hast given me," whom he describes as having believed (8th verse) and as believing at a future time (20th verse). The word is used similarly in many other passages—"The world knew him not" (John ii. 10); "Light has come into the world, and men loved darkness rather than light" (iii, 19); "The Spirit of truth, whom the world can not receive" (xvi, 17); "He will reprove the world of sin, because they believe not on me" (xvi, 8, 9); "How is it that thou wilt manifest thyself unto us, and not unto the world?" (xvi, 22.) Therefore the extent of the sacrifice is not to be limited by the narrow bounds of that intercession.

I could wish to learn from Illyricus how it can be in accordance with the justice of God, and the infinite value of Christ's sacrifice, that "prayer is expiatory and the rule of the Sacrifice [Canon Sacrificii]. "I think, not only that Christ did not ask of the Father to regard favourably his sacrifice, but that it was not possible that He should present such a petition: if that is indeed true, which our churches teach and profess with one voice, that the most complete satisfaction was made to the justice of God by the sacrifice of Christ. But that idea originated in the Polish mass, in which, also, are those words-"Canon Sacrificii."

But the words, which contain your conclusion are remarkable, and have no right meaning. What is meant by this? -- "Christ was appointed to be a ransom by the intercession and oblation of the Son." Intercession is subsequent to ransom. Therefore the latter was not appointed by the former. Oblation belongs to the ransom itself, and is therefore prior to the intercession, and could, in no way, be concerned in the appointment of the ransom. But the action itself has the character of an oblation. Hence, also, the ransom itself, as I have already often said, is prior to election. For election is unto life, which has no existence except by the oblation of the ransom; unless we may say that election is unto life, not now existing, nor as yet merited, not even in the decree of God. For he is the "lamb slain from the foundation of the world."

You proceed further, and endeavour, but in vain, to confirm the same sentiment by other arguments. They seem to have some plausibility, but no truth. You say, that "Christ is only the Mediator of those, whose character he sustained on the cross;

But he sustained the character of the elect only on the cross; Therefore he is only the Mediator of the elect." I reply to the Major, that it belongs not to the essence or the nature of Mediator to sustain the character of any one. For he is constituted a Mediator between two dissident parties. Therefore, as Mediator, he sustains the character of neither; unless, indeed, the nature of the mediation be, of necessity, such as to demand that the mediator should sustain the character of one of the parties. But this mediation has such a nature as the justice of God required. For it could enter upon no way of reconciliation with a world, guilty of sin, unless the Mediator should pledge satisfaction, and, in fact, should make it in accordance with the right of surety. This is what is said in 2 Corinthians v. 19, 21, "God was in Christ, reconciling the world unto Himself—for He hath made him to be sin" for the world, that is, a sin offering. In this sense, also, it is truly said that Christ is not a Mediator, except for those, whose character he sustained. I speak here in respect to the Sacrifice; "For every high priest taken from among men, is ordained from me," &c., (Heb. v. 5, 1.) Here, also, a distinction may be made between the act, by which reconciliation is obtained, and the completion of that act, which is reconciliation. The act, obtaining reconciliation, is the oblation of Christ on the cross. Its completion is the reconciliation. In respect to the act, he sustained our character, for we deserved death, not in respect to the completion. For the effect, resulting frown the oblation, depends on the dignity and excellence of the character of Christ, not of us, whose character he sustained. Indeed, if it be proper to use distinctions of greater nicety, in this place, I may say, that Christ sustained our character, not in respect to action, namely, that of oblation, but of passion. For He was made a curse for us, and an offering for sin. From which it is evident, that, as all men are sinners and obnoxious to the curse, and Christ assumed human nature common to all, it is probable that he sustained the character of all men.

We see this also in the Minor of your syllogism, which is "Christ sustained the character of the elect only on the cross," in which I notice a two-fold fault, that of falsity and that of incorrect phraseology. Its falsity consists in this, that Christ is said to have sustained on the cross the character of the Elect only. I prove it, from the fact that the Scripture no where says this; indeed it asserts the contrary in numerous passages. Christ is called "the Lamb of God which taketh away the sin of the world" (John i. 29) God is declared to have "so loved the world that He gave His only begotten Son" (iii, 16). Christ declares that he will give "his flesh for the life of the world" (vi, 51). "God was in Christ reconciling the world unto Himself" (2 Cor. v. 19). "He is the propitiation for our sins; and not for ours only, but also for the sins of the whole world" (1 John ii. 2). The Samaritans said "We know that this is indeed the Christ, the saviour of the world" (John iv. 42). Also 1 John iv. 14, "We have seen and do testify, that the Father sent the Son to be the saviour of the world." That, in the word "world," in these passages, all men, in general, are to be understood, is manifest from these passages and from Scriptural usages. For there is, in my judgment, no passage in the whole Bible, in which it can be proved beyond controversy that the word "world" signifies the Elect. Again, Christ it is said to have died for all, in Hebrews ii. 9, and elsewhere. He is said to be "the saviour of all men, especially of those that believe" (1 Tim. iv. 10), which declaration can not be explained to refer to preservation in this life without perversion and injury. Christ is also styled the "Mediator between God and men" (1 Tim. ii. 5). He is said to have died for those "without strength, ungodly, and yet sinners" (Rom. v. 6-8.)

What I said a little while since, is important also on this point; -- that the case of the whole human race is the same, all being alike conceived and born in sin, and the children of wrath; and that Christ assumed human nature, which is common to all men, not from Abraham only and David, as Matthew traces his genealogy, but also from Adam, to whom Luke goes back in his third chapter. He offered, therefore, the flesh which he had in common with all. "For as much then as the children are partakers of flesh and blood, He also himself likewise took part of the same, &c." (Heb. ii. 14). He offered that flesh for the common cause and the common sin, namely, for the sin of the world, in respect to which there is no difference among men, and the Apostle adds this cause in the passage just cited, "that through death he might destroy him that had the power of death." Let the dignity and excellence of the person, which could offer an equivalent ransom for the sin of all men be added to this. Let the gracious and tender affection of God towards the human race come into consideration, which, in the Scriptures, is usually spoke of by the general term filanqrwpia as in Tit. iii. 4. Which term signifies, in general terms, the love of God towards men; which affection cannot be attributed to God, if He pursues with hatred any man, without reference to his deserts and his sin.

I know that some will reply that God indeed hates no one except on account of sin, but that He destined some to His own just hatred, that is, reprobating some without reference to sin. But in that way the order of things is inverted; for God does not hate because He reprobates, but reprobates cause He hates. He reprobates a sinner, because the sinner and sin are justly hateful and odious to Him. Hatred is an affection in the Deity by which He hates unrighteousness and the unrighteous, as there is in Him also love for righteousness and the righteous. Reprobation is an act of God, internal in purpose, external in execution, and the act is, in the order of nature, subsequent to the affection. The destination of any one to hatred, however it may be considered, has necessarily these two things preceding it, hatred against unrighteousnes, and the foresight that the individual, by his own fault, will be guilty of unrighteousness, by omission or commission.

I know, indeed, that the love of God, referred to, is not in all respects equal towards all men and towards each individual, but I also deny that there is so much difference, in that divine love, towards men that He has determined to act towards some, only according to the rigor of His own law, but towards others according to His own mercy and grace in Christ, as set forth in his gospel. He willed to treat the fallen angels according to that rigor, but all men, fallen in Adam, according to this grace. For every blessing, in which also mercy and long suffering (Exod. xxxiii. 19 & xxxiv, 6-7) are comprehended, He determined to exhibit, in the deliverance and salvation of men. Some, however, may wish to do away with the distinction, which many Theologians make between the fall of angels and that of man. For they say that the angels fell beyond all hope of restoration, but that men could have a complete restoration, and they assign, as a reason, the fact that angels sinned, by their own motion and impulse, and man, by the instigation and persuasion of an evil angel. To all these things, we may add, by way of conclusion, the proper and immediate effect of the death and suffering of Christ, and we shall see that no one of the human race is excluded from it. It is not an actual removal of sins from these or those, not an actual remission of sins, not justification, not an actual redemption of these or these, which can be bestowed upon no one without faith and the Spirit of Christ; but it is reconciliation with God, obtainment from God of remission, justification, and redemption; by which it is effected that God may now be able, as Justice, to which satisfaction has been made, interposes no obstacle, to remit sins and to bestow the spirit of grace upon sinful men. To the communication of these effects to sinners He was already inclined, of His own mercy, on account of which, He gave Christ as the saviour of the world, but, by His justice, He was hindered from the actual communication of them. Meanwhile God maintained His own right to bestow on whom He pleased, and with such conditions as He chose to prescribe, those blessings, (which are His by nature,) the participation in which He, through His mercy, desired to bestow on sinners, but could not actually do it on account of the obstacle of His justice, but which He can now actually bestow, as His justice has been satisfied by the blood and death of Christ; since He, as the injured party, could prescribe the mode of reconciliation, which also He did prescribe, consisting in the death and obedience of His Son and because He has given him to us, to perform, in our behalf, the functions of the Mediatorial office. If we decide that any person is excluded from that effect, we decide, at the same time, that God does not remit his sins unto him, not because He is unwilling to do so, having the ability, but because He has not the ability, as justice presents an obstacle, and because He willed not to be able. He willed that His justice should be satisfied, before He should remit his sins unto any one, and because He did not will that His justice should be satisfied in reference to that person.

On the other hand, also, if we decide that the nature of the Mediation is such, as you seem to conceive, that the sins of all the Elect are taken from them and transferred to Christ, who suffered punishment for them, and, in fact, freed them from punishment, then obedience was required of him, who rendered it, and, by rendering it, merited eternal life, not for himself, but for them, not otherwise than if we had constituted him Mediator in our place, and through him had paid unto God our debt. We must also consider that, according to the rigor of God's justice and law, immunity from punishment and eternal life are due to the elect, and they can claim those blessings from God, by the right of payment and purchase, and without any rightful claim, on the part of God, to demand faith in Christ and conversion to him. It is not easy to tell under how great absurdities, both the latter and the former opinion labour. I will refute each of them by a single argument. In reference to the former, I argue that, if God was unwilling that satisfaction, for the sins of any, should be rendered to Himself, by the death of His Son, then faith in Christ can not, justly, be demanded of them, they can not, justly, be condemned for unbelief, and Christ can not, justly, be constituted their judge. The latter, I compute by an argument, of very great strength, taken from the writings of the Apostle. The righteousness, rendered by Christ, is not ours in that it is rendered, but in that it is imputed unto us by faith, so that faith itself may be said to be "counted for righteousness" (Rom. iv. 5.) This phrase, if rightly understood, may shed the clearest light on this whole discussion. I conclude, therefore, that Christ bore the character of all men in general, as it is said, and not that of the elect only.

I notice incorrectness of phraseology in the statement that he bore, on the cross, the character of the Elect, when no one is elect, except in Christ, as dead and risen again, and now constituted by God the Head of the church, and the saviour of them who should believe in him, and obey him unto salvation. Therefore, there were no elect, when he was yet hanging on the cross, that is, both of these events being considered as existing in the foreknowledge of God; hence He could not have borne, on the cross, the character of the Elect. On this account, likewise, it would be absurdity to say that Christ bore the character of the reprobate, because reprobation had there no place. But he bore the character of men as sinners, unrighteous, enemies to God, apart from any consideration or distinction between Election and Reprobation. It is evident, then, from this reply, that it can not be concluded, from that argument, that Christ is the

Mediator for the Elect only, the work of the Mediator being, now, restricted to the oblation made on the cross.

You advance, also, another argument to prove the truth of your sentiment, and say; -- "Whatever Christ suffered and did as Redeemer, the same things all the redeemed do and suffer in him, and with him; -- But Christ, as Redeemer, died, rose again, ascended, sat down on the right hand of the Father;

Therefore, in him and with him, all the redeemed died, rose again, ascended, sat down at the right hand of the Father." You then assume, as a position by consequence, that "The Elect only die, rise again, ascend, sit at the right hand of the Father, in and with Christ. Therefore, they alone are redeemed." We will inspect and examine both parts of this argument in order.

The Major of this prosyllogism seems to me to be chargeable with notorious falsity, as can, also, be easily demonstrated. For it confounds the sufferings and the actions, by which redemption is effected and obtained, with the completion of redemption itself, and the application of redemption. For redemption does not refer to suffering, or to any action of Christ, but to the completion, the event, and the fruit of that suffering and action; therefore, the sufferings and the actions of Christ are prior to redemption; but redemption is prior to its application. They, however, are called redeemed from the application. Therefore, that, which Christ suffered and did to obtain redemption, the redeemed did not suffer or do. For they were not at that time redeemed, but, by those actions, redemption was obtained, and applied to them by faith, and so they, as the result, were redeemed. The very nature of things clearly proves that redeemer and redeemed are things so related, that the former is the foundation, the latter, the terminus, not vice versa, and, therefore, in the former is comprehended the cause of the other, and indeed the cause, produced by its own efficiency; whence it follows that the redeemed did not that, which was done by the redeemed, since, in that case, they were redeemed before the act of redemption was performed by the redeemer, and the redemption itself was obtained. If you say that you consider the redeemed not as redeemed, but as men to be redeemed, I reply that, in whatever way, they are considered, it can never be truly said that they did, in and with Christ, what Christ did for the sake of redeeming them. For those, who were to be redeemed were not in Christ or with Christ, therefore, they could, neither in him nor with him, suffer or do any thing. You will say that "they suffered and acted in him as a surety and pledge;" but I say in him as constituted a surety not by them, but by God for them, and on him the work of redemption was imposed by God. It is true, indeed, that he assumed from men the nature in which redemption was performed; yet He, not men in him, offered it. But, if they may be said to have suffered, because their nature suffered in the form of Christ, you see that, in this way also, the redemption is general for all those to whom the same nature belongs. Perhaps you refer to those passages of Scripture, in which we are said to be "dead with Christ, buried with him and raised with him" (Rom. vi. 3, 4, 5). Your explanation is unsatisfactory, if it regards them as having reference to our present subject. For those passages treat of the crucifixion, death, burial, and resurrection, which we each, in our own person, endure and experience. But they do not pertain to the meritorious redemption, as the crucifixion, death, &c., of Christ. Again, in those passages, the subject of discussion is that of our engraftment into Christ by faith, and our communion with him, which pertain to the application of redemption; but, here, the subject of discussion is the obtainment of redemption, and the acts which pertain to it. Those passages teach, that we, being grafted into Christ by faith, received from him the power of the Spirit, by which our old man is crucified, dead and buried, and we are resuscitated and raised again into a new life. From this it is apparent that they have no connection with our present subject.

The right meaning of the Minor, is that Christ, performing the work of redemption, died, rose again, and ascended into the heavens. For he was not the redeemer, before he offered himself to death and rose again from the dead. I remark, more briefly, that Christ died and rose again in that he was Redeemer by the imposition and acceptance of the office, not by the fulfillment of the same. For the death and resurrection of Christ pertain to the function of the office of Redeemer. It now appears, from this, in what sense the conclusion is true. not in that in which you intend it, that they, whom you call "the redeemed," died and rose again in the person of Christ, but as I, a short time since, explained it, in a sense, pertaining, not to the obtainment of redemption, but to the application of the obtained redemption. For Christ is said to have "entered in once into the holy place, having obtained eternal redemption," (Heb. ix. 12), which redemption he communicates to believers, by the Holy Spirit sent from heaven.

These things being thus considered, your position by consequence does not weigh against the opinion, which I here defend. For it certainly happens to the Elect, only in the sense which we have set forth, with Christ to die, rise again, ascend, and sit at the right hand of the Father. They also, by reason of their being engrafted in Christ, and the application of the benefits of Christ, and of communion with Christ, are said to be "redeemed." "Thou art worthy to take the book, and to open the seals thereof; for thou wast slain, and hast redeemed us to God by thy blood out of every kindred, and tongue, and people, and nation; and hast made us unto our God kings and priests; and we shall reign on the earth" (Rev. v. 9, 10). So, also, in Rev. xiv. 3, 4, the same are said to have been "redeemed from the earth, and from among men." It is, however, to be observed that this position is not a consequence of the antecedents, unless there be added, to the Major, a restrictive phrase, in this way:

"Whatever Christ suffered and did this all the redeemed, and they only, suffered and did in him, and with him.

The arguments which you adduce to prove this position, are readily conceded by me, in the sense which I have explained. But that, which you afterwards present to illustrate your meaning, deserves notice. For the sins of those, for whom Christ died, are condemned in the flesh of Christ, in such a manner that they may not, by that fact, be freed from condemnation, unless they believe in Christ. For "there is, therefore, now, no condemnation to them which are in Christ Jesus, who walk not after the flesh, but after the Spirit" (Rom. viii. 1).

The error of confounding things, which should be distinct, and uniting those which should be divided, is constantly committed. For obtainment, and the act itself, which obtains, are confounded with the application, and the former are substituted for the latter.

You say, also, "the expiatory victim sanctifies those for whom he is a victim. For victim and sanctification pertain to the same persons; -- But Christ sanctifies only the Elect and believers; -- Therefore, Christ is victim for the Elect only and believers."

I answer to your Major, that the expiatory victim sanctifies, not in that it is offered, but in that it is applied. This may be plainly seen in the passage cited by yourself (Heb. ix. 13, 14). "For if the ashes of a heifer, sprinkling the unclean, sanctifieth to the purifying of the flesh—How much more shall the blood of Christ, &c." For which reason, it is called in Heb. xii. 24, "the blood of sprinkling." In the same manner, those, who, not only slew the paschal lamb, but also sprinkled the door-posts with its blood, were passed over by the destroying angel. If, then, the phrase "for whom" implies, not the oblation only, but also the fruit and advantage of the oblation, I admit the truth of the Major. But we are, here, discussing not the application of the victim Christ, but the oblation only, which, in the Scriptures, is simply said to be "for men" (Heb. v. 1). But faith must necessarily intervene between the oblation, and its application which is sanctification. The oblation, of the victim, then, was made, not for believers, but for men as sinners, yet on this condition, that He should sanctify only believers in Christ. Hence, it can not be considered, even though the Minor should be conceded, that Christ offered himself for the Elect only, since Election, as it is made in Christ, offered, dead, risen again, and having obtained eternal redemption by his blood, must be subsequent to the oblation.

You add—"Christ is the complete saviour of those, whom he saves, not only by his merits, but by efficaciously working their salvation." Who denies this? But the distinction is to be observed between these two functions and operations of Christ, the recovery, by his blood, of the salvation, which was lost by sin, and the actual communication or application, by the Holy Spirit, of the salvation obtained by his blood. The former precedes, the latter requires, in accordance with the Divine decree, that faith should precede it. Therefore, though Christ may not be said to completely save those who are not actually saved, yet he is said to be the saviour of others than believers (1 Tim. xiv. 10). I do not see how that passage can be suitably explained, unless by the distinction between sufficient and efficacious salvation, or salvation as recovered and as applied. The passages, which you cite from the Fathers, partly have no relation to the matter now discussed, and partly are related to it, but they teach nothing else than that the death and passion of Christ, which are a sufficient price for the redemption of the sins of all men, in fact, profit the Elect only, and those who believe unto salvation. What you say in reference to the application is correct; but I wish that you would distinguish between it, and those things which precede it.

From what has already been said, the decree, in reference to the bestowment of the Mediator and to the salvation of believers through the Mediator, is prior to the decree of predestination, in which some are destined to salvation in Christ, and others are left to condemnation out of Christ. But you say that "the decree of election is the cause and the beginning of all the saving gifts and works in men." I grant it, but not in view of the fact that it is the decree of election, but in that it is the desire of the bestowment of grace. In that it is the decree of election, it is the cause that grace is bestowed only on those: for it is the opposite of reprobation, and necessarily supposes it. For there is no election without reprobation, and the term elect itself signifies loved, with the contrast of not loved at least in the same mode and decree, and restricts love to those who are styled elect with the exclusion of those who are styled the non-elect or reprobate. So far, then, as saving gifts are bestowed upon any one in that act which is called election, it is properly love; in that the bestowment is restricted to some, to the exclusion of others, it is called election.

From this, it is apparent, in the first place, that the love which is according to election, would not be less towards the elect than it now is, even if God should declare the same favour, and His own love towards all men in general. Secondly, they, who make the love of God, in Christ, the cause of the salvation of men, and that alone, do no injury to grace, even if they deny that such love is according to election, that is, restricted to a few by the decree of God. They may, indeed, deny that which is true, but without injury to grace or mercy; for I presupposed that they make the same love to be the cause of salvation, as they do, who contend for election. I know, indeed, that Augustine often said against the Pelagians, that "they who make the grace of God common to all, in effect, deny grace altogether;" but this assertion is not, in all respects, true; but it was valid against the Pelagians, and all those who, at that time, made the grace of God universal. For they explained the grace of God, to be the gift bestowed equally on all by creation, in our original nature. I acknowledge, indeed, that, from the universality of grace, some consequences can be deduced, which will prove that the universality of grace may be indirectly opposed to that grace by which the elect are saved. But it should be known that those consequences are not, all of them, tenable, we examine them accurately, and I wish that you should demonstrate this.

You will thus effect much, not, indeed, in sustaining the view which you here specially advocate, but in sustaining the doctrine of election and reprobation in general. But it will be said that, by the reprobation of some, that is, by election joined with love, the elect are more fully convinced that the love of God towards themselves is not of debt, than they would be if that same love were bestowed by God upon all without any distinction. I, indeed, grant it, and the Scripture often uses that argument. Yet that love, toward us, can be proved to be gratuitous, and not of debt, and can be sealed upon our hearts, without that argument. It appears, then, that there is no absolute necessity of presenting that argument. I do not say these things because I wish that the doctrine of election should not be taught in our churches; far be it from me; but to show that this subject is to be treated with moderation, and without offense to weak believers, who, for the very reason that they hear that they can not be certain of salvation, unless they believe that which is taught concerning Election with the rejection of some, begin to doubt whether the sense of certainty of salvation, which they have at times enjoyed, is to be attributed to the testimony of the Holy Spirit, or to a certain persuasion and presumption in their own minds. I write this from experience. So much in reference to Election. Let us now consider its opposite—Reprobation.

But you define the decree of reprobation in a two-fold manner. First you say—"It is the work of divine providence, by which God decreed to pass by certain men, as to supernatural grace, that He might declare His justice and wrath in their due destruction." In my opinion, there are, in this definition, four faults, which, with your consent, I will exhibit, if I may be able to do so. The first fault is, you have made the decree of Reprobation, "the work, &c.," when, as it exists in God, it can, in no way, be called a work, which is something apart from that which produces it, existing after an act, and from an act produced by the efficaciousness or efficiency of an agent. I should prefer then to use the word "act" in this case, The second fault is you do not well describe the object of that act, when you say—"certain men are passed by," without any mention of any condition required in the object, or any reference to the fact that the men spoken of are sinners. For sin is a condition, requisite in a man, to be passed by in reprobation, or, so to speak, in one capable of being passed by. This I shall briefly prove in a few arguments.

First, the Scripture acknowledges no reprobation of men, as having been made by God, unless its meritorious cause is sin. Secondly, since reprobation is the opposite of election, it follows, if divine election has reference to sinners, that reprobation has reference to persons of the same character. But Election, as I have previously shown, has reference to sinners. Thirdly, because that supernatural grace, which is denied by reprobation, is grace necessary to sinners only—namely, that of remission of sins, and the renewal of the Holy Spirit. Fourthly, because justice and wrath can not be declared, except against a sinner, for where there is no sin there can be no place either for wrath or punitive justice, (of which you here necessarily speak). Fifthly, because punishment is due to no one, unless he is a sinner, and you say that "the wrath of God and His justice are declared in the due destruction of the Reprobate." When I make sin the meritorious cause of reprobation, do not consider me as, on the other hand, making righteousness the meritorious cause of Election. For sin is the meritorious cause of the reprobation of all sinners in general. But election is, not only of that grace which is not of debt, and which man has not merited, but also of that grace which takes away demerit. Even if the meritorious cause is supposed, the effect is not at once produced, unless by the intervention of His will, to whom it belongs to inflict due punishment, according to the merit of sin; but He has power to punish sin according to its desert, or to pardon it, of His grace in Christ. Therefore, in both cases, in election and in reprobation,. the free-will of God is considered the proximate and immediate cause. If you oppose to me the common distinction, by which sin is said to be required in the object of the execution, but not in the object of the decree itself, I reply that it is not right that God should will to condemn any one, or will to pass by him without consideration of sin, as it is not right for Him, in fact, to pass by or condemn any one without the demerit of sin. It is, then, truly said, the cause of the decree and of its execution is one and the same. Your third fault is, that of obscurity and ill-adjusted phraseology. For what is implied in the phrase "to pass by as to supernatural grace," instead of—to pass by in the dispensation and bestowment of supernatural grace? There is ambiguity, also, in the word "supernatural." Grace is supernatural, both as it is superadded to unfallen nature, bearing nature beyond itself, and as it is bestowed on fallen nature, changing it, and raising it to things heavenly and supernatural.

The fourth fault is, that you present a result of the preterition which coheres by no necessary copula, with the antecedent cause of the preterition. For sin is not presupposed to that act; sin does not of necessity exist from that act; one of which facts is necessarily required from the necessity of coherence between the act and its result. If, indeed, you say that sin necessarily results from that preterition, then you make God the Author of sin by a denial of the grace, without which, sin can not be avoided. But if that grace, which is denied to any one by preterition, is not necessary for the avoidance of sin, then a man could, without it, abstain from sin, and so not deserve destruction. If he could do this, that declaration of justice and wrath does not result from the act of decreed preterition. But you know that the parts of a definition should mutually cohere by a necessary copula, and that a result should not be proposed, which, even on the supposition of any act, does not result from that same act. For such a result would be incidental, and therefore, ought not to be found in a definition which is independent, and designed to convey absolute knowledge.

Let us, now, examine the other definition, which you have adduced, perhaps for the very reason, that you thought your former one somewhat unsound. It is this; -- "The decree of reprobation is the purpose to permit any one to fall into sin, and to inflict the punishment of damnation on account of sin." I know that this definition is used by the School-men, and, among others, by Thomas Aquinas, for whose genius and erudition I have as high an esteem as any one; but he, here, seems to me to be under a kind of hallucination. First, because he makes the decree of reprobation to be antecedent to sin, which opinion I have already refuted. Secondly, because he attributes that permission to the decree of reprobation, which ought to be attributed to a certain other, more general decree, that of providence, as I will show. An act which has reference to all men, in general, apart from the distinction between the elect and the reprobate, is not an act of reprobation; for, in that act, God had reference to the reprobate only; -- But that act of permission, by which God permitted man to fall into sin, is general, and extending to all men; for in Adam, all sinned (Rom. 5). And all are "by nature the children of wrath" (Ephes. ii. 3); -- That act, then, is not one of reprobation, but of mere general providence, regarding all men entirely without difference, and governing and administering their primitive state in the person of Adam. If you say that both are to be conjoined, the permission of the fall and the infliction of punishment, and that the whole subject, taken in a complex manner, is the proper act of reprobation, I answer that, on that principle, permission, according to which Adam, and in him, all his posterity fell, which is one and univocal, is resolved into two diverse matters, and thus becomes two-fold and equivocal; that is, into the decree of reprobation, by which the reprobate are permitted to fall, and the decree of providence, by which even the elect themselves are permitted to fall.

I add another argument, which, in my judgment indeed, is irrefutable. Reprobation and Election are spoken of as things separate and opposite; one is not without the other. Hence, no act can be attributed to one of them, the opposite of which, either affirmative or negative, may not be attributed to the other. But no act, opposite to that of permission to fall, can be attributed to Election. There is but one act which is opposite to the act of permission, namely, hindrance from failing into sin. But no man, not even one of the elect, is hindered from falling into sin. For the elect themselves sinned in Adam. Therefore, the act of permission is not to be assigned to the decree of Reprobation. If you diligently consider this argument, you will see that it is clearly evident, from it, that permission to fall was prior both to Reprobation and to Election, and therefore the decree of Permission was prior to the decree of Election and Reprobation—prior, in order and nature. Then, also, that other peculiarity of reprobation remains, and as it presupposes sin, I conclude that men, as sinners, are the object of reprobation.

You limit, moreover, the decree of reprobation to two acts. "The former is the purpose to pass by certain men, and to illustrate justice in them." But what justice, unless it is punitive? If it is punitive, then it coincides with the second act—"the ordination to punishment." Others distinguish that same decree into the negative act of preterition, and the affirmative act of ordination to punishment. If you meant the same thing, you have not expressed it well, for punitive justice superintends the ordination of punishment, but the freedom of the divine will superintends preterition. Your assertion that "this preterition has not its cause in men" will not be proved by any passage of Scripture, which every where teaches that all abandonment is on account of sin. Though this is so, yet it does not follow that "the mere good pleasure of God" is not the cause of abandonment. For God is free to leave or not to leave the sinner, who deserves abandonment; and thus, the will of God is the proximate and immediate cause of abandonment, and indeed the only cause in this respect, that when it is possible for Him not to forsake the sinner, He may yet sometimes do so. For God dispenses, absolutely according to His own will, in reference to the merit of sin, whether, in His Son, to take it away, or, out of His Son, to punish it. And how, I pray, does it "interfere with the liberty of the good pleasure"—I would prefer the word pleasure—"of God," if He is said not to be able to forsake one who is not a sinner? For it is only in view of His justice that He is able to forsake one unless he is a sinner. And liberty does not describe the objects with which God is concerned, in the operations of His will, but the mode in which He pleases to operate in reference to any object.

I could wish that you would not attribute any freedom to the will of God which may impinge upon His justice. For justice is prior to the will, and is its rule, and freedom is attributed to the will as its mode. That mode, then, is limited by justice. Yet it will not, therefore, be denied that God is completely free in the acts of His will. Since then He is completely free in the acts of His will, not because He wills all things, but because He wills freely whatever He wills, in what respect is it contrary to the freedom of God, if He is said not to will certain things? For He can not, in His justice, will them, and His freedom is not limited by a superior being out of Himself, but by His own justice. In this sense, also, the will of God is said to be "the cause of causes, and out of which, or beyond which no reason is to be sought," which is true also according to my explanation. For if any one asks, "why does God leave one, and choose another?" the answer is—"because He wills it."

If it be asked, -- "but why does He will it?" The cause is found not out of Himself. But there is a cause why He could justly will to leave any one, and that cause is sin, not effecting actual desertion, but deserving it, and making the sinner worthy of abandonment, and certainly to be abandoned, if God should choose to punish him according to his demerit, which choice is allowed to His free-will. Man is indeed as "clay in the hands of the potter," but it does not follow from this that God can justly make of that clay whatever it might be possible for Him to make by an act of His omnipotence. He can reduce to nothing the clay formed by Himself and made man, -- for this belongs to Him by supreme right: but He can not hate the same clay, or be angry with it, or condemn it forever, unless that lump has become sinful by its own fault, and been made a lump of corruption. Thus also Augustine explains the passage in Romans 9, as having reference to the lump of corruption. But you say, "if God had willed by His eternal decree to pass over men as sinners only, not as men, then He did not make them vessels of wrath, but He found them vessels of wrath, made such by themselves." I reply that ignorance of the phrase, which the apostle uses in Romans 9, is shown here. For "to make a vessel unto wrath," does not signify to sin or to make one worthy of wrath through sin; but it signifies to destine to just wrath him who has sinned and so made himself worthy of wrath, which is an act of the divine judgment, peremptory indeed, because it is an act of reprobation, but it has reference to man as a sinner, for sin alone is the meritorious cause of wrath. If you urge further that in the word "lump," men, not as made but as to be made, are signified, and that this is proved by the force of the word, shall deny that the force and radical meaning of the word is to be, here, precisely insisted upon, and shall assert that, in Scriptural use, the word is applied to men, not only as made but as sinners, and as those received into the grace of reconciliation, and transgressing of the covenant of grace; as in the prophet Jeremiah, "Behold as the clay is in the potter's hand, so are ye in mine hand, O house of Israel" (chapter xviii, 6.)

In your third argument you turn aside from the controversy, and from the real state of the case, contrary to the law of correct disputation, and, therefore, you do not come to the conclusion which is sought, unless you may say that to reject grace is the same as to sin, which two things are indeed often distinguished in the Scriptures. For the Pharisees were already, in Adam, and, indeed, in themselves, sinners before they "rejected the counsel of God against themselves, being not baptized" of John (Luke vii. 30). The Jews, of whom mention is made in Acts xiii. 46, were already sinners, in Adam and in themselves, before they made themselves unworthy of the grace of God, rejecting the word of life. But the question here is whether God passes by sinners, not whether he sees that they will reject grace.

Again, it does not follow that "reprobation, therefore, depends on men," if God reprobates no one unless reprobation and rejection is desired. For an effect can not be said to depend on that cause which, being in operation, does not certainly produce the effect. All men as sinners, but some of them, namely, the Elect, are not left; hence sin is not the cause of rejection, unless by the intervention of the damnatory sentence of the judge, in which it is decreed that sin shall be punished according to its demerit. Who does not know that the sentence depends on the judge, not on the criminal, even if the criminal has deserved that sentence by his own act, without which the judge could neither conceive, nor pronounce, nor execute the sentence. Nor does it follow "that God chooses some, and so they are chosen by Him, and that He rejects others, and, therefore, they are rejected." For sin, as to demerit, is common to the elect and the reprobate, according to the theory, which simply requires that men as sinners should be made the object of predestination, without any special distinction in the sin itself.

But you present, as a proof, that the foreseen neglect of grace is not the cause of rejection, the statement that "infants," dying out of the covenant of the gospel, have not neglected this grace, and yet are reprobate and "rejected by God." I affirm that they rejected the grace of the gospel in their parents, grand-parents, great-grand-parents, &c., by which act they deserved to be abandoned by God. I should desire that some solid reason might be presented to me why, since all his posterity have sinned, in Adam, against the law, and, on that account, have merited punishment and rejection, infants also, to whom, in their parents, the grace of the gospel is offered, and by whom, in their parents, it is rejected, have not sinned against the grace of the gospel. For the rule of the divine covenant is perpetual, that children are comprehended and judged in their parents. The fourth argument, which you draw from Romans 9, does not relate to the present subject. For the apostle there treats of the decree, by which God determined to justify and to save those, who should be heirs of righteousness and salvation, not by works, but by faith in Christ; not of the decree by which He determined to save these or those, and to condemn others, or of that by which He determined to give faith to some, and to withhold it from others. This might be most easily demonstrated from the passage itself, and from the whole context, and I should do it, if time would permit. But this being granted, yet not acknowledged, namely, that the apostle excludes works as the basis of the decree, of which he here treats, yet that, which you intend to prove, will not follow. For Augustine interprets it of works, which were peculiar to each of them (Esau and Jacob), not common to both, such as original sin, in which they were both conceived, when God spoke to Rebecca (12th verse). This interpretation of Augustine is proved to be true from the fact that the apostle regards Jacob, as having done no good, and Esau, no evil, when it was said to their mother Rebecca, "the elder shall serve the younger," as if it might be thought that Esau, by evil deeds, had merited that he should be the servant of his younger brother, who, by his good deeds, had acquired for himself that prerogative. Therefore, it does not exclude all respect of sin—sins, to which they were both equally subject. That "will" of God, in which "Paul acquiesces," is not that, by which He has purposed to adjudge any one, not a sinner, to eternal death, but by which, of those who are equally sinners, to one He shows mercy, but another He hardens; which words indeed mark the pre-existence of sin. For mercy can be shown to no one, who is not miserable; and no one is miserable, who is not a sinner. Hardening also has sin as its cause, that is, contumacious perseverance in sin.

But from your last argument, you deduce nothing against those, who make sin a requisite condition in the object of Predestination; for they acknowledge that "it is of the mere will of God that this one is elected, and that one rejected." The passage also which you cite from the author of the book "De vocatione gentium," also places sin as a condition, prerequisite to Predestination. For he is not "delivered" who has not been, first, made miserable and the captive of sin.

The second act of reprobation, you make to be "ordination to punishment," which you distinguish into "absolute and relative." There might be also a place for the same distinction, in the contrary act of election. For absolute election is a reception into favour; relative election is that, by which one person, and not another, is received into favour. You do rightly in making the will of God the cause of absolute ordination, yet not to the exclusion of sin. For it is very true that, in the Deity, there is the same cause of willing and doing that which He has decreed. Sin also has the same relation to ordination as to damnation. It has the relation of meritorious cause to damnation, hence it has also the relation of meritorious cause to, ordination. There is likewise no probable relation, to which a contrary can not be conceived. Therefore, it can not be absolutely denied that "sin is the cause of the decree of damnation." For though it may not be the immediate, proximate or principal cause, yet it is the meritorious cause, without which God can not justly ordain any one to punishment. But I should desire the proof that "sin does not precede, in the relation of order, in the divine prescience, that former act" of preterition and rejection. There is, indeed, in my judgment, no passage of Scripture, which contains that idea; I wish that one may be adduced. "Relative ordination is that by which this person, and not that, is ordained to punishment, and on the same condition." God has indeed the power of punishing and of remitting sin, according to His will, nor is He responsible to any one, unless so far as He has bound Himself by His own promises. In this, also, "the liberty of the divine goodness is exhibited," but not in this only. For the same thing is declared in creation itself, and in the dispensation of natural blessings, in this, that He determined that one part of Nothing should be heaven, another the earth, a third the air, &c. Indeed He has in creation demonstrated "the same liberty in the bestowment of supernatural blessings." For He has honoured some of His creatures with supernatural gifts, as angels and men, and others, indeed all others, He has made without super-natural gifts. He has likewise demonstrated the same freedom, not only in the creation, but in the government and care of His rational creatures, since He has made a communication of supernatural felicity, according to the fixed law and pleasure of His own will. From which angels and men could understand that God was free to communicate it to them according to His own will. This is declared by the arbitrary prescription of its condition. I make this remark that no one may think, that the act, which we now discuss, was the first act by which God evinced the freedom of His will.

Your words—"and indeed if God should destroy and damn all those who are rejected by Him, yet He would not be unjust," I can not approve, and you will not, if you compare your previous statements with them. For you said that ordination to punishment is subsequent to sin in the order of nature, and, here, you do not place sin between rejection, which is the first act of reprobation, and damnation, which is the second; while damnation does not follow rejection immediately, but it follows sin. Those words; so to speak, also contain a manifest falsity. First, because "the judge of all the earth can not do right, if He should slay the righteous with the wicked" (Gen. xviii. 25); and sin is the single and only meritorious cause of damnation. "Whosoever hath sinned against me, him will I blot out of my book" (Exod. xxxii. 33). "The soul that sinneth it shall die" (Ezek. xviii. 4). Secondly, because that rejection is the cause into which sin can be resolved, and, therefore, the cause of sin, by the mode of removal, or non-bestowment of that aid, without which sin can not be avoided. No small error is committed here, in the fact that, when you do not suppose sin to be previous to rejection and divine preterition, you yet make ordination to punishment subsequent to rejection, without any explanation of the coherence of both those acts. If you attempt this, you will fall into no less a fault; for you will make God, on account of that rejection, the author of sin, as can be shown by irrefutable arguments. The illustrations, which you propose, are not adapted to your design, and fail through want of analogy. For it is one thing to kill a beast, by which deed it ceases to exist and is not rendered miserable, or to exclude from your house one whom you do not please to admit, and a very different thing to condemn a man to eternal punishment, which is far more severe than to annihilate the same person. "The cause of this relative reprobation is the mere will of God without any consideration of sin," namely, that which may have any effect in making a distinction between different persons, but not in giving the power to ordain certain persons to punishment, which power indeed exists in God as Lord and Judge, but can not really be exercised except towards a sinner who deserves punishment from the equity of divine justice. That which you quote from Augustine and Gregory agrees with this distinction. For both make sin the meritorious cause of reprobation, and consider sin and sinners as altogether prerequisite to predestination; but attribute the act of separation to the mere will of God.

In this "second act of reprobation," you make two "steps, just rejection, and, damnation on account of sin." It is apparent, from this, that you distinguish between that rejection which you made the first step of reprobation, and this latter rejection. Yet you do not state the distinction between those two rejections, which, however, ought to have been done, to avoid confusion. Yet it may be right to conjecture, since you make the former prior to sin, that you would make the latter consequent upon sin, and existing on account of the desert of sin. You make the divine rejection two-fold, but do not explain whether you mean, here, the latter, which you consider the first step in the second act of reprobation, or divine rejection in general. It is not the former, in my judgment, for that, as it pertains to the second act of reprobation, is on account of sin; and this is considered by you to be prior to sin. Perhaps it is the same with the rejection, which is the first act of reprobation. If so, you can not in the passages now referred to, escape the charge of confused discussion.

Let us see how you explain that two-fold rejection. You say that the former is "the denial of aid, confirmation, and assisting grace, by which the first is rendered efficacious for the resistance of temptations, and for perseverance in goodness," and you style it "rejection of trial or test" and affirm that it occurs in the case of those "who have not yet forsaken God," illustrating it from the example of the first man, Adam. But I inquire of you, whether you consider that aid, confirmation, and assisting grace so necessary for perseverance in goodness, that, without it, a man could not resist temptation? If you reply affirmatively, consider how you can excuse, from the responsibility of sin, the Deity, who has denied to man, apart from any fault in him, the gifts and aids necessary to perseverance in goodness. If negatively, then indeed, tell me by what right you call this a rejection by God. Can he be said to be rejected by God, who is adorned and endued with grace, rendering him acceptable, provided with all gifts and aids necessary to perseverance in goodness, and even fortified by the help of the Holy Spirit to resist temptation? If you speak in accordance with Scriptural usage you can not call it rejection. You will say that it is not called, in an absolute sense, rejection, but in a certain respect, -- that is, so far that God affords to him, on whom He has bestowed all those things—not efficacious aid, not actual confirmation in goodness, not that assisting grace, without which the former graces are inefficacious. This is apparent, you say, from the event, since, if he had obtained also those helps, he would have been steadfast in goodness, he would not have fallen. This you express in quoting from Augustine: -- "God rejected man, not as to ability, but as to will." If he had possessed the latter, he would have maintained his integrity.

Here we enter on a discussion of the utmost difficulty, and scarcely explicable, at least by myself, as yet but a tyro, and not sufficiently acquainted with those heights of Sacred Theology. Yet I will venture to present some thoughts, trusting to the grace of Him, who gives wisdom to babes, and sight to the blind. You will assist me in part, that, by our mutual conference, the light may shine with greater brightness. For I have undertaken to write not against you, but to you, for the sake both of learning and of teaching.

I see here two things which will need explanation from me.

First, in reference to sufficient and efficacious grace. Secondly, in reference to the administration and dispensation of both, and the causes of that dispensation.

EXAMINATION OF THE ANSWER OF PERKINS TO CERTAIN ALLEGATIONS

AGAINST THE ADVOCATES OF
UNCONDITIONAL PREDESTINATION

We have, thus far, examined your doctrine of Predestination. If now it may seem proper to you to correct it according to our observations, it will, without doubt, be free from the liability to be called "Manichean," "Stoic," "Epicurean," or even "Pelagian"; though, as set forth by you, it is free from the imputation of the last error. It can not be with equal ease acquitted of the former, to him, who shall accurately compare not only your opinion, but the logical consectaries of your opinion, with the dogmas of the Manichees, and the Stoics. Some would deduce Epicureism also from the same opinion, but only by means of a series of conclusions. I wish that you had with sufficient perspicuity vindicated your doctrine from those objections. You, indeed, attempt to do this in answering the various allegations, usually made against the doctrine, set forth by you. We will consider these, with your answers in order.

ALLEGATION 1

"IT IS TAUGHT BY US THAT CERTAIN MEN, AND FEW IN NUMBER, ARE ELECTED."

It is true that your theory, manifestly includes the very doctrine which is stated in that allegation. Therefore, in that accusation, no sentiment contrary to your opinion and doctrine is attributed to you. It is also true, that the allegation contains no offense. For the Scripture in plain terms declares that "Many are called, but few are chosen" (Matt. xxii. 14).

"Fear not, little flock" (Luke xii. 32). In your reply, you show most clearly that nothing false is charged upon your theory, in that allegation. I do not, indeed, think that there is any one who can object, on this account, to that theory. For even all heretics, with whom we have become acquainted, think that the elect are few; many of them, and, I would dare to say, all of them, believe that "the few are known to God, and so definitely, that the number can be neither increased nor diminished, and they, who are numbered, can not be varied." But they offer another explanation of the term election, contrary to, or at least different from your idea. You ought, then, to have presented this allegation, not in such terms, that it could be made against you only by a foolish opponent—but as it would be stated by those who are opposed to your view. For they do not object to your theory, because you say that "certain persons, and few in number, are elected by God," but because you consider that "God, by a naked and absolute decree, without any reference to sin or unbelief, elected certain men, and that they were few; and that, by the same decree, He rejected the residue of the multitude of men, to whom He did not give Christ, and to whom He did not design that the death of Christ should be of advantage." But something shall be said of the allegation in that form, under the other allegations referred to by you.

ALLEGATION 2

"WE TEACH THAT GOD ORDAINED MEN TO HELL-FIRE, AND THAT HE CREATED THEM, THAT HE MIGHT DESTROY THEM."

In that allegation, the word "men" should have been limited and restricted to certain men, namely, to those about to perish. For no one will impute to you such an opinion in reference to all men, since all know that you except and exclude the elect from that number. You ought then, to have set forth that allegation thus; -- "We teach that God ordained some men, as men, without any consideration of sin, to hell-fire, and created them, that He might destroy them." This is, indeed, a serious allegation, and contains a great slander, if it is falsely charged upon you. If it is a true charge, you ought, by all means, to endeavour to free and relieve yourself of it, by a change of sentiment. I admit that you, and they, who agree with you in opinion, are not accustomed to speak in this way. But it is to be considered whether or not you assert what is equivalent to this, and if that shall be proved, you are held convicted of the charge. I will now, for the time, take the place of those who accuse you, yet being by no means myself an accuser; and do you see to it, whether I plead their cause well, and convict you of that charge.

He, who makes hell-fire the punishment of sin, who ordains that the first man, and in him all men, shall sin, who so, by his providence, governs that first man that he shall of necessity, sin, and shall not be able, in fact, to avoid sin, in consequence of which he, and all in him, commit sin, who, finally, certainly and irrevocably decrees in Himself to leave in Adam (i.e. in depravity) most of these, who shall sin in Adam, and to punish sin in them by hell-fire, is said, most deservedly, to have ordained to hell-fire, by an absolute decree, some, and indeed most men, as men, apart from any consideration of sin, or any demerit on their part. There is a connection between their sin and hell-fire, from the position of that law which is sanctioned by penalty, and by the decree of God in reference to withholding the pardon of their sin. Sin is also, of necessity, connected with the decree of God, and, in truth, it depends on it, so that man could not but sin, otherwise there would be no place for the decree. From which it follows, that God has absolutely ordained very many to hell-fires since He ordained men to the commission of sins and absolutely decreed to punish sin in many.

But I will prove, that you and those who agree with you, hold each of these opinions. First, you say, and truly, that hell-fire is the punishment ordained for sin and the transgression of the law. Secondly, you say that God ordained the first man, and in him, all men should sin; you not only say this, but you also adduce the reason of that decree and divine ordination, that God, in that way, might declare His righteousness and mercy, in which His glory chiefly consists, for which there could be no place except through sin and by occasion at it. Thirdly, you add that God, by His providence, so arranged the primeval state of man that, though, as far as his own liberty was concerned, he might be able to stand and not fall, yet he should, in fact, fall and commit sin. These two things are mutually connected; for that God might attain the object of His own act of ordination, it was necessary that He should so arrange the whole matter that the object should be attained. But you do not make prescience of sin the foundation of that administration; wherefore it is necessary that you should consider, as presiding over it., the omnipotence of God, to resist which, the man would have neither the power nor the will. This being so considered, you make a necessity of committing sin. To all these things you add, moreover, the irrevocable decree of God, by which he determined to punish, without mercy and of mere justice, sin committed according to that decree. From this, I think that it is most clearly evident, that when that allegation is made against you, nothing is charged upon you which is foreign to your sentiment.

I now consider the other part of the allegation, in which it is asserted that, according to your doctrine, "God created men that He might destroy them." The truth of this allegation is evident from this, that you say that God created men for this purpose, that He might declare, in these, His mercy, and in those, His justice, and indeed His punitive justice—which is the opposite of mercy—and apart from foresight. From which it follows, as punitive justice destroys men, that God created some men that He might destroy them. For punitive justice and the destruction of man are connected, and the former can not be declared except by the latter. It is evident then that nothing, foreign to your theory is charged against you in the whole of that allegation.

Indeed I think that you wished to show favour to your own sentiment, when you made the charge less than it deserved. For it is much worse that God should have ordained men to sin, and should have created them that they might sin, than to have ordained them to hell-fire, and to have created them that He might destroy them. For if sin is a worse evil than damnation, as it is, evidently, since the former is opposed to divine good, and the latter to human good, then truly is it greater to ordain one to sin than to ordain to hell, to create a man that he might sin, than that he might perish. If, however, accuracy of statement is to be sought, it should be affirmed that, if a man is ordained to commit sin, then he can not sin. For sin is a voluntary act, and the decree of God in reference to sin introduces a necessity of sinning. Further, if a man is created that he may be condemned, then he can not be condemned by God. For condemnation is the act of a just judge. But a just judge does not condemn one unless he is wicked by his own fault, apart from necessity; and he is not wicked, apart from necessity, and of his own fault, who is created that he may sin, and thus perish.

Let us now examine your answer to this second allegation. You think that you blunt and confute it by a distinction in the second act of reprobation, but it is not so. For you freely admit that God, by His absolute purpose, deserted the creature, from which desertion, sin, according to your opinion, necessarily exists; otherwise you can not connect punitive justice with desertion, except in view of a condition; namely, the contingency that man should sin after that desertion. Therefore you admit what is imputed, in that allegation, to your theory, you do not confute the charge. You also blend, in a confused way, the permission of the fall, and the permission, by which God allows one to finally fail of blessedness. For these are not the same, or from the same cause. For all have fallen by the divine permission, but many do not finally perish in their fallen condition; and permission of the fall depends on the divine providence, which is general over the whole human race; and the final permission to remain in that fallen condition depends on reprobation, and only relates to some persons. Your assertion, also, that "sin is subsequent to the desertion and permission of God," is to be understood as referring to that permission, by which He permits man to fall into sin, which pertains to providence, not to that permission by which He suffers some to finally fail of blessedness, which pertains to reprobation. For sin is the cause of this latter permission, that is, the meritorious cause, as has now been frequently stated.

We, now, examine the testimonies which you present. In the remark of Lombardus, the phrase "future demerits" is to be understood to refer to what one has different from another. But common demerits, though they may not be the moving cause, yet they are the meritorious cause, and a condition requisite in the object of reprobation. So also the assertion of Jerome is to be referred to the doing good or evil, by which the brothers were distinguished from each other, and not to sin, in which they were both conceived. This is apparent from what he says: -- "and their election and rejection displayed not the desert of each, but the will of him who elected and rejected. In the remark of Anselm that which I claim is clearly apparent. For he says, that "God does justly, if

He rejects sinners." The word "miserable," used in another remark of the same father, indicates the same thing. With these agree the remarks of Thomas Aquinas and Augustine. For the question is not whether the will of God is the cause of election and reprobation, but whether it has sin as an antecedent, as the meritorious cause of reprobation, and a requisite condition in the object both of election and of reprobation, which is most true, according to the views always held by Augustine. The word "conversion," used by Thomas Aquinas, and the word "drawing," used by Augustine, make sin the antecedent to the act of the will which "converts" and "draws." We would examine the testimonies of other School-men, if their authority was of much weight with us. But I make this remark, that there is no one of those testimonies, which excludes the sin of Adam—and that of men in common with him—from the decree of Predestination, and some of them, indeed, clearly the same in that decree. For when the words "grace" and "mercy" are used, there is a tacit reference to sin.

That "the latter act"—that of destruction—takes place "in reference to sin," is certain, but it is in reference to sin, not by any previous decree ordained to take place, but ordained to be punished in some by justice, and to be remitted in others by grace, when it has been committed. This explanation, however, does not show that "the allegation is a slander," unless you, at the same time, show that sin did not necessarily exist from that decree of reprobation or from some other.

Your second answer consists only in words. For an act, if it is unjust, is not excused by its end or object. It is unjust to destroy a man apart from sin, and it remains unjust, even if any one may say that it is done "for the declaration of judgment," or "for declaring judgment"; and that, which is added, seems absurd—that "this is done for declaring judgment in just destruction," as it can not be just unless it is inflicted on account of sin. The statement, that "God pleases to punish, with due destruction, a man, not as he is a man, but as he is a sinner," has the force of a sound answer, on the condition that the man has sinned freely, not of necessity. For the necessity and inevitability of sinning excuses from sin, and frees from punishment, him who commits that act. I say act, and not sin, because an act, which one necessarily and inevitably commits, can not be called sin. The apparent distinction, by which a man is said to sin freely in respect to himself, but necessarily in relation to the divine decree, has no effect in warding off this blow; since it can not be that one should do freely that, which he does necessarily, or that one act can be performed necessarily, that is, can not but be performed, and yet contingently, that is, can possibly not be performed. For this is at variance with the first principles of universal truth, in reference to whatever it is proper to make an affirmation or negation. I know that some defend this distinction by referring to the example of

God Himself, of whom they assert that He is both freely and necessarily good. But this assertion is incorrect. So false, indeed, is it that God is freely good, that it is not much removed from blasphemy. God is, what He is, necessarily, and if He is freely good, He can be not good, and who has ever said that those things which are in Him, of nature and essence, are in Him freely? The assertion of Cameracensis is indeed partly blasphemous, partly true. It is blasphemous to say that "God can, without loss or detriment to His justice, punish and afflict eternally His own innocent creature." It is true that "God can annihilate one of His creatures apart from sin." But punishment and annihilation are very different. The latter is to deprive of that, which had been graciously bestowed, the former is to render one miserable, and indeed infinitely miserable, and apart from any demerit on account of sin. Misery is far worse than annihilation, as Christ says—"It had been good for that man if he had not been born" (Matt. xxvi. 24). That it is contrary to the divine justice to punish one, who is not a sinner, appears from very many declarations of Scripture. "That be far from thee to do after this manner, to slay the righteous with the wicked" (Gen. xviii. 25). "Whosoever hath sinned against me, him will I blot out of my book" (Exod. xxxii. 33) "Seeing it is a righteous thing with God to recompense tribulation to them that trouble you, and to you, who are troubled, rest with us" (2 Thess. i. 6, 7). "For God is not unrighteous to forget your work and labor of love," etc., (Heb. vi. 10).

The saying of Wisdom (chapter 12), quoted by Cameracensis, likewise teaches the contrary of what he attempts to prove from it. For it treats of the perdition of unrighteous nations, and, in plain words, declares in the 15th verse—

"For so much, then, as thou art righteous thyself, thou orderest all things righteously, thinking it not agreeable with thy power to condemn him that hath not deserved to be punished." I grant, indeed, that the error of Cameracensis was caused by the fault of the old version. But you can not be excused on the account of this. For you ought to omit the testimony of an author who is led into an error by the fault of a version, since you are acquainted with it from the Greek text itself, and from translations better than that ancient one. It is true that "God is not bound by created laws," for He is a law unto Himself, He is justice itself. That law, also, according to which no one is permitted to inflict punishment upon the undeserving was not created, or made by men, and it has place not among men only. It is an eternal law, and immovable in the divine justice to which God is bound in the immutability of His nature, and righteousness. It is not universally true, that "whatever is right, is right because God so wills it," as there are many things which God wills, because they are right. It is right that God alone should be acknowledged by the creature to be the true God. We affirm that God wills this because it is right, not that it is right because God wills it. The act of simple obedience is right, not because God wills that it should be performed by the creature, but because it is such in itself, and God can not but require it of the creature, though it may belong to free-will to prescribe in what matter He wills that obedience should be rendered to Him. As far as we are concerned, also, it is truly our duty in reference to laws, divinely enacted for us, not so much to see whether that which they command is just in itself, but simply to obey them, because God prescribes and commands it. Yet this duty is founded on the fact that God can not prescribe that which is unjust, because that He is essential justice, and wisdom, and omnipotence.

I had designed to omit a more extended examination of the remarks, quoted by you, from the Scholastic Theologians; but I will say a few words. "The four signs of Francis Maro, necessary for understanding the process of predestination and reprobation" of which he speaks, are of no value, are notoriously false, and are confused in their arrangement. In the sentence from D. Baunes, the "permission by which all nature was permitted to fall in Adam" is absurdly ascribed to reprobation, as that permission, and the fall which followed it, extended to the whole human race, without distinction of the elect and the reprobate. Those "four things," which, Ferrariensis says, "are found in the reprobate," are not in him, as reprobate, and in respect to the decree of reprobation, but the latter two, only; for "the permission of the fall and sin," to use his own words, are found in the elect, and pertain to the more general decree of providence, by which God left man to the freedom of his own will, as has been before and frequently said. Therefore, arguments, other than these, should have been presented by you, for the refutation of that charge. I very much wish that you would cite Scripture for the confirmation of your sentiments and the overthrow of those allegations. The writings of the School-men, ought not to have weight and authority, especially among us; for our Doctors of Theology with one voice affirm of them, "that they have changed true Theology into Philosophy, and the art of wrangling, and that they endeavour to establish their opinions, by the authority, not so much of the Sacred Scriptures, as of Aristotle."

ALLEGATION 3

"THE PREDESTINATION OF THE STOICS, AND THE FATALISM OF THE STOICS, HAS BEEN INTRODUCED BY US: BECAUSE—THEY SAY WE ASSERT THAT ALL THINGS ARE DONE OF THE NECESSARY AND EFFICIENT DECREE OF GOD; ALSO, THAT THE FALL OF ADAM WAS ACCORDING TO OUR OPINION—AS THEY ALLEGE—DECREED AND WILLED BY GOD."

This is, indeed, a heavy charge, and yet it is set forth in a milder form by you, than by those who make it. You ought to add those things which pertain essentially to this allegation, and are charged by them upon you and your doctrine. Such are these—"It would follow from this, 'that God is the Author of sin; that God really sins; that God alone sins; and that sin is not sin,'" which Bellarmine charges against the sentiment of certain of our doctors—the sentiment also, which you seem to defend. But the reason that they present all those things, as opposed to your doctrine, is this: -- You say that all things happen by the efficacious will of God, which can not be resisted, and that events do not occur, because God, by an absolute decree, has determined that they should not occur. From this, it follows, also, that sinful acts are performed by the will of God, which can not be resisted, and that righteous acts are omitted, because God has simply and absolutely decreed that they shall not be performed; and therefore, that God is the Author of sin, and the preventer of righteousness and of good acts. From which it is inferred that God, truly and properly speaking, sins; and, since the necessity, from which men perform such acts, acquits them from sin, it follows that God alone sins, just as He alone is responsible, who strikes a blow by the hand of another person, of which he has laid hold. But since God can not sin, it follows that sin is not sin. Hence, it seems to me that no injustice is done to your doctrine by that allegation.

But let us see how you dispose of it. Neglecting the general charge, you begin your discussion with that part which refers to the fall of Adam. You admit that this occurred "not only according to the prescience of God, but also by His will and decree; yet," as you explain it—"by His will, not approving or effecting it, yet not prohibiting, but permitting it." This distinction, properly used, indeed, solves the difficulty. If it is your opinion and the opinion of others, that God did not approve, and did not effect the fall; did not incite, and did not impel Adam to fall; did not lay upon him any necessity of sinning, either by acting or not acting, but only willed not to prevent, but to permit the fall of Adam; then, I acknowledge that all those things are unjustly alleged against your sentiment. You, indeed, make this statement verbally, while in fact you so explain permission or non-prevention, that it amounts to the "efficient decree of God." This I will prove. You say, "What God does not prevent, occurs, because God does not prevent it, the reason of the non-existence of a fact, or event, is that God does not will that it should exist." I conclude, therefore, that the divine permission or non-prevention, and the event are mutually, and indeed immediately connected, as cause and effect. Thus, also, non-prevention has the relation of energetic performance. Therefore, likewise, the volition of God, and the non-existence or event of a thing are mutually connected as cause and effect, and hence, a volition that a thing shall not be done, has the relation of energetic prevention. This I show, more extendedly, in this manner.

Sin is two-fold, of Commission and Omission—of Commission, when that is performed which has been forbidden—of Omission, when that is not performed which has been commanded. There is, in your opinion, a concurrence in that act which can not be committed by a man without sin, and indeed such a concurrence that God is the first cause of the act, and man is the second, the former moving man, the latter moved by God, and, indeed, moving, in such sense, that man, of necessity, follows that motion, and consequently of necessity performs that act which involves transgression. Not to prevent sin of omission is, in your opinion, not to give that grace without which sin can not be omitted, and the contrary good can not be performed. But he, who, in that manner, concurs, and denies such grace, is absolutely the chief and efficient cause of sin, and indeed, the only cause, as the joint cause of the act—man, since he can not resist the motion of the first cause, can not sin in following that irresistible motion. But, if you can so explain your sentiment and that of others, that it shall not, in reality, differ from it, then I shall not object to it.

You will not escape by the distinction that "it is one thing to will a thing per se, and another to will it as to the event," unless, by the "event" of a thing, you understand that which results from the prolongation and the existence of the thing itself, which is not your sentiment. For you say that "God wills the event of sin," that is, "that sin should happen, but does not will sin itself;" which distinction is absurd. For the essence of sin consists in the event, for sin consists in action. God, also, wills sin itself, in the mode in which He wills that sin should happen, and He wills that sin should happen in the mode in which He wills sin itself. He does not love sin per se. He wills that sin should happen for His own glory; He wills also sin for His own glory. I speak this in the sense used by yourself. Show, if you can, the difference, and I will acquiesce.

Your assertion, that "God wills not to prevent sin," is ambiguous, unless it is explained. What! Has not God hindered sin, as far as was suitable, and according to the mode in which it is right for Him to treat a rational creature, namely, by legislation, threatening, promise, the bestowment of sufficient grace, and even the promise of His assistance, if man would consent to have recourse to it? This he could do, or we go infinitely astray. But He did not hinder sin by any omnipotent or physical action, because that would not have been inappropriate; He would have thus prevented man from using that primeval liberty in which He had placed him; and, by consequence, as we have elsewhere quoted from Tertullian, "He would have rescinded His own arrangement."

It is rightly said, that God properly, and primarily, and, we may add, immediately, willed His own permission. But it does not thence follow, that God also willed the event of sin. For it is a non-sequitur—"God voluntarily permits sin, therefore, He wills that sin should happen." The contrary is true, -- "God voluntarily permits sin; therefore, He neither wills that sin should happen, nor wills that it should not happen." For permission is an act of the will when inoperative which inoperativeness of the will may here be properly ascribed to the Deity, since He endowed man with free-will, that He might test his free and voluntary obedience. He could not have done this, if He had imposed an inseparable hindrance upon man. But the cause of the occurrence of that which God permits is not the permission, although it would not happen without that permission. He who performs the act is the proper and immediate cause, with the concurrence of the Deity, which is always prepared for him. But permission can not be resolved into a cause per se, if we are to treat this subject accurately and truthfully, but only into a cause sine qua non, or one which removes, or, rather, does not present a hindrance, and indeed such a hindrance as I have referred to, which cannot be resisted by the creature.

Your statement, "as no good thing can exist or be done, except by the agency of the Deity, so no evil can be avoided, unless God hinders it," is true, if rightly understood; that is, the agency of the Deity being that, by which He may suitably effect what is good by means of a rational and free creature, and the hindrance of God being that, by which He may suitably hinder a free creature from that which is evil. But the limit both of doing and hindering is such that it does not deprive man of freedom, but permits him, also, freely and of his own will, according to the mode of will, to do good and to abstain from evil. Otherwise good is not performed by man, and evil is not avoided by him, but an act, only, is performed or avoided, by a necessity either natural or supernatural. Those words, also, are susceptible of amendment, if any one should wish to discuss these things with greater accuracy. The statement might have been this:

"As no good is, or is done, except by the agency of God, so no evil is avoided, except by the hindrance of God." For by the agency of God, good not only can be but is done, and by His hindrance, evil not only can be, but is hindered. But if you wish to retain that word "can," you ought to have expressed your ideas in this way: "As nothing good can be, or can be done, unless God wills to do it, or to give to another the power and the will to do it, and to concur with him in doing it, so nothing evil can be avoided unless God wills to give, and actually does give strength sufficient for the avoidance of sin, and wills to call out that strength and to co-operate with it." In this sense, "not even the least thing is done without the will of God, namely, either willing that it should be done, or willing not to prevent, but to permit, that it should be done." It is not true that "providence is inactive" in permission, even explained in such a manner as to coincide neither with that will of God, by which He wills that something shall be done, nor with that by which He wills that something shall not be done. If it coincides with either of these, there is no permission, and the assertion of Augustine—"nothing is done except by the agency or permission of God," is without force.

I now examine some arguments, which you present in favour of your view. The first is deduced from several passages of Scripture. Let us see now what can be proved from these passages. The passage in Acts ii. 23, teaches, not that God willed that the Jews should slay Christ, but, that he was "delivered by the determinate counsel and foreknowledge of God" into the power of those who wished to slay him. Nothing more can be inferred from Acts iv. 28. For God predetermined to deliver His own Son into the hands of his enemies, that He might suffer from them that which God had laid upon him, and which the Jews, of their own wickedness and hatred against Christ, had determined to inflict upon him. God, indeed, "determined before" that death should be inflicted on Christ by them; but in what character did God consider them when He "determined before" that this should be done by them? In that character, surely, which they had at the time when they inflicted death upon Christ, that is, in the character of sworn enemies of Christ, of obstinate enemies and contemners of God and the truth; who could be led to repentance by no admonitions, prayers, threats or miracles; who wished to inflict every evil on Christ, if they could only obtain the power over him, which they had often sought in vain.

It is evident, then, that there was here no other action of God in this case than that He delivered His own Son into their hands, and permitted them to do their pleasure in reference to him, yet determining the limit to which He pleased that they should go, regulating and governing their wickedness, in such a manner, yet very gently, that they should inflict on him only that which God had willed that His own Son should suffer, and nothing more. This is clearly seen in the very manner of his punishment, in preventing the breaking of his legs, in the piercing of his side, in the inscription of the title, and the like. But there appears here no action of God by which they were impelled or moved to will and to do what they willed and did; but He used those who wished, of their own malice and envy, to put Christ to death, in a mode, which, He knew, would conduce to His own glory and the salvation of men.

But the reason that it cannot be said, with truth, that God and Christ, in the delivery of Christ to the Jews, sinned, does not consist, only or chiefly, in the fact that they were led to this delivery by various motives. What if Judas had done the same thing with the design that Christ, by his own death, should reconcile the world unto God, would his sin have been less heinous? By no means. It was not lawful for him to do evil that good might come. But the chief reason of the difference is that God had the right to deliver His Son, and Christ, also, had the right to deliver his own soul to death, and consequently, in doing this, they could not sin. But Judas had no power in this case, and he, therefore, sinned. There is a distinction in actions not only as to their end, but as to their principle and form. Saul was not acquitted of sin, because he preserved the herds of the Amalekites for sacrifice (1 Sam. xv. 9-22).

Again, what is implied by that inference? -- "therefore, we may also say that, when Adam ate of the forbidden fruit, he did that which the hand and counsel of God foreordained to be done?" This, indeed, never was the language of the apostles and of the church, and never could be, in matters having so much dissimilarity. For the relation of Adam and of those enemies of Christ is not the same. The former, previous to eating the fruit, was holy and righteous; the latter, before the death of Christ, were wicked, unrighteous, unfriendly, and hostile to Christ. The latter, in all their desires, sought for, and frequently and in many ways, attempted to put Christ to death. Adam was disinclined to eat of the forbidden fruit, even when he was enticed to it by his wife, who had already transgressed. The death of Christ was necessary for the expiation of sins, and was, per se, declarative of the glory of God; the fall of Adam was wholly unnecessary, and, per se, violated the majesty and glory of God. He needed not the sin of man for the illustration of His own glory. What, likewise, can be imagined more absurd than that circular reasoning? "The death of Christ was foreordained by God, that it might expiate the sin of Adam; the fall of Adam was foreordained, that it might be expiated by the death of Christ." Where is the beginning and where is the end of that ordination? Nevertheless God ordained the fall of Adam, not that it should occur, but that, occurring, it should serve for an illustration of His justice and mercy. The passage in 1 Peter iii. 17, is to be explained in a similar manner. "God wills that the pious should suffer evils," for their chastening and trial. He wills that they should suffer these evils from other men; but from men of what character? From those, who of their own wickedness and the instigation of Satan, already will to bring those evils upon them, which ill will God already foresaw, at the time when He predetermined that those evils should be inflicted upon the pious.

Therefore, they were moved, by no act of God, to will to inflict evils upon the pious; they were moved, also, by no act to inflict evils, unless by an act such as ought rather to move them from that volition, and to deter them from that infliction; such as would, in fact, have moved and deterred them, unless they had been deplorably wicked. The doctrine, life, and miracles of Christ and the Apostles, drew upon them the odium and hatred of the world. The fact that God is declared, in 2 Samuel xvi. 10, to have said unto Shimei, "Curse David," also, if rightly explained, presents no difficulty. Let Shimei, and David, and the act which may be called "the precept of cursing," be considered. Shimei was already a hater of David, of most slanderous tongue, and bitter mind, impious, and a contemner of God and the divine law, which had commanded "Thou shalt not curse the rule of thy people (Exod. xxii. 28)." David, by his own act against God and his neighbour, had rendered himself worthy of that disgrace, and altogether needed to be chastened and tried by it; he was, moreover, endued with the gift of patience to endure that contumely with equanimity. The act of God was the ejection and expulsion of David from the royal city and from the kingdom. In consequence of this occurred the flight of David, the fact that the rumor of that flight came to the ears of Shimei, and the arrangement that David and Shimei should meet together. Thus, by the act of God, David, fleeing and driven before his son, was presented to Shimei "a man of the family of the house of Saul," and an enemy of David, ready to curse him. Add, if you please, the hardening of the mind of Shimei, lest he should fear to curse David, on account of the attendants of David, that so he might, in some way, satisfy his own mind and his inveterate hatred against David. Therefore, that opportunity, by which David, in his flight, was presented to Shimei, and the hardening of the mind of Shimei, divinely produced, and also the direction of that cursing tongue, were acts pertaining to that precept of God, apart from which acts, nothing in that precept can be presented, which would not impinge on the justice of God, and make God the author of sin.

A comparison of all these things will show that Shimei, not so much as God, was the author of that malediction. Shimei was alone the author of the volition, yet it is rather to be attributed to God, as He effected that which He willed, not by moving Shimei to the malediction, but by procuring for Shimei the opportunity to curse David, and the confidence to use that opportunity. From this, it appears, most plainly, that God is without blame, and Shimei is involved in guilt.

The passages—Jer. xxxiv. 22, and1 Sam. iii. 37 -- will be explained similarly, and will present no difficulty. From an examination of these, it will appear that they have no reference to the fall of Adam, -- which was the beginning of sin; and all other evils have place, sin having now entered into the world, and men having become depraved by sin.

We proceed to your second argument, that "God voluntarily permits sin" is certain, and it is equally certain that "the will to permit is the will not to prevent." But pause here. The will to permit or not to prevent, is not the same with "the will not to bestow grace." For He permits that person to fall, to whom he has given grace sufficient and necessary to enable him to stand. Let us proceed. You say that "He, who does not will to prevent sin, which he foreknows will happen, by confirming grace when he can do it, in fact wills that the same should happen." But I deny that the volition of sin can be deduced from the nolition of preventing or hindering. For there are three things distinct from each other, no one of which includes another—"to will that sin should not be committed," that is, to will its prevention; "to will that it should occur or be committed," that is, to will its commission; and "to will to prevent or not to prevent it," that is, to will its permission or non-prevention. The former two are affirmative acts, the last one a negative act. But an affirmative act can not be deduced from a negative for there is more in an affirmative than in a negative act, and there can not be more in a conclusion than in the premises.

Further, I say that your argument, on this point, is fallacious. For God wills to permit sin in one respect, and to hinder it in another—to hinder it so far as would be appropriate, which hindrance is not followed of certainty, by the omission of sin, and to not to hinder it, in another mode, which hindrance would, indeed, be followed by the omission of sin, yet without any virtue or praiseworthiness in him who omits it, as he can not do otherwise than omit it on account of that hindrance. But I may be allowed to argue, in opposition to such a view, that He, who hates sin and by the enactment of law and the bestowment of sufficient grace wishes to hinder, wills, not that sin should happen, but that sin should not happen, which is an affirmative act of the will. You will say that this is a correct conclusion, the will being understood as that "of approval." I answer that God can not, by any mode of volition, will things which are contradictory. But "to happen" and "not to happen" are contradictory. Therefore, it can not be that God, by one mode of volition should will that an event should happen, and, by another mode of volition, should will that it should not happen. It may indeed be true that God, in His will "of good pleasure" as they style it, purposes to permit that which, in His will "of approval" or "that which is revealed", He wills should not be done. Thus your conclusion is faulty, and the remarks of Calvin and Beza, let it be said with due respect to so eminent men, are hardly consistent with the truth. But examine, I pray you, your subjoined statements, and you will see and acknowledge that you put them on paper, when you did not observe what you said. You say that "Whatever God does not hinder, He does not hinder it, either because He wills it to be done, or because He is altogether unwilling that it should be done, or because He does not will that it should be done." What is the difference between the latter two reasons? "To be unwilling that any thing should be done" is "not to will that any thing should be done;" the modifying word "altogether" is of no effect, since, in things opposed to each other, the negative can not receive any increase, as, for instance, in the phrase "not a man;" a wolf is as much "not a man" as is the earth, the air, the sky; but perhaps by the expression—"He is altogether unwilling that it should be done" you mean "He wills that it should not be done," or "because His will does not act." If the first be true, my view is correct. But the second can not be true, for it is absurd to say "God does not will to prevent any thing because He wills that it should not be done." You ought not, in that enumeration of reasons, to have introduced such a statement; for "not to will to prevent," and "to will that a thing should not be done" are opposites and from this it is certain that one can not be the cause of the other. In the investigation and distribution of causes, it is neither usual nor proper to introduce that which is the opposite of an effect. But let that pass.

You will say then, "that 'not to hinder' must be on account of one of those three causes." I grant it. "But it is not 'because His will does not act,' which is Epicureanism, nor 'because He does not will that it should be done,' therefore, it is, 'because He wills that it should be done.'" I deny the antecedent. For this is the reason that God does not hinder an event, because He neither wills that it should occur, nor wills that it should not occur, as will be more clearly evident, if you consider the matter in this light. That, which God wills to be done, He efficaciously brings to pass. That, which He wills not to be done, he efficaciously hinders. That, which he neither wills to be done, nor wills not to be done, He leaves to the creature. How is it possible that the human mind should conceive that God does not prevent, that is, permits any thing, because He wills that it should be done. Indeed the expression "He wills that it should be done" has too much comprehensiveness to admit that permission or non-hindrance should be deduced or concluded from it.

Your objection to this argument, namely, that, from it the conclusion is drawn that "such things are done, either through the ignorance or through the negligence of the Deity, is absurd; you can not defend it, even against yourself. For you have already made a distinction between "not to will" and "not to care that a thing should be done." Therefore, you can not deduce one from the other. How, also, can it be asserted that a thing is done without the knowledge of God, which is done by the permission of God, and by His will, the agent of that permission. But, it will hereafter appear, when we shall have explained, more largely, in reference to that permission, that what God permits, He does not permit without knowledge or care. It is, however, to be understood that permission is an affirmative volition, and not one that is merely negative. For God wills His own permission by an affirmative act. But in reference to the thing, which He permits, the act of His will is a negative act.

Far be it from any one to think that any decree of God is contrary to justice or equity. If God has decreed any thing, it is certain that He has justly decreed it. But it is to be considered whether, and how God has decreed it. It is not possible that any of His decrees should be at variance with His justice, as revealed to us in the Scriptures; it is, then, to be understood that it is not sufficient, in order to remove a charge from a decree which we ascribe to God, to add

"He has decreed it but justly;" for the addition of that phrase does not make the decree just, but it must be shown that the decree, which we attribute to God, really belongs to Him, and there will, then, be no question concerning its justice. Your third argument is weak. For, from the event of any thing, it can not be concluded that God willed that it should happen, but that He willed not to prevent it; and this volition, not to prevent, is also an act of the providence of God, which is present to all things and to each, and presides over them, either by effecting them, or by permitting them; yet administering and ordaining all things for just and legitimate ends, and in such a way as to "regard, not only the events of things, but also their commencements, and the principles of things and actions." It is known, indeed, that Satan and the wicked can not only not perfect any thing, but can not even begin it, except by the permission of the Deity. That which you add, "by His will," I do not concede, until you shall prove it by a greater weight of arguments than you have yet adduced. You say truly—"It is impious to affirm that any thing exists or is done, unless the holy and just God has decreed it from eternity, and indeed willed either to do or to permit it." For the decree of God is two-fold, efficacious and permissive. Neither can take the place of, or intrude upon the other. Let us consider also your fourth argument—"The decision of the ancient church." Augustine, manifestly makes a distinction between permission and efficiency. And although he says that "nothing is done unless God wills it to be done" he yet explains himself when he says "either by permitting it to be done, or by doing it Himself:" and thus, that which He permits is not an immediate object of the will, but permission is the immediate object, while that, which God permits, is the object of permission. So, also, the statements of Tertullian, Jerome and others, are to be explained, that they may not impinge on the Scriptures, which declares absolutely "Thou art not a God which hath pleasure in wickedness" (Psalm v. 4.) Hence, if I may be permitted to speak freely, I shall affirm that I should prefer that Augustine, Jerome, Catharinus and all others had abstained from phrases of this kind, which are not contained in the Scriptures, and which need lengthened explanation, that they may not be made the occasion of heresy and blasphemy.

That second distinction, according to which God is said "to will that evil may be, and yet not to will evil," has no force. For God hates evil, and hates the existence of evil; and since evil exists in action, its being done is its being, and its being is its nature. Through there may be a subtle distinction between the essence and the existence of evil, it can not be said that there is so much difference between them that God wills that sin should exist, but does not will sin itself; For since God hates the essence of evil, if I may so speak for the sake of form, He, therefore, forbids that evil should be done, and the reason that He is unwilling that sin should exist, is the fact that He hates sin itself. But He does not hate the existence of evil, or evil itself, so much that He may not permit evil to be done by a free agent, not because it is better that evil should be, than that they should not be, but because it is better first, that He should permit His rational and free creatures to act according to their own will and freedom, in which consists the trial of their obedience, than that, contrary to His own original arrangement, He should take away that freedom from the creature, or even prevent its exercise; secondly, that He should bring good out of evil, rather than not permit evil to be. But the idea that God wills that evil should exist not as such, but as the means of good, needs a more extended explanation, which by the will of God, we will hereafter present.

The first objection to which you refer is of great weight. For the will is said to be evil in view of an evil volition and that volition is said to be evil, which is directed to an object to which it ought not to be directed. But evil is an object to which it ought not to be directed. Therefore that volition is evil, by which any one wills evil, and by which he wills that evil should be done. For there is a verbal distinction, but a real agreement between those ideas. Hence, also, "it belongs to an evil will to will that evils should be done, whether that will delights in the evils, or wills to use them for a good purpose." It is not right that any one should will that evil should be done, that he may have an opportunity of using that evil to a good end. The rule, which you cite is correct, -- "Evil is not to be done," or even willed "that good may come." The first wickedness exists in the will or the volition of evil, the second in its perpetration.

Your answer does not remove the difficulty stated in this objection. Of what importance are those "two principles?" Even if their correctness is conceded, the objection is still valid. For, in reference to the first; -- As there is no evil in the nature of things, the will can not be directed to evil, per se, and it pertains to universal will, and not only to that, but to universal desire and appetite to tend to good, per se. The evil consists in this, not that the will is directed to evil, but that it is directed towards an undue good, or in reference to an undue mode and end. As to the second; -- It is true that "there is no evil which has no good joined with it." There is no supreme evil there is no evil except in that which is good. It does not, however, follow that it is good that sin should happen. For sin is so great an evil that it ought to be avoided, even if it have some good united with it: The act of fornication has this good, it is the sexual intercourse, natural to man and woman, yet it is to be avoided, because it can not be committed without sin. But the good to which you seem to refer, is not united to sin except incidentally, that is, by the intervention of the Divine will, directing that evil to a good end.

The remark of Augustine, if understood strictly, can not be admitted, but, with suitable explanation, it may be tolerated. It is not true that "it is good that evils should exist." For God effects every good. Then it would follow, according to the remark, that He effects the existence of evils. This is at variance with another statement of Augustine, in which he says—"God does some things, but permits other things to be done, as in the case of sin." How can it be said, without a contradiction in terms, of God—

"He causes that evils should exist, and permits evils to exist?" The reason, subjoined, does not prove this. For Almighty God does not, therefore, permit evil, because it is good that evil should exist, but because He knows that, in His own wisdom and omnipotence, He can educe good from the evil, contrary to its nature and proper efficacy, and this of His own pure act, either by way of just punishment or gracious remission. It is not good that evil should exist unless incidentally, namely, on account of the wisdom, omnipotence and will of God. But that, which is incidental, is not under consideration.

But let us, now, look at your answer. You say that "sin, considered universally in its causes and circumstances, assumes a two-fold respect or formality." In the first place, you say that "sin is considered not under the relation of sin, but as far as it has the relation of good in the mind of God, decreeing it." But I deny that sin has the relation of good in the mind of God decreeing it. For the acts of God, in reference to sin, altogether declare that sin is considered by God not in the relation of good, but in that of evil. For He permits sin, but effects good: He punishes sin, but He punishes that which is evil, and as it is evil. He remits sin and pardons it; but that which is pardoned is considered as an evil by him that pardons it. But God decrees the permission of sin because He knows that He can produce good results from sin, not in that sin is good, but in that it is evil. Nor is it rightly said—"sin has the relation of good in the mind of God, who decrees it, because God knows how to make sin an opportunity of good acts;" for He does not produce those acts except with the consideration of sin as sin. It is wonderful, also, that any consideration can be affixed to sin, which is contrary to its definition. The definition of sin is a transgression of the law, and, therefore, it is a violation of the Divine will. Hence it is, also, evident that it is incorrectly said that "sin has the relation of good, because it exists in that which is good, and because it tends to that which is good." For "good" is affirmed of a subject, in which sin exists as a deforming vice and as corrupting, not of sin existing in that subject. But how far God wills the subject, in which sin exists, that is, the act which can not be performed by a man without sin, we will perhaps discuss, more largely, hereafter, when we shall speak of permission in general. Sin likewise tends to good not per se, but incidentally only, because God ordains, not that it should be done, but that, having been done, it should result in good, and makes, from it, an occasion for good. God is not said—to will that sin should occur, so far as in His wonderful wisdom He knows how to elicit good from it, but He so far wills to permit and not to hinder it. For this is the reason that He permits and does not will to hinder, not that He wills that sin should occur.

You affirm, in the second place, that another relation of sin is "that, in which it is considered formally and properly, that is, as sin." Here, also, you adduce a two-fold consideration of sin, either as it is sin in respect to men, or as it is sin to God. But if you will listen to me, those are vain and frivolous distinctions, and invented, not to explain the matter, but to involve it more deeply. "In respect to men," you say, "God does not will, or approve, or effect sin, but wills as to its event, not absolutely, as in the case of those things which are good in themselves, but only by willing to permit that sin should be committed." Be it so, and this, if rightly understood, can be tolerated. I will not examine what you say in reference to a three-fold action of the divine will, since it has no bearing at all on the subject, at least against the sentiment which I defend.

What you say in the margin is true—"God wills that sin should happen, so far as it is possible that it should happen without the efficiency of God." I wish that you had discussed this subject more fully, and it would, indeed, have been evident that you have, thus far, not rightly, set forth the mode in which God wills that sin should happen. You so set it forth as not to acquit God of the efficiency of sin. You say that "sin, as such to God, is neither willed, nor approved, nor affected, nor indeed permitted by Him." I concede the first three, but deny the last, for the proper object of the divine permission is evil, as it is evil, and indeed considered by God as evil; though the reason of His permission of sin, is not the evil itself. A distinction is to be made between the object of permission and its cause. We have already demonstrated that He permits evil as evil. But you have not rightly stated the cause or reason why God permits evil, for He does not permit evil on account of a conjoined good, but because He can elicit good from evil, which good can not, on that account, be said to be conjoined to sin, because it is elicited from sin only by the action of God. But if you understand the phrase "conjoined good" to imply—not in the nature of sin itself, but in the act of God, I do not oppose you. The words of Beza, which you quote, will not bear a rigorous examination. The former is either false, or equivocal; false, if understood of the permission, of which we now treat, which is opposed not to legal prohibition, but to efficacious prevention. It is true that God by law prohibits sin as sin, and yet permits, that is, does not hinder the same sin as sin. But if it refers to the permission, which is the opposite of the prohibition, made by law, the discussion is equivocal, for we are not treating of that permission. For who does not know that God can not, at the same time, strictly require and not strictly require the same thing by law. Permission has likewise been previously defined or described by yourself as "the denial of confirming grace" not indeed as "the non-imposition of a law." The second statement of Beza is simply false. For punishments of sins are not permitted by the Deity, but are inflicted by a just judge, and have God himself for their author. "Shall there be evil in a city, and the Lord hath not done it?" (Amos iii. 6). Also, of what sin, I pray, was the first sin the punishment? Yet it was permitted. Therefore, it was not a punishment.

The remarks of Calvin, must be understood according to the interpretation already presented by us, otherwise they can not be defended. But, as it was his aim to overthrow the doctrine of the School-men on this subject, it ought not to be said by one, who has undertaken to defend his views, that "the School-men speak correctly when they do not disjoin the will from permission." This you say; they, however, state that there is this distinction between the two, -- that permission is the immediate object of the will, but sin is the object of permission. All the School-men openly acknowledge that what God permits, He voluntarily permits. Nor is the blasphemy of the Manichees to be charged upon Calvin, because though he sometimes uses unsuitable phraseology, he elsewhere clearly defends himself and his doctrine from that accusation.

The second objection, noticed by you, is this, -- "God wills contraries, if He wills that to happen, which He, in His law, prohibits." This is, indeed, a valid objection, and your answer does not remove it. For "to will anything to happen," and "to will the same thing not to happen," do not differ "in respects" only, but "absolutely and in their whole essence." Nor is there any respect or mode, according to which God can be said to will that anything should happen, and at the same time to will that it should not happen. For the divine will can not be engaged in contrary acts about one and the same object, in whatever respects it may be considered. Nor can one and the same act of the divine will be engaged on two contrary objects, such as "to happen" and "not to happen," in whatever respects those objects may be considered. "God prohibits evil as evil," but He permits the same, not as it puts on the relation of good, for it is false that sin ever puts on the relation of good, but because God knows how, from it, to elicit and produce good. The remark of Thomas Aquinas does not favour your view, and is not opposed to mine.

The third objection you have formed at your own pleasure, that you might be able more easily to overthrow it. For a boy, possessed of very little skill in Dialectics, knows that there is a great difference between the cause conse-quentiœ and the cause consequentis. The cause, indeed, can be inferred from the effect. And therefore you, properly, affirm that the Major of the syllogism, contained in the objection, "is not general." But your correction, added to that

Major, has no effect as to its truth. For it is not true that "if no middle cause intervenes between the antecedent, on the existence of which the consequent follows, and that consequent, then the antecedent is the cause of the consequent." Nor does the antecedent, therefore, cease to be the cause of the consequent, even if a middle cause intervenes. For Satan was the cause of the eating of the forbidden fruit, even if man was its proximate and immediate cause. By this, the force of your reply is weakened. If you can show that these two things are mutually consistent, that God can will that sin should happen, and that man still sins of his own free will, you have gained your case. I indeed admit that man can sin certainly, and yet freely; but to sin certainly is not the same as to sin necessarily. For the word "certainly" is used in respect to the divine prescience; but "necessarily" in respect to the decree of God, and the divine will, by which He wills that sin should happen. Hence, also, you incorrectly attribute certainty to the decree of God, when, you ought to attribute it to His prescience, and necessity to His decree. You also, afterwards, yourself acknowledge that God is the author of the sin of man, that is, by a desertion of him, and by the non-bestowment of the aid necessary for the avoidance of sins, from which it follows that man necessarily sinned. For he, who makes a law, and does not bestow the aid which is necessary for the fulfillment of the law, is the cause of the transgression of his own law.

You say, that "in this desertion, the will of man comes in, since he is not deserted, unless he wills to be deserted." I answer, that, if it is so, then the man deserved to be deserted. I ask, however, whether the man could will not to be deserted. If you say that he could, then he did not sin necessarily, but freely. If, on the other hand, you say that he could not, then the fault falls back upon God not less than before, because God is the cause of that volition, by which the man willed to be deserted, since He did not bestow the necessary grace, by which the man could will not to be deserted, and nothing can be conceived, which may intervene between this desertion on the part of God, and the volition of man, by which he willed to be deserted.

Your second answer to this objection is of no greater advantage to you; indeed you twice admit that God, by His own decree, by which He willed that sin should happen, is the cause of sin. First, you say that "sin is the mere consequent of the decree;" whence it follows that the decree is the cause of sin, unless you present some other relation in which sin may be the consequent of the divine decree, which you are wholly unable to do. You say that "the decree of God is, in such a manner, the antecedent of human sin, that it has no relation of cause, except that of deficiency. But I affirm that, in the use of this second argument, you are convicted of making God the author of sin. If that, which was deficient through the influence of the cause, was necessary to the avoidance of sin, then certainly God, by the deficiency of the operation, which was necessary to the avoidance of sin, is the cause of sin; unless you teach that man had previously deserved this deficiency of the divine operation. The words of Augustine do not sustain your opinion. For he only means that sin, which is committed contrary to the precept of God, is not committed when He is unwilling that it shall be committed, and absolutely wills that it shall not be committed, but when He permits it, and by a voluntary permission. You refer to another objection. "The decree of God is the energetic principle of all things, according to your sentiment; therefore, also, it is the principle of sin."

You acknowledge and teach that the antecedent is true. First, by the authority of the Scripture, and cite the first chapter to the Ephesians, but in a sense different from that of the Holy Spirit. For all those passages, in that chapter, refer to salutary gifts and effects which God, in His Son, and by the Holy Ghost, works in the elect, as is also proved by the word "good-pleasure." Secondly, by a reason, which is a sound one; for God is the cause of all beings and acts; yet it is to be suitably explained how He produces all acts. You deny the consequence, because sin is a "defect of being—not a real being, but only a being of the reason." It is necessary to explain, more fully, in what sense sin is a "defect" rather than "a real being." Sin is a being of the reason, because it not only has its subsistence in the mind, but also has its origin from the mind, and was produced by the mind, that it might serve to obtain for it the knowledge of things of good and evil. But a defect, even if it has no substance or fixed form, yet exists in the subject, from which the habitude of sin proceeds, and so affects the subject that it is perceived by it; and it is not understood by the mind, except in relation to its own habits, by which its limits are also determined. From which it is apparent, that sins are not purely beings of the reasons. You allow, indeed, that sin is not a being of the reason, when you say "it follows and exists, immediately and surely, from the removal of original righteousness." But though sin is, not a positive being, but a defect, yet if God is the energetic cause of that act, which can not be committed by man without sin, then He is also the energetic cause of sin. You admit this, when you say that "God is the energetic cause of all acts." You, then, do and must admit the consequent; unless you show in what way it can be effected that a man should freely perform the act, which, in respect to himself is sin, if the same act is produced by the energetic decree of God, which no one can resist. But more on this subject hereafter.

Finally, it is objected to your sentiment that it teaches that "God inclines to sin and positively hardens." I admit that this objection is made, and not without cause. It has never happened to me to see an answer, which frees the doctrine, which you advocate from that objection and charge.

You answer, that you "do not approve of a permission, separate from the will." Who does approve of such a permission? Who has ever denied that what God permits, He voluntarily permits? You say—"I do not attribute to God positive or physical action, as if He would infuse corruption and wickedness into a man." I wish, however, that you would explain how sin is committed, "necessarily in respect to the Divine decree," apart from any physical action of the Deity -whether that physical action be positive or negative—and, indeed, if you please, apart from positive action. You resolve that act, which is not performed without sin, into a first cause, in such a manner as, also, of necessity, to make God the positive cause of sin. But it is not necessary that He should infuse wickedness or corruption to such a degree that physical, or positive action can be attributed to Him; it is sufficient, if He moves, if He impels to the act, if He limits the liberty of the man, so that He can not but will and do that, which has been prohibited. You admit that "God effectively hardens;" which, indeed, I do not deny, but it is necessary that there should be an explanation, such that God may not, in any way, be made the author of sin. This we shall hereafter see.

I do not disapprove of the threefold action of Divine Providence in reference to human acts, referred to by Suidas. But consider whether that "action, which is according to the good-pleasure, by which God wills, approves, effects, and is delighted in any thing," is referred to in a sense different from that, in which you always use the word good-pleasure. For you have before said, on the authority of Ephesians 1, that "God does all things according to the good-pleasure of His own will;" of which passage, relying on its true interpretation, which you here present from Suidas, I have deprived you.

In reference to "the second action of Divine Providence, which is that of arrangement, or that of sustentation and preservation," I would have you consider whether it is so much the preservation and sustentation of motions, actions, and passions as of existence and faculties. For since the existence of things, and the faculties existing in them are the first acts, and motions, actions, and passions, resulting from them are the second acts, or from second acts, it seems, indeed, that an act of Divine Providence presides over the latter, different from that which presides over the former, It is true, indeed, that God sustains sinful nature. But it should be carefully explained how far and in what way God concurs with the creature in the performance of an action; but whatever explanation of that matter may be made, there must always be caution that a concurrence, with a second cause, may never be attributed to the first cause, such that the cause of evil can be rightly ascribed to the latter. You say—"the will can do nothing alone, yet it can act in an evil manner," and illustrate it by simile. Let us see how far it is appropriate. It is especially to be considered that it is applicable to a man, in an unfallen state, because "his pipe is not disjointed;" therefore that simile is not to be applied to his primitive state. Again, -- in "lameness," two things are to be considered, namely, walking or motion, and lameness, which is irregularity of motion." You compare walking with the act, and lameness with the irregularity of the act, in which the relation of sin properly consists. But those two things are not present in every act which is evil.

For instance, the eating of the forbidden fruit, in which it is not allowable to distinguish between the act and its sinfulness. For the act itself ought not to have been performed, and the relation of sin consists, not in the fact that he performed the act of eating in a mode, in which it ought not to have been performed, but in that he performed it at all. That illustration would have place in acts, good in themselves, but performed in a way, in which they ought not to be performed. Thus he, who gives aims, "that he may be seen of men," performs a good act, but in an improper manner, he walks, but is lame. Hence it follows that no one can be impelled to an act, the commission of which is a transgression of the law, without sin, and blame in the impeller and mover. You, also, see from this how cautiously the mode, in which God is said to be the cause of an act, but not of the sin existing in the act, is to be explained. You say that "the third action of Divine Providence is of concession, that of acquiescence or permission, by which God blamelessly effects certain things, in the evil deeds of men." It is not doubtful that this may be truly said of the Deity.

In this third action, you make also another three-fold division. You say that the first is "permission," but you explained it in such a manner, that it could not be adapted to Adam, in his original state, but to those only who have sinned, and, by their sins, deserved to be left by God to themselves, and given "over to a reprobate mind." For "God did not loose the reins upon Adam. He did not remove the impediments of sinning. He did not free him, previously bound, with cords." I have nothing at all against "the second action" and its explanation, if it be applied to sinners; yet I think that some things, highly necessary, might be added to it.

You do not seem to me to explain, with sufficient distinctness, "ordination," which is the third action. For the word is used in a two-fold sense—that of decreeing and determining that something shall be done, and that of establishing an order in that which is done, and of disposing and determining to a suitable end, things which are done. This equivocal use of the word should have been avoided, and the different significations of the word should not be confounded, as you do, in the same discussion, when you say that "God ordains sin as to its cause and principles," in which case, the word "ordain" is used, in its first signification: again—"He ordains the same thing as to its result and purposes," in which case, it is used in the second signification. The explanation, which you add, from the case of Satan, is only in reference to the ordination, as to the end and the result. If there is not a suitable explanation of the mode in which "God ordains, as to its causes and principles, an act, which can not be done by a man without sin"—I prefer to use this phraseology rather than the word sin—the cause and blame of sin will, by an easy transition, be charged upon God.

The words of Clemens Alexandrinus can only be understood of an ordination to an end, and I wish that you and all our writers would persist in the use of such language. For it is correct, and explains the action of God, who effects His own work by the evil deeds of wicked persons. In the words of Augustine, "there is the most manifest difference between "to make" and "to ordain," and the word ordain is used in its second signification, that of disposing and determining wills, evil by their own fault, to these and those purposes and to certain actions. But those words of Augustine, "God works in the hearts of men, inclining their wills whithersoever He pleases, even to evil things, according to their demerits," are to be suitably explained, so as not to impinge upon what follows; that "God does not make the wills evil." He, therefore, inclines evil wills to evil things, that is, so that they expend their wickedness upon one object, rather than upon another. If he is said to impel any one to will that which is evil, it is to be understood that He does this by the instrumentality of Satan, and, in such a way as can be easily reconciled with His justice. Fulgentius explains the matter most correctly and in a few words. For he sufficiently acquits Him of sin, when he denies that "God is the author of evil thoughts." For thoughts are the first causes in the performance of a work; and he also uses the word "ordain" in the latter signification, as can be clearly seen from his subjoined explanation. For he says that "God works good out of an evil work."

Your third answer denies, and with propriety, that the "Fate of the Stoics" is introduced by your doctrine, that is, Fate explained, as the Stoics taught concerning it. But it does not remove this difficulty, that, on the supposition of that Divine decree, which you suppose, a necessity is introduced with which liberty can not be consistent. While, therefore, the Fate of the Stoics may not be presented in your doctrine, yet a fate is presented, which places a necessity upon all things, and takes away freedom. You attempt to explain the decree of God in a way such as may not, by the divine decree, take away freedom, though it supposes necessity; to do which is, in my opinion, wholly impossible. But let us see how you present the mode of explaining and of disentangling the matter. First, you distribute that, which is necessary, into the simply or absolutely necessary, and the hypothetically necessary. The absolutely necessary—you correctly say—

"is that which cannot be otherwise, and whose contrary is impossible," but you do not, in your statement, make any distinction whether you treat of a thing which is incomplex and simple, or of a complex being. But let that pass. It is certain that there is nothing necessary in that sense, but God, and what pertains to Him. All other things are placed outside of that necessity. You say "that the necessary, of hypothesis, is that which can not be otherwise when one, or a number of things, is supposed." You do not here make a distinction in the supposition of things, between that, by which a thing is supposed to be, and that by which a thing is concluded; which latter necessity is distinguished into that of the consequent [consequentis], and that of the consequence [consequentiœ]. The latter is syllogistic, the former is that of causes, producing effects, or consequents, causes which neither are necessarily supposed, nor act necessarily as causes, but if they are supposed, and act as causes, the effect necessarily exists. For example, God does not, necessarily, create a world, but if He creates one, then it exists, necessarily, from that action. You consider that "the necessary by hypothesis is of nature, of precept, and of decree." That which is necessary of nature removes freedom and contingency. So, also, that which is necessary of precept; for that, which is rendered obligatory by law, is not left to the freedom of the creature, though, from the necessity of nature, an act is necessarily produced unless it be prevented by that which has greater power. But, by the necessity of precept, the act is not necessarily produced; there is laid upon the creature a necessity of performing the act, if it wishes to obey God, and to be accepted by Him. You badly define necessity of decree, as "that which God has foreknown and willed either to effect or at least to permit." For the necessity of prescience, and of the Divine permission is one thing, and that of efficiency is another. Indeed, we may allow that there is no necessity of prescience and of permission, but only of efficiency, or of the divine will. For, not the prescience of God, but "His will is the necessity of things," though, the prescience of God being supposed, it may follow that a thing will be, not from prescience as an antecedent [causa consequentis],but as sustaining to prescience the relation of conclusion [consequentiœ]. We shall hereafter treat of permission, at a greater length. We remark, also, that what is necessary of decree, can not at the same time, be called free or contingent in respect to the will as efficient.

In the second place, you distinguish necessity into that of coaction, and that of certainty. This is not well, for these are not opposed, as one and the same thing can be produced, by the necessity of coaction, and can be certainly foreknown. Again, they are not of the same genus. For the former belongs to the will, effecting something, and is prior, in nature, to the thing effected, while the latter is by prescience, and is subsequent, in nature, to the thing. The former coincides with the necessity of consequent, the latter, with that of the conclusion. Thirdly, there is a necessity which is nearer, as to relation, cause and genus to the necessity of coaction, and is the opposite of coaction, and from which, as its contrary, the necessity of coaction ought to have been distinguished. It is the necessity of inevitability, which term, also, indeed, comprehends the idea of coaction, but an unnamed species may be called by the name of its genus.

That this may be more clearly understood, I explain myself thus: The necessity of inevitability is two-fold, one introducing force, in things purely natural, when it is called violence, and in things voluntary, when it is called coaction; the other, inwardly moving a thing, whether it be nature or will, so smoothly and gently, that it cannot but be inclined in that direction, and will that to which it is moved. Yet I admit that the will is not carried or moved, according to the mode of the will, but according to the mode of nature, as, by the act of moving, freedom is taken away, but not spontaneous assent, while both are taken away by the act of impelling. I pass over your definition of coaction. That of certainty does not please me; for, in that definition, you conjoin things, which do not belong together. For a thing is said to happen certainly in respect to prescience, but immutably in respect to the thing itself; and immutability does not correspond with certainty. For certainty is attributed to prescience, which can not be deceived on account of the infinity of the divine nature and wisdom. You should, then, expunge that word "immutably" from your argument. For that which can either happen or not happen, can not be done immutably, yet it can surely be foreknown by Him who foreknows with certainty, all things even those which are contingent. But you rightly add an axiom to the certainty of necessity; "Every thing which is, so far as it is, is necessary." Thus far, the distinctions of necessity. You will now show how they mutually correspond. "All relations of effects are to their own causes," but either to separate causes, or to concurrent causes, and to joint causes, and to causes which act at the same time. If they are to separate causes, the effects are named from the mode, in which those effects exist from their causes. If necessarily, they are called necessary effects, if contingently, they are called contingent. But if many causes concur to produce one effect, that effect has relation to, and connection with, each of its causes, but does not receive its name, except from the mode, in which it exists and is produced from those united causes; if that mode is necessary, the effect is called necessary; if that mode is contingent, it is called contingent. It can not, however, be that one and the same effect should exist in part contingently, and in part necessarily, in any respect whatever. It is, indeed, true that, if that which is called a second cause, operates alone and of its own will, the thing might be called contingent; but, since the first cause moves the second, so that it can not but be moved, the whole effect is said to be necessary, since it can not be that the effect should not be produced, when those first and second causes are in operation.

The position that "the freedom of second causes is not taken away by that necessity," is, here, of no importance; as also your opinion that "an effect can be called free and contingent in respect to a certain cause, which is said to be necessary in respect to the first cause." For it is absurd to wish to harmonize freedom with necessity, and the latter with the former. All necessity, indeed, is at variance with freedom, and not the necessity of coaction alone. This is so true, that even any degree of vehemence can not be successful in weakening its truth. I grant that it is true, that "the decree of God ordains second causes, and, among them, the freedom of human will," but, in such a manner that freedom is not taken away by that "ordination:" but freedom is taken away, when God, either by coaction (which cannot be, both on account of the divine omnipotence, and on account of the nature of the will), or, by an easy and gentle influence, so moves the will, that it can not but be moved.

You seem to me not to discriminate between a free movement and one which is spontaneous. A spontaneous movement is so different from one that is free, that the former may coincide with a natural and internal necessity, but the latter can by no means do so. For a man spontaneously wishes to be happy, and not freely. Beasts are spontaneously borne towards those things, which are good for them, by natural instinct, but no liberty can be attributed to them. From these considerations, it is apparent that it can, in no manner, be said that "Adam fell necessarily and at the same time freely," unless you introduce the necessity of certainty, which belongs, not to the fall, but to the prescience of God, on account of His infinity. But freedom is taken away, if a decree of God is supposed, since "Adam could not resist the will, that is, the decree of God." Your answer that "as he could not, so he also would not," is refuted by the consideration that he could not will otherwise. This you confess to be true "as to the event," but not true "as to his power." But it is not the subject of disputation, whether the will of Adam was deprived of the power, which is called freedom, which was not necessary to induce the necessity of the fall, but whether the event itself, that is, the fall, occurred necessarily. When you admit this, you must admit also that he did not fall freely. For that power was limited and determined as to the act and event, so that, in the act, he could not will otherwise; else the decree of God was made in vain. Here, also, you unskillfully use spontaneous motion for free motion..

To elucidate the subject, you "distinguish three periods, -- previous, present, and future to the fall." But the present and the future are of no importance to this discussion. For the fall can not have any necessity from present and future time. Previous time only serves our purpose. You say that a at the present moment, the fall was necessary, in a two-fold respect." First, -- "on account of the prescience of God." But prescience is not a cause of necessity, nor can anything be said to be done infallibly, on account of prescience, but prescience is the cause, that a thing "which will occur, contingently, at its own time," is certainly foreknown by God. Secondly; -- "on account of the permissive decree of God." But permission can not be a cause of immutability or of necessity. For it is a negative act, not a prohibition; and from it an affirmative necessity can not exist.

The words of honourius, and Hugo do not aid you, for they treat of something wholly different, and they are not reliable authorities. But the reason, which you present, is partly fallacious, partly of no force. The fallacy, a petitio principii, consists in this sentence, "because an evil, which is permitted, can not but happen." The reason is of no force, when you say "because it can not happen otherwise than God decreed." It does not follow, from this, that it therefore happens necessarily; since, though evil can not happen otherwise than God permits it, yet that permission does not impose a necessity upon the event or sin. For the divine determination is not in reference to sin, that is, shall be committed, but in reference to the same thing, which is about to take place of its own causes, that is, shall not extend further than seems good to God. I do not accede to your definition of "permission" that "it is a negative of that grace, -- which is sufficient for the avoidance of sin." For, as has often been said, this is not to permit a man to sin freely, but to effect that he should sin necessarily. I wish also that you had explained, in what way "the necessity of the divine decree, by which He determined that Adam should sin, was evitable in respect to the freedom of the human will, when it was inevitable in respect to the event." I pass over the inconsistency of calling necessity evitable.

You do not wish that any one should think that "that necessity arose from the decree of God." But you have said so many things, in proof of it, that you now express your unwillingness in vain. Explain how that necessity follows the decree, and yet the decree has not the relation of cause, in respect to that necessity. For the decree is the cause of necessity, in the relation of consequent, not in that of consequence. Those are words and phrases, designed to avoid the force of truth, in which there is no truth, and not even the semblance of truth. For it will always remain true that whatever is necessary "of decree" has the cause of its necessity in and from the decree of God. Is not that labourious investigation and use of many distinctions a sign of falsity, when the statement of truth is simple and open? The assertion that "the predestinate are saved necessarily, and the reprobate are damned necessarily," is to be correctly understood. The fact, that any one is predestinate, is at variance with the fact of damnation, and the fact, that any one is reprobate, is at variance with the fact of salvation. But the ability to be saved or damned, is at variance with neither. For the decree is not in respect to the ability, but in respect to the fact of salvation or damnation. But those two acts, which you mention, namely, that of not showing mercy and that of damning, are subsequent to sin. For mercy is necessary, only, to the miserable and the sinner, and it is truly said that "the purpose of damning does not make any necessity of damnation unless by the intervention of sin," but by its intervention, in such a sense, that it is possible that it should not intervene. If, however, God has decreed to make and govern men, that he can not but sin, indeed, in order that He may declare His own righteousness in his destruction, that purpose introduces a necessity of sin and of damnation.

It is an absurd assertion that "from prescience that necessity follows in the same way." For what God foreknows, He foreknows because it is to take place in the future. But what He decrees, purposes, and determines in Himself to do, takes place thus because He decrees it. Also, from prescience is concluded the certainty of an event, which is a necessity of the consequence, and from the decree immutability of the same thing is concluded, which is a necessity of the consequent.

You make an objection against yourself, -- "They who are predestinated to death can not, if they will, be freed by repentance." That objection is not appropriate to this time and place. But I present you with an objection, that they, who are predestinated to death, are, also, according to your doctrine, predestinated to sin; that what God has decreed to bring upon them, namely, death, He may be able to bring upon them justly, that is, on account of sin. But indeed, if God can predestinate to sin, that He may be able to bring death upon the sinner; He is able also to bring death upon one, who is not a sinner, because he, who is a sinner in consequence of the divine predestination, is in fact not a sinner. It is far worse to predestinate a just man to sin than to predestinate an innocent man to death. Of this we have also, previously, spoken.

Your effort to charge the same necessity on the opinion "which supposes a permission of evil" is futile. I refer, here, to "permission," when rightly explained, and understood according to its own nature. But you describe permission in such a manner, as really to amount to an act of efficiency. For if "to permit is to will not to hinder," which it is in fact, and "the will not to hinder is such, that, without that hindrance, sin can not be avoided," as you assert, then, "to will not to hinder sin" is to effect sin, by a negation of the necessary hindrance.

Thus evil also necessarily exists from that permission, but by no means freely on the part of man. From which, it is clearly evident that the decree of God is not more evitable than a permission of the kind, which you have described. But, unless the distinction of the decree of God into energetic or efficacious and permissive is without foundation, -- as it certainly is not—then it is necessary that permission should be described so as not to coincide with energetic decree.

The charge of holding the Stoic and Manichean doctrine, which is made by some against you, is not made by them with the idea that your opinions entirely agree with that doctrine, but that you agree with it in this, that you say that all things are done necessarily. You ought to remove this charge from yourself, and free your doctrine from this accusation. You unite contrary things together when you say that "a man can not abstain from sinning, and yet he sins not necessarily, but freely." Nor is it sufficient to constitute freedom of the will, that it "be capable of being turned in opposite directions, and to choose spontaneously," if it shall be "determined to one directions only, by the Deity:" For that determination takes away the freedom of the will, or rather the liberty of volition. For though the will, in other things not determined by Gods may remain capable of change in any directions and free, yet the volition is not free, since it is determined precisely to one of two contraries.

The remark of Anselm presents the same idea as we have, often, presented, that a distinction is to be made between the necessity of the consequent, and that of the consequence: the former precedes, the latter follows the action. But your necessity of decree precedes the act and does not follow, while that of Anselm follows it, therefore, they are not the same. In the remark of Gaudentius there is not even a trace of the doctrine which you defend.

In your brief recapitulation, you fail, as greatly, of untying the knot. For it will always remain true that a denial of grace, necessary to the avoidance of sin, is a cause of sin, by the mode of the non-bestowment of the necessary hindrance; and it will, always be false, that he sins freely and voluntarily, who can not but sin, and that the will acts freely in that direction, to which it is determined by the certain and inflexible decree of God. It is false in the sense that freedom and determination are mutually opposed in the limits of their action. For the former has respect to two contraries, the latter to one only.

You present the example of the "angels who obey God both necessarily and freely," on your own authority, and do not at all prove what you assert. I assert that these two things are mutually inconsistent, so that, if you affirm that the angels obey God freely, I shall say, with confidence, that it is possible that the angels should not obey God. If, on the other hand, you affirm that they can not but obey God, I shall thence boldly infer that they do not obey God freely.

For necessity and freedom differ from each other in their entire essence, and in genus. And I would dare say, without blasphemy, that not even God Himself, with all His omnipotence, can not effect that what is necessary may be contingent or free, and that what is done necessarily, may be done freely. It implies a contradiction, that a thing should not be possible not to be done, and yet be possible not to be done, and it is a contradiction, opposed to the first and most general idea, divinely infused into our minds, in reference to whatever subject the truth is affirmed or denied. And a thing can not, at the same time, be and not be, at the same time, be and not be of a given character. For the fact, that God can not do this, is a mark not of impotence but of invariable power. The fact that a thing exists, depends on the actual power of God. If it should happen, at once and at the same time with the previous fact, that the same thing should not be, then the actual power of God would be either overcome, or have an equal power opposed to itself, so that it would happen that a thing, which is by the power of God, at the same time, is not. Which is the greatest of all absurdities.

DISCUSSION OF THE SUBJECT OF PERMISSION

As frequent mention of the permission of sin has been already made by us, it will be a work, not useless in itself, and not displeasing to you, if I shall distinctly set forth what I consider the true view concerning permission, in general, according to the Scriptures. You will read, weigh, and judge, freely and with candour, and if I shall, as to any point, seem to err, you will recall me to the right way, by serious and friendly admonition. I will treat, first, of permission in general, then of the permission of sin.

We know that permission pertains to action, in a generic sense, from the very form of the word, whether in itself or by reduction as they say in the schools. For cessation from act may also be reduced or referred back to the act, but it has, as its proximate and immediate cause, the will, not knowledge, not capability, not power, though these, also, may be requisite in the being, who permits. No one is rightly said to permit, who does not know what and to whom he permits, and is not capable of permitting or preventing, and finally has not the right and authority to permit. If permission is attributed to any one, who is destitute of that knowledge, or capability, or power, it is in an unusual and extended sense, which ought not to have a place in an accurate discussion of a subject.

The object of permission is both the person to whom anything is permitted, and the act which is permitted, and, under the act, I would include, also, cessation from the act. In the person, to whom anything is permitted, two acts are to be considered in respect to the person, -- first, strength sufficient to the performance of an act, unless there is some hindrance; secondly, an inclination to perform the act, for apart from this, the permission would be useless. Strength is necessarily requisite for the performance of an act; even if this is present, unless the person, to whom an act is permitted, has an inclination to the act, it is permitted to no purpose, and in vain. Indeed it can not be said, correctly, that an act is permitted to any one, who is influenced by no inclination to the performance of the act. From this it is apparent that permission must be preceded by the prescience or the knowledge of the fact that both sufficient strength and an inclination to perform the act, exist in him, to whom the permission is granted. The mode of permission is the suspension of efficiency, which efficiency is also possible to the being, who permits, either according to right, or according to capability, or in both respects, and, when used, would restrain, or in fact prevent the act. We may, hence, define permission in general, thus; -- It is the act of the will by which the being, who permits, suspends any efficiency which is possible to him, which, being used, would restrain, or, in fact, prevent an act in him to whom the permission is granted, to the performance of which act the same person has an inclination and sufficient strength. These conditions being applied to the Divine permission, by which He permits an act to a rational creature, the definition may be thus arranged: -- Divine permission is an act of the divine will by which God suspends any efficiency possible to Himself, either by right, or by power, or in both modes, which efficiency, used by God, would either restrain or really prevent an act of a rational creature, to the performance of which act, the same creature has an inclination and sufficient strength. But, since the will of God is always directed by His wisdom, and tends to good, that permission can not but be instituted to a certain end and the best end. There are two modes or species of permission, as is manifest in the definition, in which, to efficiency, if used, either the limitation of an act, or its prevention is ascribed. For the will of God is considered, in a two-fold respect, either as He prescribes something to His creatures, by command or prohibition, or as He wills to do or to prevent anything. Hence the efficiency, which is under discussion, is two-fold, on one hand, as the prescription or enactment of a law by which any act of the creature is restrained, by which restraint or limitation that act is taken away from the freedom of the creature, so that he can not, without sin, perform it, if it is forbidden, or omit it, if it is commanded; and on the other, as the interposition of an impediment, by which any act of the creature is prevented.

In the first mode, there was a limit as to the eating of the forbidden fruit of the tree of knowledge of good and evil, and as to the love due to a wife, the former by prohibition, the latter by command. In the second mode, Balaam was prevented from cursing Israel, Ahaziah from the murder of Elijah, Sennacherib from the capture of Jerusalem, and Abimelech from sin with Sarah. But since God, if He pleases, suspends this efficiency, in both modes, when and where it seems good to Him, permission is also two-fold; on one hand, as He does not restrain an act by a law, but leaves it to the decision and freedom of the creature, whether this may be on account of the simple nature of the act itself, as in that expression of the apostle "all things are lawful for me" (1 Cor. vi. 12) or, on account of another forbidden evil, an example of which may be taken from the "bill of divorcement;" on the other hand, as He does not, by His own action, interpose an impediment to an act, -- an impediment, by which the act may be really prevented, not one, by which it can or ought to be prevented. Thus He permitted Adam to eat of the forbidden fruit, and Cain to kill his own brother. Though He used impediments, by which, each of those acts could, and ought to have been prevented, yet He did not use impediments, by which the act, in either case, was prevented. We may be allowed to divide, also, the latter mode of permission which is by abstaining from the use of an impediment, which would prevent the act, according to the difference of the modes in which God is able, and, indeed, accustomed to prevent an act, to the performance of which a creature is inclined and sufficient. I do not wish, however, that such sufficiency should be ever understood apart from the concurrence of the first cause. That variety arises from the causes by means of which a rational creature performs an act. Those causes are "capability, and will, -- we, here, speak of voluntary acts, to which the permission, of which we now treat, has reference and, there-fore, the impediment is placed either upon the capability or the will of the creature; that is, God effects that the creature should be either not able, or not willing to produce that act. In the former mode He prevented the entrance of Adam into Paradise, in the latter, He prevented Joseph from polluting himself with adultery with the wife of his master.

More particularly, we must consider in how many ways God may prevent the creature from being able or willing to perform the act, to which he has an inclination and sufficient strength, that is, apart from this impediment. We consider prevention as applied, first to the capability, secondly, to the will. That the creature may be able to effect any thing, it is necessary that he should have capability; that no greater or equal power should act against him; finally, that he should have an object on which his capability can act. From this it is evident that an impediment may be placed on the capability in a four-fold manner; -- first, by the taking away of being and life which are the foundation of capability; secondly, by the deprivation or diminution of the capability itself; thirdly, by the opposition of a greater, or, at least, an equal power; fourthly, by the removal of the object; either of which ways is sufficient for prevention. We will adduce examples of each mode.

In the first mode, the capture of Jerusalem attempted by Sennacherib, was prevented by the slaughter of "an hundred four score and five thousand" men, made by one angel (2 Kings xix. 35, 36). Thus, also, the effort to bring Elijah before Ahaziah was prevented by the fire, twice consuming fifty men, who were sent to take him.

In the second mode, Samson was prevented from freeing himself from the hands of the Philistines, after his hair was cut off (Judges xvi. 19, 20), the strength of the Spirit, by which he had formerly been so mighty, having been taken away or diminished.

In the third mode, Uzziah was prevented from burning incense to the Lord by the resistance of the priests (2 Chron. xxvi. 18), and the carrying of Lot and the Sodomites into captivity was prevented by Abram with his servants, attacking the victorious kings (Gen. xiv. 15, 16).

In the fourth mode, Ahab was prevented from injuring Elijah (1 Kings xix. 3), and the Jews, who had sworn to slay the apostle Paul, were prevented from effecting their design (Acts xxiii. 10). God removed Elijah, and Paul was rescued from the Jews by the chief captain. Thus, also, Christ often removed himself out of the hands of those, who wished to take him; of those, also, who wished to make him a king.

The permission, which is contrary to this prevention, also subsists by four modes, contrary to those just exemplified, but united together. For a complete cause is required to the production of an effect, the absence of a single necessary cause, or element of the cause, being sufficient to prevent the effect. Thus it is necessary that, when God permits any act to the capability of a creature, that creature should be preserved as it is, and should live; that its capability should remain adapted to the performance of the act; that no greater or equal power should be placed in opposition; finally, that the object, to be operated upon, should be left to that capability. It appears, from this, that this divine permission is not inactive, as so many actions of the providence of God are requisite to that permission, -- the preservation of being, of life, and the capability of the creature, the administration and government, by which a greater or an equal power is opposed to the creature, and the presentation of the object. We may be allowed, also to adduce similar examples of permission. Thus God gave His Son into the power of Pilate and of the Jews. "This is your hour and the power of darkness" (Luke xxii. 53). Thus He gave Job into the hands of Satan (Job i. 12), Zachariah into the hands of his murderers (2 Chron. xxiv. 21), and James into the hands of Herod (Acts xii. 2). Let us now consider how God may prevent a creature from a volition to perform an act, to which he has an inclination and sufficient strength. An impediment is placed by the Deity, upon the propensity and the will of a rational creature, in a two-fold mode, according to which God can act on the will. For He acts on the will either by the mode of nature, or according to the mode of the will and its freedom. The action, by which He affects the will, according to the mode of nature, may be called physical impulse; that, by which He acts on the same, according to the mode of the will and its freedom, will be suitably styled suasion. God acts, therefore, preventively on the will either by physical impulse or by suasion, that it may not will that, to which it is inclined by any propensity. He acts preventively on the will, by physical impulse, when He acts upon it, by the mode of nature, that, from it may necessarily result the prevention of an act, to which the creature is inclined by any propensity. Thus the evil disposition of the Egyptians towards the Israelites seems, in the judgment of some, to have been prevented from injuring them. God acts, preventively, on the will by suasion, when He persuades the will by any argument, that it may not will to perform an act, to which it tends by its own inclination, and to effect which the creature has, or seems to himself to have, sufficient strength. By this, the will is acted upon preventively, not of necessity, indeed, but of certainty.

But since God, in the infinity of His own wisdom, foresees that the mind of the rational creature will be persuaded by the presentation of that argument, and that, from this persuasion, a prevention of the act will result, He is under no necessity of using any other kind of prevention. All the arguments, by which the reason can be persuaded to the performance of an act, can be reduced to three classes—that which is easy and practicable; that which is useful, pleasant, and delightful; and that which is honest, just and becoming. Hence, also, God, by a three-fold suasion, prevents a person from the will to perform any act. For He persuades the mind that the act is either difficult to be performed, or even altogether impossible; or useless and unpleasant; or dishonest, unrighteous and indecorous.

By the argument from the difficult and impossible, the Pharisees and chief priests were, often, prevented from laying violent hands on Christ: for they knew that he was considered a prophet by the multitude, who seemed prepared to defend him against the efforts of his enemies. The Israelites, pursuing the king of Moab, when they saw that he had offered his eldest son, as a burnt offering, and, from this fact, knew that he was strengthened in his own mind, departed from him, thinking that they could not take the city without very great difficulty and much slaughter (2 Kings iii. 23-27). Sanballat and Tobiah, and the other enemies of God's people, endeavouring to hinder the building of the walls of Jerusalem, were prevented from accomplishing their design, when they heard that their plots were known to Nehemiah (Neh. iv. 15). For they despaired of effecting any thing, unless they could take the Jews by surprise. By the argument from the useless, the soldiers, who crucified Christ, were prevented from breaking his legs (John xix. 33), because he was already dead, and it would have been useless to break his legs, as this was designed, and usually done to hasten death; and, at this time, the Jews desired that their bodies should be taken down from the cross before sunset. But God had declared, "a bone of him shall not be broken" (John xix. 36). By the same argument—of inutility—Pilate was prevented from releasing Christ. "If thou let this man go, thou art not Caesar's friend" (John xix. 12). Thus, also, Pharaoh did not wish to let the people of God go (Exod. chapters 5, 6 and 7). By the argument from the unrighteous or dishonest, David was prevented from slaying Saul, when he had fallen into his hands; "The Lord forbid that I should stretch forth my hand against the anointed of the Lord" (1 Sam. xxiv. 6).

It is sufficient, for the prevention of an act by the argument of suasion, that the act should seem to be impossible, useless, or unrighteous to those, by whom God wills that it should not be performed, even if it is not so in reality. Thus the Israelites were prevented from going up into the promised land, when they learned, from the spies, the strength of the nations, and the defenses of the cities, thinking that it would not be possible for them to overcome them (Num. 13 and 14). Thus David was prevented from fighting, for the Philistines, against Saul and the Israelites; for the Philistines said to their king—"let him not go down with us to battle, lest, in the battle, he be an adversary to us" (1 Sam. xxii. 4).

Thus Ahaz was prevented from asking a sign of the Lord, at the suggestion of Isaiah, the prophet; for he said, "I will not ask, neither will I tempt the Lord (Isa. vii. 12). To this last argument pertain the revelations of the Divine will, whether they are truly such, or are falsely so esteemed. Thus David was prevented from building the temple of the Lord, by the Divine prohibition in the mouth of Nathan (2 Sam. vii. 5 &c.), though he had purposed, in his own mind, to do this for the glory of God. Thus Laban was prevented from speaking "to Jacob either good or bad," for, he said, "it was in the power of my hand to do you hurt" (Gen. xxxi. 29). The king of Babylon being prevented by the oracle of his own gods, which he consulted, from attacking the Ammonites, marched against the Jews, whom God wished to punish. Each of these is not always used separately, from the others, by God to prevent an act which He wishes should not be performed, but they are some times presented, two or three together, as God knows may be expedient, to the prevention of an act which He wishes to prevent.

We do not, in this place, professedly discuss what that action is, by which God proposes suasory arguments, designed to act preventively on the will, to the mind of the creature, inclined to the act and having strength adequate to its performance. Yet it is certain, whatever that act may be, that it is efficacious for prevention, and will certainly prevent, which efficacy and certainty depends, not so much on the omnipotence of the divine action as, on the prescience of God, who knows what arguments, in any condition of things or at any time, will move the mind of man to that, to which God desires to incline him, whether on account of His mercy or of His justice. Yet, in my judgment, it is lawful so to distinguish that action as to say that, on the one hand, it is that of the gracious and particular providence of God, illuminating, by His Holy Spirit, the mind of the man who is regenerate, and inclining his will, that he may will and not will that which God purposes that he should will and not will, and that, indeed, of a pure inclination to obey God; on the other hand, it is that of more general providence, by which He acts on men as men, or as only morally good, that they may not will, and may will, as God purposes that they should not will and should will, though not with this event and purpose, that they should, in their nolition or volition, obey God.

We now deduce, from this, the modes of permission, the opposite of prevention, which are not to be separated like those of prevention, but are to be united. For, as a single argument can act preventively on the will, that it may not will what God purposes to prevent; so it is necessary that all those arguments should be absent by which the will would be persuaded to an act of nolition, otherwise, there would be no permission. Therefore, the permission, by which God permits a rational creature to perform an act, to the performance of which he has inclination and adequate strength, is the suspension of all those impediments, by which the will was to have been persuaded, and in fact moved to a nolition. For it can be that God, being about to permit an act to the will of the creature, should so administer the whole matter, that not only some arguments of dissuasion, but all conjoined, may be presented to the will of a rational creature; yet, as persuasion can but result from that presentation of arguments, which is also known to God, it is from this fact that the presentation of arguments, is most consistent with the permission of that thing to dissuade from which they were used.

Let us illustrate the subject by examples. God permitted the brethren of Joseph to think of slaying him; (Gen. xxxvii. 18;) and at length they sold him, not caring that he was their brother, and that they were forbidden, by the laws of God, to commit murder, or to sell a free person into slavery. So, also, He permitted the enemies of His Son to condemn him, though innocent and unheard, and finally to slay him, setting at naught their own law, which not only had been imposed on them by the Deity, but was called to their remembrance, by Nicodemus, Joseph and others, in the inquiry, "Doth our law judge any man before it hear him?" They obtained false witnesses, and found that "their witness agreed not together" (Mark xiv. 56). Yet they did that, which their envy and hatred against Christ dictated. Thus God likewise permitted Saul to persecute David (1 Sam. 23 and 24), making no account of the fact that he had been taught and convinced of David's innocence by his own son, and by personal experience. From this discussion, it is apparent that a difference must be made between a sufficient and an efficacious impediment, and that the permission of which we here treat, is a suspension of efficacious impediment. A sufficient impediment is used, by God, partly to declare that the act, to prevent which He takes care that those arguments should be proposed, and presented, is displeasing to Himself, partly that they may be more inexcusable, who do not permit themselves to be prevented; and even that He may the more, on account of their iniquity, incite them to the act which is so eagerly performed. Then we have this three-fold permission of the Deity—first, that by which God leaves any act to the decision of a rational creature, not restraining it by any law; secondly, that by which He permits an act, in respect to the capability of the creature; third, that by which He permits the act, in respect to the inclination and will of the creature. The last two can not be disjoined in a subject, though they can and ought to be suitably distinguished from each other. For it is necessary that an act, which God does not will to prevent, should be permitted both to the capability and the will of the creature, since, by the sole inhibition, either of the capability, or of the will, an impediment is presented to the act such that it is not performed.

Some may say that the species or modes of prevention are not sufficiently enumerated; as no act is prevented in its causes only, but also, in itself. It is necessary to an act, not only that God should bestow both the power and the will, that he should produce the effect itself, and without the intervention of means. It must follow, therefore, that an act will not be certainly produced, even if God should bestow the power and the will, and hence, it is possible that an act should be prevented, even if God does not present an impediment to the capability or the will, that is, if He withholds from the creature his own concurrence, either active or motive, which is immediately necessary to produce the act. From this, it can be deduced, also, that an act is not fully permitted, even if it is left by God to the capability and will of the creature, unless God has determined to unite immediately to produce the same act, by his own act, motion, or concurrence. I reply, that I do not deny the necessity of that concurrence or immediate act of God to the production of an act; but I say that it has once been determined by God, not to withhold, from His creatures His own concurrence, whether general or special, for the producing those acts, to perform which He has given to His creatures the power and the will or which He has left to the power and will of His creatures; otherwise, He has, in vain, bestowed the power and the will, and He has, without reason, left the act to the capability and the will of the creature. I add that an example of an impediment, of that kind, can not be given, that is, an impediment, placed by God, in the way of an act permitted to the capability and will of a creature, by withholding from the creature His own immediate concurrence.

I, therefore, conclude that the modes or species of prevention, and there-fore, of permission, have been sufficiently enumerated. I grant that not only much light, but also completeness, will be added to the doctrine of the divine permission, if it not only may be shown how God prevents acts, for which rational creatures have an inclination and sufficient strength, but may be explained, with accuracy, how God produces and effects His own acts and His own works, through His rational creatures, whether good or bad. In which investigation, many learned and pious men have toiled, and have performed labour, not to be regretted; yet I think that so many things remain to be solved and explained, that no genius, however surpassing, can be sufficient for all of them, and so it can be truly said that the mine of this truth is not only deep and profound, but also inexhaustible. Yet, if we descend into it with soberness, and, following the thread and guidance of the Holy Scriptures, there is no doubt that it will be granted unto us to draw thence so much as God, the only fountain and giver of the truth, knows will conduce to the salvation of the church, and to the sanctification of His name in this world, to whom be glory for ever, through Jesus Christ. Amen.

Having thus discussed the subject of permission in general, let us now consider the permission of sin. At the outset, it must be understood that sin is not permitted in the first mode of permission, for it is sin in that it is forbidden by the law, therefore, it can not be permitted by the law; else, the same thing is sin and not sin; sin in that it is forbidden, and not sin, in that it is permitted, and not forbidden. Yet, since it is said truly that sin is permitted by God, it is certain that it is permitted in some way, which will, generally considered, be a suspension of all those impediments by the interposition of which sin could not be committed by the creature. But the impediments by which sin, so far as it is sin, is prevented, are the revelation of the divine will, and an act moving or persuading to obedience to the divine will. From which it is evident that permission of sin is a suspension of that revelation, or of that suasion, or of both.

It may be stated, here, from the general definition of permission, that revelation, motion, or suasion have so much efficacy, that if they are used and applied, the sin would not, in fact, be committed. I say this, then: Let no one think that God performs no act sufficient to prevent sin, when sin is not, in fact, prevented, and thence conclude that God wills sin; and again, let no one judge that, when God perform one or more acts, sufficient to prevent sin, that He unwillingly permits sin. In the latter of which remarks, we see that they are frequently mistaken, who do not consider the subject with sufficient accu-racy. For the sole consideration of efficacious prevention, by the suspension of which, permission is properly and adequately defined, effects, in view of the use of some, though inefficacious, impediments, that we should understand that God does not will sin, nor yet that he permits it unwillingly, because He has, in addition to those sufficient impediments, also efficacious ones in the storehouse of His wisdom and power, by the production of which, sin would be certainly and infallibly prevented.

That, what has been thus said by us, in general terms, may be more evident, let us explain, with a little more particularity, in reference to differences of sin. Sin is either of omission or of commission. Sin of omission is a neglect of an act, prescribed and commanded by law; sin of commission, is a performance of that, which is forbidden and prohibited by law. But since, in a preceptive law, not a good act, only, is enjoined, but its cause, mode and purpose, also in a prohibitive law, not a bad act, only, is forbidden, but also the cause and purpose of the omission, it is apparent that sin, both against a preceptive law, and against a prohibitive law, is two-fold: against a preceptive law if the enjoined act is omitted, and if it is performed unlawfully as to manner and purpose; and against a prohibitive law, by performing an action, and by not performing, but omitting it with an unlawful reason and purpose. The examples are plain. He, who omits to bestow alms on the poor, sins in omitting a prescribed act. He, who bestows alms on the poor that he may be seen of men, sins in omitting the due reason, and purpose of the bestowal. He, who steals, sins in committing a forbidden act; he, who abstains from theft, that his iniquity may be covered for the time and may afterwards more deeply injure his neighbour, sins in omitting the forbidden act with a wrong purpose. The divine permission is to be accommodated to each of the modes both of mission and of commission.

Sin is distributed, in respect to its causes, into sin of ignorance, of infirmity, and of malice; and by some, an additional distinction is made, namely, sin of negligence or thoughtlessness, as different and separate from the former, while others think that this is embraced in the three species previously mentioned.

The divine permission is also adjusted to these differences. It would be an endless work to present all the divisions and differences of sin, and to show how the divine permission is related to each class. But we must not omit that, in sin, not it alone but the act also, blended with it, is to be considered, as in sin there is the transgression of the law, and the act, that is the act, simply as such, and the act, as forbidden or prescribed, the omission of which prescript is sin. But permission can be considered, either in respect to the act, or to the transgression, for sin is prevented in the prevention of the act, without which sin can not be committed. Again, the act is prevented in the prevention of the sin, which necessarily inheres and adheres to the act, so that the act itself can not be performed without sin. For one may abstain from an act, towards which he is borne by his inclination, because it can not be performed without sin; another, on the contrary, abstains from sin because he is not inclined to the act itself. When he abstains from the act because it is sin, he abstains from sin per se, from the act incidentally: but when he abstains because the act is not pleasant to him, he abstains from the act per se, from sin incidentally. When also an act, is permitted as an act, it is permitted per se, sin is permitted incidentally. When sin is permitted as sin, it is permitted per se, the act is permitted incidentally. All of which things are to be diligently considered in reference to the subject of permission, that it may be understood what efficiency God suspends in that permission, and what efficiency He uses to no purpose—to no purpose in relation to the event, in that sin is not omitted, not to no purpose in relation to the objects which God has proposed to Himself, the best and the most wisely intended, and most powerfully obtained. But though we have already discussed the permission of acts in general, it will not be superfluous to treat here of the same, so far as those acts are blended with sin, and sin with them; though, in the mean time, the principal reference in this discussion, must be to the permission of sin, as such. For, as these two are so connected, that they can not be separated in an individual subject, the very necessity of their coherence seems to demand that we should speak of the permission of both in connection, though of the permission of sin per se, and of the act incidentally. But since the relation of sin appears, most plainly, in an act committed against a prohibitive law, as omission of good may be often comprehended under it by synecdoche, as in the definitions of sin, -- "it is that which is done contrary to the law,"—also, "a desire, word, or deed against the law,"—it will not be irrelevant to show, in the first place, how God permits that sin, whether as it is a sin, or as it is an act, which He permits, or in both relations.

We will present the modes of permission corresponding to the contrary modes of prevention, as before. The murder which Ahab and Ahaziah intended to perpetrate on the prophet Elijah, was an act, which, being performed would have taken away the life of Elijah, and it was a sin against the sixth commandment of God. God prevented that murder, not as a sin, but as an act. This is apparent from the mode of prevention, for in one instance, he took Elijah out of the hands of Ahab, and in another He consumed, with fire sent down from heaven, those who had been sent to take the prophet (2 Kings 1). The former case was according to the fourth mode, heretofore mentioned; the latter was, according to the first mode, in opposition to the power of Ahaziah and in this case prevented the effect. David, being instigated by his followers to slay Saul, his persecutor and enemy, refused, being restrained from that act, not as an act, but as a sin, for he said "The Lord forbid that I should stretch forth my hand against him, seeing he is the anointed of the Lord" (1 Sam. xxiv. 6).

The mode of prevention was by a revelation of the divine will, and by a persuasion to obedience, and was suitable to the prevention of sin as such. The defilement of Sarah, the wife of Abraham when she was brought to Abimelech, would have been an act, by which, as the violation of Sarah's chastity, would have caused great grief to Abraham, and would have been a sin against the seventh precept of the Decalogue. It was divinely prevented, if you consider the mode of prevention, as far as it was sin. For God, in a dream, revealed to him that she was "a man's wife" (Gen. xx. 3), and he could not, without sin, have carried out his design. If you examine the design and reason of the prevention, it was both in respect to the act and to the sin; as an act, because it would have caused indelible grief to Abraham, and from this God wished to spare his servant; as sin, because God knew that Abimelech would have done this "in the integrity of his heart" (6th v.) and He, therefore, withheld him from sin, in adultery with the wife of his friend.

Let us look at the opposite modes of permission in examples, also selected from the Scriptures. The sale of Joseph, made by his brethren, (Gen. 37), was an act and a sin; also, the affliction by which Satan tried Job, the man of God (Job. 1 & 2). Both were permitted by God. Was this in respect to the act or to its sin? This can not be gathered from the mode of the permission, for God abstains from all modes of restraint when He permits any thing, and if He did not so abstain, He would prevent, and then would, consequently, be neither the act nor sin. But, from the end and the mode of effecting the permitted act and sin, a judgment may be formed of the respect according to which God has permitted the act of sin. From the sale of Joseph resulted his removal to Egypt, his elevation to the highest dignity, in that land from which, food, necessary for his father's family, could be procured, in a time of most direful famine. God declares that He sent him into Egypt for this purpose. All this resulted from the sale, not as it was a sin, but as an act. In the affliction of Job, God desired that the patience and constancy of His servant should be tried, and it was tried by the affliction not as a sin but as an act. On the other hand, God permitted David to number the people (2 Sam. 24), and Ahab to slay Naboth (1 Kings 21), in which cases the numbering of the people, and the murder were acts, but were permitted as sin. For God purposed to punish Israel, and that Ahab should fill up the measure of his crimes. It is, indeed, true that God also wished to take pious Naboth from this vale of sorrows to the heavenly land; this was effected by the murder, not as it was a sin, but as an act. Yet the proper, immediate, and adequate reason that God permitted Ahab to perpetrate that murder, is that of which I have spoken—the measure of his crimes was to be filled. For God could, in some other way, without human sin, have called Naboth to Himself. Again, God permitted Absalom to pollute, by incest, the wives or concubines of his father, and this was done in respect to both. For it was permitted both as an act, and as sin. As an act, it served for the chastisement of David who had adulterously polluted the wife of Uriah; as a sin, it was permitted, because God wished that Absalom, by his crime, should cut off all hope of reconciliation with his offended father, and, in this way, hasten his own destruction, the just punishment of rebellion against his father. In both respects, also, God permitted Ahab to go up to Ramoth-Gilead contrary to the word of the Lord; as a sin, because God wished to punish him; as an act because God wished that he should be slain in that place, to which he came by the act of going up. From these examples a judgment may be formed of similar cases. Thus far in reference to permission of sin, which consists in the perpetration of an act, prohibited by law.

Let us now consider sin, as it is committed when an act, forbidden by law, is not performed, but omitted not from a due reason and purpose. Here the act is prevented, but sin is not prevented. There is, then, in this case, the permission of sin only, as such, and the mode of permission is a suspension of the revelation of the divine will, or at least of suasion and motion to obedience to the known will of God. For the creature omits the act, not because God has forbidden it, but for some other reason. Thus the brothers of Joseph omitted to slay him, as they had determined to do, not because they began to think that this crime would displease God, but because, from the words of Judah, they thought it useless, and that it would be better to sell him into bondage (Gen. 37). Absalom, after thousands of followers had been collected, omitted to pursue his fleeing father as Ahithophel counseled him, not because he considered it wrong to pursue his father, for he was wholly hostile to him, but he followed the counsel of Hushai, because he considered that the curse, advised by Ahithophel, would be dangerous for himself and the people. In this and similar examples, we see that God restrained an act, which had been forbidden and therefore was sin, and yet did not prevent sin, which was committed by those, who omitted that forbidden act; but he permitted them to sin in the mode of omitting the forbidden act. The reason is manifest, as by the act, a person, whom God purposes to spare, would be injured, but no one but the sinner himself is injured by sin committed in an undue omission of an act, as is just. Indeed by the prevention of an act, there is prepared for the persons, who have omitted an act, the punishment due to them both on account of this sin of undue omission, and for other reasons, as happened to Absalom.

We now proceed to the permission of sin, which is committed in the mere omission of an act, which has been commanded. This is permitted by God, as it is an omission of an act, and as it is sin. God, I assert, permits that act, which the law commands to be omitted, either as it is an act, or as it is sin.

God permitted the sons of Eli to disobey the admonitions of their father, (1 Sam. ii. 25); Saul, to spare the king of the Amalekites, (1 Sam. xv. 8); the Israelites, when the statement of the spies had been made, to refuse to go up into the promised land, (Num. xiv. 4), the citizens of Succoth and Penuel, to deny bread to the army of Gideon, (Judges viii. 6 & 8); Ahab, to send away Benhadad alive, a man devoted to death by the Lord, (1 Kings xx, xxxiv,); Festus, before whom Paul was accused, not to pronounce sentence against him, and in favour of the Jews, (Acts xxv. 12); &c. He permitted all these things partly as they were omissions of acts, partly as they were sins, that is, omissions contrary to a preceptive law, which imposed commands, partly in both respects. In reference to the sons of Eli, the Scripture says—"they hearkened not unto the voice of their father, because the Lord would slay them." The permitted omission of obedience thus far was sin. The omission by Saul of the slaughter of those, whom God willed and commanded to be slain, was permitted as it was a sin, not as it was the omission of an act, by the performance of which they would have been deprived of life. For God had determined to take away the kingdom of Saul from him, and had already denounced this against him, by the mouth of Samuel, because he had sacrificed, not waiting for Samuel, (1 Sam. xiii. 9-14). Agag, also, was afterwards hewed in pieces before the Lord by the prophet Samuel. The fact that the Israelites omitted to go up into the promised land, as they had been commanded by the Lord, occurred because God purposed that their bodies should fall in the wilderness, as they had so often tempted God, and murmured against Him. Then that omission was permitted as a sin. God permitted the citizens of Succoth and Penuel to withhold bread from the army of Gideon, partly that He might test the constancy of those, who were "pursuing after Zebah and Zalmunna," partly that He might prepare punishment for the citizens of Succoth and Penuel. In this case then, the omission of the act was permitted as it was such, and as it was sin. For as, being provided with food, they would have been strengthened, who were pursuing the Midianites, so the omission of the act, as such, on their part, was grievous and to be worthy of punishment. The sending away of Benhadad, or his release from death was permitted by God, as a sin—a sin, committed against an express command—for God purposed that Ahab should heap up wrath against the day of wrath, on account of his heinous sins; and also as an act, as He purposed that Benhadad, in the prolongation of his life, by the omission of an act commanded by God, might fight afterwards with Ahab, and, after his death, with the Israelites, and besiege Samaria to the great injury of its inhabitants. Festus was permitted by God, to refrain from acquitting Paul—according to law and right as he could be convicted of no crime—in respect to the act as such, and not as sin. For, from that omission resulted a necessity for the appeal of Paul to Caesar, which was the occasion of his departure to Rome, where God willed that he should bear testimony concerning His Son.

In respect to sin, when a prescribed act is performed unduly as to manner and design, it is certain that it is permitted as such, for in it nothing is permitted except the omission of a due mode and purpose, which omission is purely sinful. This is evident from the mode of permission, which, in this case, is certain; namely, the suspension of efficiency by which sin, as sin, is permitted. Joab performed many distinguished deeds and those prescribed by God, in fighting bravely, against the enemies of the people of God, in behalf of Israel, that it might be well for the people of God; but God did not incline his mind to do this from a right motive. It is apparent that he sought his own glory, in those deeds, from the fact that he, by wicked treachery, destroyed men, equal to himself in bravery and generalship, that he might be alone in honour. For the man who defends any cause, only that it may be defended, and for the glory of God, will not be vexed that as many as possible, endued with skill and bravery, should be united in its defense; indeed, he would most deeply rejoice and be glad on this account.

As to the differences of sin in view of its causes—ignorance, infirmity, malice, negligence—there is in respect to these a clear distinction in their permission. For the permission of a sin of ignorance arises from the suspension of the revelation of the divine will; of malice, from the suspension of the act by which the perversity of the heart is corrected and changed; of infirmity, from the withholding of strength to resist temptation, of negligence, from the suspension of the act by which a serious and holy care and anxiety is produced in us to watch our faculties, and to walk in the law of the Lord. For God knows, when it seems good to him to perform a work, by the acts of rational creatures, which can not be committed by them without sin, how to suspend His own efficiency, so as to permit His creatures to perform their own acts. He willed that His church should be proved and purged by persecutions, and indeed by the act of Saul, a man zealous for the law, who, from inconsiderate and preposterous love towards his own religion, wished that the sect of the Nazarenes, so called should be extirpated. That this might be effected through him, He suffered him to be some time in ignorance, without which, as he was then constituted, he would not have persecuted the church. For he says that he "did it ignorantly" (1 Tim. i. 13). In the case of Julian the apostate, a most foul persecutor of the church, God did not correct his willful and obstinate hatred of Christ and his church. For when he was convinced of the truth of the Christian doctrine, he could have persecuted it only through willful malice. God's procedure, in not correcting that hatred, was deserved by him, who, willingly and of his own fault, had apostatized from Christ. God purposed that Peter, presuming too much on himself, should come to a knowledge of himself, and He suffered him to deny his Master, from fear of death, not affording him such support of His Spirit, as to move him to dare to profess Christ openly, despising the fear of death. David, being freed from his enemies, and having conquered many neighbouring kings and nations, began to guard his steps with too little care, and heedlessly gave himself up to negligence, especially because he had Joab, a distinguished general and skilled in military duties, in whom, on account of consanguinity, he could trust; from this it happened that he fell into that shameful adultery with the wife of Uriah. But God permitted him to fall into that negligence, and on that occasion to commit sin, that he might be more diligently watchful over himself, mourn on account of his own sin for an example to others, afford a distinguished specimen and example of humility and repentance, and rise more gloriously from his sin. It would be tedious to remark the same thing in each kind of sin; but let these suffice, as exhibiting the means and mode of forming a correct judgment in reference to permission. But though the whole complex matter, which is made up of act and transgression, may be permitted by God, through a suspension of all divine acts, by the use of which, on the part of God, the act, either as an act or as sin, would have been prevented, yet it is useful to consider, distinctly, in what respect that permission may be given by God, and what efficiencies, and of what kind, He suspends, that He may not hinder the commission or omission of an act prescribed or forbidden. For in this the divine goodness, wisdom and power, and even justice is seen as distinctly as possible, and it is most clearly proved how God, in all his own action, restraint and permission, is free from blame, and without sin, and by no means to be considered the author of sin. In showing which, it is so much the more evident how easily they may fall into absurdity and blasphemy, who refer, indeed, to a providence, acting, restraining, permitting, but not with sufficient distinctness, accuracy, and diligence, bringing together and comparing them, and distinguishing each from the others.

The individual causes of permission, in its variety and in that of the permitted acts, and of sins, are, at the same time, various and manifold, and not generally explicable, which can, perhaps, in some way, be demonstrated by those, who have their senses exercised in divine things, and are accustomed to consider them with earnest study. Two general or universal reasons can be presented for the fact that God permits events in general, and why He permits any particular event. One is the freedom of the will, which God bestowed on rational creatures, and which He designed as the mistress and the free source of their actions. The other is the declaration of the divine glory, which is of such a character as not only to effect and prevent that which can be effected and prevented, for his own glory, but also so to reduce to order the acts of rational creatures which are permitted, and which frequently deviate from the order, prescribed to them, that from it the praise of the divine goodness, mercy, patience, wisdom, justice and power may shine forth and be revealed. To which pertains that, which is beautifully said by Augustine, "God has judged that it belongs to His own omnipotent goodness to bring good out of evil rather than not to permit evil to exist."

The creature is likewise to be considered, to whom is granted the permission of an act of commission or of omission, which can not, without sin, be committed or omitted; namely, as to his character at the time when that act is permitted to him, whether, as only created, and remaining in his primeval integrity, or as fallen from that state; again, whether made a partaker of grace, or invited to a participation of grace; whether brought to that state, or resisting grace, or not sufficiently solicitous to receive it, and to continue in it, and the like. For God can deny to any creature, considered as such, action, motion, efficiency, concurrence, either general or special, of nature or of grace, of providence or predestination—though I do not dare to make a confident assertion in reference to the act of Predestination—which act and concurrence, which motion and efficiency He could not, without injustice, deny to the same creature considered in a different relation. But a permission of sin depends, as we have before seen, on a suspension of the divine act, motion, efficiency, &c.

He, however, who wishes to discuss fully and thoroughly the subject of permission must, of necessity, treat of the general providence of God, and of that special providence, which preserves, governs, rules, effects, prevents and permits. For, as permission is opposed to prevention, by the mode either of privation or of contradiction, so it is opposed to efficiency by negation; and it is the nature of permission to have, antecedent to itself, various acts of God concerning the same creature, to which permission is granted, and concerning that act which is permitted. If these acts of God are not accurately explained, it can not be understood what that efficiency is, in the suspension of which, permission properly and immediately consists. This, also, is the reason that many, when they hear any thing concerning permission, immediately, in their own minds, conceive of inactive quiet, and abstinence from all effort on the part of providence; others, considering the power and efficacy of that providence, which is present in and presides over all things and acts, either reject the idea of permission, or acknowledge it only in word, in the mean time, so explaining it as to resolve it into a certain act of God, and into the efficiency of providence. But these errors are both to be avoided, lest we should take away, from the divine providence, acts which belong to it, or should attribute to it things foreign to it, and unworthy of His justice. In reference to the remarks, already made, some one will object that I attribute to permission not only the illegality and the irregularity of the act, but also the act itself; and thus remove from the operation of the divine will and efficiency, not only the illegality of the act, but the act itself. He will say that, in this, he perceives a double error; first, because I attribute sin, simply and taken in any respect, to permission, and remove it from the divine efficiency and will; when it ought, in a certain respect, to be attributed to the divine efficiency and will; secondly, because I take away, from the efficiency and the will of God, the act which is the first and supreme cause of all being. Let us examine a little more closely both objections. We explain the former by the sentiments of the objector himself. In sin there are three respects; for there is, first, guilt; second, punishment; third, the cause of other sins. Indeed God is not, they say, the cause of sin in respect to its guilt, but to its punishment, and to its being the cause of other sins. They affirm that God is, without controversy, the cause of punishment, because that is an act of justice, by which sin, deviating from the law of the prescriptive justice of God, is brought under the rule of divine punitive justice. That sin is of God, as it is the cause of other sins, they, also, prove from the acts of blinding, hardening, giving over to a reprobate mind, which are acts of God and are causes of sins. I answer; -- to the first, that the objection is not valid against all sins. For the first sin, committed by a creature, can not be the punishment of another sin. There are also many sins which are not, in fact, the causes of other sins; for God may so administer and dispense the fall and the sins of His creatures, as that they may result in good, that is a greater odium against sin, and a more diligent solicitude and anxiety to guard their own steps. Therefore many sins, contrary to this objection, come to partake of an opposite character, by the permission of God, and in no respect by His efficiency. It will be said, in reply, that there are, nevertheless, many sins which must be considered in those three respects: of these at least, it may be proper to say, that in the last two respects they have God, as their cause and author. I answer secondly, that there is no act or sin, which has, at the same time, the relation of guilt, of punishment, and of the cause of another sin, if these things may be correctly and strictly considered. I confess that this is usually said, and is common with many who treat of this subject.

I will prove my assertion, first by argument, then by presenting examples of blinding and hardening. That no act at the same time, sin and punishment, is certain, since sin is voluntary, punishment is involuntary; sin is action, punishment is passion; by punishment sin is brought into subjection, but sin is not brought into subjection by sin; but by punishment, I say, differing from sin or guilt, not in relation only, but in the thing and subject which is the act. When this is said by learned men, a reason ought to be assigned for this opinion. I acknowledge it; but let us consider the sense in which this is said and understood by them. They say that sin is the punishment of sin, because, on account of previous sin, God permits the sinner to commit another sin, and, indeed, suspends some of His own acts, and performs others, in which case the creature will sin of his own wickedness, and will commit other sins, on account of which he deserves greater punishment and condemnation, and thus, as sin deserves greater punishment, it is said to be the punishment of sin by a metonymy of cause and effect. In this sense they understand their own declaration, or it can not be sustained. But that no sin is, at the same time, guilt and the cause of another sin, is also true, if it may be rightly understood; that is, a proximate and immediate cause. It is, indeed, the meritorious cause of another sin, that is, it deserves that God should afterwards suspend some act, and perform other acts, which being performed, he will, of his own wickedness, as said before, commit some sin; it is also the preparatory cause of the perpetration of other sins: for by sin the conscience is wounded, desire for prayer, and confidence in it are destroyed, a habit of sinning is prepared, a power over the sinner is granted to Satan, from which an easy lapse into other sins readily follows; yet it is not the proximate and immediate cause of another sin. "It is nevertheless a cause," some may say, "though remote and meritorious." What then? By this very distinction the whole force of the objection is destroyed. By it, God is made the cause of some acts, the creature will, of His own wickedness, deservedly add another sin to the former, and God is absolved from the charge of being the cause of sin, which deserved that He should perform those acts of sin, as it is the cause of another sin. For the action of the Deity intervenes between the sin, which is the cause of another sin, and that consequent sin. In that objection, however, it was inferred that God is the cause of sin, in that He is the occasion of the second sin. That error arises from the confusion and the inaccurate consideration of those acts. Sin, in the relation of guilt, is first in order, then follows demerit or conviction to punishment, from the justice of God; which is the act of God, who punishes that sin by merited desertion, and blindness. But "blindness," you say, "is sin or guilt, and the punishment of previous sin, and the cause of subsequent sin, and God is the cause of blindness." The truth of what has been previously said may be demonstrated in this example. That blindness, judicially produced by God, is correctly said to be the punishment of previous sin, and can, if rightly understood, be said to be the cause of consequent sins, that is, by a removal of restraining grace, and by the performance of some acts, from which it will follow that the creature, thus blinded and left, will, of his own wickedness, commit sin. But that blindness is not sin or guilt. A distinction is to be made between the blindness as the act of God to which man is judicially subjected, and the blindness of man himself by which he renders his own mind hard and obstinate against God, which is the act of man, produced by wickedness and obstinate pertinacity. These acts indeed concur, but do not coincide, nor are they one single action, made up of the efficiency of those concurrent actions, which together make up one total cause of that act, which is called blindness. Learned men often speak in such a manner, I grant, but not with sufficient distinctness; and perhaps in a sense which agrees with my explanation, and is not contrary to it. For they use the term blindness, in a complex and indistinct manner, for the act and its result, or the work and its effect, which is, thereby, produced in the person made blind, which may be called passive blindness, produced by that active blindness. Of blindness, thus confusedly and indistinctly considered, it may be said that it is sin, the punishment of sin, and the cause of sin, but this is not at variance with my opinion, for I deny that God is the cause of that blindness, so far as it is sin and guilt. Active blindness—as we now term it, by way of distinction—which is produced by a man, making himself blind, is sin, for it is a great crime to harden one's own mind against God. Active blindness, which proceeds from God, is the punishment of previous sin, by which the sinner has merited to himself desertion, and privation of grace. The active blindness, which is from man, and that, which is from God, concur to the same effect, which is passive blindness, which is, properly, punishment. Finally, the active blindness of man, blinding himself, and that of God, blinding man, is the cause of the accumulation of other sins with those previously committed, by the blinded sinner, but in the mode of which I have spoken. I answer, that if it is true that one and the same act is sin or guilt, the punishment of sin, and the cause of subsequent sin, then it can not be true that God is its cause, according to the last two relations, and not according to the first, for a twofold reason. First, this distinction of relation can not effect that God should be the cause of one thing, and not of another, in fact, joined to it, unless in that mode, which will be hereafter explained, which they exclude from this subject, who say that blindness, produced by God, is sin, and the cause of sin. These respects are useful to a mind, intelligent and able to discriminate between things most intimately connected, which constitutes actually and numerically, one thing, but considered in different relations, they can not have place in actual efficiency, the limit of which is real existence. God inflicts punishment on a person who is a sinner, and His creature; the act of infliction does not distinguish the creature from the sinner, but the mind of Him, who punishes, makes the distinction, for it knows how to punish the creature, not as such, but as sinful. This error is frequently committed, that relations are carried further than their nature may permit. Secondly, because of those three relations, order, nature, and causality, the former is that in which sin is considered as guilt, the latter two are those in which it is considered as punishment, and the cause of consequent sin. God is the first cause of all effects, which He produces with or by His creatures; but, in this case, He will be a subsequent cause, for He will produce, in the relation of subsequent respects, an act, which the creature produces in the relation of prior respect, which is absurd, and inverts the order of causality and efficiency, which exists between first and second causes. There may, indeed, be supposed to exist a concurrence, which we shall hereafter explain; but they, who say that the blindness, inflicted by the Deity, is the cause of consequent sins, and at the same time a sin, deny that this concurrence has any place here. These things, indeed, I have thought, ought to be explained, somewhat fully, on account of the difficulty of the subject itself, and of preconceived opinions.

Let us proceed to the second objection, which we thus set forth, according to the meaning of its authors. "In sin there are two things, the act and its illegality, or violation of law. As an act, it is positive; as a violation of law, it is privative: the latter has the will of the creature for its cause; the former must necessarily be referred back to the first cause, and, in this relation, God is the cause of that act which, in respect to man, or as it proceeds from man, is sin. Therefore it is wrong to remove the act, which is not performed by a man without sin, from the divine will and efficiency, and attribute it to the divine permission, since that act, as such, belongs to efficiency, but as it violates law, it belongs to the divine permission. I reply, first, that it can not be said truly, and universally of all sin, that in it there are these two things, namely, the act and the violation. For, sometimes, it is the act itself which is prohibited, and sometimes, not the act itself, but some circumstance in reference to the act. Thus the eating of the fruit of the tree of knowledge of good and evil was prohibited, not any circumstance connected with it; and, therefore, the act of eating, itself, was undue, unlawful and inordinate; it was, indeed, in itself a deviation from the rule, that is, from the law which forbade the eating. That act, of and in itself, apart from the law, is a natural act and has, in itself, no inordinacy. But after the enactment of a law which prohibits eating, that act, can not be considered as good, agreeably to its natural relations, as there is added to it the fact of inordinacy, on account of which it ought to be omitted; for it is then to be omitted, of itself and on its own account, because it is forbidden by the divine law, and because to eat is to sin, the whole inordinacy consisting in the fact that the act of eating, referred to, has a place in the number and series of human actions, which place it ought not, on any account, to have, and the number of which ought not to increase, but it ought to be wholly omitted, and to be kept under restraint, and to be never carried into effect.

The simile of a lame horse, which very many adduce to illustrate this matter, is not applicable to an act, which is prohibited by law. For in lameness there is the gait, and there is the limping or irregular gait; and a defect is added to the gait or motion on account of weakness or injury of a leg, which defect, though it may not, in fact be separated from the gait itself, can, nevertheless, be readily distinguished from it; and hence it may occur that the same horse, after the cure has been effected, can walk properly, and so lameness will be separated from his gait. But in the eating of the forbidden fruit, it was not the eating and the defect of eating, which was forbidden, but the eating itself, wholly and solely, had the relation of sin, because it was committed contrary to the law. That simile would be applicable in sin, which is committed against a law which prescribes the act itself, but prohibits some circumstance of the act; which sin consists in the fact that an act, good, according to, and prescribed by the law, is performed in a manner, which is not right, as when alms are given to a poor man, from ambition and pride, that he, who bestows them, may appear unto men to be liberal and a lover of the poor, and even religious. That act is good and may be illustrated by the gait, but the defect in it is like the lameness produced by disease or injury, and causes the act to limp, and to be displeasing to God, yet it is not to be omitted, but to be performed, only in a due and right manner, all defectiveness being avoided and omitted, which, rightly and in fact, can and ought to be separated from it. I acknowledge that the question or objection is not satisfied by that answer; for some one may affirm, that, "eating is nevertheless, a positive act, and, therefore, has an existence, though forbidden, and since all existence has God as its cause, God also is the cause of that act of eating; and so, also, of other positive acts, though they may be committed against a prohibitory law; and consequently, sin, as an act can not be removed from the efficiency of God."

I reply, that I, by no means, take from the efficiency of God an act, which is not perpetrated by the creature without sin; indeed, I openly confess that God is the cause of all acts, which are perpetrated by His creatures, but I desire this only that the efficiency of God should be so explained as not to derogate any thing from the freedom of the creature, and not to transfer the fault of his sin to God; that is, to show that God may, indeed, be the effector of the act, but only the permitter of the sin; and that God may be at once the effector and permitter of one and the same act. This subject is of most difficult explanation, yet we may make some effort towards its elucidation.

I remark, then, that God is, either mediately or immediately, the cause of an act which proceeds from a creature. He is the mediate cause, when He exerts an influence upon the cause and moves it to cause the act. He is the immediate cause, when He exerts an influence on the act and, with the creature, is the whole cause of that act. When God moves the creature to cause anything, since the creature, as the second and subordinate cause, is determined by the first moving cause to a particular act, which has its form from the influence and motion of the Deity, that act, whatever may be its character, can not be imputed, as a fault to the creature; but if the act can be called sin, God is necessarily the cause and the author of that sin. But since the latter idea can never be true, it is certain that the explanation can not be found in that mode of the mediate action of the Deity, how God is the cause of the act, which is not performed by man without sin, and the permitter of the sin. When God is the immediate cause of an act, which proceeds from a creature, then the second cause, if it is free, and we are now treating of free agents has it in its own power either to exert its influence in the act, or suspend that influence so that the act may not take place, and to exert its influence so that one act, rather than another, may be performed. Hence it follows, that, when a second cause has freely exerted its influence to produce all act, and when, by its particular influence, it has determined the general influence of God to this particular act, and has disposed the form of the act, the second cause is responsible, and the act may be deservedly called "sin" in respect to the second cause; but God is free from responsibility, and, in respect to Him, the act can not be called sin.

The concurrence and influence of the Deity bestows nothing upon the free will of the creature, by which he may be either inclined, or assisted, or strengthened to act, and it does not in the first act, but in the second, dispose the will, and therefore it presupposes, in the will, whatever is necessary for acting, even without the exception of the concurrence of the Deity itself. Though the will of the free creature may not, in reality, have that concurrence, except when he puts forth activity, yet he has it in his own power before he performs that which is prepared for, and imposed upon him. If this is not so, the will can not be said to have the act in its own power, or in its proximate capability; nor can the cause of that act be called moral but natural only, and therefore necessary, to which sin can, by no means, be attributed.

In this way that difficulty is solved, and it is shown how God can be the cause of an act, which can not be performed by the creature without sin, so that neither He may be the author of sin, nor the creature be free from sin; that He, indeed, may be only the permitter of sin, but the creature may be the proper cause of sin. For God leaves to the choice of a free second cause the disposition of its own influence to effect any act, and when the second cause is in the very movement and instant of exerting its influence, God, freely and of His own choice, joins His influence and universal concurrence to the influence of the creature, knowing that, without His influence, the act neither could nor would be produced. Nor is it right that God should deny His concurrence and influence to the creature, even if He sees that the influence of the creature, exerted to effect an act, which he is just ready to perform, is joined to sin, and is committed contrary to His law. For it is right that the act, which He left to the freedom of man, when the law had not yet been enacted by which that act was afterwards forbidden, should be left to the freedom of the same creature, after the enactment of the law. A law would be imposed, in vain, on an act, for the performance of which God should determine to deny His own concurrence. In that case, it could not be performed by the creature, and therefore no necessity would exist that its performance should be forbidden to the creature by a law. Besides God, in His legislation, designed to test the obedience of His creature; but this He could not do, if He determined to deny, to the creature, His concurrence to an act, forbidden by law; for apart from that concurrence, the creature can not perform that act. Why should God, in reference to an act, to which, as naturally good, determined not to deny His concurrence, deny that same concurrence, when the act has been made morally evil by the enactment of law; when He declares and testifies in His own legislation, that He wills that the creatures should abstain from that act, in that it is morally evil, and not in that it is an act, in its natural relations. But He wills that the creature should abstain from the act, as evil, when He imposes upon him a prohibitory law, to which he is bound to yield obedience. When, however, He determines to deny His concurrence, He wills that, in its natural relations, it shall not be performed by the creature. For the former is a kind of moral hindrance, the latter is a natural hindrance; the former, by the enactment of law; the latter, by the denial of concurrence; -- by the enactment of law, in view of which that act can not be committed without sin, and by denial of concurrence, in view of which the act can not be committed at all. If the latter impediment, that of the denial of concurrence, exists, there is no necessity that the other, that of the enactment of law, should be interposed.

It is apparent, from this explanation, that the creature, committing sin, commits it in the full freedom of his will, both as to its exercise, and as to the form of the action, to which two things the whole freedom of the will is limited. Freedom, as to its exercise, is that by which the will can put forth, and suspend volition and action. Freedom, as to the form of action is that, by which, it wills and performs this rather than that action. We will show that freedom, in both respects, exists, in another manner, in the act of sin, which the creature performs with the general concurrence of God. In the act of sin, its existence and its essence are to be considered. The existence of the act depends on the freedom of the will, as to its exercise. That its essence should be of this rather than of that character—that it should be rather a forbidden act than one not forbidden, against this precept rather than against that, depends on the freedom of the will as to the form of action. That the act should exist, the creature effects by its own free influence, by which it wills to do rather than not to do, though not without the influence of the divine concurrence, uniting itself freely to the influence of the creature at its very first moment and instant. But that the act should be of one character rather than of another, the second cause effects, freely determining its own act to a certain direction, to this rather—than to that—that it should be one thing rather than another. If any one says that, on this supposition, the divine concurrence is suspended on the influence of the creature, I reply, that this does not follow from my statements. Though God may not concur unless the creature wills to exert his influence, yet the exertion of that influence depends purely, on his own freedom; for he can omit that exertion.

It may be clear from this, how God is both the permitter of sin, and the effector of an act, without which the creature can not commit sin; the permitter of sin, in that He leaves to the creature the free disposition of His own influence; the effector of an act, in that He joins His own concurrence to the effort of the creature, without which the act could not be, at all, performed by the creature.

If any one takes exception to this distinction, on account either of the difficulty of the subject or of the defect of my explanation, and so contends that efficiency in sin is in some respect to be ascribed to God, because He is the effector of that act, I wish that he would consider that God can, on the same principle, be called the permitter of the act, because He is the permitter of the sin, and, indeed, far more justly, since, in His own prohibition, He declares that He is unwilling that the act—already permitted, not only to the freedom and the ability of the creature, but also to its right and power—should be performed by the creature; by which prohibition, that act is removed from the divine efficiency, only so far as that ought to avail to deter the will of the creature from performing that act; and, on the other hand, the efficiency of that act is, so much the more, to be ascribed to the freedom of the will, as it can be understood to have, more vehemently willed that which is forbidden by the divine law. But, in whatever way that subject may be explained, it is carefully to be observed, both that God be not made the author of sin, and that the act itself be not taken away from the efficiency of God; that is, that the whole act, both as an act merely, and as sin, may be rightly made subject to the providence of God—as an act to efficient providence, as a sin to permissive providence. If, however, there shall still be an inclination in the other direction, there will be less error, if the act is taken away from the divine efficiency, as an act, than if sin is attributed to the efficiency of God, as a sin. For it is better to take away an act from the Deity, which belongs to Him, than to attribute to Him an evil act, which does not belong to Him; so that a greater injury is charged on God, if He is said to be the cause of sin, than if He is regarded as an unconcerned spectator of an act.

ALLEGATION 4

"WE TEACH THAT THE GREATEST PART OF THE HUMAN RACE ARE LEFT WITHOUT CHRIST AND WITHOUT ANY SAVING GRACE."

The meaning of this allegation, is that God, by His own eternal and immutable decree, has determined, of His mere will to elect some, but to reprobate others, and those the more numerous. Since the elect can not be brought unto salvation, as having become sinners in Adam, unless satisfaction to the justice of God, and expiation for sin should have been made, therefore, God determined to give his own Son to them, as Mediator, Reconciler, and Redeemer, who should assume human nature, for them only, should die for their sins only, should reconcile them only to the Father, should meritoriously obtain the Holy Spirit and eternal redemption for them only, should offer, according to His purpose, grace to them only, should call them, only, to faith, and should bestow, by an internal vocation, faith on them, only, &c., to the exclusion, from all these things, of those whom He reprobated, so that there should be to them no hope of salvation in Christ, because God had willed from eternity that Christ should not be made man for them, or die for them, apart from any consideration of their unbelief; and when He arranged that the gospel should be preached also to them, it was not done for their benefit, but because the elect were intermingled with them, who, by that preaching, were according to the decree of God, to be led to faith and salvation. You should, indeed, have answered whether you admitted that allegation as made truly against your doctrine, or whether you think your doctrine to be not amenable to it. You seem to admit that this is truly your sentiment. It ought, indeed, to be admitted by you, if you wish to be consistent with yourself, and to speak in harmony with your doctrine.

You answer, then, that what is charged against your doctrine in that allegation, is not a crime, but let us see how you show and prove this. First, you say that "it is not hard that they should be left without Christ," because "they might at the first, in Adam, have received saving grace, righteousness, and a life of blessedness, together with the ability to persevere in the same, if they had only willed it." I affirm that very many persons are absolutely left without Christ, who never were, and never will be partakers of the saving grace of Christ. For the grace, bestowed on Adam and on all his posterity in him, was not the grace of Christ, which was not, at that time, necessary. But "God could," you say, "without injustice, at that time, have condemned all, and not have bestowed, on a single individual, grace through Christ. Who denies it? The point in dispute is not—whether God, when man, with all his posterity, sinned of his own fault: and became obnoxious to eternal death, was obligated to give His own Son to the world as a mediator—but whether it can be truly said that, when God willed that His own Son should become a man and die for sins, He willed it with this distinction, that he should assume, for a certain few only, the human nature which he had in common with all men; that he should suffer for only a few the death which could be the price for all the sins of all men, and for the first sin, which all committed alike in Adam; whether God purposed to proceed according to the rigor of His justice, and to the strictness of the law, and the condition made requisite in the law, with the largest part of the human race, but according to His mercy and grace with a few, according to the gospel and the righteousness of faith, and the condition proposed in the gospel; whether He proposed to impute, even to a certain few, the sin which they had personally committed in Adam, without any hope of remission. This, I assert, is the question: you reply affirmatively to this question, and, therefore, confess that the allegation is made, with truth, against your doctrine, nor can you escape by the plea, that "it is not wonderful that they should be left without Christ, since they had rejected the grace offered in Adam." Your answer has reference to the justice of the act, and the question is concerning the act itself; your answer has reference to the cause, and the question is concerning the existence of the thing, the cause of which you present. That your answer may not, to some, seem too horrible, you present, secondly, another answer, namely, "Christ may be said to have died for all," but you subjoin an explanation of this kind, which perverts the interpretation, and absolutely nullifies your apparent and verbal confession. For you add that "he did not die for all and for each equally in reference to God, in the same sense for the lost and for the elect, or efficiently on the part of God." Let us linger here, and weigh well what you say. The Scripture declares explicitly, and in plain terms, that Christ died even for those who are lost, (Rom. xiv. 15; 2 Pet. ii. 1). Not equally, you say, in respect to God. But what is the meaning of the phrase "in respect to God"? Is it the same as "according to the decree of God?" Indeed, Christ, "by the grace of God tasted death for every man" (Heb. ii. 9). By the command of God, Christ laid down his life "for the life of the world" (John vi. 51), and "for the sheep" (John x. 15). He can not, indeed, be said to have died for any man, except by the decree and the command of the Father. You will say that you do not now refer to the decree, by which God, the Father, imposed upon His Son the office and duty of expiating sins by his own death; but to the decree, by which He determined to save the elect through Christ. But I assert that the latter decree is, in its nature, subsequent to the death of Christ, and to the merit obtained by that death.

You add then, that "he died not equally for the reprobate" (you ought to use that word, and not the word "lost") "and for the elect." You consider these things in the wrong order. For the death of Christ, in the order of causes, precedes the decree of election and reprobation, from which arises the difference between the elect and the reprobate. The election was made in Christ, dead, raised again, and having meritoriously obtained grace and glory. Therefore, Christ also died for all, without any distinction of elect and reprobate. For that two-fold relation of men is subsequent to the death of Christ, pertaining to the application of the death and the resurrection of Christ, and of the blessings obtained by them. The phrase, "Christ died for the elect," does not signify that some were elected before Christ received the command from God to offer his life, as the price of redemption for the life of the world, or before Christ was considered as having died, (for how could that be, since Christ is the head of all the elect, in whom their election is sure?), but that the death of Christ secures for the elect only, the blessing which is bestowed through an application of Christ and his benefits.

Hence, also, the phrase used by the school-men, is to be understood thus, that "Christ died for all men sufficiently, but, for the elect and believers only, he died efficaciously." Your phrase, "efficiently on the part of God," is, in my judgment, irrelevant. What is the meaning of the statement—"Christ died efficiently, on the part of God. for the elect, and not for the reprobate"? This phraseology can not be used in any correct sense. I know that you wished to give the idea that the efficacy of Christ's death is applied to some and not to others. If you mean this, you ought to speak so that this might be understood to be your meaning. If your affirmation and that of the school-men, be rigidly examined, it will be seen that they can not be used without injury to the death of Christ and its merit. For they attribute sufficiency to the death of Christ, but deprive it of efficacy, when, indeed, the death of Christ is a sufficient price for the life of the world, and was efficacious for abolishing sin and satisfying God. We do not speak, you say, of the efficacy of his death, but of that of its application. The contrary, however, is clearly manifest; for you deprive of efficacy that to which you attribute sufficiency—and you attribute sufficiency to the death of Christ. If this, also, is examined rigidly, it will be seen that you do not even attribute sufficiency to the death of Christ. For how shall that be a sufficient price which is no price? That is not a price, which is not offered, not paid, not reckoned. But Christ did not offer himself, except for a few only, namely, the elect. Certainly, my friend, those are words and evasions, sought for the purpose of avoiding the stroke of truth.

You, then, bring some passages of Scripture to prove your proposition. "Christ says to the reprobate, 'I never knew you,' therefore, he never acknowledged them for his own." What then? Did he, therefore, not die for them? That certainly, is an inconclusive argument. For it is necessary that, by his own death, he should redeem unto himself those whom he was to have for his own: but those whom he has not as his own, he did not know as his own, or acknowledge for his own. But, as he acknowledges some for his own, it is not sufficient that he should die for them, and, by the right of redemption, prepare them for himself, but also should make them his own in fact, by an efficacious application of blessings. Hence, it is apparent that there are, here, the fallacies of ignoratio elenchi and causa non causa. The other argument which you adduce is not more valid. "If all and each are efficaciously redeemed, all and each are also reconciled to God; -- But all are not reconciled, nor do all receive the remission of their sins; -- Therefore, not all and each are efficaciously redeemed." What if I should say that I concede all this, if it is only correctly understood, and that your conclusion does not belong to the question? You confound the result with the action and passion, from which it exists. For the offering of Christ in death, is the action of Christ, by which he obtained redemption. You then confound the obtainment of redemption with its application: for to be efficaciously redeemed, means to be a partaker of the redemption, made and obtained by the death of Christ. You confound, also, reconciliation made with God by the death and sacrifice of Christ, with the application of the same, which are plainly different things. For "God was, in Christ, reconciling the world unto himself, and hath committed unto us the word of reconciliation" ('2 Corinthians v. 19). We are said to have been "reconciled to God, when we were enemies" (Rom. v. 10), which cannot be understood of the application of reconciliation. But your statement—"remission of sins and satisfaction belong together," is not, in all respects true. For satisfaction precedes, as consisting in the death and obedience of Christ, but remission of sins consists in the application of that satisfaction by faith in Christ, which may possibly, not actually follow the satisfaction which has been rendered. Christ, indeed, obtained eternal redemption and the right to remit sins, but sin is not remitted except to those who really believe in Christ. The remark of Prosper is entirely in accordance with these statements. For, by the word redemption, he understands the act both in its accomplishment and in its application. This your second argument, therefore, aside from the purpose, and, on account of confusedness and equivocation, proves nothing.

Your third argument is also inconclusive. For, even if the antecedent is granted, the consequent does not follow. It is true that "Christ gave himself, that he might obtain, from the Father, the right of sanctifying those who should believe in him," and these are thus immediately joined. But, as he obtained the right, he also, in fact, used that right, by his Spirit and the application and sprinkling of his own blood, sanctifying to himself a peculiar people, and redeeming and freeing them from their own depraved condition, which right pertains to the application of the benefits, obtained for us by the death of Christ. But it does not, thence, follow that, because all do not, in fact, become partakers of that sanctification, therefore, Christ did not give himself for them as the price of redemption; for the action of Christ is confounded with its result, and the application of benefits with their obtainment.

The fourth argument labours under the same fault—that of confusedness. It is true that "the redemption, which has been accomplished, and, therefore, sonship, are destined for those who believe in Christ; "but it is necessary that the act should precede, by which Christ must obtain for us redemption and sonship, which act, in the order of causes, precedes the entire purpose of God in reference to the application of the redemption. In the fifth argument, you commit the same fallacy. For the point in dispute, is, "Did Christ die for all without any distinction of elect and reprobate?" and you present, as an argument, the assertion—"his death and the benefits of his death are not applied to all without distinction." You say that "we may grant that they are, on the part of God, freed from condemnation; yet they are not so far the recipients of grace as that sin no longer reigns in them." I reply that if you grant the former, the latter must also be conceded. For these two benefits, obtained for us by the death and resurrection of Christ—freedom from the condemnation of sin, and from its dominion—are conjoined. One can not be bestowed without the other, on any person.

You, lastly, produce some testimonies from the old writers, but they all, it rightly explained, agree with these things which we have said. For Ambrose plainly speaks of the advantage resulting from the application of Christ's passion, when he says "he did not descend for thee, he did not suffer for thee," that is, "not for thy benefit." Whence, also, I pray, does faith come to us? Is it not from the gift of the Spirit which Christ has merited for us? Therefore, the passion and the descent of Christ must have preceded our faith, and, therefore, they can not be limited by that faith. But faith is the instrument of that application. Augustine, also, treats of "deliverance" not as obtained, but as applied. Thus, also, Bernard, Haimo, and Thomas Aquinas. If any of the fathers or school-men seem, at any time, to speak differently, their words must be so explained as not to impinge the truth revealed to us in the Scripture.

Let us now look at some of the objections to your doctrine which you notice. The first is this—"The Scriptures assert that Christ redeemed the world." Why did you not use the word suffer for rather than the word redeem, so as to avoid ambiguity; especially, when the question has reference not to the application of Christ's passion, but to that passion itself, and the death of Christ. But let us consider the objection, as it is presented by yourself. I say that a distinction is to be made between redemption obtained and redemption applied, and I affirm that it was obtained for the whole world, and for all and each of mankind; but that it was applied only to believers, and to the elect. First, I show that if it was not obtained for all, faith in Christ is, by no right, required of all, and if it was not obtained for all, no one can be rightly blamed, on account of rejecting the offer of redemption, for he rejects that which does not belong to him, and he does it with propriety. If Christ did not die for all, then he can not be the judge of all. The latter idea is conceded, on both sides. But I say that, in the remark of Augustine, the subject discussed is the application of reconciliation, and actual salvation.

The second objection is—God "will have all men to be saved, and to come unto the knowledge of the truth." But you do not subjoin the conclusion. It may, indeed, be deduced from the antecedents. But it is of much importance, how that conclusion is formed. For one concludes, "therefore all men universally, will be saved, and will come to the knowledge of the truth. For who hath resisted his will?" Another infers "then there is no predestination, according to which God wills that some should believe and be saved, and that some, being alien from the faith, should be condemned, and this, also, from His decree." A third deduces this conclusion:

"Therefore, there can be no will of God by which He absolutely and without reference to sin in man, wills that any should be condemned and not come to the knowledge of the truth." The first conclusion is not legitimate. For they are not always saved, whom God wills to be saved. The second, also, can not be deduced from the text. But of the third, I think that it can be said with truth that it can and must be deduced from those words. I give a plain and perspicuous reason. No one can be condemned for rejecting the truth unless he has been called to it, either in his own person, or in the person of his parents, grand-parents, great grand-parents, &c. No one is called to it, if God does not will that he should come to it; and all men who shall be condemned, will be condemned because "light has come into the world, and men loved darkness rather than light" (John iii. 19).

Let us consider your reply. You present this in a four-fold manner. The first is this: "The word all does not embrace all the descendants of Adam, but is used in reference to men in the last age of the world." This, indeed, is truly said, the circumstance of this passage being considered, which treats of the amplitude of the grace exhibited, in the New Testament, in Christ; but the truth of the same words extends itself even further. For that is the perpetual will of God, and had its beginning in the first promise of the blessed Seed, made in paradise. That God did indeed suffer the Gentiles to walk in their own ways, does not contravene this declaration. For they were alienated from the covenant of God, and deprived of the promises by their own fault—by their own fault, committed either in themselves or their ancestors. It ought, then, to have been conceded by you that God willed, through all ages, that all men, individually, should come to the knowledge of the truth and be saved, so far as they were embraced in the divine covenant, not, indeed, when they had in themselves, or their parents, departed from it.

Your second answer is—"God willed that all men should be saved who are saved," which, indeed, does open violence to the phraseology, and holds up to ridicule the apostle, who if that explanation is correct, presents so foolish an argument. The design of the apostle is to exhort that "prayers should be made for all men, and for all that are in authority." This reason is "this is good and acceptable in the sight of God, who will have all men to be saved, &c." It is here apparent that the word all is used, in the same sense, in the statement of the reason, as in the exhortation. Otherwise, the connection of the parts is destroyed, and there are four terms in the syllogism. But if it is intended, in the statement of the reason, to refer to all who will be saved, then it must be taken in the same sense in the exhortation also, and then the exhortation of the apostle must be understood in this sense: "I exhort that prayers and supplications be made for all who are to be saved, for God wills that all, who are to be saved, shall be saved." What is doing violence to the meaning of the apostle, if this is not? "But Augustine so explains it: "What then? We do not rest in his authority." Also, we prove this by a collation of a similar passage: "This I deny. For the passage in 1 Corinthians xv. 22, "in Christ shall all be made alive," is not similar. For the emphasis may, here, be placed on the words "in Christ," and then it will read thus: "all, who are made alive, will be made alive in Christ, and no one out of Christ." The emphasis, indeed, belongs on those words, as is apparent from the contrast of the other member, "as in Adam all die." But in the passage, in the first epistle to Timothy, there is nothing similar to this. For it says, "God wills that all men should be saved," in which that repetition and reduplication can not have any place. Does not the Scripture teach that we must pray for all, even for those who are not to be partakers of salvation? So far, at least, as it is not evident to us whether they have or have not sinned unto death; for those of the former class, and them only, prayer is not to be made.

Your third answer is that "the phrase means not single individuals of classes, but classes of single individuals;" as if the apostle had said "God wills that some of all classes, states and conditions of men should be saved." This answer you defend from the diverse use of the word all, which is taken, at one time distinctively, at another collectively, which is, indeed, true, although you have interchanged the distributive and collective use of the word. For all the animals were, in a distributive sense, in Noah's ark, and all men, in a collective sense. Even if the use of that word is two-fold, it does not thence follow that it is used in one and not in the other sense, for it can be used in either. In this passage, however, it is used not for classes of single individuals, but for single individuals of classes; for the will of God goes out towards single individuals of classes, or to single human beings. For he wills that single men should come to the knowledge of the truth and be saved, that is, all and each, rich and poor, noble and ignoble, male and female, &c. As the knowledge of the truth and salvation belong to single human beings, and is, in fact, prepared, by predestination, for the salvation of single individuals, not for classes, and is denied, by reprobation, to single individuals, not to classes, so, also, in the more general providence of God, antecedent, in the order of nature, to the decree of predestination and reprobation, the divine will has reference to single individuals of classes, not to classes of single individuals. For providence, having reference to classes of single individuals, pertains to the preservation of the species, but that, which refers to single individuals of classes, pertains to the preservation of individuals. But that providence which ministers salvation and the means necessary for salvation, pertains to the preservation and salvation of individuals. Besides, if this passage is to be understood to refer to classes, then the apostle would not have said "for all in authority," but "for some, at least, in eminent positions," but he openly says "that prayers should be made for single individuals in that relation." Nor is there any necessity of any other acceptation of that word, for there is no need of that plea to avoid this consequence, "therefore, all and each are saved." For the salvation of all would not follow from the fact that God wills that any one should be saved, by his will, approving and desiring the salvation of all and of each, but it would follow, if He, by an efficacious volition, saves all and each. To this effect, also, is the distinction made by Damascenus, which we will examine at somewhat greater extent.

Your fourth answer is, "Paul here speaks according to the judgment of charity, not according to the judgment of secret and infallible certainty." This is really absurd, unless you refer to the charity of God. For Paul here treats of the will of God to which he attributes this volition, that He wills the salvation of all men; not of His will according to which He earnestly desires the salvation of all. But it is, in the mean time, true that God does not will this infallibly or certainly, so that it can not, or at least will not happen otherwise. This, however, is not said by those, who use this passage to sustain a positive contrary to your sentiment. It is settled, then, that from this passage it is a fair inference that "God can not be said, without reference to sin in men, to will that any should err from the truth, or should not come to the truth, and should be condemned."

We may now consider the distinction, made by Damascenus, in which He regards the will of God, as antecedent and consequent. It is of special importance to observe, when the antecedent and consequent wills are spoken of relatively, in what relation they receive those appellations. This relation is that of the will to the will, or rather that of the divine volition, to the divine volition, the former as antecedent, the latter as consequent—for God puts forth one volition before another, in the order of nature, though not of time—or it is that of the divine volition to the preceding or subsequent volition or act of the creature. In respect to the latter, the divine will is called antecedent; in respect to the former, consequent. But these two relations do not greatly differ, though I think that the relation to the volition and act of the creature, either subsequent to or preceding the divine volition, was the cause of the distinction. If we consider the order of volitions, which God wills previous to any act or volition of the creature, we shall see, in that order, that there are some antecedent, some consequent volitions, yet all previous to any act and volition of the creature. And, since that volition, which exists of some cause in us, may be called consequent, it is certain that the distinction was understood by Damascenus, its first author, in the sense that it was in relation to the act or volition of the creature.

The will of God, then, may be called antecedent, by which He wills anything in relation to the creature (our discussion, a rational creature) previous to any act of the creature whatever, or to any particular act of it. Thus He willed that all men and each of them should be saved. The consequent will of God is that, by which He wills any thing in reference to a rational creature after any act or after many acts of the creature. Thus He wills that they, who believe and persevere in faith, shall be saved, but that those, who are unbelieving and impenitent, shall remain under condemnation. By His antecedent will, He willed to confirm and establish the throne of Saul forever; by His consequent will, He willed to remove him from the kingdom, and to substitute in his place a man better than he. By his antecedent will Christ willed to gather the Jews as a hen gathers her chickens; by his consequent will, he willed to scatter them among all nations.

You, indeed, approve this distinction, but do not approve the example of antecedent will, presented by Damascenus himself. Let us examine the reasons, in view of which you form this decision.

First you say, "It would follow from this that there is in the Deity weakness and limited power." I deny this sequence; for the divine power is not the instrument of the divine inclination, or desire, or velleity, but of free volition, following the last decision of the divine wisdom, though God may use His power to obtain what He desires within proper limits. Nor is it true that, if one desires or seriously wills any thing, he will effect the same in any way whatever, but he will do it in those ways, in which it is suitable that he should effect it. A father may desire and seriously propose that his son should obey him, but he does not violently compel him to obedience, for it would not be obedience. A father seriously wills that his son should abstain from intoxication, yet he does not confine him in a chamber, where he can not become intoxicated. A father seriously wills to give the paternal inheritance to his son; and by a consequent volition, namely, one that follows the contumacious and obstinate wickedness of the son, wills to disinherit him, nor yet does he do all things, within the scope of his power, that his son may not sin. For, it was possible for the father to keep his son bound and lettered with chains, that he might not be able to sin. But it was as suitable that the father should not use that mode of restraint, as it was to will the patrimony to his son.

The illustration taken from the merchant desiring to save his goods, yet throwing them into the sea is well adapted to its purpose. God seriously wills that all men should be saved, but compelled by the pertinacious and incorrigible wickedness of some, He wills that they should suffer the loss of salvation—that they should be condemned. If you say that the analogy fails, because God could correct their wickedness, but the merchant can not control the winds and the waves, I reply that it may, indeed, be possible to absolute omnipotence, but it is not suitable that God should in that way correct the wickedness of His creatures. Therefore God wills their condemnation because He does not will that His own righteousness should perish.

They, who object that this will may be called conditional, do not say all which might be said, yet they say something. Not all, because this inclination by which God desires the salvation of all men and of each, is simple, natural, and unconditional in God. Yet they say something, since it is true that God wills the salvation of all men, on the condition that they believe, for no will can be attributed to God, by which He may will that any man shall be saved in a sense, such that salvation will, certainly and infallibly, come to him, unless he is considered as a believer, and as persevering in faith even to the end. Since, however, that conditional volition may be changed into an absolute one, in this manner—God wills that all believers should be saved, and that unbelievers should be condemned, which, being absolute, is always fulfilled, this volition may be said not to pertain to this distinction of the will. For, in that volition, He wills nothing to His creature but He wills that these two things, faith and salvation, unbelief and condemnation, should indissolubly cohere. Yet, if it seems proper for any one to consider this an example of antecedent volition, I will not contradict him, yet the application is only by a volition, consequent on the act of faith and perseverance, of unbelief and impenitence.

Your conclusion that "the will of God must be in suspense until the condition is fulfilled, and that the first cause is dependent on second causes," is not valid. For, concerning the former part, I remark that inclination in God is natural towards His own creature, whether the man believes or not. For that inclination does not depend on faith, and uncertainty can not be attributed to the will of Him who, in His infinite wisdom; has all things present to himself, and certainly foreknows all future events, even those most contingent. Nor is the first cause, consequently, dependent on second causes, when any effect of the first cause is placed, in the order of nature, after an effect of the second cause, as that effect, consequent in order, belongs to the mere will of the first cause. It is absurd to say that the condemnation of those, who perish, depends on themselves, even if they would not perish unless by their own demerit. For they willed to merit perdition, and not to perish, that is, they willed to sin and not to be punished. Therefore that punishment depends on the mere and free will of God, yet it can inflict it only on sinners, the operation of power being suspended by justice, agreeably to which that power ought to be exercised. It is no more a valid conclusion that, by this distinction, the free choice of faith or unbelief is attributed to men. For it is in entire harmony with that condition that no one has faith except by the gift of God, though there can be no doubt that man has the free choice not to believe.

You say, secondly—"this conditional will of God is inactive because it belongs to infinite power, and because He can do whatever He will." But it is not suitable that He should use His infinite power to effect that, to which He is borne by natural desire, and it is useful for man, that this will of God should be presented to him as conditional, indeed, rather than as absolute, as was previously said; for it seems as an argument to persuade him to believe. For if he wishes to be saved he must believe, because God has appointed that men shall be saved only through faith.

Your third reason, referring to angels, can be made doubtful by the relation of the antecedent, and even if this is conceded, the consequent does not follow. For the relation of angels and of men is not the same. I am, indeed, fully of the opinion that it is most true that God, by antecedent volition, willed that all and each of the angels should be saved, but only in a due mode and order. Three divine volitions in reference to angels may be laid down in order: the salvation of angels, the obedience of angels, the condemnation of angels. God wills the first from love for His creatures; the second from love for righteousness and the obedience due to Him from His creatures, and, indeed, in such a sense, that He more strongly wills that the second should be rendered to Himself, than the first to His creatures; the third He wills from the same love for justice, whose injury He can not leave unpunished, since punishment is the sole mode of correcting disorder.

Your statements, under your fourth reason, are correct, "and God might will that all sinful men as such should be condemned," if He had not from love towards men determined to lay their sins on His Son, to this end that all who should believe in him, being freed from their sins, should obtain the reward of righteousness. It may indeed be said that God willed that all sinners, as such, should be condemned; but not all sinners are, in fact, condemned, because believers, though they have sinned, are considered not as sinners, but as righteous in Christ.

Fifthly, you say that "the antecedent will of God is absolute." What then? I do not wish to hinder you from regarding the antecedent will in your own way, different from the sentiment of Damascenus. You should, however, consider that you are not then arguing against him. But who has ever defined absolute will—"that which can not be resisted"? Absolute will is that which is unconditional. For example, God willed absolutely that Adam should not eat of the forbidden tree; yet he did eat of that tree. The will, which can not be resisted, is called efficacious. It is not allowable to arrange things defined, and their definitions, according to our own choice. "But," you may say, "it is not possible to resist the antecedent will." I deny it. You assert, as proof, that "the will, referred to in Romans 9, is antecedent will, and that it can not be resisted." It is for you to prove that assertion. The very statement declares, since the subject, in that passage, is the will of God, by which He hardens, and has mercy, which are divine effects, following acts of the creature which are sinful, called sin, that the will, here spoken of, is consequent not antecedent.

Another method, which you use to prove the same thing, is equally weak. For, it is not true that "God, simply and absolutely, wills that some should believe and persevere, and others be deserted, either not believing or not persevering." He does not will to desert them, unless they desert themselves; and He is even gracious to those, who do not think of Him. The argument from the event is futile. For some things occur by the will and the efficiency of God, some by His permission. Therefore it can not be concluded from any event that God willed it. But it has been previously shown how an event may take place, not because God may be unwilling to prevent it; though it would not happen, if God should will efficaciously to prevent it. Therefore that conclusion can not be thus deduced. It is, indeed, true that the reason can not be given why God should afford to one nation the means of salvation, and not to another, why he should give faith to one man, and not to another, which facts may not be resolved into his will. Yet it is not thence concluded, and it is not true, that the will, in that case, is antecedent, even though it precedes all causes in men.

Sixthly, you say that the foundation being destroyed, the edifice falls. But the foundation of that opinion in reference to the antecedent will, which desires the salvation of all men and of each, is the passage in 1 Timothy ch. 2, which has been already discussed by us, and that is incorrectly understood by Damascenus. I reply, first; -- Not only that passage, but many others, most clearly sustain that distinction of the will into antecedent and consequent. "How often would I have gathered you together," is an example of antecedent, and "your house is left unto you desolate" of consequent will (Matt. xxiii. 37-38). "And sent forth his servants to call them that were bidden to the wedding," is a case of antecedent will, "they which were bidden were not worthy" and were destroyed, of consequent will. He, also, was invited, according to antecedent will, who, being afterwards found, not having on a wedding garment, was cast out, according to consequent will (Matt. xxii. 3, 7, 8, 12 and 13). According to antecedent will, the lord commanded his servants to reckon their talents, and to use them for gain for their master; by consequent will, the talent, which he had received, was taken from the wicked and slothful servant (Matt. 25). By antecedent will, the word of God was first offered to the Jews; by consequent will, the same word was taken from them and sent to others (Acts 13). The same distinction is proved by a consideration of the attributes of God; for since God is good and just, He can not will eternal death to His own creature, made in His image, without reference to sin; He can not but will eternal salvation to His creature. The immutability of God necessarily requires the same thing. For since His providence has given to all His creatures means, necessary and sufficient, by which they can attain their designed end, but the designed end of man, made in the image of God, is eternal life, it hence follows that all men are loved by God unto eternal life by antecedent will; nor can God, without a change of His own arrangement, deny eternal life unto men, without reference to sin; which denial, being consequent on the act of man, pertains to consequent will.

The views of Augustine are not opposed to Damascenus. Augustine, indeed, denies that this passage refers to efficacious will; but Damascenus makes no such assertion; he even concedes the very same thing with Augustine; -- "God does not will efficaciously to save all and each of mankind." The second interpretation of Augustine is rejected by us on sure grounds. Nor is Prosper opposed to Damascenus. For he, who says that "God wills antecedently that all men should be saved," does not deny that He can, by a consequent will, pass by many men, to whom He does not impart the grace of vocation. Thomas Aquinas, also, is, no more than the others, opposed to Damascenus, for he, in commenting on this passage, speaks of efficacious and of consequent will; and elsewhere he approves of the distinction of Damascenes, and makes use of it, in explaining the passage, which is in controversy. Hugo clearly agrees with Damascenus, if his views are suitably explained.

The third objection is this: "Whatever any one is bound to believe is true; -- But every one is bound to believe that he has been efficaciously redeemed by Christ; -- Therefore, it is true that every one has been efficaciously redeemed by the death of Christ; and, therefore, even the reprobate have been redeemed,

since they also are bound to believe this." Since this objection is of great importance, and alone sufficient, if it is true, it is necessary that we should examine it
with diligence, and at the same time your answer to it. The truth of the Major is
manifest, for truth is the foundation of faith, nor can one be, in any way, bound
to believe what is false. But you make a distinction in reference to truth and say,
that "what is true, is either: true, as to the intention of God, who obligates us to
believe, or as to the event." But that distinction is of no importance. I affirm that
what is true, according to the intention of God, must be believed according to
that intention. What is true, according to the event, must be believed according
to the event; and the intention of God can not obligate any one to believe any
thing to be true according to the event, which is not true according to the event.
In general, it is true that we are bound to believe that which is true in that mode
in which it is true, not in any other mode; otherwise, we should be bound to
believe what is false. You see, then, that there is no need of that distinction
in the Major; indeed it is most clearly evident that you, lest you should say
nothing, wished, by that minute distinction, to avoid this effective blow.

Let us consider the Minor. Its phraseology is bad, because the efficacy of
redemption pertains to its application, which is made through faith. Therefore
faith is prior to efficacious application, and the object of faith is prior to faith
itself. We may correct it, and it will read thus, "But every one is bound to believe
in Christ, the saviour, that he died for his sake, and obtained for him reconciliation and redemption before God." This is, indeed, most true. For they can not
be condemned, for want of faith, who were not bound to believe this. But here
also you use a distinction, but one which is irrelevant and ridiculous—pardon
my freedom of speech—and you do great injustice to yourself, and your own
genius, when you endeavour to disguise the plain truth, by so puerile distinctions. You say that the elect are obligated to believe, so that, by faith, they may
be made partakers of election, the reprobate are obligated to believe, so that,
by neglecting to do so, they may be without excuse, even in the intention of
God. But what is the difference whether one is bound to believe to this or that
end, provided he is only bound to believe. From which obligation to believe,
the truth of that which any one is bound to believe may afterwards be inferred.
The expression -"that they may be made partakers of election," is absurd. It
should be corrected thus—"that they may be made partakers of the blessings
prepared for them in election," or, if we wish to confine ourselves to the limits
of the objection, -- "that they may, in fact, be made partakers of the redemption
prepared for them by Christ." But the reprobate are also bound to believe for
the same reason. If it be said that they, absolutely, can not be made partakers,
I will say that, for this very reason, the reprobate are not obligated to believe.
For the end of the exercise of faith is the application of redemption, and of all

the blessings, obtained for us by the merit of Christ. The end of the command and the requirement of faith is that the application may be possible. But how absurd is the declaration that the reprobate are under obligation to believe, so that they may, by not believing, be rendered inexcusable. Unite, if you can, these things, so inconsistent, and widely distant as heaven and earth. This, however, has been before referred to. You proceed with your distinctions, and say—"one command has reference to obedience; another, to trial." But what relation has this to the present matter? For whether God commands, with the purpose that man should, in fact, obey, or with the purpose, only, of testing his obedience in the effort to execute the command, the man is always obligated to perform what God commands, as is apparent in the offering of Isaac by Abraham. Nor has this command, in the relation of that, any analogy, with what you subjoin, -- "God does not sport with men, even if He, by the preaching of the word, calls those whom He does not purpose to save." Indeed we have already said enough in reference to those and similar evasions. I will say, in a word, -- that no one can confess that he is guilty for rejecting a promise made verbally, if the mind of the promiser has determined that the promise does not belong to the person addressed; or rather if he, who verbally promises, has, by a fixed decree, determined that the promise may not and can not belong to the other person.

You present an objection, as an adversary to yourself, thus -"but you will say that it could not belong to him." Not only may that objection be urged, but also another—"How do you confute that statement, so that it may not follow from it that he is without blame, who could not receive the salvation offered to him?" You will say that such inability is voluntary, and born with us, and therefore undeserving pardon. You err here, and confound inability to keep the law, propagated in us from Adam, with inability to believe in Christ, and to accept the grace of the gospel, offered us in the word. By what deed have we brought this inability upon ourselves? Not by a deed preceding that promise; then it was by a deed following it, that is, by a rejection of the promise of the gospel; which rejection also can not be imputed to us as a fault, if we were unable to receive it at the time when the promise was first presented to us. The answer, then, amounts to nothing, because the two kinds of inability are confounded, in which is the fallacy of ignoratia elenchi, also that of equivocal use of terms.

You reply, in the second place, that "what any one is obligated to believe is true, unless he may have placed before himself an obstacle by not believing." Is this correct? Can any one place before himself an obstacle, by his own unbelief, that what he is bound to believe may not be true? Absurd. One can, by his own unbelief, place before himself an obstacle, so as not to be able afterwards to believe, that is, to deserve hardening in unbelief on account of rejecting the truth offered to him. One can, also, by his own unbelief, deserve that God should change that good will, by which He offered His Son as the redeemer, into wrath, by which He may will to punish him without remission or pardon.

Thirdly you reply that "the argument twice depends on assertion, in both parts." But who compelled you to so reduce that argument into an illogical syllogism, when it might have been put in a legitimate form and mode, in this way, "That which every one is bound to believe, is true; -- That Christ is his redeemer, who, by his own death, meritoriously obtained the divine grace, and the pardon of his sins, is what every one, called in the gospel, is bound to believe; --

Therefore it is true, that Christ is the redeemer of all, who are called by the gospel and commanded to believe. But among them are many reprobate persons. Therefore it is true that Christ is the redeemer of many reprobate persons. If we consider vocation to be that by which any one is called, either in himself or in his parents, then all men, universally, are or have been partakers of that vocation, and therefore all have been redeemed by Christ." But the form, also, in which you have put it is the same in effect, though you have so arranged the words, that they seem to have a different meaning. I see that you wrote those things with a hurried pen, without an examination of the syllogism as you have proposed it.

The fourth objection, from the fathers, is valid against you, nor do you reply in accordance with the terms of the sentiment hostile to you. The amount of the objection is this, "Christ died for all sufficiently, both as to the common nature of the human race, and as to the common cause and sufficient price of redemption." You have introduced efficacy into the argument or objection, while they, who make this objection against you, know that there is the clearest distinction between the death of Christ itself and its application. You say, "and thus far in reference to the extent and efficacy of Christ's death," when the discussion has been hitherto in reference not to its efficacy, but to its sufficiency, and its oblation and the universality of that oblation. You, now, proceed to treat of the amplitude of grace, but what you present does not much affect the point at issue. The question is not, whether all and each of the human race are, in fact, regenerated and renewed, but whether God has reprobated any man, without respect to sin as a meritorious cause; or whether He has determined absolutely to deny to any man the grace of remission and of the renewal of the Holy Spirit without reference to unworthiness, in that he has made himself unworthy of that grace—unworthiness, not resulting from original sin, but from the rejection and contempt of that offered grace. The distinction of sufficient and efficacious grace might have been well adapted to this subject, as we have also previously demonstrated. Yet there is one thing of which I may admonish you. You seem to me not correctly to deprive, of supernatural grace, the image of

God, consisting of righteousness and holiness. For though the former gift was bestowed on man at his creation and at the same time with nature itself, for so I now consider it, yet it is supernatural, and surpasses the nature of man itself, as I prove from the act of regeneration, which belongs to supernatural grace. For, since there is need of regeneration for the recovery of that righteousness and holiness, which regeneration is a supernatural act, it is necessary that the same should, originally, have been bestowed on man, by a supernatural action. I wish, also, to know what those supernatural things are which man is said to have lost in the fall, his natural qualities having become corrupt. Thus far, in reference to these things.

I think, indeed, that it is sufficiently evident from what we have thus far discussed that the view of Predestination which you have presented can not be proved by the Scriptures; that it can not be defended against strong objections; that it can not be acquitted of manifold absurdity. It ought then to be abandoned by you, and another should be sought from the Scriptures, which may harmonize with them, and may be able to sustain without injury the onset of assailant objections.

AN EXAMINATION

OF THE TREATISE OF WILLIAM PERKINS CONCERNING THE ORDER AND MODE OF PREDESTINATION

PART 2
CONCERNING PREDESTINATION

In the first part of our treatise, we have examined, most learned Perkins, your sentiment concerning Predestination, and have proved that it is, by no means, consistent with the Holy Scriptures. Another labour now remains to us, to consider how you refute the opinion which you say is different from yours.

You, briefly, set forth that opinion, diligently gathered from the writings of others, consisting of four parts—

First, "God created all and each of mankind in Adam unto eternal life."

Secondly, "He foresaw the fall."

Thirdly, "Since He is good by nature, He seriously wills that all men, after the fall, should be saved, and come to the knowledge of the truth; and therefore He wills to bestow, on all men, all the aids both of nature and of grace that they might be saved, but indefinitely, that is if they should believe. This will of God" (they say) "is predestination, and is the same with that embraced in the gospel. The rule of this will is—'He that believeth shall be saved, but he, that believeth not, shall be damned.'"

Fourthly, "Election is according to foreknowledge of future faith—to fail of which is possible, wholly, as some, or finally, as others claim, -- and Reprobation is according to foreknowledge of unbelief or contempt of the gospel."

I can not speak, with certainty, in reference to the statement of that theory, whether it agrees with the views of its authors or not, because you are silent concerning the authors from whom you have taken it: yet, with your permission, I may say that it does not seem to me to have been staged by you with sufficient correctness. Omitting the first two propositions, I think that, in enunciating the third, you make a frivolous statement, which will, I believe, be scarcely admitted by those, whose sentiment you profess to present. For what is the meaning of this—"God wills that all men should come to the knowledge of the truth, but indefinitely, if they should believe"? Is not faith itself the knowledge of the truth? Therefore the enunciation is deceptive and ridiculous—"God wills that all men should come to the knowledge of the truth, but indefinitely, if they should come to the knowledge of the truth, or he wills that all men should come to faith, if they should believe." The next sentence is of a similar character, -- "God wills to bestow, on all men, all the aids both of nature and of grace, that they may be saved, but indefinitely, if they should believe," when faith itself holds a distinguished place, among the aids of grace by which salvation is obtained. From the passage of the gospel, which is quoted, "He that believeth shall be saved," &c., it is apparent that they, whose sentiment you present, would, in this third proposition, have stated not that which you say, but this, "God determined to save, from the fallen human race, only those who should believe in His Son, and to condemn unbelievers."

The fourth proposition is not, I think, expressed sufficiently in accordance with the views of those authors. For, if I am not mistaken, their sentiment is this, --

"Election to salvation is according to foreknowledge of future faith, which God has determined to bestow of His own grace upon them by the ordinary means ordained by Himself. But Reprobation is according to foreknowledge of unbelief or contempt of the gospel, the fault of which remains, entirely, in the reprobate themselves." I admit that there may be need of some explanation of that sentiment, but you do not seem to have explained it correctly. You should have considered not one view only, adverse to your own view, but the others, also, which are opposed to it, and you should have refuted all of them, that, in this way, it might be evident that no view, other than yours, is true.

We may, now, consider in what way you refute that theory. You enumerate very many errors which, you think, result from it, which we will examine in order.

The first error; -- This either is not an error, or can not be deduced from that theory. It is not an error, if its hypothesis be correctly understood. For it is universally true that "God wills that all men should be saved, if they believe, and be condemned if they do not believe." That is, God has made a decree for electing only believers, and for condemning unbelievers. "But this," you say "is an error because it makes Election universal, and from it universal Reprobation is inferred, that is, by the added condition." But that sentiment makes neither Election nor Reprobation universal, which can not be done, but it establishes the particular Election of believers, and the particular Reprobation of unbelievers. Innumerable passages of Scripture present this Election and Reprobation. "He that believeth on the Son hath everlasting life," &c. (John iii. 36). "If ye believe not that I am he, ye shall die in your sins" (John viii. 24). "To him give all the prophets witness, &c." (Acts x. 43). "Seeing that ye put it from you, &c." (Acts xiii. 46). "He, that hath the Son, hath life; and he, that hath not the Son of God, hath not life." (1 John v. 12). That Election and Reprobation is, therefore, evidently proved by many passages of Scripture. It does not follow, from this, that; "God always acts in the same manner towards all men." For though He may seriously will the conversion and salvation of all men, yet He does not equally effect the conversion and salvation of all. "What nation is there so great, who hath God so nigh unto them, &c." (Deut. iv. 7.) "The Lord thy God hath chosen thee to be a special people unto Himself, &c." (Deut. vii. 6). "He hath not dealt so with any nation" (Psalm cxlvii. 20). "It is given unto you to know the mysteries of the kingdom of heaven" (Matt. xiii. 11). "Who, in times past, suffered all nations to walk in their own ways" (Acts xiv. 16).

But you have not distinguished, as you ought to have done, between the decree of God, by which He determined to save those who should believe in His Son, and to condemn unbelievers, and that by which He arranged with Himself in reference to the dispensation of means, ordained by Him to faith and conversion. For those decrees "I will to give life to him who believes," and "I will to give faith to this man" are distinct. Faith, in the former, holds the place of subject, in the latter, that of attribute. If you had made this distinction, you would not have laid the burden of such an absurdity on that theory.

The second error; -- I remark that the highest and absolute design of the counsels of God "is not regarded by the authors of that theory to be the communication of the divine goodness in true happiness, to be made to all men." For they say that God destined salvation for believers alone; and, though He may not impart his goodness, and life eternal to a large number of persons, as unbelievers, yet they do not say this "without reference to the divine purpose." For they assert that one part of the divine purpose is that, by which He determined to deny eternal life to unbelievers. Therefore this is alleged in vain against that opinion. "But" you say "the ultimate design of the counsels of God either has an uncertain event, or is proposed in vain,"—which ideas coincide, and should not have been expressed distinctly—if "the theory is received." Its supporters will deny that conclusion. For the ultimate design of the divine counsels is not the life of one and the death of another, but the illustration of the goodness, justice, wisdom and power of God, which He always secures. Yet allow that the eternal life of these, and the death of those is the ultimate design of those counsels: it will not follow that it has an uncertain event, or is proposed in vain, if the former is bestowed upon no one, apart from the condition of faith, and the latter awaits no one, apart from unbelief. For God by His own prescience, knows who, of His grace, will believe, and who, of their own fault, will remain in unbelief. I wish that you would consider, that certainty of an event results properly from the prescience of God, but its necessity results from the omnipotent and irresistible action of God; which may, indeed, be the foundation of the prescience of some events, but not of this event, because He has determined to save believers by grace; that is, by a mild and gentle suasion, convenient or adapted to their free-will, not by an omnipotent action or motion, which would be subject neither to their will, nor to their ability either of resistance or of will. Much less does the damnation of some proceed from an irresistible necessity, imposed by the Deity.

The third error; -- You ought, here, first to have explained what is meant when it is said that "the will of God depends on the will of man." It may be that you extend that phrase further than is proper. It is, indeed, certain that the will of God, since He is entirely independent, -- or rather His volition— can not depend on the will of man, if that phrase be correctly understood, as signifying "to receive its law or rule from the volition of man." On the other hand, it is certain that God does will some things, which He would not will, if a certain human volition did not precede. He willed that Saul should be removed from the throne; He would not have willed it, if Saul had not willed to be disobedient to God. God willed that the Sodomites and their neighbours should be destroyed; He would not have willed it, if they had not willed to persevere obstinately in their sins. God willed to give His own Son as the price of redemption for sinners;

He would not have willed it, if men had remained in obedience to the divine command. God willed to condemn Judas; He would not have willed it unless Judas had willed to persist in His own wickedness.

It is not true, indeed, that "the will of God depends on the will of man." Man would, if he could, effect that the volition of God should not follow his own antecedent volition -- that punishment should not follow sin. Indeed God is purely the author of His own volition. For He has determined in His own free-will to follow a volition of His creature, by His own volition of one kind and not of another; the faith of His creature by the remission of sins and the gift of eternal life; the unbelief of the same, by eternal damnation. This is the meaning of that opinion, which you undertake to refute, and you therefore, with impropriety charge this absurdity upon it.

You, however, make an allegation of much greater weight, against this sentiment, that "by it the creature is raised to the throne of God, the Omnipotent
Creator." How do you sustain that allegation? "It is claimed" you say "that God
wills that all men should be saved through Christ, and that many of them are
not saved because they, of themselves, refuse." But, good sir, does that doctrine
say that "God wills that all men should be saved through Christ, whether they
will or not? It does, indeed, assert that "God wills that they should be saved
and come to the knowledge of the truth" which last can not be done, apart
from their free-will. For no one can, if he is reluctant or unwilling, come to
the knowledge of the truth, that is to faith. If God should will, absolutely and
apart from any condition, that all men should be saved, and yet some should
not be saved because they refused, then it would follow that the divine will was
overcome by the human will, and the creature was raised to the throne of the
Creator. But as God wills that His own volition, joined, in due order and mode,
with the volition of man, should precede salvation, it is not wonderful that
a man, who should deny his own assent unto God; should be excluded from
salvation, by that same determination and purpose of the divine will. "But God"
you say "ordains and disposes the action of the second cause; the divine will is
not ordained by the will of the creature." Who denies these statements? That is
not the doctrine which you here oppose. Therefore, here also, you attempt, in
vain, to overthrow it by this absurdity.

You add another absurdity, as consequent on this opinion. "If that sentiment is true, then men elect themselves, by accepting the grace of God, which
is offered to them, by the common aid of grace, and are reprobated by themselves, by rejecting offered grace." Let us examine this. Even if a man should,
by accepting common grace, through the aid of common grace, make himself
worthy of Election, and another, by rejecting the same, should make himself
worthy of Reprobation, it would not follow that Election and Reprobation
belong to the man, but to God, who judges and rewards worthiness and unworthiness. It is also entirely true, in reference to Reprobation, that man is the
meritorious cause of his own damnation, and therefore of Reprobation which
is the purpose of damnation. Wherefore he may be called the maker of his own
damnation, in reference to its demerit; although God can, if He will, remit to
him this demerit. But the relation of Election is different; for it is merely gratuitous, not only unmerited, but even contrary to the demerit of man. Whether
the grace, which is offered to man, may be also received by him by the aid of
grace, which is common to him with others who reject the same grace, or by
grace peculiar to him, is perhaps in controversy. I do not, indeed, see that the
sentiment, which you have presented, has given any prejudgment concerning
that matter. It is a strange assertion that "God would not be extolled, if men

should obtain his blessing merely by the aid of common grace." Who has deserved that a blessing should be offered to him? Who has deserved that grace of any kind should be bestowed on him to the obtainment of that blessing? Do not all these things pertain to gratuitous divine favour? If so, is not God to be extolled, on account of them, with perpetual praises by those, who, having been made partakers of that grace, have received the blessing of God? Of what importance to this matter is it, whether he may have obtained the offered blessing by the aid of common or of peculiar grace, if the former, as well as the latter, has obtained the free assent of man, and it has been foreknown by God that it certainly would obtain it? You will say that, if he has apprehended the offered grace by the aid of peculiar grace, it is, then, evident that God has manifested greater love towards him than towards another to whom He has applied only common grace, and has denied peculiar grace. I admit it, and perhaps the theory, which you oppose, will not deny it. But it will assert that peculiar grace is to be so explained as to be consistent with free-will, and that common grace is to be so described, that a man may be held worthy of condemnation by its rejection, and that God may be shown to be free from injustice.

The fourth error; -- The knowledge of God, as it has relation to his creatures, may be regarded in two modes. In one, as God knows that He can make those creatures, and at the same time that they can be made in this or in that mode, that they may not only exist, but may also be able to serve this or that purpose. This knowledge, in the Deity, is natural and precedes the act or the free determination of the will, by which God has determined in Himself to make the same creatures at such a time. In the other mode, as God knows that those creatures will exist at one time or another; and, regarded in this light, it depends on the determination of the divine will. This knowledge can be referred to the acts of the creatures themselves, which God has determined either to effect or to permit. Knowledge, considered in the former mode, refers to all acts in general, which can be performed by the creatures, whether God is efficient in them, or only permits them. From this, follows the decree to effect these and those acts, and to permit them, which decree is followed by the knowledge, by which God foreknows that those acts will occur, at any particular time. This latter knowledge, which is rightly called prescience, is not, properly, the cause of things or acts. But the former knowledge, with the will, is the cause of things and acts. For it shows the mode of operating, and directs the will. The will, however, impels it to execution. It is, therefore, certain that there is no determinate or definite prescience in reference to culpable evil, unless it has been preceded by a decree to permit sin.

For without this, sin will not exist. Prescience has also reference to things future and certainly future; otherwise, either it is not prescience or it is uncertain. These things are rightly said by you, and the order, which you have made in prescience and decree, is correct; but it is not contrary to the hypothesis of the doctrine, which you oppose, but so consistent with it, that it can not be defended without this order. For it states that God, from eternity, knew that it was possible that man, assisted by divine grace, should either receive or reject Christ; also, that God has decreed, either to permit a man to reject Christ, or to co-operate with him that he may accept Christ by faith, then, that God foreknows that one will apprehend Christ by faith, and that another will reject him by unbelief. From this follows the execution of that decree, by which he determined to justify and save believers, and to condemn unbelievers, which is an actual justification of the former, and a condemnation of the latter. It is, therefore, apparent that you improperly allege such absurdity against that doctrine. Your statement that "God permits evil, always, with respect to or on account of a conjoined good," deserves notice. Those words can be understood to mean that God would permit, an evil on account of a good, conjoined with the evil, which sentiment can not be tolerated. For the good, which comes out of evil, is not conjoined with the evil, but is wonderfully brought out of evil, as its occasion, by the wisdom, goodness and omnipotence of God. For He knows how to bring light out of darkness. The knowledge, also, by which God knows that he can use evil to a good end, is also the cause of the permission of evil. For, as Augustine well says, "God, in His goodness, never permits evil unless, in His omnipotence, He can bring good out of the evil."

The fifth error; -- Here three things must be properly distinguished. The acts and sufferings of Christ, the fruits and results of those acts and suffering, and the communication and application of those fruits, Christ, by the sacrifice of his own body, by his obedience and passion, reconciled us unto God, and obtained for us eternal redemption, without any respect or distinction of elect and reprobate, of believers and unbelievers; as that distinction is, in the order of nature, subsequent. That reconciliation and redemption is applied to us, when we, having faith in the word of reconciliation, believe in Christ, and in him are justified, or regarded as righteous, and are, in fact, made partakers of redemption. Hence it appears, according to that theory, "that not many of those, to whom reconciliation and redemption is, in fact, applied, by faith, are lost." Therefore, it will not follow, from this, that "sin, Satan, the world, death, hell, are more powerful than Christ the Redeemer. For, they could not, in the first place, prevent Christ from offering himself to the Father in sacrifice, obeying the Father, and suffering death; and, in the second place, that he should not thereby obtain reconciliation and eternal redemption before God. In reference to the application of these blessings, it is true that sin, Satan, the world, and the flesh, prevent many from believing in Christ, and being made partakers of them. Yet God is not overcome by these, both because it has seemed good to God not to use His omnipotent and irresistible power to cause men to believe, and because God has determined that no one shall be a partaker of those blessings, who does not believe in Christ. It is not true that "God is mutable, according to this hypothesis." For the theory does not state that God, absolutely and simply, wills to save all men, but conditionally: and according to His own prescience, He has determined to condemn, eternally, those who will not incline themselves to this counsel. This is also, finally, performed in fact without any charge. It is not sufficient to charge absurdity on any doctrine; it must be proved, by fair inference, to be a consequence of that doctrine.

The sixth error; -- I am very certain, from the Scriptures, "that saving grace is" not "universal" in the sense that it can be said to have been bestowed on all and each of mankind in all ages. But you ought to have said that "saving grace is stated to be universal" by that doctrine. You neglect to do that, and are much engaged in proving something else. I do not, indeed, object to this, but the other thing was equally necessary to reach the object, which you had proposed to yourself. But also, at this point, there are some things deserving consideration. You do not, with sufficient accuracy, regard the distinction between "the ability to believe, if one wills," and "the ability to will to believe." For each of these, the latter, as well as the former, must, and indeed does pertain to those, who will continue in unbelief. For unless they have the ability to believe, and, indeed, the ability to will to believe, they can not rightly be punished for their unbelief. Besides one includes the other, for no one can believe, unless he can will to believe. No one believes, without the exercise of his will. But the actual exercise of the will to believe is a different thing from the ability to will to believe; the latter belongs to all men, the former to the regenerate only, or rather to those enlightened by the grace of the Holy Spirit. Hence, you see that you ought to make corrections in many particulars, and that in place of "the ability to will to believe," should be substituted "the will to believe," which is most closely connected with the act of faith, while the other is removed to the greatest distance from actual faith. The distinction between the ability, the will, and the act, is here especially necessary: but not only is it to be suitably explained, but also the causes are to be referred to, by which it may be given to men to be able to will, and to act. In your third argument, in which you prove the speciality of grace, you use the disjunctive correctly in your expression, "who had not the knowledge of faith, or did not retain it." There is a greater emphasis, in that disjunctive, than one would, perhaps, at first, think. For, if they did not "retain it," they lost it by their own fault; they rejected it, and are, therefore, to be punished for the rejection of the gospel. If they are to be punished for this, they were destined to punishment, on this account. For the cause of the decree is not different from that of its execution. You present an objection to your own doctrine, deduced from the usual saying of the school-men, "A man can not be excused for a deficiency of supernatural knowledge, from the fact that he could, and indeed would, receive it from God, if he would do so according to his own ability, and since he does not do this, he is held guilty of that deficiency. You reply to this objection, but not in a suitable manner. For it is not a sufficient distinction that "grace is given either of merit or of promise:" nor, indeed, does it agree with the contrary or opposite parts. For God can give this, without either merit (I should have preferred the word debt), or promise, but of unpromised grace, since He does and gives many things of grace, which He has not promised. Let us look at that promise, which was made immediately after the fall; it was made, neither of debt, nor of promise, but of grace preceding the promise. For God gives life "to him that worketh," of promise and of debt (Rom. iv, 3, 4). But consider whether a promise is not contained in that declaration of Christ, "Unto every one which hath shall be given," by which God pledges himself to illuminate, with supernatural grace, him who makes a right use of natural grace, or at least uses it with as little wrong as is possible for him.

The argument, from idiots and infants, is wholly puerile. For who dares to deny that many idiots and infants are saved? Yet this, indeed, does not happen to them, apart from saving grace. Some remark is to be made in reference to the passages which you cite, though it may, perhaps, be irrelevant. In Romans ix. 16, where it is said "not of him that willeth, nor of him that runneth, but of God that showeth mercy," the word "righteousness" is understood. For the discussion in that place is in reference to those, to whom righteousness is properly imputed, not to them that work, but to them that believe, that is, righteousness is obtained not by him that willeth or that runneth, but by him to whom "God showeth mercy," namely, to the believer. Matt. xiii. 11, proves that grace is not given equally and in the same measure to all, and, indeed, that the knowledge of "the mysteries of the kingdom of heaven" is not divinely bestowed on all. In the other passages, the things which are opposed, do not belong in this relation. "The Spirit breathes not upon all, but on whom he wills" (John iii. 8). What if He wills to breathe upon all? From the statement, "he breathes where he wills," it does not follow that he does not breathe on any one, unless it is proved that he does not will to breathe upon him. So, also, "The Son revealeth the Father to whom he will" (Luke i. 29). What if he will to reveal himself to all? Not all believe, but those who are drawn" (John vi. 44). But, what if all are drawn? You see that those things are not rightly placed in opposition, though it may be true that the Spirit does not breathe upon all; that Christ does not reveal the Father to all; that all are not drawn by the Father.

I wish, also, that your remarks in reference to the disparagement of efficacious grace, had been more extended. First, indeed, the nature of grace itself, and its agreement with the free-will of man, then its efficacy, and the cause of that efficacy, ought to have been more fully explained. For I consider nothing more necessary to the full investigation of this subject. Augustine, because he saw this, treats, in very many places, of the agreement of grace and of free-will, and of the distinction between sufficient and efficacious grace. I remark here, in a word, that by efficacious grace is meant, not that grace is necessarily received and can not be rejected, which certainly is received, and not rejected, by all, to whom it is applied. I add that it is not to the disparagement of grace, that the wickedness and perversity of most men is so great that they do not suffer themselves to be converted by it unto God. The author of grace determined not to compel men, by his grace, to yield assent, but to influence them by a mild and gentle suasion, which influence, not only, does not take away the free consent of the free-will, but even establishes it. Why is this strange, since God, as you admit, does not choose to repress the perverse will, that is, otherwise than by the application of grace, which they reject in their perversity. I do not oppose those things which you present from the fathers, for I think that most of them can be reconciled with the theory which you here design to confute.

You also present certain objections, which can be made against you, and in favour of that doctrine, and you attempt to confute them. The first is this, "the promise, in reference to the Seed of the woman, was made to all the posterity of Adam, and to each of the human race, in Adam himself." This, indeed, is true, nor do those things, which are stated by you, avail to destroy its truth. For the idea that the promise pertained to all men, considered in Adam, is not at variance with the idea that the Jews were alone the people of God. These ideas are reconciled by the fact that the people of other nations were alienated from the promise by their own fault or that of their parents, as may be seen from the whole tenor of the Holy Scriptures.

The second and third objections are made by those who do not think that historical faith in Christ is necessary to salvation. Your refutation of these pleases me, and those objections are of no moment. You also meet, with a sufficient reply, the objection from the fathers. But that objection is not presented, oppositely to the views of those, whom, in this treatise, you oppose. For they admit that the grace, by which any one is enabled to will to be converted, and to will really to believe in Christ, is not common to all men, which idea they do not regard as opposed to their own sentiment concerning the election of believers, and the reprobation of unbelievers. The seventh error; -- Should I say that this dogma is falsely charged upon that doctrine, you will be at a loss, and indeed will not be able to prove your assertion. For they acknowledge that the rule of predestination is "the will and the decree of God." This declaration—"Believers shall be saved, and unbelievers shall be condemned"—was made apart from any prescience of faith or unbelief, by God, of His own mere will, and they say that in it is comprehended the definition of Predestination and Reprobation. But when the Predestination of certain individuals is discussed, then they premise the foreknowledge of faith and of unbelief, not as the law and rule, but as properly antecedent. To which view, the passage in Ephesians 1, is not opposed. For believers are "predestinated according to the purpose of Him who worketh all things after the counsel of His own will." The purpose, according to which Predestination is declared to have been made, is that of adopting believers in Christ to sonship and eternal life, as is apparent from many passages of Scripture, where that purpose is discussed (Rom. 8 and 9). From this, it is also evident that your first argument against those who hold that opinion, amounts to nothing.

In the second place, you assert, that "divine Election is rule of giving or withholding faith. Therefore Election does not pertain to believers, but faith rather pertains to the elect, or is from the gift of Election." You will allow me to deny this, and to ask for the proof, while I plead the cause of those, whose sentiment you here oppose. Election is made in Christ. But no one is in Christ, except he is a believer. Therefore no one is elected in Christ, unless he is a believer. The passage in Romans xi. 5, does not serve to prove that thesis. For the point, there discussed, is not the election of grace, according to which faith is given to some, but that, according to which, righteousness is imputed to believers. This may be most easily, proved from the context, and will be manifest to any one, who will more diligently inspect and examine it. For the people, "which God foreknew, (verse 2d,) that is which He foreknew according to His grace, is the people, which believed, not that which followed after righteousness by the works of the law (Rom. ix. 31). This people God "hath not cast away." For thus is to be understood the fifth verse, "there is a remnant according to the election of grace," that is, they, only, are to be esteemed as the remnant of the people of God, who believe in Christ, as they alone are embraced in the election of grace, the children of the flesh, who followed after righteousness by the law, being excluded. That, which follows, teaches the same thing, "if by grace, then it is no more of works." What is that which is "by grace "? Is it election to faith? By no means; but it is election to righteousness, or righteousness itself. For it is said to be "by grace" not "by works." For it is not, here, inquired whether faith, but whether righteousness belongs to any one by works. Consider also the next verse "What then? Israel hath not obtained that which he seeketh for, but the election hath obtained, and the rest were blinded." What is that which Israel had sought for, and had not obtained? Not faith, but righteousness. See the end of the 9th and the beginning of the 10th chapters. They rejected faith in Christ, and endeavoured to obtain righteousness, by the works of the law, and this is the reason that they did not attain "to the law of righteousness." It is the same thing, also, which the elect are said to have obtained, not faith, but righteousness.

You will ask—"Is not faith, then, given according to Election?" I answer faith is not given according to that election, which is there discussed by the apostle, and therefore that passage does not conduce to your purpose. But, is there, then, a two-fold Election on the part of God? Certainly, if that is Election, by which God chooses to righteousness and life, that must be different, by which He chooses some to faith, if indeed he does choose some to faith: which, indeed, I will not now discuss, because it is my purpose only to answer your arguments.

Your third argument is equally weak, for prescience of faith and of unbelief has the same extent as predestination. In the first place, unbelief is a negative idea, that is, want of faith, and it was foreseen by God, when He decreed unto damnation. Secondly, the infants of believers are considered in their believing parents, and are not to be separated from the people of believers.

Your fourth argument is answered in the same way as the second. Faith is not the effect of that election, by which some are elected to righteousness and life. But it is this election to which they refer, in the examination of whose doctrine you are now engaged. The passage, in Ephesians 1, regards faith, as presupposed to predestination. For no one, but a believer, is predestinated to adoption through Christ - - "as many as received him, to them gave he power to become the sons of God." The passages, adduced from the fathers, sustain the idea that faith is the effect of election, but, without doubt, that election is referred to, by which God makes a distinction among men in the dispensation of means, by which faith is attained, which will perhaps not be denied by those, with whom you are now engaged, if it may only be correctly explained according to the Scriptures.

The fifth argument amounts to this: -- "Election is not according to the foresight of faith, since the cause of the divine foresight of faith in one, and not in another, is the mere will of God, who purposes to give faith to one, and not to another." Your opponents would reply that faith is, in such a sense, of the mere will of God, that it does not use an omnipotent and irresistible influence in producing faith in men, but a mild suasion and one adapted to incline the will of man, according to the mode of the human will: therefore the whole cause of the faith of one, and the unbelief of another, is the will of God, and the free choice of man.

To the sixth argument, he, who acknowledges that faith can be wholly lost, will reply that the rule or rather the antecedent condition of election is not faith, but final perseverance in faith: of that election, I mean, by which God chose to salvation and eternal life.

The eighth error; -- That true and saving faith may be, totally and finally, lost, I should not at once dare to say: though many of the fathers frequently seem to affirm this. Yet the arguments, by which you prove that it can be, neither wholly nor finally, lost, are to be considered. Your first proof is deduced from Matt. xvi. 18 -- "upon this rock I will build," &c., and you argue in favour of your doctrine in a three-fold manner from that passage. Your first proof is equivocal on account of the double meaning of the word faith. For it means either the confession of faith made by Peter concerning Christ, or trust resting in that confession and doctrine of faith. Faith, understood in the former sense, is the rock, which remains unshaken and immovable, and is the foundation of the church; but faith, understood in the latter sense, is inspired in the members of the church, by the spirit and the word, by which they are built upon the rock as their foundation. Therefore the word faith is used in the antecedent in a sense, different from that, in which it is used in the consequent.

Your second proof is this; -- "They, who have been built on the rock do not wholly fall from it; -- But those, who truly believe, are built upon the rock; -- Therefore, they do not utterly fall from it." Answer. The Major of this proposition is not contained in the words of Christ, for he says not that "those built on the rock shall not fall from the rock," but "the gates of hell shall not prevail against it (the rock, or the church)." It is one thing that the gates of hell should not prevail against the rock, but another that those who are built upon the rock shall not fall from it. A stone, built upon a foundation, may give way, and fall from it, while the foundation itself remains firm. If Christ referred to the Church, I say, even then, that to assert that those who are built upon the rock shall not fall from it, is not the same as to declare that the gates of hell shall not prevail against the church. For the act of falling pertains to the free will of the person who falls; but if the gates of hell should prevail against the church, this would occur on account of the weakness of the rock on which the church is founded. The Minor does not repeat the same idea as was contained in the Major. For, in the Minor, it is stated that believers are built, not having been built, completely, on the rock, on account of the continuation and confirmation of the work of building, which must, necessarily, continue while they are in this world. But while that continuation and confirmation lasts, believers do not seem to be out of danger of falling. For as any person may be unwilling to be built upon the rock, so it is possible that the same man, if he begins to be built, should fall, by resisting the continuation and confirmation of the building. But, it is not probable that Christ wished to signify, by those words, that believers could not fall, as such an assertion would not be advantageous. Since it is necessary that they should have their own strength in the rock, and therefore, that they should always bear upon and cling to the rock, they will give less earnest heed, in temptations, to adhere firmly to the rock, if they are taught that they can not fall from it. It may be sufficient to animate them, if they know that no force or skill can throw them from the rock, unless they willingly desert their station.

As to your third proof, even if it should be evident that Christ declared, that the gates of hell should not prevail against the church, yet it would not follow that no one could fall away from the faith. If any one should fall, nevertheless the church remaineth unshaken against the gates of hell. The defection of an individual, as was before said, is not caused by the power of hell, but by the will of him, who falls, in reference to the inflexibility of whose will the Scripture says nothing; the use of argument, presenting such consolation, would not be useful for the confirmation of the faithful. In reference to the sentiments of the fathers, you doubtless know that almost all antiquity is of the opinion, that believers can fall away and perish. But the passages, which you present from the fathers, either treat of faith in the abstract, which is unshaken and immutable, or concerning predestinated believers, on whom God has determined to bestow perseverance, who are always to be distinguished, according to the opinion of the fathers, and especially of Augustine, from those who are faithful and just, according to present righteousness.

Your second argument proves nothing, for, though it is true that he that asketh may be confirmed against temptations, and may not fall away, yet it is possible that he may not ask, and thus may not receive that strength, so that defection may follow. Hence arises the constant necessity of prayer, which does not exist, if one obtains that assistance from God, without daily prayers, nor is it, here, declared that believers may not intermit the duty of prayer, which must necessarily be presupposed to that conclusion, which you wish to deduce from prayer.

That "Christ undertakes to confess the elect" (Matt. x. 32) is true. But "elect" and "believers" are not convertible terms according to the view of the fathers, unless perseverance be added to faith. Nor is it declared, by Christ, in Matt. xxiv. 24, that the elect can not depart from Christ, but that they can not be deceived, by which is meant that though the power of deception is great, yet it is not so great as to seduce the elect: which serves as a consolation to the elect against the power and artifices of false Christ's, and false prophets.

Your third argument can be invalidated in many ways. First, "entire defection from true faith would require a second engrafting, if indeed he, who falls away, shall be saved." It is not absolutely necessary that he, who falls away, should be again engrafted; indeed some will say, from Hebrews 6 and 10, that one, who wholly falls away from the true faith, can not be restored by repentance. Secondly, There is no absurdity in saying that they may be engrafted a second time, because in Romans xi. 23, it is said of branches, which had been cut or broken off, that "God is able to graft them in again." If you say that the same individuals are not referred to here, I will ask the proof of that assertion. Thirdly, It does not follow from the second engrafting that "a repetition of baptism would be necessary" because baptism, once applied to an individual, is to him a perpetual pledge of grace and salvation, as often as he returns to Christ: and the remission of sins, committed even after baptism, is given without a repetition of baptism. Hence, if it be conceded that "baptism is not to be repeated," as they, with whom you now contend, willingly admit, yet it does not follow that believers can not wholly fall away, either because those, who wholly fall away, may not be entirely restored, or because, if they are restored, they do not need to be baptized a second time. It does not seem that your fourth argument, from 1 John iii. 9, can be easily answered. Yet Augustine affirms that, here, they only are referred to who are called according to the divine purpose and are regenerated according to the decree of the divine predestination. If you say that it is here said of all, who are born of God, that they do not sin, and that the seed of God remains in them, I will reply that the word "remain" signifies inhabitation, but not a continuance of inhabitation, and that so long as the seed of God is in a person, he does not sin unto death, but it is possible that the seed itself should, by his own fault and negligence, be removed from his heart, and as his first creation in the image of God was lost, so the second communication of it may be lost. I admit, however, that this argument is the strongest of those which have been hitherto referred to.

To the fifth, I reply, that the seed of the word of God is immortal in itself, but it can be removed from the hearts of those, who have received it (Matt. xiii. 19, etc).

The Sixth argument. So long as the members abide in Christ as the branches in the vine, so long they can not indeed perish, as the vivifying power of Christ dwells in them. But if they do not bear fruit, they shall be cut off (John xv. 2). It is possible that the branches, even while abiding in the vine, may not bear fruit, not from defect of the root or of the vine, but of the branches themselves. Romans 6, is also an exhortation of the apostle to believers, that they should not live any longer in sin, because they, in Christ, are dead to sin. This admonition to Christians would be in vain, if it were not possible that they should live in sin, even after their liberation from its dominion. It is to be considered that the mortification of the flesh is to be effected through the whole life, and that sin is not, in a single moment, to be so extinguished in believers that they may not at some time bear the worst fruit, provoking the wrath of God, and deserving the destruction of the individual. But, if a person commit sins, deserving the divine wrath, and destruction, and God remits them, only on condition of contrition and serious repentance, it follows that those, who thus sin, can be cut off, and indeed finally, if they do not return to God. That they should return, is not made necessary by the efficacy of their engraftment into Christ, although that return will certainly occur in those, whom God has determined, by the immutable decree of His own predestination, to make heirs of salvation.

The Seventh argument. "All who are members of Christ attain the stature of a perfect man." This is true, if they do not depart from Christ. This they can do, but it is not included in the internal and essential definition of members, that they should not be able to recede and fall away from their head. It is declared, in John 15, that the branches which do not bear fruit are taken away; and in Romans 11, some branches are said to have been broken off on account of unbelief.

You, then inquire, as if you had fully proved that faith can not be wholly lost, -- "What is the reason that faith may not utterly fail?" and reply—"It is not from the nature of faith, but from the gift of grace, which confirms that which is promised to believers." You, here, incorrectly contrast faith itself, and confirming grace, when you ought to contrast a man, endued with faith, on one hand, and the gift of grace on the other. The reason that faith can not wholly perish, or rather that the believer can not wholly lose his faith, is found, either in the believer himself, or in grace, which confirms or preserves faith, that the believer may not lose it. It is not in the believer himself, for he, as a human being obnoxious to error and fall, can lose his faith. But if God has determined that he should not lose his faith, it will be preserved through the grace by which He strengthens him, that he may not fall. "Simon, I have prayed for thee, that thy faith fail not" (Luke xxii. 32). The faith, then, of Peter could have failed, if we consider his strength. But Christ, by his intercession, obtained for him that grace, by which its preservation was secured. The covenant of God, of which mention is made in Jer. xxxii. 40, does not contain in itself an impossibility of departure from God, but a promise of the gift of His fear, by which, so long as it shall continue in their hearts, they shall be restrained from departing from God. But the Scripture nowhere teaches that it is not possible to shake off that gift of fear, nor is it profitable that promises of such a character, should be made to those in covenant with God. It is sufficient that they should be sustained, by the promises, against all temptations of the world, the flesh, sin and Satan, and that they may be made strong against all their enemies, if they will only be faithful to themselves and to the grace of God.

You add another question: "How far can believers lose grace and the Holy Spirit?" You reply that this question can be solved by a two-fold distinction, both in believers and in grace. In the distinction, which you make among believers, those, whom you mention first, do not at all deserve to be called believers; for hearing and understanding the word, if approbation of the same is not added, do not constitute a believer. They, who occupy the second order, are called believers in an equivocal sense. For true faith can not but produce fruit, convenient to its own nature, confidence in Him, love towards Him, fear of Him, who is its object. You distinguish believers of the second and third order in such a manner as to make the latter those who "apprehend Christ the redeemer by a living faith unto salvation" which you deny in reference to the former; in the mean time conceding to both not only an approbation of evangelical truth, heard and understood, but also the production of certain fruits, when you ought, indeed, to have considered the declaration of Christ; "without me ye can do nothing; as the branch can not bear fruit of itself, except it abide in the vine, no more can ye, except ye abide in me" (John xv. 4, 5).

Can any one indeed abide in Christ, unless he apprehends him as a redeemer, by a living faith unto salvation. Therefore that whole distinction among believers is futile, since the last class only ought to receive this name. If you can prove that these can not fall away and perish, you fully accomplish your purpose. The other classes can not be said to lose grace and the Holy Spirit, but rather to reject grace and to resist the Holy Spirit, if they do not make further progress; though the hearing, understanding and approbation of the word may tend to this that they should, apprehend Christ Jesus as their Redeemer, by a living faith unto salvation.

Let us now come to your distinction of grace, and see how you from this distinction meet the question above presented. You say that "Grace is of a two-fold character. Primary grace is the gratuitous favour of God, embracing his own in Christ unto eternal life." Be it so. You also say that "some fall from this grace, in a certain manner, that is, according to some effects of that grace of which they must be destitute and the contrary of which they must experience, when they commit any grievous sin; not according to that grace, when God always preserves His paternal feelings towards them, and does not change His purpose concerning their adoption, and the bestowment on them of eternal life." But these things need more diligent consideration. The effect of grievous sin committed against the conscience is the wrath of God, the sting of conscience, and eternal damnation. But the wrath of God can not be consistent with His grace in reference to the same thing, at the same time, and in respect to the same person, so that he should, in reference to him with whom He is angry, in that very wrath, yet will eternal life. He can will to bestow on him certain effects of grace, by which he can be brought back to a sound mind, and, again to bestow on him, thus restored, that grace of God unto eternal life. An accusing conscience—one really accusing, can not be consistent with grace and the gratuitous favour of God unto eternal life. For, in that case, the conscience would not really accuse. God does not will to bestow eternal life on one, whom His own conscience testifies, and truly, to be unworthy of eternal life; unless repentance shall intervene, which, of the gracious mercy of God, removes unworthiness. God does not will to bestow eternal life on him who has, by his sin, merited eternal damnation, and has not yet repented, while he is in that state. Therefore he truly falls from that grace which is designed to embrace him unto everlasting life. But, since God knows that such a man wills; by those means, which He has determined to use for his restoration, rise from the death of sin, he can not be said to wholly fall from the Divine grace. But a distinction is to be made here in relation to the various blessings which God wills to bestow on such. He wills eternal life only to the believing and penitent. He wills the means of faith and conversion to sinners not yet converted, not yet believers. And it does not seem to be a correct statement that "God regards sin, but not sinners with hatred," since the sin and the sinner are equally odious to God. He hates the sinner on account of his sin, of which he is the author, and which, except by him, would not be perpetrated.

In the description of that primary grace, there is that, which weakens the answer itself. "It is the favour by which God embraces in Christ his own. He embraces no one in Christ, unless he is in Christ. But no one is in Christ, except by faith in Christ, which is the necessary means of our union with Christ. If any one falls from faith, he falls from that union, and, consequently, from the favour of God by which he was previously embraced in Christ. From which it is also apparent, that in this explanation there is a petitio principii. For the question is this, "Can believers fall from this primary grace, that is, from the favour of God, by which he embraces them in Christ?" It is certain that they can not, while they continue to be believers, because so long they are in Christ. But if they fall from faith, they also fall from that primary grace. Hence the question remains—"Can believers fall from faith?" But you concede that believers, do fall, so far as themselves are concerned. I conclude, then, that God does not remain in them, and that neither the right of eternal life, nor filiation belongs to them, according to the declaration, "as many as received him, &c." (John i. 12). Hence, if you had wished to make your statements consistent, it was necessary to deny that believers fall from faith, or, if you concede this, to concede, at the same time, that they can fall from the favour of God by which He embraces them in Christ unto eternal life. But, as I said, this whole subject may be elucidated, if the grace of God is suitably distinguished from its various effects.

Let the passages of Scripture, which you cite, be examined. "Neither shall any man pluck them out of my hand" (John x. 28). Who will deny this? But some say—"The sheep can not be taken out of the hands of the shepherd, but can, of their own accord, depart from him." You affirm that "this is a weak statement." By what argument? "Because when they fall, they are taken by the Devil." Truly indeed, they are taken, when they fall, and it is not possible, that it should be done in any other way. For unless the sheep are in the hands of the shepherd, they can not be safe against Satan. But the question is—Does not the act of departure and defection in its nature, precede their seizure by Satan? If this be so, your answer is vain and futile. You argue again in this manner, "'If ye continue in my word, ye are my disciples indeed,' (John viii. 31), therefore, he who continues to be one of the flock, and does not fall, is truly one of the flock." Answer.—In the first place, there is ambiguity in the word continue. It signifies either present observance of Christ's word, or continuous observance, without defection from that word. Present observance, if it is sincere, makes one a disciple of Christ, or rather proves that one is a true disciple of Christ, otherwise one can never be truly called a disciple of Christ, unless when he has passed the limit of this life, when defection will be no longer to be feared, which is absurd. In the second place, I affirm that in the phrase "my disciples indeed" there is a two-fold sense; it signifies either that one, who at any time falls away from the word of Christ, was never a disciple indeed, though he may, at some time, have kept his word in sincerity; or that one, who at any time has kept the word of Christ and then obtained the name of disciple, if he yet falls away, is afterwards unworthy of the name of disciple. Therefore, if the relation of his present state is considered, He is "a disciple indeed;" if the relation of his subsequent state, he is not a disciple indeed, or does not deserve that name, because he, at some time, deserts it, unless one may say that no one has ever sincerely observed the word of Christ, who falls from it. This assertion needs proof. The passage in Romans 8, "Who shall separate us from the love of God?" is wholly irrelevant. For it is the consolation by which believers are strengthened against all present and assailing evils. None of these can at all effect that God should cease to love those, whom He has begun to love in Christ. Romans xi. 29 is not better adapted to your purpose. For though "the gifts of God are without repentance" yet one can reject the gifts of God, which he receives. Your quotation from (2 Tim. ii. 19,) "The Lord knoweth them that are His," does not favour your design. The Lord knoweth His own, even if some believers do fall away from faith. For it can be said that God has never known them as His own, by the knowledge, which is the handmaid of Predestination now under consideration. The distinction of Augustine may be applied here;-" some are children according to present justification, some according to the foreknowledge and predestination of God."

Secondary grace, you say, is either imputed or inherent. The phrase imputed grace does not sound well in my ears. I have heretofore thought that grace is not imputed, but imputes, as in Romans iv. 4, "the reward is not reckoned of grace, but of debt." Righteousness is said, in the same chapter, to be imputed of grace, without works. But, passing by this, let us examine the subject. The question proposed was—"How far may believers lose grace and the Holy Spirit?" You answer—in respect to imputed grace, which consists in justification, a part of which is the remission of sins—"The remission of sins is not granted in vain." Be it so. But believers may, after remission of some sins has been obtained, commit sin and grievously backslide. If, then, they should not repent of that act, will they obtain remission? You answer in the negative. I conclude from this, that they can lose that grace of the remission of their sins. But you reply—"It can not be that they should not repent." I know that this is asserted, but I desire the proof—not that the elect indeed, can not depart hence without final repentance, but that they, who have once been believers, can not die in final impenitence. When you shall have proved this, it will not be necessary to recur to this distinction of grace, for then you would be permitted to say that the believer never finally loses his faith and dies in impenitence.

You make a distinction in inherent grace, as "faith" and "the consequent gift of faith." In faith you consider "the act and the habit of faith." From this distinction, you answer the proposed question, thus—"Faith, considered in respect to habit and ability, can not be lost, on account of confirming grace, (though it can per se be lost,) but faith, in respect to any particular act, can be lost." First, I ask proof of your assertion. "Faith, in respect to habit, can not be lost, on account of confirming grace." I also inquire—"Is that act of faith, in respect to which faith can be lost, necessary or not, that any one may apprehend Christ? If it is, then a man can fall from grace, if he loses, as you say, the act of apprehension of Christ, or, rather, if he does not apprehend Christ by that act. If it is not necessary, then, it was indeed, of no importance to have considered that act, when the loss of grace was under discussion.

You attempt to prove, both by the example of David and by the opinions of the fathers, that the habit of faith and love can not be lost. The example of David proves nothing. For, should it be conceded that David, when he was guilty of adultery and murder, had not lost the Holy Spirit, it does not follow from this that the Holy Spirit can not be lost. For another might sin even more grievously, and thus lose the Holy Spirit. If, however, I should say that David had lost the Holy Spirit when he committed that adultery and murder, what would you answer, You might reply that it is evident that it was not so from the 51st

Psalm. That Psalm, I reply, was composed by David after he had repented of those crimes, having been admonished by Nathan. God, at that time, according to the declaration of Nathan, restored the Holy Spirit to David (2 Sam. xii. 13). In reference to the assertions of the fathers, I consider that the case of Peter is not to the prejudice of the opinion, which states that faith can be destroyed. For Peter sinned through infirmity, which weakens faith, but does not destroy it. I pass over Gratiaus. It would be proper to discuss, at some length, the sentiment of Augustine, if it had been proposed to present it fully. If, however, any one wishes to know what was the opinion of Augustine concerning this matter, let him look at the following passages: "De Predestinatione Sanctorum" (lib 1, cap. 14), and "De Bono Perseverantiae" (lib. 2, cap. 13, 16, 19, 22, 23). Let some passages be added from Prosper, who holds and every where defends the opinions of Augustine, e.g. Ad cap. Gall. respons. vii, Ad objectiones Vincentinas, respons. 16; De vocatione Gentium, lib. 2, cap. 8, 9, and 28. From these passages, it will, in my judgment, be apparent that Augustine thought that some believers, some justified and regenerate persons, some, on whom had been bestowed faith, hope and love, can fall away and be lost, and indeed will fall away and be lost, the predestinate alone being excepted.

You quote some objections to the foregoing explanation. The first objection is this: "Sin and the grace of the Holy Spirit can not subsist together." You reply, that "this is true of reigning sin, or sin with the full consent of the will." But you deny that the regenerate sin with the full or entire consent of the will. I answer, first, that "reigning sin" is not the same as that which has the full consent of the will. For the former belongs, generically to quality or habit, the latter pertains generically to action, and by the latter is prepared a way for the former. From this, it is clearly manifest that reigning sin can not subsist with the grace of the Holy Spirit. It is also true that sin does not reign in the regenerate. For, before this can take place, it is necessary that they should reject the grace of the Holy Spirit, which mortifies sin and restrains its power. We must, then, examine the other mode of sin, and see whether some of the regenerate may sin or not with the full consent of the will. You deny this, and deduce the reason for your denial from the beginning and successive steps of temptation. You consider the beginning of temptation to be concupiscence or native corruption, and you say that "it exists alone in the unregenerate man, who is entirely carnal. That, in the renewed man, there is, at the same time, flesh and Spirit, but in various degrees, so that he is partly carnal, partly spiritual;" from which you conclude that "concupiscence can subsist with the grace of the Holy Spirit, but not reign." I reply that though I have but little objection to that conclusion, yet I can not altogether approve those things which precede. For some of them are not true, and the statement is imperfect.

It is not true that "an unregenerate man is wholly carnal," that is, that there is in him only the flesh. For by what name shall that truth be called which the wicked are said to "hold in unrighteousness" (Rom. i. 18)? What is that conscience which accuses and excuses (Rom. ii. 15)? What is the knowledge of the law by which they are convinced of their sins (Rom. iii. 20)? All these things can not be comprehended under the term flesh. For they are blessings, and are adverse to the flesh. Yet I admit that the Holy Spirit does not dwell in the unrenewed man. The statement is imperfect, because it omits the explanation of the proportion, which exists between the flesh and the Spirit in the renewed man, as the Spirit predominates in the regenerate person, and because, from the predominating element, he receives the name of spiritual man, so that he can not come under the term carnal. But observe, moreover, that your conclusion has reference to concupiscence, which is a quality, while the question related to actual sin, namely—"Can actual sin consist with the grace of the Holy Spirit?" You refer to "five steps, of temptation." You concede that the first step may pertain to the regenerate, also the second, and it is, indeed, true. But it can never be proved that Paul, for such a reason, "complained of his own captivity, because he could delight in sorrowful meditation in reference to the commission of sin." For he is treating there, of sin already committed. "The evil which I would not, that I do."

The third step, which is "the consent of the will to the perpetration of sin," you attribute also to the regenerate, "but a more remiss consent, according to which they will, in such a sense, that they are even unwilling to commit sin," and you think that this can be proved from the example of Paul in Romans 7. I wish you to consider, here, how these things harmonize together, that, in reference to one and the same act, the will or volition may be two-fold, and, indeed, contrary to itself, even at the very moment when the act is performed. Before the act, while the mind is yet in doubt, and the flesh is lusting against the Spirit, and the Spirit against the flesh, this might be affirmed: but, when the flesh carries out its concupiscence into action, that is, does that which it has lusted against the Spirit, then, indeed, the Spirit has ceased to lust. The position must then be assumed, that the renewed man commits sin from the concupiscence of the flesh, the Spirit in vain lusting against it, that is, the flesh is stronger than the Spirit, and the desire of the Spirit is overcome by the flesh, contrary to the declaration of Scripture—"greater is he that is in you, than he that is in the world" (1 John iv. 4), and contrary to the condition of the regenerate, in whom the Spirit predominates over the flesh, nor does it occur that the flesh should conquer, unless when the Spirit is quiet, and intermits the contest.

"But the Scripture affirms (Rom. 7) that the renewed man would do good, yet does it not, and would not do evil, yet does it." I answer. in that passage, reference is made not to a regenerate person, but to a man under the law. But, even, if this point be conceded, I affirm that it is not possible that there should be volition and nolition, at the same time, concerning the same act; hence, that volition, which is followed by an act, is a pure and efficacious volition; the other is not so much volition as velleity, which is produced, not by the Holy Spirit striving against the flesh, but by the conscience, or the law of the mind, existing in man, which ceases not to struggle against the flesh, until it is seared, and deprived of all feeling. That struggle of the conscience does not effect that the man should not sin with his full consent, but rather aggravates the sin, and declares how vehement is the consent of the will to a sin, presented by the concupiscence of the flesh, when not even the conscience, exclaiming against it, has not power to restrain the will from that consent.

It is, then, an injurious and most dangerous opinion, which holds that the renewed man does not sin with full consent, when he feels the sting of conscience, opposing the sin which the will is about to perpetrate. As this happens to all, who are affected by any sense of right and wrong, it will be very easy for them to persuade themselves that, as they do not sin with the full consent of the will, they have a certain indication of their own regeneration. Therefore, if the full consent of the will to sin can not consist with the grace of the Holy Spirit, it is certain that the regenerate sometimes lose the grace of the Holy Spirit, because they sin with the full consent of the will, when they sin against the conscience.

You consider the fourth step to be "the carrying out of an evil work into an act." This is correct, but the distinction which you make, can not be proved from the Scriptures. When the regenerate person commits sin, he commits it being overcome by the concupiscence of the flesh, while the Spirit of regeneration is quiescent, and not testifying against the sin, unless before the sin, when the consent of the will has not yet been gained by the suasion of concupiscence, and after the sin when the Spirit has begun to revive. But the "testifying," of which you speak is nothing else than the act of the conscience accusing the person both before and after the commission of sin. The whole man, then, sins, but "not according to that principle by which he is renewed." This was unnecessarily added; for who would ever call this in question? This, also, can be said of a man placed under the law, as he does not sin according to the law of his mind, that is, of his conscience approving the law, but only according to the flesh. Hence, you see that the distinction in this case, ought to have been of another character. Nor does it seem necessary to concede, "that an action, performed by a regenerate person, may be less sinful than if performed by him in whom sin reigns."

For the fault and sinfulness of an action is to be judged from the strong consent of the will to the sin. But he is borne more vehemently towards sin, who rejects the act of the Holy Spirit striving in the contrary direction, and follows the concupiscence of the flesh, than he, who, opposing the concupiscence of the flesh by his conscience alone, at length yields. Thus the sin of David, committing adultery and murder was far more heinous than that of a heathen man committing the same sins; the inhabitants of Bethsaida and Chorazin sinned more grievously than the citizens of Tyre and Sidon, because the former, committing their sins, resisted more influences, adapted to restrain from the commission of sin, than the latter. You say that the last step is "when a sin, confirmed by frequent repetition, becomes a habit." That step or degree was called, you remark, by the Greeks to< ajpotelei~n But you will allow me to deny that the Greeks used that word, in that sense. For your fourth step was equivalent to ajpotelei~v the same as to commit sin. But this last step is a degree, not so much in sin, as in sinners, of whom some advance further than others. You deny that this step can happen to the regenerate.

This needs proof. In all those distinctions, there is a continual assumption of the point to be proved. For they, who say that the regenerate can lose the grace of the Holy Spirit, say, also, that the regenerate may not only sin, but may persevere in sin, and contract the habit of sin.

The second objection, which you adduce, is this: "Adam, being yet pure, fell wholly, therefore, much more may they fall, who, having been born and renewed after the fall of Adam, have believed." The force of the argument depends on the parity or equality of the conditions of the parties; that of Adam, in respect to which he was created in righteousness and true holiness; and that, of his descendants, in respect to which they have been renewed in righteousness and true holiness. You attempt to solve the difficulty by showing the dissimilarity of the cases. But the dissimilarity, which exists between the two conditions, does not effect that the regenerate may not be able, altogether, to fall away. Nor, indeed, is this affirmed, in the passage, which you cite from Augustine. For, though the regenerate may have the will to do according to their ability, of which gift Adam was destitute, according to the sentiment of Augustine, yet it does not follow that they can not repudiate and willingly reject this gift. You were permitted to add other things, in which the condition of believers in Christ differs from the original state of Adam in righteousness. Among other things, this is peculiar, that the latter state had not the promise of the remission of sins, if it should happen that Adam should ever once commit sin; but that of believers is rendered more blessed by the promise—"their sins will I remember no more" (Heb. viii. 12). Hence it is that the faith of God is not made "without effect," even if those in covenant with him do sin (Rom. iii. 3). For the covenant is one of grace and faith, not of righteousness and works. Yet make whatever differences you please between the two states, it will be always necessary to admit that perseverance, voluntary, free, and liable to change, was necessary to salvation in both states. Man does not persevere, either in the former or the latter state, unless freely and willingly. This is so far true "that God does not take away even from those, who are about to persevere, that liability to change, by which they may possibly not choose to persevere," as is affirmed in the treatise "De vocatione Gentium, lib. 2, cap. 28." You refer to a third objection, "This member of a harlot is not a member of Christ—But the believer, who is a member of Christ, can become the member of a harlot; -- Therefore, the believer may cease to be a member of Christ." You reply to this objection by making distinctions in the term member. But those distinctions are unnecessary. First, the subject of discussion is a member not in appearance, but in truth. An apparent member is, in an equivocal sense, a member, and therefore, does not belong to the definition; and there would be four terms to the syllogism. Nor is the subject of discussion a member, which is such in its destination, for we know that all men, who are in destination members of Christ, are, universally, members of Satan, before they are in fact brought to Christ, and united to him. Since, therefore, members, which are really such, are referred to in the objection, to what purpose are these niceties of distinction sought? "In reference to those who are really members," you say, "some are living, others are half dead. But both are members, according to election." If this be so, you attain your object; for who is so foolish as to say that the elect may finally be lost? But they whom you consider your opponents, will deny that all true members of Christ are such by predestination. They will affirm that some are such according to their present state, their righteousness and present engraftment in Christ. Let us however, consider your answer, in the supposition of the truth of that distinction. You assert that "a true and actual member, and one that remains such cannot be a member of a harlot." That, indeed, is not strange. For it is an identical proposition, and, therefore, amounts to nothing. The member of Christ, that remains such, is not a member of a harlot, but this does not answer the question—Will a living member of Christ always remain alive? It was affirmed in the objection that a living member of Christ may become a member of a harlot, and may, therefore, not remain a member of Christ. The point, to be proved, is again assumed in your answer to that argument. But you say that "the half dead may, as far as they are concerned, at any time, lose the Holy Spirit." But, from what state do they become half dead? Is it not from being wholly alive? You would not indeed say that any one is half dead, at the time, when he is engrafted in Christ. You see that such an assertion is absurd. The state of the case, according to those who argue against you, is like this. At the beginning of faith in Christ and of conversion to God, the believer becomes a living member of Christ. If he perseveres in the faith of Christ and maintains a good conscience, he remains a living member. But if he becomes indolent, has no care for himself, gives place to sin, he becomes, by degrees half-dead: and proceeding in this way he at length wholly dies, and ceases to be a member of Christ. You ought to have refuted these statements, which, so far from refuting, you rather confirm by your distinctions. You have indeed treated this subject, with less care than its dignity, and your learning deserved. The ninth error; -- That, which is so styled by you, is erroneously charged on the sentiment adverse to you: for they do not say this, nor can it, in any way, be deduced from their sentiment. This is their opinion. "A man, by his own freewill, receives the grace, which is divinely offered to him, whatever it may be." For as grace preserves, so the free-will is preserved, and the free will of man is the subject of grace. Hence it is necessary that the free-will should concur with the grace, which is bestowed, to its preservation, yet assisted by subsequent grace, and it always remains in the power of the free-will to reject the grace bestowed, and to refuse subsequent grace; because grace is not the omnipotent action of God, which can not be resisted by the free-will of man. And since the state of the case is such, those same persons think that a man can reject grace and fall away. From which you see that you have undertaken a futile task, when you refute the error which you charge on that sentiment. Yet we may consider, also, those same things: perhaps an opportunity will be afforded to note something, which will not be unworthy of knowledge. "This sentiment," you affirm, "attributes a free will, flexible in every direction, of grace, to all men." Do you deny that the free will is "flexible in all directions"—I add, even without grace? It is flexible by its own nature: and as it is addicted to evil in its sinful state, so it is capable of good, which capability grace does not bestow upon it; for it is in it by nature. But it is, in fact, only turned to good by grace, which is like a mold, forming the ability and capacity of the material into an act, though it may be, of itself, sufficiently evil. Augustine (de predestin Sanctorum, cap. 5) says, "It belongs to the nature of man to be able to have faith and love, but it pertains to the grace of believers to actually have them." But you may be dissatisfied that this is said "to exist in all men," but that dissatisfaction is without cause. Their meaning is not that grace is bestowed on all men, by which their free will may be actually inclined to good; but that in all there exists a will which may be flexible in every direction by the aid of grace. But they teach, you say, that "it is in the will of man to apply itself to the grace which is bestowed by the aid of universal grace, or to reject the same by the inability of corrupt nature." What do you desire at this point? You will answer "that for the phrase 'universal grace' should be substituted 'particular grace.'" But who has ever said that "a man can apply himself to particular grace by the force of universal grace"? I think that no one can be so foolish: for the man is led to the use of particular grace, offered to him, by the free-will, assisted by particular grace. The expression, "to reject the same by the inability," &c., is ineptly used; for inability does not reject; a passive non-reception pertains to it, while it is the province of depravity to reject. When, therefore, you have introduced, according to your own judgment, the phrase "universal grace," you fight against your own shadow. For it is evident that "the ability to believe is not carried out into action, unless by the aid of other subsequent grace, which we call particular or special, since it does not happen to all and to each of mankind.

The passages of Scripture, which you adduce, do not answer your purpose. For the former two are adapted to prove that the faithful do not fall away from Christ; and let it be remembered that, according to Augustine and the author of the book, "De vocatione Gentium," that perseverance pertains only to believers, who are predestinated to life. The passages from Augustine show that the grace, prepared for the predestinate, will certainly incline their hearts, and will not be rejected by them because God uses such persuasions with them, as He knows to be suitable to them, and adapted to persuade them. This he calls efficacious grace, and always distinguishes it from efficient grace. You, however, in quoting Augustine, with sufficient superciliousness, repudiate that distinction. But what arguments do you use? You say that no grace is sufficient for conversion, which is not efficacious. I deny it, and nature itself exclaims against your assertion, while she distinguishes sufficiency from efficacy. God is sufficient for the creation of many worlds, yet He does not efficaciously perform it. Christ is sufficient for the salvation of all men, yet he does not efficaciously accomplish it. But you perhaps understand by efficacious cause that which can effect any thing, and so make it identical with efficient cause. But they who distinguish between sufficient and efficacious define the latter as that, which really produces the effect.

You do not prove that which you intend, when you say that "man has not free-will in spiritual things." Granted. But if grace may restore the freedom of the will, is it not then in the exercise of free-will, that he either can do sufficiently, or really does efficaciously? Nor is it to the purpose to say that "we are dead" (Col. iii. 3), and that "our sufficiency is of God" (2 Cor. iii. 5). This is not denied by those, who speak of sufficient grace. Nor does that three-fold inability do away with sufficient grace. They, who make the distinction, say that sufficient grace is able to remove that three-fold inability, and to effect that a man should receive offered grace, should use it when received, and should preserve it.

You endeavour to prove, in the next place, as the necessary consequence of "the five-fold nature of grace, preeminent, preparative, operative, co-operative, and persevering," that no single grace can be sufficient, because "no one of those five kinds of grace is alone sufficient for salvation, since all joined together are necessary." It is not a sound conclusion, that there is no sufficient grace because no one of those five kinds of grace is sufficient alone. The reasoning here is from a particular case to a general conclusion, and therefore is not valid; there is here also the fallacy of Composition. But the first two kinds of grace, namely, prevenient and preparative, are either sufficient or efficacious. For God precedes (by His grace) sufficiently and efficaciously; He also prepares sufficiently and efficaciously. It may be questioned, also, whether the same can not be said of operative and co-operative grace. Yet let us concede that those terms properly pertain to efficacious grace. Nevertheless they who defend the use of the phrase "sufficient," will say that these latter kinds of grace are prepared for and offered to all those, who have suffered themselves to be moved by prevenient and preparative grace, which is sufficient in its character, in the direction intended by that grace; and afterwards the gift of perseverance is also bestowed. Hence you have not, by that argument, disproved sufficient grace so far as it is distinguished from efficacious grace. But we will not examine the definitions of that five-fold grace, because this does not pertain to the scope of this discussion. You also endeavour to refute the same distinction by a simile. But in it there is a great want of analogy. For an inert mass is moved, naturally and necessarily, by the application of forces, which exceed the force of its gravity; but we, as human beings, are moved according to the mode of freedom, which God has bestowed on the will, from which it is called free-will. At this point, the similitude, which Cardinal Contarenus uses in reference to predestination, and the opposite of your simile, may be not ineptly mentioned. He supposes a two-fold gravity in a stone, one natural, the other adscititious. The strength which is sufficient to raise a stone, tending downwards by natural gravity alone, will not be sufficient, if that adscititious gravity shall be added, and the efficiency of sufficient strength will be hindered by the adscititious gravity. We see this clearly in athletes, engaged in wrestling. One endeavours to raise the other from the earth, and to prostrate him, thus raised up. Either of them would be able in a moment to effect this in reference to his antagonist, if the latter should only offer the resistance of the native weight of his body, but because he does not wish to be raised, he depresses himself and his adversary as much as he can, by using the strength of his nerves and bones, which far exceeds the weight of his body alone. So there is, in man, by derivation from the first sin of the first man, a weight, which is, or may be called, native. There is, in addition to this, another produced in each person by his own wickedness, which does not so much exist in him, as is present with him, serving as a hindrance that the power of that grace, which is sufficient to overcome the natural tendency, may not effect that which, without the interposition of that impediment, it would effect. Nor is the flexibility of our will, nor our power of choice taken away by the concurrence of those five gifts, but, by that concurrence, it is effected that the will, which by its own nature is flexible in every direction, and the choice, which is able to elect freely between two different things, should incline certainly and infallibly in that direction, towards which the motion of the five-fold grace impels it. Hence, also, I wish that instead of "inflexible inclination," you had said "certain and infallible inclination." For, if we do not say that the mind of a man may possibly be inclined in another direction, even at the time when it is inclined in a given direction by efficacious grace, it follows that the will of man acts not according to the mode of liberty, but according to the mode of nature, and thus not the free-will, but the nature of man, will be saved. But the free-will, at least as to its exercise, will be, in that case, destroyed by grace, while it belongs to grace not to take away, but to correct nature itself, wherein it has become corrupt.

Nor is what is said concerning the promised Spirit opposed to these views. For the "Spirit, who effects that, in fact, we may walk," does not take away the freedom of the will and of human choice, but he acts upon the flee-will, in such a manner, as he knows will be suitable and adapted to it, that it may be, certainly and infallibly, inclined. I wish that the same thing may be understood of the phrase, "the Father draweth." Those things, which follow, have not the effect of weakening this doctrine. For, by the supposition of "efficacious grace acting in those, concerning whom God, certainly and infallibly, wills their conversion and salvation," the existence of sufficient grace is not denied: nor indeed is that, which you infer, included in that supposition, namely, that they, who are truly believers, can not but persevere. We may be permitted to infer from it the certain, but not the necessary existence of an effect. Ignorance of this distinction is the cause of your idea that you must deny sufficient grace.

Next follows the explanation of some passages of Scripture, which they who hold to sufficient grace are accustomed to use in proof of it. You seem to have selected them from Bellarmine, who presents them, in the same order, as you use. We will consider your refutation.

The first passage is from Isaiah 5. Bellarmine deduces from that passage a two-fold argument in proof of sufficient grace. The first is like this, when put in a syllogistic form: "He, who did all things for his vineyard which were necessary that it might be able to bear fruit, used sufficient culture for its productiveness; -- But God, &c.; - - Therefore, &c." The truth of the Major is plain from its very terms. It consists in a definition, and is itself a definition. For sufficient culture is that in which all things necessary for fruitfulness are used." The truth of the Minor is contained in the text. For he, who has done all things which he might do for fruitfulness, has used all necessary means.

God could not, with justice, speak in such terms if He had not used all necessary means. Therefore the conclusion is a correct one. You reply by making a two-fold distinction in sufficiency, and in the nature of the vineyard; the sufficiency of external means, and that of internal grace; also of a good and bad vineyard. In the first part of this reply, you concede what is proved in the passage under consideration. For, if the external means are of such a character, that men would be sufficiently invited and led by them unto salvation, unless their minds were so perverse and depraved, as you say, then it follows that those means would have been sufficient. For is it necessary, in order that sufficiency, by those means, may be attributed to grace, that internal grace, certainly changing the bad vine into a good one, should be added. Indeed it can be said that so much internal grace, as would be sufficient for a change of heart, was not wanting, or at least would not have been wanting, if they had not, in their perversity, rejected the external means. The distinction between the good and the bad vineyard is of no importance in this place. For this is the very thing, concerning which God complains that His vineyard was so perverse that it would not respond to the sufficient culture which had been bestowed upon it.

The second argument of Bellarmine is like this. If God had not bestowed on that vineyard all things necessary for the production of grapes, then He would have said absurdly that He "looked that it should bring forth grapes;"—But He said, well and justly, that He "looked that it should bring forth grapes;"—Therefore he had bestowed on it all things necessary for the production of grapes. The truth of the Major is certain. For God knew that a vineyard could not produce fruit, which was destitute of any of the means necessary for fructification, and if He knew this, He knew, also, that it would be futile, nay, foolish to look for grapes from a vineyard, which could not bear grapes. The Minor is contained in the text. Therefore the conclusion is valid, that sufficient grace was not wanting to the vineyard.

It is worth the while to consider what is the meaning of that divine looking for or expectation, and how it may be correctly attributed to the Deity. An expectation, by which an act is looked for from any one, depends on a proper knowledge of the sufficiency, necessary for the performance of the act, which either exists in Him or is present with Him, on whom the act is incumbent, else, the expectation would be unreasonable. No one looks for figs from thistles, or roses from a thorn-bush. This divine expectation, therefore, if we do not wish to call it unreasonable, which would be blasphemy, depends on the same knowledge. Nor does the fact that, in the infinity of His knowledge, God knows that no effect will follow, from the sufficiency of those forces, to prevent us from attributing that expectation to Him. For that knowledge does not at all interfere with the sufficiency of causes on which depends the justness and reasonableness of the expectation. It is, indeed, true that the divine knowledge effects that God can not be deceived. But he, who looks for fruit in vain, and to whose expectation the event does not correspond, is deceived. From this, it is easy to infer that expectation is attributed to God only by anthropopathy. But, if even this be conceded, it will nevertheless follow from the consideration that expectation is attributed, with this appropriate qualification, to the Deity, that sufficient strength was present with the individual from whom something was expected. But if, in that expectation, we consider not only the knowledge referred to, but also the highest desire, with which, he, to whom expectation is attributed, demands the production of fruits, in that respect expectation is most properly attributed to God. For he desires nothing so much from men; in nothing is He equally delighted. This also is most plainly expressed in that parable. Let us now return from this digression.

To that second argument you make no reply, but propose another case which you think will be more easily managed. But let us examine this, also, with your answer. The case is this: "If he did not bestow grace to bear fruit, which could not be had, except by His gift, then God had no just cause of expostulating with the Jews." The reply consists in a denial of the consequence, for the denial of which, a three-fold reason is assigned. The first is this; "as He did not owe that grace, He was under obligation to no one." Secondly, "because they rejected it when offered to them in their parents." Thirdly, "because they did not, after having rejected it, seek it anew, or have any care concerning it." Indeed to one, who carefully considers the matter, the reason is a single one, though consisting of three parts. For the reason assigned that God could rightly expostulate with those, who do not bear fruit in this, that "they had grace sufficient for this purpose but rejected it." To confirm and strengthen this reason, it is added that God would not be obligated to give grace a second time, and that, even should He be obligated, He would not deny it to those desiring it, but He would not give it to those not desiring it, and not having any care whatever concerning that grace. That reason for just expostulation is to be examined, and even so much more diligently, as it is more frequently used. It is asked, then, "Could God rightly expostulate with them because they do not bear good fruit, who have rejected the grace received in their first parents, which is necessary for the production of those fruits, or rather who have lost it, by a judicial removal of it, on the part of God?"

For the discussion of this question, it is necessary to consider, first, "whether God could demand fruit from those who have, as a punishment from

God, lost the grace necessary for that production, which was received in their first parents," that is, who are destitute of necessary grace, though by their own demerit. From this will readily follow the answer of the question "whether He can justly expostulate with such persons, if they do not produce fruit. We remark, then, -- every divine demand, by which He requires any thing from a creature, is prescribed by law. But a law consists of two parts, command and sanction. The command, by which an act is prescribed or forbidden, ought not to exceed the strength of him, on whom the command is laid. The sanction contains a promise of reward to the obedient, a denunciation of punishment against the transgressor. Hence it is evident that the demand of the law is two-fold, of obedience and of punishment. That of obedience is prior and absolute; that of punishment is subsequent, and has no place except when obedience is not yielded. Hence, also, there is a two-fold satisfaction of the law; one, in which the obedience, prescribed by the law, is rendered; the other, in which the punishment, required by the law is inflicted. He, who satisfies the claim of the law in one way, is free from its demands, in the other. He, therefore, who pays the penalty laid down in the law, is entirely free from obligation to render obedience. This is true, universally, of every kind of punishment. If the punishment of disobedience comprehends within itself a privation of that grace, without which the law can not be obeyed, then, indeed, by a two-fold right, he seems to be entirely free from obligation to obedience, both because he has suffered due punishment, and because he is deprived of that strength without which the law can not be obeyed, and deprived, punitively, by God Himself, the enacter of the law, which fact is of much importance. For thus is excluded that argument, which some present, saying, that the servant is bound to render obedience or servitude, even if he has cut off his own hands, without which he can not render it. The case is not analogous. For the fault and sin of the servant consists in the fact that he has cut off his hands, but in the other case, God himself the lawgiver, takes away the strength, because it has not been used by him, who had received, according to the declaration, "to him that hath shall be given, &c." That servant, indeed, deserved punishment by that crime, and if he should suffer it, his master could not afterwards demand from him service which he could not render without hands. Therefore it seems necessary to conclude that God can not demand fruit from those, whom he has deprived, though on account of their own demerit, if the strength necessary for producing fruit. Let us take the illustration of a tree. The tree, which does not bear fruit, deserves to die, but when that punishment has been inflicted upon it, no one can, by any right demand fruit from it. Hence, therefore it follows secondly "God can not justly expostulate with those, who do not bear fruit if they are destitute of grace necessary for this, even by the punishment of God. It is of no consequence that God is not obligated to restore grace to them. For as He is not obligated to bestow grace, so He can not demand the act of obedience; and, if He wills to demand an act, He is obligated to restore that grace, without which the act can not be performed. Thus also it is not to the purpose that they do not seek the grace, which they have lost. For thus they twice deserve not to receive grace, both because they have lost it, of their own fault, and because they do not seek it when lost. On this very account, God has not the right to demand an act, not susceptible of performance. These things are in reply to your answer to the case proposed.

The second passage is in (Matt. xxiii. 37). "How often would I have gathered thy children together, and ye would not." From this passage Bellarmine, to prove that there is sufficient grace, thus argues, "If Christ did not desire that the Jews should be able to will, then he could not, justly complain that they would not. But he did justly complain that they would not. Therefore he desired that they might be able to will." This reasoning is based on the supposition that no one can justly complain of any person that he has not performed an act, for the performance of which he had not sufficient strength.

Your reply to that argument is two-fold. The former part, which refers to the distinction of the will into that of good-pleasure, and that of sign or revelation has nothing whatever to do with the subject of the argument. For Bellarmine does not say that Christ wished to gather them according to his good-pleasure, but he openly denies it, and affirms that he can sustain that position from the passage itself. For a gathering, which is made according to the will of good-pleasure is not only sufficient but also efficacious. Let the gathering together here referred to, be according to the will, which is styled that of sign or revelation, and from it follows that, which is deduced by Bellarmine. For, in no mode of the will, does he wish to gather them unless he assists or is ready to assist, that they also, whom he wishes to gather, may be able to will; and thus it is a false assertion, that "God can, by the will of sign, will to gather the Jews together, though He may not aid them to be able to will." For the necessary consequences or effect of this will is sufficient aid, by which also the Jews themselves might be able to will. It is a contradiction in terms, though indirectly, to assert that "He wills to gather, and wills not to give sufficient aid by which the Jews may be able to will to be gathered, who can not, except by their own will, be gathered." You add, to this reply, that which has also been said in reference to the first argument, and its repetition is unnecessary. The latter part of your reply is, "Christ does not here speak as God, but as the minister of the circumcision." Granted. Then he wished to gather them together as the minister of the circumcision, and as a minister who had power to baptize with the Holy Ghost. Therefore, in that declaration of his will he showed that he either had given or was ready to give sufficient grace to them, without which they could not be gathered together. But in the passage in Isaiah 5, God Himself speaks, who is able efficaciously to soften and convert hearts, and says—"What could have been done more to my vineyard?" Who would reply, according to the meaning of your answer, "Thou mightest have softened their hearts and have converted them and it was suitable that thou shouldst do this. For thou art God, and speakest there as God." Therefore that distinction is absurd and not adapted to solve that objection. We see indeed on how weak foundations, that opinion rests, which can not present other answers to meet those arguments.

The third argument is from the 7th chapter of the acts, 51st verse. "Ye do always resist the Holy Ghost." From this passage Bellarmine argues in a two-fold manner. First, --

"Those, in whom good desires are not inspired, can not be said to resist the Holy Spirit, -- But the Jews are said to have resisted; Therefore good desires were inspired in them, by which they could have been converted." Secondly— "They, who can not but resist, can not be justly accused on account of their resistance; -- But the Jews were justly accused by Stephen; -- Therefore they were able to resist." From these two syllogisms can be deduced as a consequence, -- "They had grace sufficient to enable them not to resist and even to yield to the Holy Spirit." The latter argument is the stronger. Though something may be said against the former, yet a small addition may give to it also strength to withstand any opposition.

Let us examine your reply. It seems to us, not at all pertinent, and in part very ridiculous. For Bellarmine concedes that this is not said of "the efficacious operation of the Spirit." For he clearly distinguishes between sufficient and efficacious grace or operation. Indeed he does this very thing by quoting passages to show that there must be a division of special grace into sufficient and efficacious. "But this passage," (Acts vii. 51), you say "refers to the external ministration of the prophets." True; but that ministration was one, by which the Spirit chose to work; otherwise the man, who opposed that ministration, could not be said to resist the Holy Ghost. These things are co-ordinate and conjoined so far that the Spirit wills to work at least sufficiently through that ministration. The interpretation of Peter Lombardus is truly worthy of the parent of the Scholastic Theology, and unworthy of an introduction to the light by you, without stern reprehension. I do not add a refutation of it, because its perversity appears, on its very front, to those who examine it. The fourth passage, which you have made third in order, is from the 3d chapter of Rev. 20th verse. "I stand at the door and knock." On this Bellarmine remarks—"He, who knocks at a door, knowing with certainty that there is no one within, who can open, he knocks in vain, and indeed is a foolish person. Far from us be such an idea in reference to the Deity. Therefore when God knocks, it is certain that the man can open, and consequently he has sufficient grace." Your answer does not touch this argument of Bellarmine, for he does not wish to infer the universality of grace but that there is such a thing as sufficient grace, and this you do not, in your answer, contradict. Whether, indeed, that sufficient grace is universal, that is, is bestowed on all and each of mankind universally, is discussed, in another place, by Bellarmine, whose defense, indeed, I have not undertaken, and I am not desirous to do so, yet it is necessary to love the truth, by whatever person it may be spoken.

The tenth error; -- This, in your estimation, is that "the hypothesis, which you oppose, is at variance with itself." This is indeed a valid mode of confutation. But how do you prove the liability of that theory to the charge of self-contradiction? You very injuriously charge it with the opinion that "God determined to bestow all natural and gracious aids upon all men." Who can hold such an opinion, when he acknowledges that there is an "efficacious grace which God does not impart to all?" Indeed you are not consistent with yourself in the statement of their doctrine. For you say that it affirms that "God bestows all aids upon all men," and afterwards say that it asserts that "God does grant to all not actual perseverance, but the ability to persevere or to will to persevere." Is not the gift of actual perseverance one among all aids? How shall both these assertions be made without contradiction? Correct your error, and when you have corrected it, you will see that you ought to have made the remark "without which no one actually obtains salvation," as explanatory of efficacious grace. Yet God is not wanting to those to whom He gives the grace, by which they can be saved, though He may not give the grace by which they will actually be saved. Those words "by persevering, to obtain salvation," should have been arranged thus "to persevere and obtain salvation." You erroneously confound act with ability and efficacy with sufficiency.

The eleventh error; -- In this, you allege against this doctrine that "it introduces heresies long condemned," namely, those of the Pelagians. This assertion you indeed afterwards seem to soften down, because the Pelagians attribute the faculty of doing well either wholly to nature, or only in part to grace, while the doctrine attributes it wholly to grace. You, however, find fault with it because "it makes grace universal, and thus involves itself in yet greater difficulty." Something has been heretofore said on this point. Yet of what weight is your refutation? For what if any one should say that all men universally, have the power of believing and obtaining salvation, if they will, and that this very power is bestowed, divinely, upon the nature of mankind, by what argument will you disprove the assertion? It does not follow, from this statement, that nature and grace have an equally wide extent. For the ability to believe pertains to nature, actual belief is of grace. So with the ability to will, and actual volition, "It is God, which worketh in you, &c." (Phil. ii. 13). "Unto you it is given to believe, &c." (Phil. i. 29). You seem to do injury to the truth, when you say that it is a Pelagian idea that "a man can, by the opposition of his will, resist grace." There is no page in Scripture, where this is denied. Is a man a mere log that, by pure necessity of nature, he must yield to grace? If this is not true, then a man consents freely, and therefore has the ability not to consent, that is, to resist. Otherwise to what purpose are threats and promises? The opinion that "a man has ability in the exercise of the will, to yield to the grace of God, when explained to refer to remote ability, and which may, otherwise, be called capacity to receive active and immediate ability, by which any one can will to yield to grace," is not Pelagian. Would that they, who, at this day, hold the dogma of Predestination, might prove that it does not introduce, by fair inference, the idea of fatal necessity. You say also that the Papists formerly held these views. The fact that a similar crime is charged on both does not prove a similarity in other respects. It is possible that they, when you oppose, may differ from the Papists, and that the latter defend a doctrine which is obnoxious to your objections.

The twelfth error; -- You affirm that "this doctrine is in harmony with the Papish view of predestination. If that should be conceded, is the doctrine therefore false? You, indeed, present a statement of it, but do not refute it. You think that it is so absurd that it may be sufficient to have presented it—that the statement itself will be a sufficient refutation. But, if some one should undertake to defend that doctrine, how would you refute it? We may make the attempt, "God foresaw from eternity the natures and the sins of men; this foresight preceded the decree by which he gave Christ to be the saviour of the world." I should say—

"The foresight of most sins," for He did not foresee the sin of the crucifixion of Christ, until after that decree was made. You have given a careless statement of that doctrine, as you have not made that necessary distinction. Then God decreed "to give, for the sake of Christ, sufficient grace, by which men might be saved." To all? The Papists do not assert this. Then, "He predestinated to life those who, He foresaw, would finish their life in the state of grace, which was prepared for them by the predestination of God;" this is indeed not very far from the doctrine of Augustine.

Your theory is "God did not reveal Christ for all and each of mankind." This theorem is not of much service to you in proving the speciality of predestination and of grace, since those, with whom you contend, even on the supposition of its truth, meet you with a two-fold argument. First, -- the reason that God did not reveal Christ to all and to each of mankind was the fact that their parents rejected the word of the gospel; -- on which account He permitted both the parents and their posterity to go on in their own ways, and this, for so long a time, as the divine justice and their sins seemed to demand.

The second argument is, that, in the mean time, while they were destitute of the knowledge of Christ, God "left not himself without witness" (Acts xiv. 17) but even then revealed to them some truth concerning His power and goodness, and the law also, which He kept inscribed on their minds. If they had made a right use of those blessings, even according to their own conscience, He would have bestowed upon them greater grace, according to that declaration, "to him that hath shall be given." But by abusing, or not using, those blessings, they made themselves unworthy even of the mercy of God, and therefore were without excuse, and not having the law they were condemned, their own thoughts accusing them (Rom. ii. 14, 15). But that God concealed the promise of the Messiah from any man, before that, rejection can not be proved from the Scriptures. Indeed, the contrary can be proved from those things which are narrated of Adam and his posterity, and of Noah and his children in the Scriptures. The defection from the right way gradually progressed, and God is not bound at any particular time to send a new revelation to men, who do not rightly use the revelation which they already have.

From this, it is manifest what judgment must be passed on those consectaries.

To the first; -- The reason that the promise of the blessed seed was not revealed to all men is both the fault of their parents in rejecting it, and of themselves in holding the truth, which they now have, in unrighteousness.

To the second; -- The answer is the same.

To the third; -- All men are called by some vocation, namely, by that witness of God, by which they may be led to feel after God that they may find him (Acts xxvii. 27); and by that truth, which they hold in unrighteousness, that is, whose effect, in themselves, they hinder; and by that inscription of the law on their hearts, according to which their thoughts accuse one another. But this vocation, although it is not saving in the sense that salvation can be obtained immediately from it, yet it may be said to be antecedently saving, as Christ is offered for them; and salvation will, of the divine mercy, follow that vocation, if it is rightly used. To the fourth; -- It is stated that "no one has said that the prescience of faith or unbelief is the rule of predestination," and this charge is futile. But that some may be condemned, by the law alone, is most true, and on account of their impenitence, though not on account of their rejection of Christ.

INDEX OF SCRIPTURE REFERENCES

Genesis

1 1:31 2:16 2:17 2:17 5:3 5:3 9:6 14:15 14:16 18:25 18:25 18:25 20:3 31:29 37 37 37:18

Exodus

5 6 22:28 26:6 32:33 32:33 32:33 33:19

Numbers

13 14:4 23:19

Deuteronomy

4:7 7:6

Judges

8:6 16:19 16:20

1 Samuel

2:25 2:30 3:37 13:9-14 15:8 15:9-22 22:4 23 23:12 24:6 24:6

2 Samuel

7:5 12:13 16:10 24

1 Kings

19:3 21

2 Kings

1 3:23-27 19:35 19:36

2 Chronicles

24:21 26:18

Nehemiah

4:15

Job

1 1 1 1:12 2 2 4:18

Psalms

1:6 5:4 5:4 5:4 11:7 15:3 15:3 33:11 47:20 80:11-12 81:13 118

Proverbs

8:31

Ecclesiastes

7:27 7:29

Isaiah

5 5 5:4 5:4 5:4 6 6:10 7:12 40:17 40:22 55:11 59:2 59:2

Jeremiah

32:40 34:22

Ezekiel

18:4 18:23

Hosea

1:6

Amos

3:6

Malachi

3:6

Matthew

1:2 1:21 1:21 7:17 10:32 11:25 11:26 11:28 11:28 12 13:11 13:11 13:19 16:18 22:2-8 22:3 22:7 22:14 23:37 23:37 23:37-38 24:24 25 25 25 25 25 25:12 25:29 25:34 26:24 26:39 30

Mark

14:21 14:56

Luke

1:29 2:14 7:30 7:30 7:30 7:30
12:32 22:32 22:53

John

1:3 1:4 1:12 1:12 1:12 1:29 1:29
1:29 1:29 2:10 3:8 3:16 3:16
3:18 3:19 3:36 3:36 4:42 6:44
6:51 6:51 7:37 7:38 8 8:24 8:31
8:34-36 8:44 10:15 10:28 12:39-
40 15 15:2 15:4 15:5 16:13 17:9
17:9 19:12 19:33 19:36

Acts

2:23 2:38 2:39 4:28 4:28 4:28 7
7:51 10:43 12:2 13 13:46 13:46
13:46 13:46 14:16 14:17 15:18
23:10 25:12 27:27 28:26 28:27

Romans

1:18 2:4 2:14 2:15 2:15 3:3 3:8
3:20 4:4 4:4 4:5 4:5 4:16 4:25
5 5:6-8 5:10 6 6:3 6:4 7 7 8
8 8 8 8 8 8 8:1 8:3 8:17 8:20
8:20 8:29 8:29 8:29 8:29 8:39 9
9 9 9 9 9 9 9 9 9 9 9:7-11
9:11 9:11 9:11-13 9:15 9:16 9:18
9:20 9:21 9:21 9:22 9:22 9:22
9:22 9:31 10:5 10:6 10:9 11 11:5
11:23 11:29 12:3 14:15

1 Corinthians

1:21 1:24 2 2:8 2:14 3:7 4:7
5:19 6:12 13:9 15 15:19 15:22
15:24 15:28 15:44 15:45

2 Corinthians

3:5 3:8 5:19 5:19 5:19 5:19 5:19
5:21 5:21

Galatians

2:20 3:9 3:9 3:10 3:10

Ephesians

1 1 1 1 1 1 1 1 1 1 1 1 1
1:3-6 1:4 1:4 1:4 1:4 1:4 1:5 1:5
1:5-6 1:10 1:10 1:10 1:11 1:11
1:22 2:3 2:3 2:3 4 4 4:24 5:25

Philippians

1:29 2:13

Colossians

1 3 3 3:3 3:10 3:10

2 Thessalonians

1:6 1:7

1 Timothy

1:13 2 2:5 2:5 2:5 2:6 4:8 4:10
5:21 5:21 14:10

2 Timothy

2:13 2:19

Titus

3:4

Philemon

1:2

Hebrews

1:2 1:14 2:9 2:9 2:9 2:9 2:14
2:14 2:14 2:16 5:1 5:1 5:1 5:1
5:5 6 6:10 6:10 7:10 8:6 8:12
9:12 9:13 9:14 9:22 11:6 12:24

James

1:17

1 Peter

1:18 1:18-20 1:19 2:7 2:8 3:17

2 Peter

1 2:1 3:9

1 John

2:2 3:4 3:8 3:8 3:9 4:4 4:14
5:12

Revelation

3:4 5:9 5:9 5:10 14:3 14:4 20

Lightning Source UK Ltd.
Milton Keynes UK
UKOW02f1324301014

240861UK00001B/310/P